FOUNDATIONS FOR OFFENDER MANAGEMENT

Theory, law and policy for contemporary practice

Anne Robinson

Leeds Trinity
University

First published in Great Britain in 2011 by

The Policy Press
University of Bristol
Fourth Floor
Beacon House
Queen's Road
Bristol BS8 1QU, UK
t: +44 (0)117 331 4054
f: +44 (0)117 331 4093
tpp-info@bristol.ac.uk
www.policypress.co.uk

North American office:
The Policy Press
c/o International Specialized Books Services
920 NE 58th Avenue, Suite 300
Portland, OR 97213-3786, USA
t: +1 503 287 3093
f: +1 503 280 8832
info@isbs.com

The author would like to thank Fergus McNeill for his kind permission to reproduce the two figures in Chapter Four.

British Library Cataloguing in Publication Data
A catalogue record for this book is available from the British Library.

Library of Congress Cataloging-in-Publication Data
A catalog record for this book has been requested.

ISBN 978 1 84742 764 9 (paperback)
ISBN 978 1 84742 765 6 (hardcover)

Cover design by Qube Design Associates, Bristol.
Front cover: photograph kindly supplied by iStockphoto.
Printed and bound in Great Britain by Hobbs, Southampton.

Contents

List of figures and tables iv

About the author v

Introduction vi

Part One: Offender management: key considerations 1

one Respecting rights and diversity 3

two Modernisation and changing structures 17

three Partnership and inter-agency working 35

four Reducing re-offending 51

Part Two: Offender management: key law and policy 67

five Human rights 69

six Equalities 83

seven Dealing with risk and danger 103

eight Safeguarding children 119

nine Procedures at court 143

ten Community sentencing 157

eleven Custodial sentencing 173

twelve Engagement and enforcement 187

Part Three: Offender management: key areas of practice 205

thirteen Work with victims 207

fourteen Youth justice 221

fifteen Substance use and misuse 245

sixteen Mentally disordered offenders 263

seventeen Sex offenders 283

eighteen Indeterminate sentence prisoners 299

References 315

Appendix: List of probation circulars 339

Index 341

List of figures and tables

Figures

2.1	The team around the offender	29
4.1	Programmes in context	55
4.2	Preconditions for change	58
8.1	Referral	133
8.2	What happens after the child protection conference, including the review process?	137
9.1	Court system in England and Wales	144
14.1	Youth justice disposals	234
16.1	Matching practitioner contact with severity of mental illness symptoms and risk of harm and re-offending	277

Tables

4.1	Engagement model	63
7.1	Risk management activity	110
7.2	MAPPA categories 2003/04 to 2008/09	112
10.1	Requirements under the Criminal Justice Act 2003	166
10.2	Requirements on community orders made in 2007	170
13.1	Conventional versus restorative forms of justice	219
14.1	Young people in custody 30 June 2010	237
15.1	Misuse of Drugs Act 1971 penalties	249
15.2	Classification of substances under the Misuse of Drugs Act 1971	250
15.3	Comparing drugs courts and DTTO review courts	258
17.1	Sex Offender Register notification periods	286
17.2	Sex Offender Treatment Programme (SOTP)	291
18.1	Sentences of life imprisonment 1995-2008	302

About the author

Anne Robinson qualified as a probation officer in 1993 and worked in a variety of probation and prison settings, before spending four years in management roles, both operational and strategic, in youth offending services. Since joining the Department of Law, Criminology and Community Justice at Sheffield Hallam University in 2005, she has been involved in professional development courses for youth justice practitioners and youth workers, as well as teaching on the Diploma in Probation Studies qualifying course for probation officers. Working with colleagues in the Hallam Centre for Community Justice, her research and evaluation projects have focused on resettlement, Prolific and Priority Offender schemes, offender accommodation and police commuity support officers. She is currently Course Leader for the programme established under the new Probation Qualifying Framework and leads on the law and policy elements of the teaching. Her academic interests are youth justice, criminal justice interventions with women offenders, women involved in sex work and policy development in criminal justice.

Introduction

'Offender management' is a relatively new term for what probation officers and others would recognise as supervision or case management. As with many new terms, it represents a re-branding of familiar processes. After all, the law breakers who come within the ambit of offender management are no different to those who would previously have been 'put on probation', and the social circumstances and disadvantages that they face have changed little. It is true that criminal justice agencies have initiated change as a result of legal mandate or in response to public opinion, but in essence they still retain their own characteristics. What is different, however, is the complexity of the practice context in which work with offenders takes place, and the variety of professionals involved in 'offender management', which is no longer the sole preserve of the probation service.

This book charts and provides a critical commentary on this practice context. It starts from two basic premises, the first being that practitioners who are confident in their knowledge and understanding of the legal and practice frameworks that govern their professional world will be better able to negotiate its more tricky aspects, to deal with complex ethical questions and to work constructively with both criminal and non-criminal justice agencies. They will therefore be more equipped to go beyond the technical and bureaucratic skills increasingly required for the different elements and roles within the offender management process, and will be able to maintain their professional purpose and identity in multi-agency contexts.

The second premise is that practitioners should be adept at working within the established frameworks for practice, but should at the same time be prepared to ask questions about where these frameworks have come from and the values and beliefs that inform them. Developing as professionals – practitioners able wisely to exercise discretion and judgement – involves fostering critical and political perspectives on the social world and the organisational context we inhabit. It also entails challenging existing practice and exploring new approaches to promoting behavioural change and reducing harm.

Having laid out that position, it might then seem incongruous to use the term 'offender' throughout a book that advocates nurturing a political sensibility, because the concept of being an 'offender' is so loaded. It is not applied equally to all individuals who break the law, but is used selectively to identify, and becomes the defining characteristic of, particular social groups, adding to the exclusion and marginalisation – and often downright discrimination – that they already experience. So the term here is not assumed to be neutral and unproblematic. It is used with an awareness of power relations and the impact that the status of offender might have on an individual, often alongside the stigma and disadvantage associated with, for instance, poverty, mental illness or heroin dependency. Additionally, it is also used here because it reflects the terminology from official documents and practice guidance, terminology that exposes particular views and moral assumptions.

The main focus of the book is an account of the legal provisions and policy established in relation to the core areas of offender management practice, putting these in historical and social context and offering a critical view from the human rights perspective. However, the detail of law and policy makes little sense without some preliminary scene setting. Part One of the book, therefore, invites the reader to consider:

- a value base for work with offenders;
- the organisational context for offender management;
- partnerships and the professional challenges presented by work in multi-agency and inter-agency settings; and
- the emerging debates about processes by which offenders desist from crime and how offender management relates to these.

Together these four chapters argue for a rights-based approach to offender management that can be adopted as a way of thinking and a rationale for decisions and actions across all agencies and organisations involved. This incorporates key notions from developing approaches to practice focusing on the strengths and resilience that offenders possess, rather than the skills and qualities that they lack.

Part Two moves on to outline law and policy in relation to core offender management practice, continuing the themes outlined in the opening chapters, beginning with human rights and equalities. Further chapters cover risk and dangerousness, practices to safeguard children, court processes and both community and custodial sentencing. The section finishes with a critical chapter on engagement and enforcement, rounding off the discussions about appropriate values and approaches to practice that balance attention to offenders' rights and needs with legitimate use of authority and actions to protect the public.

Part Three comprises six chapters focusing on particular areas of practice, beginning with an analysis of the development of policy in relation to victims of crime and witnesses, and exploring the implications for offender management. Other areas include provisions in relation to youth justice, substance misuse, mentally disordered offenders (MDOs), sex offenders and prisoners serving indeterminate sentences.

Knowledge and understanding of these frameworks is important to develop not just as a practitioner but as a critically reflective practitioner, 'who is not only self-aware, but also socially and politically aware' (Thompson and Thompson, 2008, p 29). This involves an approach 'characterised by questioning and not taking things for granted – especially social arrangements that are based on inequality and disadvantage' (Thompson and Thompson, 2008, p 27). Practitioners occupy a powerful position in the criminal justice world, although for many it may not feel that way in the grind of day-to-day business. But offender managers and others who are knowledgeable and aware are in a prime position to ameliorate aspects of practice or of organisational arrangements that are potentially damaging or simply lacking in sensitivity, working in the best interests of the individual but balancing professional accountabilities. On the other hand, the risk is that practitioners without wider perspectives may implement even quite enlightened policies in ways that disable and further stigmatise offenders. This book seeks to inform developing practitioners and to nurture the growth of critical and political perspectives on practice and practice requirements, with the ultimate aim of influencing interventions in a positive rather than a punitive direction.

Part One
Offender management: key considerations

ONE

Respecting rights and diversity

In 1994, Ward and Spencer described probation service work with offenders as an inherently 'moral activity' (1994, p 97). Since that time, criminal justice interventions have changed in many ways, with more agencies and a wider range of professionals now involved in increasingly structured forms of offender management. Of necessity, probation officers have learned to share parts of the professional territory that was previously theirs alone. The moral nature of the activity remains, yet the moral positions and values of the various participants are less clear than ever, given the diversity of their professional backgrounds, qualifications and levels of experience. This chapter opens up debate about whether it is possible to establish an underpinning value base and to develop practice approaches which have the potential to be endorsed and used across all agencies involved in offender management, rather than being the exclusive property of any one.

Why talk about values?

The business of offender management is certainly not value-neutral. Values are acted out in personal interactions, in operational decisions and in organisational arrangements. Values are also evident in the legal framework and the policy directives governing offender management, even though policy makers themselves may not explicitly refer to them.

Yet these values and beliefs are often taken for granted, with little thought given to the assumptions and presumptions about people and about the social world that they imply. It is possible to work within the offender management framework without thinking too deeply about why the system has developed in the way that it has and which influences have been most salient. However, improving and developing practice requires more curiosity and a willingness to explore the value-laden context in which offender management takes place, and to ask questions about what values might form the most promising base on which to build approaches to work with offenders that actually make a difference. As Mike Nellis observes,

> There is patently room for argument about the exact nature of those values, not least because there are various types of crime and criminals, and different degrees of danger and harm. Nevertheless, we must find as much consensus as possible about what "the right thing" to do actually is. (2005, p 33)

The first question, of course, concerns what we mean by 'values'. Much has been written on that topic, but here, rather than entering into more abstract debates, three simple points might be used to guide us through a discussion of values and into a reflection of what they mean in practice:

1. Used as a verb, *to value* means to esteem or to hold in regard.
2. *Value* as a noun refers to the worth, merit or importance placed on, for instance, a particular characteristic or quality.
3. *Values* are also a set of normative beliefs or standards held by a social group.

What is valued or held in high regard is likely to be prioritised or given more attention or resources. For example, there are values active and interacting with beliefs about impact and effectiveness underlying the current preference for cognitive behavioural over other types of intervention in the criminal justice system and providing the driver for decisions about huge investment in accredited programmes.

The aims of an activity or of an organisation – what it sets out to achieve – also relate to values. As expressed by Canton (2007a), this is a reciprocal relationship: values entail aims or, at the very least, an aim of realising those values or putting them into practice; aims entail values, because, even at the most basic level, there are values involved in choosing those particular aims and not others. This is not necessarily straightforward as there may be conflicts or tensions between different aims and values, as we shall see at numerous points in the policy discussions in later chapters.

In addition, values inform and guide actions that should give expression to the values that are articulated. In considering any value statement and how it relates to practice, there are two critical questions:

• what sort of actions and approaches are consistent with the value; and
• what sort of actions or approaches would contradict the value or violate it (Canton, 2007a)

And this link between values and actions applies at all levels of practice, because 'there is a tight conceptual connection between values and action: the litmus test of what someone believes is how they behave' (Canton, 2007a, p 241). This can be seen even in the minute details of interactions between professionals and offenders or between colleagues. Again, this is not necessarily straightforward, as values may suggest codes of behaviour or ways of doing things that are difficult to fully realise in practice. However, they may still be important in defining ethical and other standards that can be worked towards and which are, in that sense, aspirational (as with the rights-based framework introduced later in this chapter). Essentially,

> Values are personal moral commitments (like a passion for justice) –
> beliefs about what it is right to do and good to be. They are expressions

of character and conscience, manifestations of what a person stands
for or stands against. (Nellis, 2007, p 239)

Values as a set of normative beliefs or standards are also significant. Such collective
values are not set in stone and are constructed (and constantly re-constructed or
re-negotiated) within social or professional groups (Dalrymple and Burke, 1995).
Through these processes, they may alter over time and in response to particular
circumstances or general social attitudes. So, for example, changes in society's
values and views of sexuality and sexual orientation are reflected in recent UK
equalities legislation and the introduction of civil partnerships for same-sex
couples. More specifically, criminal justice practitioners may be challenged to
adapt the professional values to which they have previously subscribed as they are
thrown together in different configurations in inter-agency structures. This can
be seen in youth offending teams (YOTs) (Souhami, 2007) and, more recently,
in Integrated Offender Management Units.

A second and most intriguing question is why the values or normative beliefs
of the probation service have not been at the forefront as offender management
practices have developed. Surely the probation service has a long history of
constructive interventions with offenders? Might it not be expected to lead the
way in new developments, contributing not only skills and experience, but also
putting forward a coherent set of values and principles as a foundation for work
within new offender management frameworks? After all, offender management
may be seen as a natural, if more structured, development of the case management
practices long embedded in the service (Faulkner, 2008). In practice, however,
the probation influence has been largely drowned out by managerial discourses
(Gelsthorpe, 2007) and centrally devised initiatives that have neither facilitated
work with offenders as whole people nor paid attention to the context of their
lives (Brayford et al, 2010). So why is this the case?

What happened to 'probation values'?

For more than two decades, the probation service has struggled to find its voice
and to clearly articulate an internally generated and sustained sense of values for
its work with offenders that fits comfortably within the contemporary criminal
justice world (see Nellis and Gelsthorpe, 2003; Gelsthorpe, 2007; Whitehead, 2010).
It has therefore found itself having to respond to external challenges, not least
from the Home Office in the mid-1990s, as it began to ask awkward questions
about the exact nature of the 'social work values' that the probation service was
then seeking to defend (Gelsthorpe, 2007). These values are not easily defined,
but Mike Nellis encapsulates their spirit when he writes that:

> In essence they have been about respecting the dignity and worth
> of individuals, seeking to reconcile individuals and the communities
> in which they live, empowering individuals to resist forms of

discrimination and oppression which have structured their lives and perhaps shaped their very sense of who they are. (2001a, p 34)

By the mid-1990s, the probation service had been decisively recast as 'punishment in the community' by the Criminal Justice Act 1991, with its longstanding focus on rehabilitation of offenders featuring as only one of three official aims, alongside reduction of crime and protection of the public (Nellis, 2001b). This represented a significant change for the service in its philosophical base that it was ill-placed to resist (Raynor and Vanstone, 2007). In the more intolerant penal climate that came about under Michael Howard's stewardship of the Home Office during that mid-1990s period, references to anti-discriminatory practice and the traditional social work values of the service seemed jarringly out of step (Nellis, 2007). The focus of probation concerns have since changed to the extent that Philip Whitehead (2010) asks whether probation has abandoned its traditional constituency among the poor and vulnerable in order to ensure its survival regardless of the cost to its original ideals, values and organisational integrity.

Crucially, until the 1990s, the values of the service had been significantly informed and influenced by its practitioner base. In stark contrast to other criminal justice agencies, the commitment to anti-discriminatory practice and anti-racism was undeniable, although undoubtedly uneven across the service, and dependent on the efforts of individuals and the driving force of the union, Napo, rather than consistent organisational buy-in (Vanstone, 2005). This is very different from the position today where the talk at practitioner level about values is more uncertain and arguably less optimistic than previously. Twenty years ago, if probation practitioners had been asked to identify the principles and beliefs that underpinned their practice, they would have had ready recourse to the language of social work. Perhaps there was less consensus about social work values and concepts than their most passionate advocates suggested (Nellis and Gelsthorpe, 2003). Perhaps also they were adopted rather naively by some probation officers, without being fully thought through or translated into meaningful actions in day-to-day practice. Such values and concepts are slippery, and notions close to the hearts of many probation officers, such as empathy, empowerment, respect for persons, the agency and autonomy of individuals, were often asserted rather than analysed (see, for instance, Timms, 1983). Nevertheless, the language was there and practitioners could confidently refer to what was almost a formula, a set of, if you like, ready-made values to which they could attribute the foundations for their practice.

No such easy formula exists for offender managers today. Academics writing about the probation service have proposed various possibilities as a basis for a new understanding and commitment to values, and these include:

- human rights (Hudson, 2001);
- citizenship and democratic participation (see, for example, Faulkner, 2002);

- community justice – a mixture of community safety, reduction of custody and restorative justice (Nellis, 2001);
- 'constructive' work with offenders – referring to both positive practice approaches and more theoretical perspectives on how social reality is socially constructed and interpreted (Gorman et al, 2006).

None of these has had an impact to any significant extent in the practice context, although policy makers are seemingly now beginning to heed the messages about the importance of relationships and more person-centred approaches in helping individuals achieve change. This might, then, be an appropriate point to reframe the question so that, instead of asking what probation service values should be, we ask whether there could be a common set of values adopted across the criminal justice system that could guide and inform frameworks for offender management. A subsidiary question then becomes, how can the probation service draw on its history of humanitarian concerns and work with offenders to assist the process of identifying, embedding and sustaining such values in practice? A further question might be, what could the voluntary and community sector contribute from its own different history and traditions? Finding a common language to talk about values is critical and a useful starting point is to look at areas where there may already be a degree of common interest between the different agencies.

Could 'risk' or 'public protection' be a sufficient value base?

In thinking of common areas of interest, both risk and public protection spring to mind as prominent concerns for all criminal justice agencies. Could these form the basis of a common set of values? At first glance, this might seem attractive and potentially achievable. Re-orientating itself towards risk has enabled the probation service to avoid some of the conflicts that might otherwise have arisen with other agencies and to establish common purposes. Hudson (2001) also points out that it has gone some way to enabling the service to resolve some of the internal tensions about its role and to justify its existence as both part of the penal system and as an agency that seeks to work with a constituency of offenders who often face extreme disadvantage and social exclusion. Although these tensions do still exist, a focus on risk has brought the probation service closer to other criminal justice agencies within partnerships and other integrated practice frameworks.

Nevertheless, there are limitations and critical contradictions in seeking to deploy risk or public protection as a common value base. Not least of these is the fact that reducing or managing risk and protecting the public may more accurately be seen as aims or objectives, rather than values in themselves. Fundamental points of difference might arise in relation to the values and understandings underlying the commitment of particular agencies to risk and public protection. These may include:

- lack of clarity and common understanding of key concepts, such as 'risk' and 'harm' (Kemshall, 2008; Baker, 2010);
- the meaning of public protection as a justification for work with offenders because it is such an 'elastic' term and can be linked to a range of other, potentially disparate, objectives, such as reducing offending or social inclusion (Robinson and McNeill, 2004);
- ideas about how to achieve the aims of reducing risk or public protection and specifically where the emphasis should be in terms of the use of intervention and support or control measures;
- perspectives on individual motivation and capacity to change;
- understandings of who and what public protection is aiming to protect and the nature of communities, including key questions about social exclusion or inclusiveness (McCulloch and McNeill, 2007).

These areas, once examined, expose what may be critical aspects of difference between statutory and voluntary agencies or even individuals working within agencies. These may be debated to greater or lesser degrees in practice settings, but the language of risk and public protection does not lend itself to a full and frank exploration of the nature of the relationships between the state and individuals – both those who break the law and those who do not – as well as critical questions about expectations and obligations.

Such relationships need exploration and consideration: if risk and public protection are not the best starting points from which to establish shared understandings and values, is there another approach that might be more promising? For some years commentators (see, for example, Hudson, 2001; Gelsthorpe, 2007) have argued that the concept of rights and rights-based frameworks might provide the most useful platform for debating ideas and working towards a normative set of values. More recently, thinking has developed about how a rights-based approach could be applied to criminal justice practice (Connolly and Ward, 2008). The following sections look at these arguments in more detail and start to explore the proposition that offender management should be centrally concerned with the rights of all key parties, that a rights-based approach could be incorporated into practice and that it is important in recognising the individuality and diversity of the many individuals coming within the ambit of offender management.

Value of rights-based thinking

It is necessary first to outline the benefits of looking at criminal justice generally, and offender management specifically, from the perspective of rights, before examining in more detail what a rights-based approach might entail. This goes significantly beyond the human rights enshrined in international conventions and legislation, and involves developing a culture that is open to questions of rights and seeks to work in inclusive ways that recognise and respect rights.

In legalistic terms, rights are often conceived as existing in three tiers, with *first tier rights* such as the right to life and freedom from torture being 'absolute' and therefore applicable in every case. *Second tier rights* include the right to a fair trial and the right to security of the person, and these must be adhered to in most cases, but can be limited in exceptional circumstances. *Third tier rights* – freedoms, for instance, relating to expression, assembly and thought and religion – may more easily be suspended or curtailed particularly when they impinge upon the rights of others (Hudson, 2003). These groupings of rights and their implications are explored in more depth in Chapter Five. However, here it is important to note that a rights-based approach to offenders is centrally concerned with promoting access to these third tier rights, which are often referred to as civil or participatory rights. Such rights are significant in securing social inclusion and cohesion, with offenders (as well as other marginalised groups) being encompassed in communities rather than cast out from them.

The obvious and immediate benefit of focusing on rights is that all agencies across the criminal justice system are concerned with rights and have obligations under human rights legislation. Therefore the 'language of human rights' can be shared across agencies in contrast to the probation service's way of talking about its social work values or the different discourses from parts of the voluntary and community sector (Gelsthorpe, 2007).

Although it is often assumed that rights-based approaches are focused only on the rights of the individual, as thinking and policy on human rights has developed there has been increasing recognition of the rights of particular groups, for instance based on ethnicity or culture (McLaughlin, 2003; Connolly and Ward, 2008). This can provide an interesting basis for considering the rights of other marginalised populations, for instance, sex offenders or groups of young people vulnerable to criminalisation.

Rights-based thinking, far from giving an offender's rights precedence over the rights of other parties, is concerned with finding an appropriate accommodation between the interests of all parties. It is therefore capable of dealing in a sophisticated way with complex situations where individual parties have competing rights and needs:

> Punishment and crime prevention cannot escape rights conflicts. The question is not whose rights may be disregarded, but what is the balance of rights to be struck in individual situations. (Hudson, 2001, p 111)

Dealing with such tensions is central to offender management, and thinking in terms of rights can provide a consistent and ethical basis for practice decisions and actions.

A rights-based approach is essentially socially inclusive and forms sound foundations for practitioners to build strong and collaborative relationships with offenders (Connolly and Ward, 2008). There is also a strong fit with desistance and strengths-based approaches currently being developed (for instance, the Good

Lives Model; see Ward and Maruna, 2007), and with techniques such as pro-social modelling (Trotter, 2006).

A focus on rights, however, does not mean losing focus on the management of risks, not least because those affected by crime have rights:

> Taking rights seriously means taking risks seriously because it means providing for the full enjoyment of rights and preventing infringements. This may entail punishment or control of those who threaten others' enjoyment of rights. On the other hand, rights impose restrictions on what may be done in response to actual or anticipated harm. (Hudson, 2003, p 224)

Accordingly, in Connolly and Ward's (2008) account of rights-based work with offenders, it would seek to (a) reduce risk to the community and (b) promote offenders' core interests and social 'goods'. There is therefore attention to both sides of the equation and attempts to balance the rights of the offender with those of the community in an explicit and reasoned way (Connolly and Ward, 2008).

Human rights approaches may also reap benefits in terms of promoting legitimacy, accountability and defensibility in practice, as well as transparency in dealing with offenders.

Finally, a rights-based approach may be conducive to the involvement of a diverse voluntary and community sector as it assumes a more significant role in service delivery. From a probation service perspective, a human rights approach is consistent with the service's humanitarian ethos and tradition. Adopting a rights-based culture may represent a significant shift for other statutory criminal justice agencies, but should be more easily accepted into probation practice, particularly as recent research on the values held by practitioners and trainees in the service have indicated that a strong person-centred focus still remains (Annison et al, 2008; Deering, 2010). A consistent human rights orientation may give the probation service and voluntary agencies a stronger voice and influence on developing offender management practice through which they may be able to draw on their reserves of experience in working with offenders to better effect than to date.

Rights and obligations

This section outlines some key considerations in a rights-based approach, focusing not on the pursuit of human rights under law, but the wider aspects of rights to which we may judge there are moral claims.

Discussions of rights are necessarily complex, and there is no space here to rehearse in full the many and varied debates about the nature of rights and the different types of rights. For the purposes of this book, drawing on Connolly and Ward (2008), the concept that is used is that of a right as an entitlement, something that we can rightfully claim. Human rights are those rights that are claimed by virtue of the fact that we are human and are therefore a moral agent (even if we are unable to exercise moral agency, for instance, in childhood). They are the basic conditions that are needed to enable us to function and to develop as autonomous human beings, and they cluster around the twin core values of freedom and well-being (Connolly and Ward, 2008).

Rights are regarded as having significant moral status, underpinned by moral concepts such as the inherent dignity of human beings and recognition of individual worth. So when a claim is made on the basis of rights, it is often held to have precedence over – or to 'trump' – other moral considerations. Such powerful claims impose duties on the individuals receiving the claim, obliging them to act in certain ways or to allow the claimant to pursue his or her goals so long as the rights of other people are not infringed.

The notion of rights and duties is particularly significant because all adults hold rights and at the same time have duties towards other people by virtue of their own respective rights. For instance, parents have duties towards their children, because of the children's moral claims on them in relation to food, security and developmental needs. This notion of duties, however, is different from the coupling of 'rights and responsibilities' in New Labour policy around anti-social behaviour, for example. This particular coupling assumes that citizenship is earned, rather than being given as of right (Cook, 2006), and that the benefits of citizenship – participation, having a voice, being taken seriously – can justifiably be withdrawn from offenders, a position that is directly opposed to a rights-based perspective (Gelsthorpe, 2007).

The current penal climate is, on the whole, unsympathetic to the idea of promoting the rights of offenders (Hudson, 2003) and, apart from improvements in prison conditions, developments have tended to erode, rather than uphold, offender rights. It is true that rights are tricky in relation to offenders, who may simultaneously:

- be the holder of rights as a human being;
- bear duties towards the human rights of others, perhaps within the family or local community; and
- violate the human rights of others (adapted from Connolly and Ward, 2008).

Particular rights of offenders may legitimately be restricted as a result of sanctions after conviction or as a response to risk assessment. However, they do not and should not forfeit all rights as human beings because of their status as offender. In fact, there is a central contradiction in attempts to encourage offenders to recognise the rights and interests of others where the process of doing so actually violates their own rights (Connolly and Ward, 2008).

A rights-based approach, then, seeks to ensure that:

- offenders are treated within the criminal justice system in line with the European Convention on Human Rights (ECHR) and the UK Human Rights Act 1998;
- processes and practices in offender management respect the rights of offenders as being of equal importance to those of victims and other parties;

- offenders are recognised as having rights and, at the same time, duties in respect of other people and their rights;
- constraints and controls on offenders are proportionate, defensible and impinge on their rights only insofar as is necessary to protect the rights of others;
- access to civil or participatory rights is actively promoted.

Respecting individuality and difference

It hardly needs saying that offenders are diverse and reflect many different aspects of society, although with significant distortions and disproportions in the presence of particular groups, such as African Caribbean young men, in criminal justice statistics (Smith, 2009). While 'race' and gender have been specific and longstanding concerns for criminal justice agencies, again there has been an absence of a powerful common language with which to promote system-wide initiatives to achieve greater equality. The 'old' social work discourses around anti-discriminatory practice have tended not to resonate with other agencies. Although the practices themselves are as valid as ever, the language in which they were framed long ago outlived its usefulness for the probation service in the light of a harsher penal climate (Nellis and Gelsthorpe, 2003; Nellis, 2007).

In recent years, 'respecting diversity' has become the preferred term in official documents, more politically neutral than anti-discriminatory or anti-oppressive practice and less focused on structural sources of discrimination and inequality (Lancaster, 2008). It does have the benefit of not singling out different characteristics, such as sexual orientation, gender and ethnicity, and treating them as separate entities, but is a rather nebulous term (Nellis and Gelsthorpe, 2003). There is presumably wide agreement that 'respecting diversity' is a generally 'good thing'. However, the vagueness about what that phrase actually means makes it difficult to identify significant steps towards that goal beyond managerial targets such as quotas for recruiting staff from minority ethnic groups.

A rights-based approach is underpinned by a value base for work that is capable of responding to diversity more meaningfully, because it starts from the premise that each person should be recognised as an individual with specific needs and circumstances. This may have multiple benefits at practitioner level in terms of:

- attention to the unique experiences of each individual, including any unwarranted impacts on their rights;
- recognition that multiple sites of discrimination and difference may impact on any one individual because 'we are rarely just men or women, black or Asian or white, but situate ourselves on a number of social or cultural planes' (Gelsthorpe and McIvor, 2007, p 323);
- more individualised responses to particular situations but, critically, based on reasoned judgement, rather than personal subjectivity;
- collaboratively agreed actions with offenders to tackle areas of life where they face additional difficulties or discrimination;

- negotiated changes to offender management or interventions to take account of different needs or circumstances. This is what Gelsthorpe and McIvor refer to as 'legitimate differentiation' (2007, p 322).

This last point is of particular significance and relates to the appropriate use of discretion and to accountability. Offender managers are, of course, working within a defined framework set by national standards and other practice directions that place constraints on the use of discretion in order to achieve greater consistency and equity of treatment. Nevertheless, areas of discretion still exist, and confident practitioners can use that leeway to recognise and respond to difference, not arbitrarily but in ways that they are able to account for. At the same time, they must be clear about the areas where there is no room for negotiation and the limits of their discretion. Offenders, then, should be enabled to make choices about specific aspects of their supervision. Offering a degree of self-determination may encourage individuals to see themselves as participants in the offender management process, rather than passively subject to it.

Accountability is of particular note here. Managerial accountability through national standards and performance management frameworks undoubtedly increased during the period of the New Labour administration (Canton and Eadie, 2009), and this creates tensions for practitioners in their use of discretion. Important as this accountability is – and certainly the National Offender Management Service (NOMS) and the Ministry of Justice place great value on it – it cannot override the equally important question of accountability to offenders. Gelsthorpe (2001) argues that where practitioners act in ways that demonstrate respect for social and cultural differences, this promotes a sense of accountability that may, in turn, positively impact on offenders' beliefs about the legitimacy of the criminal justice system. A belief in legitimacy is an essential foundation for building relationships that can assist individuals in moving towards change and building a better life both for themselves and in terms of reduced harm to others.

Building better lives

Offender management conceived as something that is done to offenders, rather than with them, is significantly less effective in bringing about sustained changes in behaviour and in protecting the public. It is also less respectful of their rights, human dignity and needs. In contrast, the approach outlined here is one in which practitioners seek to build collaborative working relationships that 'engage offenders in the demanding process of lifestyle change' (Ward and Maruna, 2007, p 106). Central to this is encouraging motivation and identifying incentives for making changes, recognising that it can often be extremely challenging and even frightening for offenders to move away from familiar ways of behaving or relating to their social world.

Incentives, of course, may be negative and change may be motivated by, for instance, wanting to avoid a further prison sentence or the imposition of an

Anti-social Behaviour Order (ASBO). However, positive incentives may be more powerful in the long term, and it is useful to end a discussion of values and rights-based thinking by introducing key ideas and concepts around strengths and positive levers for change.

The notion of the *good life* is particularly relevant here. This has been developed as a specific clinical model (the Good Lives Model – see, for instance, Ward and Stewart, 2003; Ward and Maruna, 2007 ; and discussed further in Chapter Four). It is not suggested here that a full Good Lives Model can be adopted for the general body of offenders under supervision, but that certain of its ideas, principles and values could usefully be employed within offender management. In particular, it proposes a different way of conceptualising risk that then informs the choice of appropriate and more holistic responses (Ward and Marshall, 2004).

In essence, drawing on understandings from psychology, the Good Lives Model proposes that all individuals share the same basic needs and are similarly driven to satisfy those needs or to gain these *primary human goods*, which may include:

- *healthy living* – this involves healthy physical living in terms of both physical and sexual health;
- *knowledge* – having an area of knowledge that you feel is varied and important to you;
- *excellence in work and play* – feeling that you have mastered something or that there is something you excel in;
- *excellence in agency* – feeling that you have some self-direction and independence or self-sufficiency;
- *inner peace* – freedom from emotional turmoil and stress;
- *relatedness* – this includes intimate, romantic, family and community relationships;
- *spirituality* – finding meaning and purpose in life;
- *happiness* – engaging in activities that make you personally happy;
- *creativity* – engaging in creative ways of thinking or behaving and increasing/developing ways in which you engage with the world. (Murphy, 2001, cited in Ireland and Worthington, 2008, p 185)

This intersects with a rights-based approach in recognising that individuals have the right to access these *primary human goods* and to work towards a fulfilling or '*good life*'. In this sense, a '*good life*' does not necessarily equate to a morally good or ethical life. Nor does it refer to a life that is good in the sense of being full of pleasure. Rather, it means a life that encompasses a range of elements that together contribute to well-being or fulfilment. Again, there is a link with the core elements or values of a rights-based approach (freedom and well-being).

However, although all individuals may seek the same sorts of *primary human goods*, internal (psychological) or external (social) factors, such as poverty or labour market conditions, may affect the ability to access these goods by legitimate means. Individuals may therefore engage in activities which are anti-social or criminal in order to fulfil their goal of gaining particular goods. For instance, young men who are unemployed and do not have a work-based social network may involve themselves in a street-based gang and in aggressive behaviour in order to enhance their sense of belonging, identity and status as young men.

What is important about the Good Lives Model is the underpinning idea that all human beings are similarly motivated towards the goals of achieving a collection of *primary human goods*, although each individual may prioritise and give different value to these goods. In this respect, there is no distinction between offenders and non-offenders. It does not treat offenders as a breed apart, with intrinsic moral or social defects. In contrast, it takes as its starting point a belief that their pursuit of goods is legitimate, even if their means of achieving these goods are not. It therefore follows that correctional intervention should focus on assisting offenders to identify the functions that offending has served in their lives and to adopt ways of achieving the goods that they desire more pro-socially. Within a therapeutic or forensic context, Ward and Stewart (2003) explain that work focuses on providing offenders with the necessary conditions in terms of skills, values, opportunities and social supports, to enable them to meet their human needs in more adaptive ways in the belief that this will then reduce the likelihood of future harm to self or others.

Naturally, this is value-laden and it is useful to identify what is prioritised and given value within a broad *good lives* approach:

- the inherent worth of individuals and their personal identities (Ward and Stewart, 2003);
- a belief that human beings are more likely to function well if they have access to a range of *primary human goods* (Ward and Maruna, 2007);
- the significance of the social and environmental context of offenders' lives and their subjective experiences (Ward and Marshall, 2004);
- offenders' own priorities and goals in relation to achieving *primary human goods*;
- recognition and respect for social and psychological needs;
- collaborative work with individuals and formulating agreed plans of action.

From this, it can be seen that there is a good fit between a rights-based approach and the values that underpin the notion of *good lives*, which can be legitimately and reasonably borrowed from the Good Lives Model to enhance the debate that has been started here about an appropriate value base for offender management.

The discussions started here and developed in the next three chapters are certainly not the end word in terms of values and work with offenders. In some senses, the ideas are still quite raw, but this reflects the complexity of the practice context that is outlined in Chapter Two and the developments in offender management that are, in important respects, consistent with the history of probation casework practice and, in other respects, represent new departures.

Summary

This chapter asked whether the language of rights and, to a lesser extent, *good lives*, could be used to develop a common understanding among the various agencies involved in work with offenders about an appropriate set of values and principles for offender management. A focus on rights could form the basis of a practice approach that could be endorsed across different statutory and voluntary agencies, promoting consistency and defensibility in practice decisions and actions. This would balance the rights of direct victims and the community in general with those of offenders and would provide a sound basis for responding to risk. A positive rights agenda would seek to ensure that the social and civil rights of offenders are actively promoted and given equal value to those of other citizens. The approach described is socially inclusive and based on establishing collaborative relationships with offenders which are better able to encourage motivation, helping them build lives that are more fulfilling for themselves and less harmful to others.

Further reading

Canton, R. (2007) 'Probation and the tragedy of punishment', *The Howard Journal of Criminal Justice*, vol 46, no 3, pp 236-54.

Gelsthorpe, L. (2007) 'Probation values and human rights', in L. Gelsthorpe and R. Morgan (eds) *Handbook of probation*, Cullompton: Willan, Chapter 17.

Hudson, B. (2001) 'Human rights, public safety and the Probation Service: defending justice in the risk society', *The Howard Journal of Criminal Justice*, vol 40, no 2, pp 103-13.

TWO

Modernisation and changing structures

Work with offenders does not take place in a vacuum, but is located within specific organisational arrangements. This chapter explains the agency structures and the current frameworks for offender management, putting them in context and highlighting the critical factors that influenced New Labour's developments and the new drivers of change under the Coalition government. As indicated in Chapter One, offender management is value-laden. Values – whether implicit or overt – are very much present in the political and policy decisions that are made and the way policies are implemented. The discussion, therefore, moves on to identify the values underpinning NOMS and the Coalition's promised 'rehabilitation revolution', pointing to tensions and opportunities in relation to a rights-based approach.

An overriding culture of risk

The probation service, as the main agency working with offenders in the community, has a long tradition of pursuing welfare-based, humanitarian interventions. In recent years the emphasis of work has shifted considerably towards those individuals whose offending causes greater concern because of its seriousness or persistence. The prison and police services have also more explicitly targeted their efforts and resources on 'risky' offender populations (Philips, 2008). This is not a chance happening; rather, it is a response to a social world preoccupied by risk and fear of crime. The implications of this are clearly signalled by Mike Nash:

> Just as governments have to respond to global risks, even though they are often powerless to do anything, so must criminal justice agencies respond to crime concerns…. Risk management has thus become a core and over-riding function….
>
> It is clear that a climate of fear and insecurity will alter the way in which criminal justice practitioners work on a daily basis. This change has probably been greater for the probation service than any other organisation in the sector. Their concern with risk shifts its focus on the offender from one of rehabilitation to one of risk management and control. (2005, p 17)

The orientation towards risk in criminal justice as elsewhere has happened over a period of years, although with a sharp escalation in the pace of change since New Labour came to power in 1997. Risk and prevention of risk is now central to the relationship between the state and its citizens, and increasingly takes precedence over its role in protecting individual rights. The ramifications for individual citizens in the modern state are profound, as evidenced in new legislation aimed at potential terrorism and the pervasive use of CCTV surveillance: 'The price of protection from greater risk is literally greater intrusion and a weakening of individual rights' (Kemshall, 2003, p 33).

The probation service has responded to the 'rise of risk' (Kemshall, 2003) by aligning more decisively with other criminal justice agencies and moving away from its more traditional links with social work departments, community organisations and local authorities generally. It has always had to position itself somewhere on the spectrum between care and control, but recent years have seen a significant shift towards the control axis. From the mid-1990s, it has progressively loosened its commitment to the social inclusion of offenders and the promotion of their welfare, in favour of an agenda dominated by public protection concerns (Bailey et al, 2007).

The prison service has also shifted emphasis and practices, engaging in more systematic delivery of structured interventions or programmes with offenders and allowing more community-based services through its doors. The coupling of the prison and probation services within NOMS is therefore less anomalous than it would have been at previous points in their respective histories, although they are still markedly different in terms of organisation, culture and primary tasks (Whitehead, 2010).

It is significant that the creation of NOMS in 2004 took place amid a particular political climate and ways of thinking and talking about risk that had developed over at least the previous decade. This period was dominated by a social policy agenda focused on managing, rather than seeking to reduce or to eliminate, the risk through broad social programmes. In terms of criminal justice, this logic suggests that agencies should concentrate on controlling or displacing 'risky or dangerous populations' (Kemshall, 2003). At the same time, the majority 'non-risky' population should be protected from 'risky' individuals, such as young, unemployed males, sex offenders and drug users – an exclusionary but politically attractive strategy.

This has affected criminal justice practices in a number of ways. For instance, it has provided the momentum for the adoption of standardised assessment tools allowing offenders to be classified according to their assumed level of risk and for resources to be targeted accordingly (Philips, 2008). Although these tools are presented as technical aids and value-free, this is not the reality: they take a pseudo-scientific approach founded on the belief that risk is predictable, that it can somehow be measured and then dealt with, given the 'right' methods and efficient implementation of procedures. The emphasis on accredited programmes and the categorisation of offenders within Multi-Agency Public Protection Arrangements (MAPPAs) are driven by the same beliefs. Kemshall (2003) characterises this as an artefact approach that tends to objectify risk, and contrasts it with perspectives that recognise the subjective nature of risk thinking and how it is shaped through social interactions and processes.

There is certainly a clear rationale for adopting practice based on research evidence, and assessment tools such as the Offender Assessment System (OASys) are good examples of this. However, while recognising the benefits of practice frameworks and structured ways of working, practitioners should also nurture a critical awareness of the way that politics, the media and other social factors influence what or who is viewed as 'risky' at any given time. Criminal justice agencies are under pressure to respond to these concerns and have increasingly targeted their resources at sex offenders, young people engaged in anti-social behaviour and, even more recently, perpetrators of domestic violence. The danger is that riskiness is then being judged on the basis of membership of these designated groups, instead of the individual's behaviours and social circumstances.

A modernising agenda

Although the explicit focus on managing risk has significantly influenced policies and practice in criminal justice, it is far from being the only driving force behind developments. Before coming into office in 1997, New Labour had signalled its intention to focus on the modernisation of the criminal justice system. Youth justice was singled out for special attention (Muncie, 2009), with one of their five election pledges relating to persistent young offenders (PYOs). However, and importantly, the ideas and approaches developed in the reshaping of youth justice have informed wider changes in the organisation and delivery of criminal justice (Senior et al, 2007). These include the creation of multi-agency structures at both operational and strategic levels, with the aim of moving towards a model of more 'joined-up justice'.

Consistent features of the modernising agenda for criminal justice are:

- emphasis on performance management and performance targets;
- developments in technology and use of ICT (information and communications technology), in particular to improve communication between agencies;
- challenge to the previous dominance of criminal justice professionals and their expert status, alongside significant changes in criminal justice personnel. This is evident, for instance, in the introduction of police community support officers into the police and the growing population of probation service officers within probation;
- pursuit of policy priorities identified by central government (such as the focus on 'what works' [Mair, 2004] and delivery of accredited programmes, and also the initiatives around prolific offenders);
- new structures for governance, with criminal justice agencies coming together in strategic bodies such as Community Safety Partnerships (CSPs) (adapted from Raine, 2001).

Changes in governance structures have been particularly significant. First, the role of the state, operating at local level through partnership structures, has moved increasingly towards establishing priorities and frameworks for action and then coordinating and monitoring delivery by a range of providers. This has been described as 'the emergence of a differentiated polity, wherein government institutions become less concerned with rowing (delivering actual services on the ground) and oriented more towards steering (establishing overall policy frameworks)' (Loader and Sparks, 2007, p 87).

Second, service delivery, which was previously the monopoly of the statutory criminal justice agencies, has shifted towards a more mixed economy of provision, with an enhanced role for voluntary and community organisations in particular, but also private companies (Senior et al, 2007). This trend is clearly set to continue under the Coalition administration.

Alongside competition and expansion within the sector, responsibilities in relation to crime prevention have also been spread across government departments and agencies with no historical focus on crime but with a potential contribution to make. There are therefore a greater number of players whose efforts and activities must be aligned and coordinated.

Third, the ideal of governance through devolved partnership structures implies an increase in accountability, because agencies are answerable to their partners in terms of their performance and the adequacy of their responses to local situations. However, the extent to which this will happen in practice is highly dependent on the politics of local relationships and working practices.

Finally, the way that power and decision making has been devolved to local areas is fundamentally paradoxical, in that alongside this drive for decentralisation was a powerful centralising tendency in New Labour policy (Senior et al, 2007). The setting of performance targets and tight timescales for activity at a national level may well have undermined the trust and cooperation necessary for effective partnership working in localities (Hughes, 2007). The emphasis on localism and reducing and simplifying performance targets announced by the Coalition government should ease these tensions (Ministry of Justice, 2010a) although there may be consequences in terms of looser coordination and fragmentation of delivery.

A managerialist twist

Although the modernisation agenda is rather wider in its concerns, New Labour's moves towards modernisation took a highly managerialist form. In the probation context, Gelsthorpe and Morgan (2007) noted a significant change in values, with the system and its operation assuming importance while the individuals within it became less important (very different from the traditional person–centred casework model of the service). There are undoubted benefits brought by a managerial approach that emphasises efficiency, accountability, open enquiry and transparency in processes and decision making. But there are also potential downsides where audits, performance targets and mechanistic application of procedures inhibit innovation and responsiveness to offenders and victims (Gelsthorpe, 2007).

Managerialist approaches tend towards pragmatism and are concerned with efficiency and effectiveness more than with matters of principle. That is not to say that managerialist practices are necessarily unprincipled: however, they are not driven by principles and often look to technocratic and utilitarian solutions to complex human situations. Interestingly, however, while managerialism is capable of providing a rationale for particular practices, in itself it cannot offer a sufficient moral justification for criminal justice activity because of the narrow – if extremely powerful – range of its concerns. It is not a value base in itself (Green et al, 2008), and this creates opportunities for accommodating different values within a managerial framework. Of course, such values could potentially espouse goals that are exclusionary and punitive. However, there is also room for developing the sorts of rights-based approach discussed in Chapter One, and furthering those associated values within current practice frameworks. There will naturally be points of tension but the two are not wholly at odds, and the potential is there to be exploited in order to prevent 'the development of bureaucratic power ... from controlling rather than serving the organisation and its values' (Whitehead, 2010, p 88).

Charting the changes

The first indications of major change for correctional services came in 1997 with *The prisons and probation review* (Home Office, 1997a), followed a short time later by a Green Paper, *Joining forces to protect the public* (Home Office, 1998a). Although stopping short of recommending a merger of prisons and probation, both expressed concerns about what they saw as a fragmented and uncoordinated probation service.

At that time there were 54 probation services, each under the control of a probation committee made up of magistrates, and each still operating in a relatively autonomous fashion, despite increasing central direction. This all changed as the Criminal Justice and Court Services Act 2000 created a national service, with a national director, in order to give more coherence and strategic oversight. The 54 services were slimmed down to 42 probation areas, each coterminous with police force areas, and probation committees were replaced by probation boards, with a more limited remit and a lesser role for the magistracy. A new agency, the Children and Family Court Advisory and Support Service (Cafcass), swept up the divorce and family court business, leaving probation to focus on criminal matters.

The probation service was only just beginning to settle after this re-organisation when Patrick Carter, now Lord Carter of Coles, was engaged to conduct a review of correctional services. His report, *Managing offenders, reducing crime* (Carter, 2003), identified structural difficulties impacting on the management of sentences and the tendency of both prison and probation services to work 'in silos' without sufficient reference to each other. The report concluded that a new approach was needed, with:

- 'end-to-end management of offenders' through a new NOMS replacing the prison and probation services;
- greater use of competition from private and voluntary providers; and
- a purchaser/provider split, with regional offender managers contracting rather than managing services on an equal basis from the public, private and voluntary sectors.

The New Labour government accepted most of the recommendations of the Carter review, which were broadly consistent with its modernising agenda. The crux of the proposed changes was the intention to make greater use of the private and voluntary sector in the delivery of offender services and to challenge the probation service monopoly in community provision.

Commissioning and contestability were seen as key elements in establishing the NOMS framework (Home Office, 2004c), as was the Offender Management Model (OMM) outlined later in this chapter. This required significant organisational change backed by primary legislation, in order to establish and support separate structures for commissioning and for delivery.

National Offender Management Service – the early years for probation

The initial period in the existence of NOMS proved to be 'rife with uncertainty and not inconsiderable controversy' (Robinson and Burnett, 2007, p 320). NOMS began by building on the findings of the 2002 report by the Social Exclusion Unit, *Reducing re-offending by ex-prisoners* (2002), and identifying seven 'pathways' or areas of work to support the rehabilitation of offenders. These were

- accommodation
- education, training and employment
- mental and physical health
- drugs and alcohol
- finance, benefit and debt
- maintaining relationships with children and families
- attitudes, thinking and behaviour

These contained considerable scope for partnership working and for the involvement of private and voluntary sector agencies in delivery (Burnett et al, 2007). National plans for work on the seven pathways were spelt out in the *Reducing re-offending national action plan* (Home Office, 2004a), and each region was required to develop its own regional plans. Meanwhile, work to progress the development of *end-to-end offender management* was taking place via a pathfinder scheme in the Northwest region (PA Consulting Group and MORI, 2005). However, legislation to facilitate competition and contestability was proving more difficult, with concerns about the impact on morale in the probation service if it had to face another re-organisation and the viability of the 'business case' for the proposed changes. Although an initial draft Bill had made more modest proposals, the final Offender Management Bill put before Parliament suggested a centralised commissioning structure operating through the regional offender managers. The existing probation boards would become probation trusts which could then compete for contracts to deliver offender management services alongside the voluntary and private sectors. This was not a popular model, but the Home Office was determined to press forward, with the Home Secretary of the time, John Reid, expressing a belief that there was a wider range of providers who could become involved in managing offenders and that creating a more varied mix of services and service providers would help improve standards (Home Office, 2006). Despite this political impetus, the legislation eventually passed in July 2007 contained a much less radical approach than that originally proposed, significantly different in terms of the scale of competition to be introduced.

The first six probation trusts came into existence in April 2008, with other probation areas quickly following suit in two later tranches. A small number of probation areas merged to create larger trusts and the whole of Wales combined to form a single trust, but there was certainly not the large-scale transfer of business originally envisaged. And trusts are now able to commission services locally, rather than all commissioning taking place on a national or regional basis.

Under Schedule 3 of the Offender Management Act 2007, the trusts took over the duties of the previous probation boards in relation to both the Children Act 2004 and YOTs under the Crime and Disorder Act 1998. They also continue to participate in a range of multi-agency partnerships, so in many respects there has been little apparent change. The move to trust status, however, created more independent bodies with – at least in theory – greater freedoms and flexibilities than the previously directly managed probation boards. Each trust is constituted with a board whose members must be approved by the Secretary of State. Membership includes one local authority representative, where practicable, but after the initial transitional period, no magistrates are able to sit on trust boards – a symbolic severing of a historical link between the magistracy and probation.

Update on NOMS

It should already be clear that the progress of NOMS has not been straightforward, and that the New Labour vision of a NOMS structure entirely focused on commissioning from a mixed economy of providers rather than itself delivering offender services has been fundamentally compromised. That model was criticised as being impractical and as posing an unfair and, in fact, unnecessary threat to the probation service that had responded to the call to improve efficiency and to deliver on performance targets.

In April 2008, a restructuring of the Ministry of Justice was announced, which involved re-branding NOMS as an executive agency within the department, responsible for both commissioning and delivering adult offender management services in custodial and community settings (Ministry of Justice, 2008a). The executive agency was charged with:

- Ensuring that prison and probation services coordinate their work in managing offenders even more closely, and work in partnership with the police and others in support of truly joined-up offender management; and
- Working with local government, the NHS, Learning and Skills Councils, Youth Justice Board and others to secure the housing, health, employment, training and other pathways to offender rehabilitation more effectively. (Ministry of Justice, 2008a p 7)

This restructuring of NOMS ensured that the distinct purchaser–provider split represented by the regional offender manager structure was abolished and regional offender managers were replaced with directors of offender management in each region of England and Wales.

The probation service does not have a rigid and readily understandable organisational structure and purpose, as the prison service does. Its work is largely a mystery to the general public and, while it does have its advocates, it has notably lacked political influence in comparison to other criminal justice agencies. This has left it particularly 'reform vulnerable' (Senior et al, 2007, p 103) and consequently subject to constant change over the past 15 years. Uncertainties for the service and its staff have been further increased by the shifting vision for the NOMS project and the status of the service within it, which has been arguably downgraded in the NOMS restructure (Whitehead, 2010) and the subsequent slimming down of central government structures under the Coalition government. It was therefore not surprising that research in 2007 among employees in four probation areas showed varying degrees of knowledge and intellectual engagement with the change process (Robinson and Burnett, 2007). The threat to probation certainly has not gone away with a new government, as the Coalition has shown renewed interest in contestability and opening up the criminal justice marketplace to the private and voluntary sectors. In this context the future of NOMS itself is unclear.

The NOMS vision

It is interesting to analyse the explicit statements from NOMS about the principles informing its work and its vision, particularly in relation to the earlier discussion of managerialism. In its *Strategic and business plans 2009-2010 to 2010-2011*, it sets out its statement of purpose:

We work to protect the public and reduce re-offending by delivering the punishment and orders of the courts and by helping offenders reform their lives. (Ministry of Justice, 2009a, p 2)

It is revealing that the same document also says that:

What work needs to be done and who does the work is based on evidence and driven by ensuring value for money. (Ministry of Justice, 2009a, p 2)

This locates concerns about efficiency and effectiveness at the heart of the NOMS agenda and it can be inferred that this attention to evidence of impact and cost is a primary means by which NOMS will seek to achieve its vision of building public confidence in its ability to protect the public and to reduce re-offending.

Turning to the values identified for the delivery of prison and probation services, these are presented as:

- be objective and take full account of public protection when assessing risk;
- be open, honest and transparent;
- incorporate equality and diversity in all that we do;
- value and empower staff, and work collaboratively with others;
- treat offenders with decency and respect;
- embrace change and innovation; and
- use our resources in the most cost effective way. (Ministry of Justice, 2009a, p 2)

These are framed more as objectives than fleshed out value commitments, not helped by being presented in a bullet-pointed list. There is no indication of what terms such as 'decency', 'respect' and 'honesty', for instance, actually mean here, and what beliefs and understandings will guide practitioners in their attempts to treat offenders, colleagues and others decently, respectfully and honestly. This may provide opportunities for the rights-based approach introduced in Chapter One, and this is worth looking at in relation to the framework for offender supervision adopted by NOMS, which gives a firmer indication of standards and values in practice.

National Offender Management Model (OMM)

One of the key elements of NOMS is a case management model designed to operate across the probation service, private and public prisons and any other delivery agency working with offenders. Case management is certainly not new to the probation service (Faulkner, 2008), but is a developing practice elsewhere, and the OMM is an attempt by NOMS to create a more consistent understanding of what *end-to-end offender management* means in practice and to promote its implementation, essentially creating a new framework for case management within a criminal justice context, where offenders move between different agencies in the penal system, sometimes within the same sentence.

One of the significant pieces of evidence underpinning the development of the OMM was a study of case management systems conducted by Sarah Partridge (2004). This identified particular features as helpful, irrespective of whether the predominant case management model in place was specialist, generic or a mixture of the two (Partridge, 2004, p 5):

- models need to acknowledge offenders' experiences and needs;
- continuity of contact with the same case manager and other staff was essential to building confidence and rapport with the offender, particularly during the initial stages of supervision;
- the greater the level of task separation the more offenders were confused by why they were undertaking different elements of their supervision, particularly where contact with the case manager had been limited;
- face-to-face contact with a small case management team was beneficial for both staff and offenders;
- openness, flexibility and support were key motivating factors for offenders.

Accordingly, the OMM developed by Tony Grapes (NOMS, 2006) focuses not on the complex overall network of agencies and large-scale provision required to manage numbers of offenders, but on the processes involved in the design and delivery of individual sentences across agencies. Furthermore, its use of the term 'offender management' also refers to the work of the offender manager at the centre of the process and his or her interactions with the individual offender.

Version 2 of the OMM

- The NOMS Offender Management Model describes an **evidence-based, offender focused** approach to work with individual offenders
- It is a **human service** approach because the main impact of correctional services is considered to arise from the **personal relationships** developed with an offender
- A **single, universal, core end-to-end process** which transcends the separate contributions of the main providers is defined using a **single language**
- A **one offender: one manager** structure is considered to be necessary for its effective delivery
- Based upon a **thorough assessment** an Offender Manager draws up a single **sentence plan**, in collaboration with the offender and providers of interventions. Resources and interventions, *commissioned and purchased by the Regional Offender Managers*, are engaged, using a **brokerage approach**. Personal **supervision** helps the offenders to comply and co-operate

- A transparent framework within the Model ensures that different resources and styles are applied to different cases, producing a highly **individualised** service capable of adapting to the **diverse needs, risks and circumstances** of individual offenders
- In order to deliver the required coherence to an offender, the model incorporates a **new concept of teamwork**
- Finally, it is a **whole system approach** requiring that organisational support functions support the core business process of Offender Management.

Source: NOMS (2006, p 12)

Note: The italics denote the change in commissioning arrangements that featured in the Offender Management Act as explained previously.

The OMM has attempted to respond to the characteristics identified by Partridge, and it is heartening to note the return to relational values and emphasis on continuity of contact with one key person and collaboration with the offender. This is in line with the growing body of work around successful desistance developed by Farrall (2002) and McNeill (2003, 2006a), for instance. Similarly, it is welcomed by Gwen Robinson (2005), who comments that:

> It is interesting to recall that much of the early Home Office–sponsored "what works" literature emphasised the importance of a consistent relationship between case manager and offender as a complement to what later became accredited programmes ... it is now generally accepted, however, that in a rush to implement programmes and achieve referral targets, this area of "effective practice" has been neglected. Furthermore, it is increasingly being recognised that poor case management may well have compromised the effectiveness of such programmes. (2005, p 312)

Recognising that services have become fragmented and that greater coherence is required, the OMM has adopted the notion of four Cs, these being:

- consistency
- commitment
- consolidation
- continuity.

And goes on to comment on the significance of process:

> Since both the "what" of offender management and its "how" are of equal importance, it is essential that the framework of standards, measures and targets conveys this message and steers behaviour accordingly. (NOMS, 2006, p 18)

Aspects of the OMM

Tiering framework: relating risks to resources

The first key feature of the OMM to note is the concentration on targeting resources according to levels of risk, which is predicated on accurate and detailed assessment of risks and needs. This practice of categorising offenders according to risk is very much a product of the artefact approach to risk discussed earlier.

According to the OMM, there are four tiers of intervention, each building on the previous layers. The notion of tiers is borrowed from the drugs, mental health and childcare fields, where increasing risk and need are reflected in assignment to a higher tier of intervention, involving more resources and services. Offenders are allocated to one of these four tiers according to their risk assessment and are subject to the approaches relevant to that tier but also interventions or approaches from the tiers beneath, so that at Tier 4, for instance, there may be a complex mix of measures designed to constrain behaviour, promote change and offer assistance. This can be seen as:

Tier 1 = PUNISH
Tier 2 = PUNISH and HELP
Tier 3 = PUNISH and HELP and CHANGE
Tier 4 = PUNISH and HELP and CHANGE and CONTROL

Under the principle that *resources follow risk*, this means that interventions, particularly at Tiers 3 and 4, have the potential to be varied and creative, once the offender is engaged. Interventions for those at Tiers 1 and 2 are likely to be much more limited and less flexible (Burnett et al, 2007), and there may be missed opportunities to deliver change-related or much needed welfare services to offenders categorised as low risk (Maguire, 2007). There may additionally be implications for particular groups, such as women offenders, proportionately less likely to feature at Tier 4 and therefore less likely to attract significant resources (Gelsthorpe and McIvor, 2007)

Interventions

The acronym, ASPIRE, captures the core of the offender management process:

Assess → Sentence → Plan → Implement → Review → Evaluate

Once the offender manager has assessed and decided which tier is appropriate for the individual offender, then a series of interventions should be delivered aimed at dealing with identified risks and needs. Two further concepts come into play here:

- Sequencing – arranging a coherent series of interventions so the timing of each is appropriate and builds, where possible, on the previous interventions.
- Brokerage – making sure the offender has access to services and interventions from elsewhere in the probation or prison services or from partner agencies, in order to provide a balanced and holistic package of interventions.

Key roles

The implication of the above is very clearly that supervision should involve more than intervention from the supervising officer/offender manager, and in this respect the OMM pushes the boundaries of probation practice. The NOMS structure, if operating as intended, should encourage closer working between the prison and probation services for offenders in custody and the greater use of partnership resources. The OMM therefore talks of *a team around the offender*, which is brought together by the offender manager. An offender supervisor may offer an important relationship, particularly where an offender is in prison, for instance, and therefore not in regular contact with the offender manager. Other key roles are *case administrator* and *key workers*, who may be drugs workers or group tutors, for example. The relationships are illustrated in Figure 2.1.

There are parallels with professional developments in other fields and particularly the *lead professional* role in the children's services, who, in a similar way to the

Figure 2.1: The team around the offender

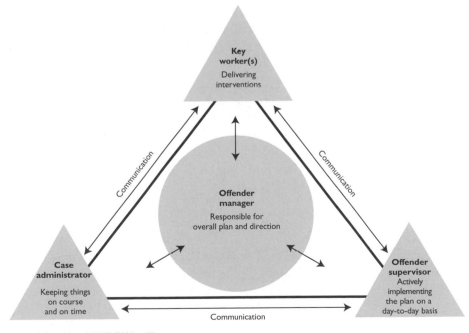

Source: Adapted from NOMS (2006, p 41)

offender manager, conducts assessments, brokers interventions and resources from elsewhere, ensures the coherence and integrity of the package of interventions and acts as the conduit for key communications.

Burnett et al (2007, p 237) neatly sum up the transformations in practice when they say that:

> In contrasting traditional and contemporary assessment, supervision and intervention, the most overt changes in each of these three areas of practice respectively are: the transition from unstructured and arbitrary assessment decisions to the use of systematic and validated assessment tools; the movement from one-to-one casework as the principal modus operandi to a team-based offender management approach; and the progression from exceptional and arbitrary use of interventions to the systematic usage of a package of interventions, sequenced and delivered in accordance with an end-to-end sentence plan.

But they go on to sound a cautionary note:

> Perhaps the greatest change of general applicability to practice – now formalised in the principle of "resources following risk" – is that those subject to "offender management" are higher-end offenders and therefore the stakes have been raised. (Burnett et al, 2007, p 237)

Implementation of the OMM

Implementation of the OMM was phased and linked to the sentencing provisions of the Criminal Justice Act 2003, with the probation service starting to apply the model to Community Orders and licences from April 2005, and custodial institutions coming on board at a later date. The intention had been to establish the OMM as the normal operating model for all sentenced offenders by April 2009 (NOMS, 2006), but in practice that date was significantly delayed.

That initial account of implementation rather underplays the complex process of bringing a supervisory framework of this type into operation across such a large and complicated system and with two very different agencies at its heart. It is instructive perhaps to look at the findings from the North West Pathfinder (PA Consulting Group and MORI, 2005) which were encouraging in terms of offender feedback, particularly from the young offender institutions in the study, where most of these young people were clear about their sentence plan and were aware of the different elements involved. For the community sample, there was less clarity about the sentence planning process but most understood the purpose and the constituent parts of the work to be undertaken on their orders.

For staff, however, there were problems arising in working across the prison/ probation divide, with offender managers in probation sometimes describing themselves as unsure of how to operate effectively within the prison environment – perhaps understandable concerns in terms of adjusting to new cultures and building skills. There were further concerns expressed about what was meant by sequencing in the OMM and how meaningfully to put this into practice. Finally, gaps in provision of interventions had a potentially serious impact on the extent to which the OMM was effective for individual cases (PA Consultancy Group and MORI, 2005).

Research in 2007 with prison staff in both public and private sectors indicated a generally positive attitude to the concept of *end-to-end offender management* and how it might enhance the prison officer role. However, the levels of knowledge and awareness among staff about NOMS and the OMM varied considerably, and this was exacerbated by an over-reliance on information technology to communicate key developments (Burnett and Stevens, 2007). This general lack of knowledge reflected the delays in implementation of the OMM and the effective bringing together of prison and probation staff in the management of individual cases.

All these are issues that the prison service and probation trusts have had to tackle in implementing the OMM. Availability of appropriate interventions has been – and will continue to be – particularly problematic at a time of budgetary constraint. What is presented as an optimistic and potentially helpful framework for working with offenders is sadly often being confounded by other organisational pressures, particularly financial, and by low morale among the probation and prison staff being asked to implement the OMM.

Looking at possible impacts and social functions of NOMS and offender management processes, Philip Whitehead highlights the potential for offender managers to 'operate as the good guys of the criminal justice system who represent a set of values rooted in personalist ethics' (2010, p 103). However, offender management can lend itself to different approaches with varying impacts involving, for instance, expressive knee-jerk reactions to individuals and events; punishment and exclusion; social control; a focus on bureaucracy and technical processes; and even a role as 'disciplinary regulators and normalisers, the eyes and ears of the courts and an increasingly centralised and authoritarian state' (Whitehead, 2010, p 104). The question for those involved in offender management is how to work constructively and be 'the good guys' within the OMM framework, conscious of, and able to resist, organisational or wider political pressures to veer towards these alternative modes.

Further changes ahead

At the time of writing, the Coalition government's Green Paper, *Breaking the cycle: Effective punishment, rehabilitation and sentencing of offenders* (Ministry of Justice, 2010a), has just been published. This promises both continuity and change, with a tilt towards private and voluntary sector provision, but a continuing core strategic role for probation trusts. The proposals were open for consultation until March 2011 and it is unclear what will eventually reach the statute books, but the key elements are:

- decentralisation;
- targets for criminal justice agencies focused on outcomes rather than measuring multiple processes;
- the closer working of key criminal justice agencies in integrated offender management;
- tougher approaches that will see an emphasis on work in prisons, an increase in curfews and electronic monitoring, and more intensive community payback delivered by the private sector;
- rehabilitation services opened up to competition from the private and voluntary sector;
- a move towards local rather than central or regional commissioning of services;
- a focus on access to employment, drug rehabilitation and mental health diversion schemes.

Some of the proposals – revisions to national standards to allow more practitioner discretion, fewer short prison sentences, restorative justice – are to be welcomed, but others raise serious questions. The most controversial element will undoubtedly be the proposals for 'payments by results' (PBR), whereby agencies will receive payments according to the outcomes they achieve. The Green Paper describes this as:

> A radical and decentralising reform which will deliver a fundamental shift in the way rehabilitation is delivered. It will make the concept of justice reinvestment real by allowing providers to invest money in the activity that will prevent offending rather than spending money on dealing with the consequences. (Ministry of Justice, 2010a, p 38)

This will apply to selected activities and offender groups, and certainly not the most high-risk offenders. It will be piloted and the criteria that form the basis of payment will be developed over time. Nevertheless, it represents a huge cultural shift and a real challenge for both the statutory and voluntary sectors that will be asked to evidence and justify their interventions in a quite different way. PBR has already or is being established in other areas of social policy, consistent with the ideological drive of the Coalition government. Yet criminal justice is a particularly sensitive area and it remains to be seen how far and in what ways it will encroach on core offender management functions.

Summary

This chapter has outlined the current context for offender management and the way that the prison and probation services have been brought together – not without controversy – within NOMS. These changes have been influenced both by responses to the 'rise of risk' and artefact approaches to risk (Kemshall, 2003), and by a modernising agenda with a distinctly managerial flavour. In comparison to the prison service and other criminal justice agencies, the probation service has found itself particularly 'reform vulnerable' (Senior et al, 2007, p 103) and consequently subject to successive organisational changes. One such change is the adoption of the OMM as a framework for practice across all agencies involved in offender management and the requirements to work more collaboratively with partners in a *team around the offender*, with the offender manager coordinating and brokering interventions and services. Although still evidencing an explicitly managerial concern for processes and procedures, the OMM has established itself as a human services model and highlights the importance of quality and consistency of relationships. There are opportunities within this, as well as challenges, for developing a rights-based approach and this is explored further in the following two chapters.

Further reading

Kemshall. H. (2003) *Understanding risk in criminal justice*, Maidenhead: Open University Press.

Senior, P., Crowther-Dowey, C. and Long, M. (2007) *Understanding modernisation in criminal justice*, Maidenhead: Open University Press.

THREE

Partnership and inter-agency working

As indicated in Chapter Two, the modernisation agenda has placed a high premium on collaborations and partnerships between criminal justice agencies and the pursuit of more 'joined-up justice'. This chapter outlines the impacts this has had at the macro (strategic) and meso (middle or operational) levels as well as looking at the micro level in terms of what practitioners might meet as they engage with other agencies. This engagement may take place within multi-agency structures, where different organisations come together to pool expertise and resources, or in more integrated (and frequently co-located) inter-agency teams. Within such teams, practitioners face challenges in terms of occupational identities and cultures, as well as role boundaries and allocation of tasks. These issues are explored with reference to the learning from the integration of children's services under the *Every Child Matters* agenda and the experience of YOTs.

Partnership work is an intrinsic part of the OMM in terms of both the *team around the offender* and the additional services and interventions that an offender manager may broker as part of a sentence plan. Confidence in working with other agencies is therefore a critical element of an offender manager's skill set: in P. Williams' (2002) terms, an offender manager needs to be a 'competent boundary spanner'. This chapter therefore ends with a discussion of brokerage and inter-relationships with practitioners from other agencies, and goes on to explore the potential for using rights-based thinking and the language of rights as a basis for developing joint work.

What do we mean by partnership?

It is useful to begin by outlining key terms used in relation to partnerships. Reference is often made to:

- *coordination:* efforts to bring the aims and activities of different organisations closer together, to achieve greater synergy;
- *collaboration:* representatives of different agencies working together to improve coordination in practice;
- *partnership:* collaboration involving a longer-term agreement about coordination and joint planning to achieve greater coordination. This entails the development of relationships of trust and inter-dependence (adapted from Payne, 2000, p 27).

Partnerships, of course, can take different forms, particularly in the complicated social world that we currently inhabit. A bewildering array of partnership arrangements have sprung up in recent years, reflecting 'growing appreciation that complex social problems, including crime, cannot be adequately addressed by the uncoordinated efforts of well-intentioned organisations working in isolation' (Rumgay, 2007, p 551).

A great deal of faith has been placed in partnerships by those making and those implementing policy and, in early days of the New Labour administration, the increase in their popularity clearly outstripped the growth in knowledge about what contributes to successful partnership working (Rumgay, 2003). Fortunately, this knowledge base is expanding and it is now possible to identify skills and capacities critical in the partnership context.

In the criminal justice world, the main areas of development have been:

- statutory partnerships where agencies are legally mandated to work together (for example, CSPs);
- contractual partnerships, where one agency commissions a service from another (often a voluntary or community organisation);
- problem-solving partnerships, where agencies come together over an area of joint interest or common targets (for example, YOTs and Connexions jointly working to identify hard to reach young people and to reduce the NEET [not in education, employment or training] population);
- partnerships aimed at wider social problems or provision (for example, Supporting People).

Partnership work is an expanding area for the prison service but is nowhere near as active or as diverse as it is for the police and for probation. However, there was a tension between the demands of the managerialist framework set by New Labour for the criminal justice system and the local autonomy required to pursue partnership working enthusiastically – performance targets could encourage agencies to be inward rather than outward looking and could thus work counter to the spirit of partnership working (Gilling, 2005). In the case of probation, this has been particularly – and regrettably – so in terms of the emphasis on delivery of accredited programmes (Rumgay, 2004a), which has resulted in the service concentrating partnership activity on the first three areas listed above, and giving relatively little attention to partnerships focused on wider social problems, such as housing or employment-related skills (Rumgay, 2007). The irony of this is that the probation service has historically sustained an interest in social justice and inclusion and, as the key agency that connects with both the criminal justice arena and social welfare provision, should be best placed to argue the needs and interests of offenders and other marginalised populations (Rumgay, 2004a).

Setting and tackling strategic priorities

New Labour policy established partnership working at all levels, particularly focusing in early legislation on building structures for agencies to come together at a local authority level. In terms of criminal justice, developments were informed by the influential Morgan Report (Home Office, 1991), which introduced the concept of 'community safety' and advocated the development of multi-agency crime prevention partnerships with a clear statutory coordinating role for local authorities, and participation from public, private and voluntary sectors. These suggestions had not been taken up by the then Conservative government, but the idea of joint ownership and joint activity was attractive to New Labour as it came into office in 1997, seeking a broader and more holistic response to crime and social exclusion.

Subsequently Section 5 of the Crime and Disorder Act 1998 established Crime and Disorder Reduction Partnerships (CDRPs), which included the police, the local authority, primary care trusts, providers of probation services and the Fire and Rescue Service as 'responsible authorities', with others such as housing organisations, Victim Support and courts being co-opted on to the partnership on a local basis. These bodies have provided strategic oversight of crime and disorder activities in local authority areas, driving forward the anti-social behaviour agenda and monitoring performance of the key criminal justice agencies. From April 2010, under Section 108 of the Policing and Crime Act 2009, their remit has expanded to include an explicit focus on reducing re-offending as well as crime prevention, so creating a more central role for probation trusts. This is reflected in a change of name to Community Safety Partnerships.

From 2003, National and Local Criminal Justice Boards (LCJBs) have brought together senior managers from the main criminal justice agencies to align strategies and provide a concerted push to bring more offenders to justice. LCJBs have an important role in overseeing prolific and other priority offender (PPO) schemes and the development of Integrated Offender Management initiatives, and, unlike CSPs, are organised around criminal justice service rather than local authority boundaries.

Other strategic partnerships include:

- Strategic Management Boards (SMBs) overseeing MAPPAs;
- Supporting People – focused on developing and funding supported housing provision;
- Learning and Skills Partnerships;
- Local Safeguarding Children Boards (LSCBs);
- Children's Services Partnerships.

This proliferation of partnerships can be understood as a distribution of responsibilities for crime and criminal justice management from statutory agencies towards a wider constituency of organisations and communities (Senior et al, 2007). It may also be understood as an attempt to harness a greater variety of skills and resources to help resolve complex situations. A further argument relates to the attempts to integrate fragmented systems and service delivery (Rumgay, 2007). The extent to which each of these happen in practice is unclear, and partnership working can be fraught with pitfalls and problems. Agencies do not necessarily meet on equal terms and there may be marked power differentials between organisations (Gilling, 2005). This in turn may determine who has the power to define the problem that has brought partners together and to influence the choice of intervention and allocation of resources to address it (Rumgay, 2004a). Alternatively, difficulties may arise and result in much wasted effort when aims, objectives and agency contributions are poorly defined (Rumgay, 2003), or where there is insufficient focus on outcomes (Rumgay, 2007).

So what contributes to successful strategic partnerships? These qualities are not so very different to partnerships operating at other levels, and include:

- collaborative styles of leadership, reflecting the fact that relationships are not hierarchical and, that within most partnerships, agencies do not have authority over each other (P. Williams, 2002);
- trust and interdependency (Gilling, 2005);
- clarity of communication;
- explicit understandings of roles, responsibilities and agency contributions;
- ability to recognise and resolve conflict (Rumgay, 2003);
- appropriate resourcing;
- attention to the process of implementation;
- sustainability or durability (Gilling, 2005).

What is also interesting to note is that, contrary to the push for standardisation and consistency in most policy areas, the drive for partnership working expects a degree of difference and innovation in localities. Partners need to find ways to accommodate both the demands of 'top-down' direction and 'grassroots' initiatives, striking 'a balance between central policy making and implementation guidance and local flexibility' (Rumgay, 2004a, p 132).

Joined-up programmes

Beneath the strategic bodies outlined above, there is a developing range of programmes bringing agencies together at operational level to coordinate their work in relation to specific targeted groups. These are:

- PPO schemes (discussed in the next section);
- MAPPAs;
- Drugs Intervention Programmes (DIPs);
- Integrated Offender Management.

All of these programmes depend on effective and timely exchange of information between agencies, and for each scheme partners have had to develop protocols and systems to enable the sharing and storage of information about individuals. Naturally, this raises issues in relation to the rights of individuals and their personal information, and also in relation to data protection. Section 115 of the Crime and Disorder Act 1998 does allow for disclosure of information for such purposes as preventing commission of an offence, but practitioners should be guided by local protocols as to when and how much information it is appropriate to pass on.

One other feature that these programmes have in common is the targeting of individuals not necessarily under statutory supervision. For instance, PPO schemes may identify offenders on release from short prison sentences as 'in scope', and DIPs attempt to make contact with offenders in the police station by virtue of arrest referral schemes. The rationale is clearly to offer services to populations of offenders who otherwise might slip through the safety net of service provision, but, alongside these benefits, there is a perceptible increase in control measures and surveillance (enhanced by the availability of new technologies).

While there are obvious gains to be made, there are also critical concerns about the extent of joint working in these programmes and the potential blurring of agency boundaries and identities. Some blurring of what could be rigid demarcations clearly contributes to successful inter-agency work, but commentators have warned that there are implications for the distinct identity of the probation service, through a process of gradual 'policification' (Kemshall and Maguire, 2001, p 252). Others have also talked about the creation of a strange hybrid creature called the 'polibation officer' (Nash, 1999). Similarly, concerns have been raised about threats to the diversity and innovatory potential of the voluntary sector as it enters more significantly into service provision through contractual arrangements (Gough, 2010).

Prolific and other priority offender programme

It is worth looking at the development of one national programme in more detail. The PPO programme arose against a background of increased public anxiety over risk and concern about petty persistent, often young, offenders. This was fuelled in part by press coverage of 'bail bandits' and out-of-control youth, exemplified by almost mythologised characters such as 'Rat Boy'. However, there was evidence to suggest that a minority of offenders did commit a disproportionate volume of crime. The Home Office document, *Criminal justice: The way ahead* (2001), cited research indicating that approximately 100,000 or 10 per cent of the total offending population were responsible for almost half of the crime in England and Wales.

Many probation areas had tried to develop prolific offender schemes during the 1990s, but these had varied considerably in approach and in the target group. By 2000, more consistent and strategic measures were already being taken within the youth justice system in relation to PYOs, intending to speed their processing through the court system. Turning the attention to adults, the Home Office instigated a Persistent Offender programme in 2002, which in 2004 became the PPO programme. This initially came within the Narrowing the Justice Gap (NJG) initiative. NJG was essentially the coming together of criminal justice agencies to work towards a more effective operation in the criminal justice system in order to ensure that more offences were successfully prosecuted through the courts. The jargon used was Offences Brought To Justice, or OBTJ, and targeting the most prolific offenders was seen as important to achieving a higher conviction rate and closing the considerable gap that existed between the numbers of reported offences and successful convictions.

There are three elements to the programme:

- Catch and convict   Lead agency: Police
- Rehabilitate and re-settle   Lead agency: Probation
- (Prevent and) deter   Lead agency: YOTs

The 'catch and convict' strand was already well developed because of the work that had taken place under the NJG initiative, so that when the Home Office issued new guidance in July 2004, that stream of work continued to progress. One aspect of this was – and still is – the Premium Service given to defendants identified as prolific or priority offenders throughout their prosecution, so that cases are charged and taken to court more quickly. Local agreements are established between the relevant agencies specifying responsibilities, actions and timescales.

Work within 'rehabilitate and re-settle' began more slowly. Following Home Office guidance, supervisory practices were based on the concept of *end-to-end offender management* (Millie and Erol, 2006), although a recent inspection found inconsistencies in the application of the OMM (CJJI, 2009). Local schemes established management and operational groups at different levels to oversee the scheme and accessed staff and resources from the police and probation primarily, but also services from other relevant agencies.

One of the vexed questions for the PPO schemes is whether they have been successful in targeting the 'right' offenders. Each CDRP/CSP has a defined number of offenders to register on the scheme and to work with, making their own decisions about the appropriate blend of support and surveillance. Local areas have more flexibility now about who to work with in this way than they did at the outset (Farrall et al, 2007), but decisions remain heavily dependent on police information and intelligence.

The findings of the impact assessment of the programme published in 2007 suggested that the local schemes were managing to identify at least some of the most prolific offenders (Dawson, 2007). The indications from the national evaluation are that there has been a significant impact on offending, although it is unclear how much of this was due to the interventions delivered by the schemes (Dawson and Cuppleditch, 2007). Interestingly, an earlier joint inspection of PPO schemes (Home Office, 2004b) had indicated that prolific offenders have needs similar to other offenders, but that typically each has a greater number of (criminogenic) needs.

This last finding points to the value of maintaining good inter-agency links and specifically involving housing, health and other providers in the partnership networks around the schemes, although there is certainly a challenge in engaging the voluntary sector in such partnerships driven by statutory agencies (Millie and Erol, 2006). This wide range of provision is largely justified in terms of its potential impact on offending rates. However, there is also a strong argument that these offenders tend to be particularly socially disadvantaged and that interventions should work in an inclusive way to enable them to receive appropriate services and to have the opportunity to build social capital.

PPO schemes were quite varied, as local areas were given freedom to develop their own models, although all include a mixture of intervention and oversight from the police and probation services. As these schemes merge with the DIP and form Integrated Offender Management Units, there are still considerations about the balance of help versus the restrictive elements being offered, and issues in terms of rights, particularly as selection criteria for the schemes are rather clearer and more rigorously applied than de-selection/de-registering (Dawson, 2007; CJJI, 2009), so it is easier for an individual to get onto the schemes and achieve a label of prolific offender than it is to prove that he or she has changed and that the label is no longer appropriate! There are also issues about what is offered to offenders leaving the intensive support of the schemes and how they are enabled to maintain progress.

Enforcement is an additional concern for those on statutory supervision, as there are extensive commitments associated with the schemes and that also means many opportunities to miss appointments or activities. However, many offenders engage on a voluntary basis, and this represents a different challenge for practitioners, particularly for the police who may be more familiar with the enforcement stick than the engagement carrot.

Writing in 2002 in relation to the prolific offender schemes that pre-dated the PPO programme, Anne Worrall comments that the historical tensions between the police and probation had not disappeared but tended to take new forms within those schemes. Certainly overt ideological conflicts seem less evident as partnership work has become more embedded, even routine (Gilling, 2005). However, while there may be apparent consensus over pragmatic responses to the demands of central government (Rumgay, 2007), this may mask a variety of underlying ideas, assumptions and values about offenders, anti-social behaviours and the nature of society.

Relationships in multi-agency work

At the micro or 'grassroots' level the ability to work with other agencies is becoming essential for competent practitioners as multi-agency practice has come to represent a new orthodoxy in criminal justice initiatives. Multi-agency teams can identify and address a diverse range of needs through more coherent and holistic service delivery and this is attractive to a criminal justice system that increasingly recognises the complex nature of offending behaviour and seeks proactive, efficient strategies in response (Souhami, 2008).

Operating confidently in a multi-agency context can be challenging for practitioners, and training has not tended to equip staff with the necessary range of skills and understanding (Rumgay, 2003) (although, for probation practitioners, this will receive more attention within their new training arrangements).

Specific challenges may arise in relation to:

- decision-making processes, which may be subject to collective distortions or 'group-think' (see for instance Munro, 2008; Beckett, 2010). This may result, for instance, in risk of harm being grossly under- or over-estimated;
- the blurring of professional boundaries – some flexibility is needed to make multi-agency arrangements work, but if roles become too indistinct or 'fuzzy', important tasks or functions may be neglected (Kemshall, 2008);
- delegation of tasks – agencies generally do not have the authority to require other agencies to take on tasks and multi-agency processes are often dependent on the commitment and willingness of participants to agree to undertake tasks or provide information (Wood and Kemshall, 2008);
- the nature of accountability – individual practitioners have accountability to their own organisation and its professional priorities, but there is a more complex network of peer accountability within multi-agency groups;
- the 'baggage' that individuals may bring with them into the partnership arena from their professional or organisational background (Gilling, 2005). This may include issues relating to past histories of disputes or problems between agencies;
- conflict and tensions over the aims of the group or the means of achieving those aims (for example, what actions are needed to protect the public).

In relation to this latter point, Wood and Kemshall comment in a MAPPA context that:

> The key test should be risk management that is based on robust research evidence about the most effective ways of reducing risky behaviours in the community, and not necessarily the pursuit of risk management strategies that most comply with the value-base or routine work patterns of the individual agencies concerned. (Wood and Kemshall, 2010, p 56)

This is an interesting point: practitioners are exactly that, not academics who can quote quantities of research studies, but it does highlight the need for offender managers and others entering multi-agency groups to be informed and to draw on (and be willing to share) their professional understanding and knowledge.

This leads on to further critical points about trust and openness in collaborative relationships. Naturally how much and what information is made public is a matter of professional judgement. While there may be relatively little argument about factual matters, practitioners have discretion about the extent to which they disclose information about themselves, their background and their values, and also make choices about what aspects of the internal workings and dynamics of their organisations they might reveal. Some disclosure on both counts would seem to be necessary to invite the trust and inter-dependency that oil the wheels of partnership.

Partnership working is a sophisticated enterprise and engages a different range of skills and personal qualities than traditional single agency work. Of course, in entering the multi-agency arena, practitioners need to be confident in their occupational identity and knowledge of the core business of their organisation. However, over and above that, in order to get the most from that arena,

> The skills and competency profile of individuals who are focused on the management of inter-dependencies will not be professional or knowledge-based, but rely more on relational and inter-personal attributes designed to build social capital. (P. Williams, 2002, p 106)

Paul Williams is referring to managers within a multi-agency context, but given the nature of the offender manager's role in bringing together the *team around the offender* and in brokering services in complex and high-risk cases, the desirable qualities that he identifies for a *competent boundary spanner* are highly relevant. These include the ability to communicate and to seek shared meaning with partners, an appreciation of the connections and inter-relationships at different stages of the partnership process, and an ability to offer negotiation and compromise (without being compromised!). He comments that:

> Brokering effective deals epitomises, perhaps, the essence of a successful boundary spanner as it depends on the employment of a range of competencies and skills – an acute understanding of inter-dependencies between problems, solutions and organisations; an interpersonal style that is facilitating, respectful and trusting; and drive to devise solutions that make a difference to solving problems on the ground. (P. Williams, 2002, p 117)

Inter-agency teams: what can we learn from children's services?

The joining up of services is not unique to the criminal justice world, but formed a theme in the development of multiple policy areas under New Labour. There was a particular impetus for the integration of children's services following the inquiry into the death of Victoria Climbié (Laming, 2003). The move towards integration has been more circumspect in children's services than in criminal justice, and the learning about the formation of inter-agency teams is instructive. It should be noted that the literature tends to use 'multi-agency', 'inter-agency' and, sometimes, 'inter-professional' as interchangeable terms, but here a clearer distinction is made between:

- multi-agency collaborations that are more loosely structured, even where legally mandated (as in MAPPA, for instance); and
- inter-agency structures that involve higher degrees of integration and formation of (primarily co-located) teams involving professionals from different agencies.

This analysis draws heavily, but not exclusively, on Economic and Social Research Council (ESRC)-funded research based at the University of Leeds and known as the MATCh Project (Multi-Agency Teamwork in Services for Children). This research looked at the experiences of practitioners in five inter-agency teams as they came together and formed 'communities of practice' (Wenger, 1998), which developed through interactions and shared experiences in the team context, and were given concrete expression in new organisational practices and procedures (Frost and Robinson, 2007).

The formation of these new teams was by no means easy, and it was clear that the emotional impact involved had not been sufficiently recognised in the preparation beforehand:

> For many professionals, a physical move to work in a multi-professional team can be a debilitating experience ... suddenly you do not know where you fit any more. You do not know where you are. (Anning et al, 2002, p 96)

There is clearly physical disorientation, but also practitioners may feel disempowered and deskilled as the beliefs, habits and boundaries of their previous professional world are challenged and 'destabilised' (Anning et al, 2002). In the early stages, professional identities may feel under attack, particularly as specialist knowledge and roles are redefined and practitioners are required to learn generic skills relating to their new practice context (Frost and Robinson, 2007).

Inter-agency teams by their very nature raise questions about role boundaries and specific dilemmas in relation to the expertise of team members and who is competent and qualified to do what (Anning et al, 2002). These judgements may be contentious but ultimately powerful in deciding the balance between specialist working and genericism within the team. Abbott et al (2005) refer to concepts of *role release* (transfer of skills and sharing of expertise) and *role expansion* (training in the language and concepts of another discipline). Clearly, if an inter-agency team develops in a healthy fashion, participants will feel empowered to engage in both and will view this as enrichment, rather than a threat.

Inter-agency teams may be differently structured and the core functions of line management, coordination and professional supervision (Anning et al, 2002) may be configured in different ways. Medical practitioners, for instance, may continue to receive clinical supervision in their parent agency. Secondment and line management arrangements may vary considerably. However, it does appear that if teams are to work in an integrated way, there must be a sense of membership and allegiance, with the development of group norms and culture (Miller et al, 2001). This is not necessarily easy to establish as individuals come together with

---

different occupational expectations and values and also explanatory models for the social problems being addressed. These may be taken for granted in a single-agency context but in an inter-agency team may need to be revealed and explained to colleagues (Frost et al, 2005). In these research studies, for instance, there were contested areas around social or medical models of disability (Abbott et al, 2005) and psychological or social understandings of offending (Robinson and Cottrell, 2005). Robinson and Cottrell remark that:

> Professionals in multi-agency teams are often challenged to contain and embrace diversity, often within a dominant team model, while not sacrificing those personal beliefs which underpin their own commitment. They were challenged to reflect on which of their beliefs about practice are imbued with core values, and which can be modified through the development of new, shared knowledge within the team. (2005, p 551)

On a related point, other researchers from the MATCh Project noted that:

> A key enabler of professionals' continuing participation in the teams in our study was that the professionals could hold on to their "balanced view" despite disagreements with other team members. There are core values retained by team members that help maintain their identity in a complex multi-disciplinary environment. (Frost and Robinson, 2007, p 192)

Naturally, for this to happen, practitioners must be secure in their value base on entering the inter-agency team and able to 'live with difference' (Frost et al, 2005, p 190). But values, of course, are not static, and practitioners must also be receptive to the negotiation and establishment of key shared values within their inter-agency team.

All these factors are of relevance to the development of effective inter-agency working in a criminal justice context. One final idea is worth consideration and that is the notion of *open teamwork*, as developed by Malcolm Payne (2000). This suggests that a strong and outward-looking core team will have around it an active network of other participants, who may be members of the community, volunteers or other professionals, for instance, or in a criminal justice context, offenders themselves. So relationships in the inter-agency team are not just focused internally, but are capable of 'going out and drawing in' (Payne, 2000, p 3). This is useful in relation to offender management, where diverse and flexible groups of people may need to come together to work on complex situations and human problems. And of course, those skills necessary to create wider connections and networks are no different from the skills and personal qualities needed to engage creatively and positively in core inter-agency teams.

Inter-agency work in the criminal justice system

Many of the points highlighted in the children's services literature are also evident in the development of inter-agency work in the criminal justice arena. Anna Souhami's (2007) study of the first year of a YOT in the Midlands is particularly revealing, and explores dilemmas and tensions that many practitioners may face as they enter different inter-agency contexts. Again, a cautionary note on terminology – what Souhami refers to as a 'multi-agency team' is classified within this chapter as a 'co-located inter-agency team'.

The specific focus of Souhami's research was the nature of occupational identity and the issues thrown up in the changing and ambiguous context of the formation of a new team. Echoing the findings from the wider literature, she noted the tensions that developed for practitioners who were expected to contribute their professional expertise and at the same time to undertake more generic team tasks. She commented that, for workers in multi-agency teams, achieving an appropriate balance between the specialist and 'generic' elements of their role was vital both for job satisfaction and a sense of team membership (Souhami, 2008). Finding such a balance was not easy, and the social processes involved:

> Threatened to disrupt practitioners' accustomed sense of occupational and identity and membership. Yet at the same time, the extent to which staff retained a distinct professional identity within a YOT put in question the success of the reconfiguration of youth justice services. Without some degree of generic YOT identity, the absorption of staff from different agencies into a single team created scope for inter-agency conflict. (Souhami, 2007, p 24)

The blurring of professional boundaries and negotiation around core tasks had particular implications for social workers, which may be pertinent for probation practitioners as allied professionals. In practice, in the Midlands YOT there was reasonable clarity about the specialist roles for education and health workers, for instance, because of their knowledge base and professional connections. However, there was more ambiguity about what social work offered that was entirely distinct from other professions. Souhami uses the concept of 'functional territory' (Huntington, 1981) to ask:

> What is the "functional territory" of social work with young offenders?
> What do youth justice workers actually do? (2007, p 58)

Social work essentially operates through the medium of purposeful relationships but exactly how such relationships are developed and how they are used can be difficult to articulate. In addition, building relationships is essential for education workers and other professionals, enabling them to perform their specialist tasks but also providing a basis for them to engage with the generic supervisory tasks of the YOT. The inherently ambiguous nature of social work – and also key aspects of probation work – is clearly of benefit within inter-agency teams, because its basic skills and values can be put to various purposes. However, the qualities of flexibility and elasticity in the social work (and probation) role can result in a loss of its distinct identity and contribution within inter-agency teams, particularly where practitioners are less secure in their professional identity and value base.

In Souhami's Midlands YOT, the basis of the team was the pre-existing youth justice social work team that was joined in stages by representatives of other agencies. The narrative of the team development noted the initial dominance of social workers and their practices and, over time, interesting in-group and out-group dynamics, in part reflecting resistance to change and pre-existing assumptions about other agencies. The key enablers for change and establishment of a new YOT identity included significant markers, such as team events or meetings and the move to new office premises. And the team moved on significantly as joint work took place around implementation of new orders and new areas of practice, enabling the team to begin establishing different routines, norms and identities.

What is also significant in the development of the Midlands YOT is that the team reached a point where the feelings of threat seemed to diminish and this happened at the stage where working relationships were established with the local secure estate. Souhami explains this as:

> A change in the way the staff perceived the power and status of the YOT. Instead of being vulnerable to encroachment, it was the YOT that could now penetrate more deeply into other agencies and even influence the ethos of their work. In this way, the new state of flux in the membership of the team no longer seemed to be a source of overwhelming anxiety. Instead it appeared to be accompanied by a new confidence in the possibilities of expansion. (2007, p 169)

Souhami's work and the emerging literature from the children's services field are highly relevant to the experience of criminal justice practitioners entering inter-agency teams and, particularly, in the formation of new teams. The recent popularity of multi-agency and inter-agency work seriously underplays the challenges and the complexity of these practice contexts. However, as indicated in the quote above, the results of inter-agency work may be extremely powerful in promoting the interests of a specific offender group and reaching beyond the spheres of the individual agencies' influence.

Returning to rights

This chapter has looked at the strategic framework bringing partners together and both multi-agency initiatives and inter-agency teams. Partnership is, of course, also relevant within the OMM in terms of coordinating the roles of offender supervisors and key workers involved in individual cases and also in accessing wider opportunities and services for offenders.

All of these contexts require the ability to work with individuals from different organisations and/or with different roles. Previous discussions identified the importance of:

- being clear about core values;
- being clear about areas of norms and values that are open for negotiation and adaptation;
- open and transparent dealings with other professionals;
- clear communication and, in particular, ensuring that there is a common understanding of terms in use;
- finding shared language to explore beliefs and attitudes and to resolve differences;
- being willing to work towards establishing a productive *community of practice*.

It may be helpful to locate discussions in the language of rights rather than the sometimes obscure and exclusive terminologies used by individual professions. This could allow individuals from different agencies to make explicit their own values and priorities, and to seek areas of mutual understanding and agreement that could then form a platform for action.

Reference has been made at several points to the need for practitioners to be confident about their values in partnership work of all kinds. A strong sense of core values can act as an important bulwark against the pressures to conform to the priorities and world view of other dominant partners or even personalities. Values are the critical determinant for practitioners as to what is acceptable and what is, effectively, a line that cannot be crossed. Adopting a set of values based on rights, practitioners would be able to respond to decisions and proposed actions on the basis of their judgement about the impact on the rights of different parties. And this would also provide a clear stance that other agencies could understand and appreciate.

There are particular opportunities where close working relationships exist in offender management teams around individual offenders for all professionals involved to work in a rights-based way and, through these practices, for a rights-based approach to be disseminated across agencies.

Summary

The exploration of partnership work in this chapter has focused on macro (strategic) and meso (operational) levels, as well as looking at the micro-environments of inter-agency teams. Various qualities and competencies have been identified as necessary in the *competent boundary spanner* (P. Williams, 2002), which may be different to the skills and aptitudes required in a single agency setting. The question of values is particularly significant in a partnership context, because values guide decisions and actions and it is therefore important to establish sufficient commonality to be able to move forward collectively. For individual practitioners, this means having to be clear about their core values – what cannot be subject to compromise – and what areas are negotiable and available for adaptation in order to make partnership 'work'. Consideration of rights and the values associated with a rights-based approach may have a particular utility in that regard. Rights may also form the basis of a common language between agencies, enabling the development of shared understandings and new *communities of practice* (Wenger, 1998).

Further reading

Anning, A., Cottrell, J., Frost, N., Green J. and Robinson, M. (2002) *Developing multi-professional teamwork for integrated children's services*, Maidenhead: Open University Press.

Pyecroft, A. and Gough, D. (eds) (2010) *Multi-agency working in criminal justice*, Bristol: The Policy Press.

Souhami, A. (2007) *Transforming youth justice: Occupational identity and cultural change*, Cullompton: Willan.

FOUR

Reducing re-offending

Previous chapters introduced discussions about the values that might underpin offender management, the organisational context and the skills needed to work successfully with the complexity of partnership, multi-agency and inter-agency arrangements. This chapter seeks to apply these understandings to practice and to start a debate about what they might mean in 'real world' criminal justice situations. After exploring recent thinking about the change process and the role of 'helpers' in facilitating change, it considers the rights and Good Lives Model framework developed by Connolly and Ward (2008) as a basis for intervention with offenders in a clinical setting. A possible model adapting this for use within the OMM is then sketched out, with further discussion of the challenges this might present in work with offenders primarily at more intensive levels of intervention. Such intervention typically involves a range of other agencies, and the chapter ends by exploring the potential for using the engagement model proposed as a common approach across agencies to help promote the sort of consistency and collaboration implicit in the concept of *end-to-end offender management*.

Risk-need-responsivity as a basis for action

As noted in Chapter Two, the criminal justice system has become orientated towards identification and control of risk and dangerousness, within what Kemshall (2008) refers to as a community protection model. This is essentially a criminal justice model that tends to operate on negative assumptions about offender motivation and denial, rather than positively seeking collaboration with offenders in assessing and managing risk. It employs technology and multi-agency strategies to increase surveillance and containment of offenders in the community, with rapid enforcement actions in the event of any breach of conditions placed on the offender. Clearly there is a rationale for this type of approach in a modern society concerned with risk and specifically risk of offending. Clearly also it is politically attractive, appealing to the 'moral majority' and promising explicit actions aimed at their protection.

However, the community protection model has the potential to be discriminatory and divisive, tending to dichotomise the interests of offenders and victims and communities (McCulloch and McNeill, 2007). Furthermore, McNeill notes that 'there is a paradox at the heart of protection and there are risks with risk. Whenever we promise to protect, we confirm the existence of a threat; we legitimise and reinforce fear' (2009a, p 22). There are dangers in this for criminal justice agencies, because risk cannot be completely eradicated as this community protection approach implicitly suggests, thereby creating a situation where their best efforts will invariably fall short of success. This may have serious consequences for all criminal justice agencies, but particularly so for the probation service whose political standing and claims on public resources may seem to be most justified by promising to manage and reduce risks and so to enhance security. Yet, whenever offender management commits itself to the assessment and management of risks, it opens itself to the inevitability of failure (McNeill and Weaver, 2010), and additionally creates further obstacles in terms of building the positive relationships with offenders critical to its work.

Nevertheless, best practice within the community protection model can counteract some of these concerns. Certainly this is the case where interventions are based on accurate assessment and management of:

- risk of harm and likelihood of offending;
- offender needs, particularly as they interact with risk;
- offender responsivity – including motivation, readiness to change and suitability of specific interventions.

The risk–need–responsivity (RNR) approach has been developed using evidence from empirical studies and, looking back to Chapter Two, it is clearly based on an artefact view of risk (Kemshall, 2003). Research has pointed to particular personal and social factors associated with greater risk of harm or of re-offending (*risk factors*) and other factors that seem to ameliorate or to reduce risk (*protective factors*). The presence of risk factors which can change and are therefore *dynamic*, and protective factors which can be enhanced, can guide decisions about targeting resources and choice, intensity and specific focus of interventions. This is obviously useful for practitioners and has assisted the development of much sharper and more defensible practice. However, in essence, it is a pragmatic approach not driven by explicit values and core principles. It treats concepts such as 'risk' and 'harm' as though they are objective and unproblematic, whereas in fact they present a number of problems, being extremely subjective and value-laden. Furthermore, it understands risk as residing in the individual and neglects the influence of social contexts on risk and whether the potential for 'risky' events ever plays out (McNeill, 2009b).

Critics of the RNR approach have also argued that it only takes practitioners so far in their quest to reduce offending in specific cases, largely because the findings from risk factor research have been generalised from large populations of offenders. Any one individual may not conform to the pattern of behaviour typical for a group of offenders with similar characteristics. Moreover, the RNR approach has a limited view of:

- the complexity of the psychological processes of change as offenders move towards a non-offending lifestyle and *desistance from crime*;
- the significance of the *agency* an individual can exercise (through his or her choices and actions) and of identity;

- the wider range of human and social needs (because it focuses almost entirely on needs that relate to offending, referred to as *criminogenic needs*);
- the role of the worker and how the relationship between worker and offender can influence change (Ward and Maruna, 2007).

These are significant criticisms of the dominant approach to risk in the criminal justice system. Recent thinking and writing about what motivates and facilitates changes in behaviour and desistance from crime give interesting insights into how these limitations of RNR might be addressed. Specifically, there is renewed interest in the role of one-to-one supervision and the relational aspects of work with offenders (Maguire and Raynor, 2010; McNeill and Weaver, 2010) which were neglected in the era when accredited programmes were viewed as the 'magic bullet'. It is important not to jettison RNR entirely and to lose the benefits that it has brought in terms of a clear focus on risk and more structured assessment, planning and intervention. However, RNR, 'despite its undeniable contributions, points us to only one part of the picture' (Porporino, 2010, p 63) and should be incorporated into rather broader and more holistic approaches, such as the engagement model suggested later in this chapter.

Processes of change and transformation

It is summarising rather crudely, but essentially the What Works movement from the 1990s onwards has been premised on an optimistic belief that offending will be reduced by applying the 'right' intervention to offenders. Researchers analysing large numbers of evaluations of interventions with offenders were able to identify characteristics that seemed to be associated with positive reductions in offending. Their messages were hopeful: there were certain methods that 'worked', particularly those that used cognitive behavioural methods to help offenders develop important problem-solving and other skills. This was good news and enthusiastically received by probation services in the UK and elsewhere who were struggling to justify their existence in a harsh penal climate and saw benefits in taking on new approaches based on evidence of effectiveness. However, in the impetus to deliver these evidence-based programmes accredited by the Home Office, the messages from research became simplified, and important aspects of the supervisory processes needed to support the programmes were neglected.

Undoubtedly the prison and probation services adopted the focused and structured interventions promoted by the What Works movement with the best of intentions. However, the orientation towards accredited programmes and a prescriptive agenda that seeks to change the offender may have blinded them to other possibilities, other ways of approaching the challenge that treats offenders with greater respect and recognises that they are themselves the experts regarding their own processes of change (Porporino, 2010).

The What Works movement arose from empirical research on the effects produced by criminal justice interventions. In contrast, the body of knowledge around desistance has recently drawn on more qualitative studies that:

> Start at a different place. Instead of asking "what is the impact of what we do on rates of recidivism?" desistance research asks "why do people stop offending?" prompting the further question, "what can the criminal justice system do to assist (or at least not disrupt) these processes?" (Farrall, 2007, p 93)

There are different strands within the debate on desistance, not least what we mean by desistance and whether/how long an individual should be crime-free to 'qualify' as a desister. Overall, however, the focus is on change as a process – something that happens over time and involves the offender moving through a stage or stages in which he or she is changing potentially harmful or damaging behaviour (*primary desistance*) and towards a more fundamental creation of a new self-image dissociated from offending (*secondary desistance*) (Maruna and Farrall, 2004). Progress in this journey tends not to be linear, but can take a zigzag path (see, for instance, Piquero, 2004), and is often characterised by ambivalence about change and significant vacillations along the way (Burnett, 2004).

An important part of this change process for the offender is belief in the possibility of change, and this may be enhanced by a positive relationship with key professionals. Fergus McNeill, in summarising what offenders have revealed in successive research studies, identified that the most positive relationships are those characterised by optimism, trust and loyalty. They are also most helpful when the offender is encouraged to be active and participative within the relationship and where the practitioner establishes clarity of purpose and roles, boundaries and expectations of each other (McNeill, 2003).

Interestingly, Shadd Maruna (2001) identifies crucial differences in the attitudes of what he calls 'persisters' and 'desisters', who tend to adopt 'condemnation scripts' and 'redemption scripts' respectively:

> In the condemnation script the active offender typically occupies the role of the "condemned victim", one who, perceiving their life script to have been written for them some time ago, generally considers themselves to be "doomed to deviance". By contrast, the accounts of the desisters revealed a different narrative in which the individual actor, normally with the support of a significant other, assumes the role of change agent and is no longer merely the object of outside forces. (McCulloch and McNeill, 2008, p 157)

Practitioners involved in offender management can act as those significant others, demonstrating a belief that the individual has the capacity to change, to manage the legacy of a previous 'spoiled identity' (Farrall and Calverley, 2005) and to master a new personal identity dissociated from offending (Rumgay, 2004b). And, at the end of the transformation process, Maruna et al (2009) refer to an uncoupling of the offender label, a kind of 'delabelling'. They also highlight how practitioners can be significant in giving official recognition or 'certification' of a new non-offending identity, something that seems different and more powerful than recognition from the individual's immediate social group (important as that may be).

The fit between offender management and desistance

The above discussion gives a hint of how complex the process of changing an offending lifestyle might be. Yet the majority of even the most persistent offenders do stop or reduce offending over time. Criminal justice interventions may play a part in this, but there are much wider influences associated with growing up, investing in significant relationships, achieving social status, changes in self-image or life goals, for instance, that may have much more impact on the choices and behaviours of individuals:

> Desistance resides somewhere in the interfaces between developing personal maturity, forming new or stronger social bonds associated with certain life transitions, and individual subjective narrative constructions which offenders build around these key events and changes. It is not just the events and changes that matter; it is what these events and changes *mean* to the people involved. (McNeill, 2003, p 151)

The RNR model and associated What Works approach tend to place the emphasis on correctional interventions, the danger being that programmes are treated as though they constitute the change process itself, rather than being one aspect of support for the change process (McNeill, 2009a). Instead, case management or offender management can be represented as located within the wider process of change and desistance, with programmed work sitting inside as one component of offender management. These relationships might be illustrated as in Figure 4.1.

Figure 4.1: Programmes in context

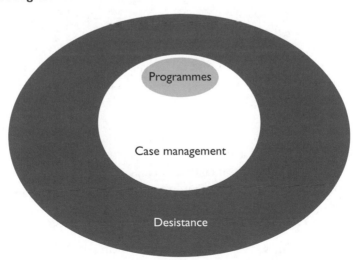

Source: McNeill (2009b, p 17)

Elsewhere (McNeill and Weaver, 2010), this model has been developed to include a further outer ring, suggesting that there are additional processes of community reintegration that take place beyond secondary desistance. This gives a useful sense of the context for offender management and suggests that it is most powerful where it recognises and facilitates the processes taking place around and outside its own activities, rather than being focused solely internally on the delivery of specific interventions.

Enhancing human and social capital

Programmed work is significant in enabling offenders to build inter-personal and problem-solving skills and other capacities associated with, for instance, self-control and awareness. However, research by Farrall (2002) with former probationers has suggested that focusing on this development of *human capital* without reference to social context and environment is not sufficient to facilitate the move to desistance. Farrall, in common with other writers, identified that both offenders and the disadvantaged areas from which they typically come are lacking in *social capital*.

While there is some debate about the meaning of the term, social capital is dependent on: trust, the type and quality of our social networks; social status or standing in the wider world; influence, power and prestige; the extent and quality of resources available to the individual or community; and capacity to effect change (see for instance Putnam, 2000).

In terms of work with offenders, a further distinction is useful between:

- *bonding capital*, which is about friendship, relationships and peer groups that provide a sense of belonging;
- *bridging capital*, which is about creating links with people outside our immediate circle, broadening opportunities and horizons;
- *linking capital*, which is about access to influential others and power structures (adapted from Boeck, 2007).

Boeck further comments that 'bonding social capital is good for "getting by" but bridging networks are crucial for "getting ahead"' (Boeck, 2007, p 296). From another perspective, Putnam describes bonding social capital as a kind of sociological superglue, whereas bridging social capital is more like a "sociological WD40" (2000, p 23).

Critically, offenders may have certain types of social capital but may lack the forms of bridging and linking capital that can help them progress beyond the range of opportunities present in their immediate environment. Monica Barry reflects on this in her Scottish research on young offenders, and comments in particular on the role of bonding capital for young people in terms of peer group relations:

> Starting offending revolved predominantly around the need for identity
> and status within their immediate circle of friends as they moved from

relative dependence on the family to the more autonomous milieu of the friendship group. (2006, p 75)

Her other findings suggest that:

- in the absence of other forms of capital, a further type of *symbolic capital* may assume increased importance for young people;
- this can mean status from offending, risk taking, position in the gang and early involvement in sexual relations;
- the onset of offending is most associated with relationships with others, particularly for females (Barry, 2007), that is, *bonding capital*;
- over time the social capital returns from offending decrease, that is, the short-term gains are not sustained due to the lack of bridging and linking capital;
- stopping is often associated with increased involvement in the criminal justice system, that is, *hassle and stigma that further reduces social capital for offenders*;
- stopping can be a 'zigzag' rather than linear process;
- it is important to be able to expend as well as accumulate capital in order to make progress in life (Barry, 2006).

This latter point is important when thinking of bridging rather than bonding capital. For instance, offenders may gain substantial income from offending and can use it to buy consumer goods that might impress within their immediate social circle, but they cannot use illegal earnings to obtain a mortgage or borrow money from a bank in order to start a business. Similarly, being the leader of a delinquent gang may bring status but cannot be put on a CV in the way that gaining a Duke of Edinburgh Award, doing voluntary work or taking a position of responsibility in an arts or sports project might be. Some forms of social capital gained from offending can therefore give short-term gains but will ultimately lead down a criminal career cul-de-sac. Desistance research suggests that offenders may need assistance to find alternative routes to make progress in life and build new (pro-social) identities (and, thinking back to previous discussions, find means of securing their *primary social goods*).

More broadly also, offender management needs to foster collaborative partnerships that can enhance the resources available in offenders' communities. For the probation service, this may involve a return to the sort of community cohesion work that it engaged with in previous decades (Farrall, 2002; McCulloch and McNeill, 2008). This has the potential to increase jobs, accommodation and other facilities for offenders but also to change attitudes and enhance the potential for acceptance and reintegration into communities, hard as this may be in the current climate of intolerance. The present position of the probation service seems a long way from this, but if it is to make an impact on both crime rates and fear of crime – which are not the same thing – it would do well to listen to the messages from writers on desistance and critical thinkers on risk.

Working to promote change

So what are the factors that can increase the possibilities of meaningful desistance, and how can offender management enhance those factors? How can practitioners in their different roles make a contribution?

McNeill (2009a, p 25) has identified three factors that need to be present before change can take place:

- motivation
- capacities or skills
- opportunities.

He has represented these diagrammatically (see Figure 4.2), and has indicated roles or functions associated with each. Within the model he refers to *human capital* or capacities, and these could be the sorts of skills that offenders might gain from accredited programmes or from basic literacy classes, for instance. He also refers to *social capital* as being the currency or assets that the individual has to move around and 'trade' in the social world.

Figure 4.2: Preconditions for change

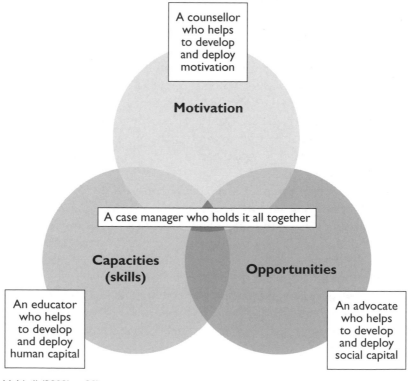

Source: McNeill (2009b, p 39)

Within the OMM, the identified roles may be taken on by a range of individuals such as offender supervisors or key workers, but it is the responsibility of the offender manager to ensure that there is an appropriate balance of all three elements and that there is coherence to the whole. Helpfully, McNeill has suggested that the diagram could be looked at as a cross-section of a rope:

> The rope won't be strong enough to pull the person towards change unless the strands are woven together. Someone needs to do the weaving and keep hold of the rope – especially when there is a strain in the process or an obstacle that the person needs to be pulled over. (2009a, p 25)

The role of offender manager, then, is significant in bringing the supervisory process together and ensuring that the various elements are relevant and meaningful to the offender. It is also critical in terms of ensuring that all the individual practitioners involved in the process – *the team around the offender* – communicate effectively and achieve an appropriate level of consistency. However, over and above this, the offender manager can be the most significant driver in terms of the values expressed through the approach to offender management, and of the beliefs and assumptions about human rights, needs and capacities that underpin it.

More about the Good Lives Model

The essential elements of the Good Lives Model have already been introduced. This model has been adopted, mainly in the US, as an alternative way of working with high-risk offenders, particularly sex offenders. Rather than concentrating on problems and controls such as the community protection approach, it is based on an assumption that:

> In order for individuals to desist from offending they should be given the knowledge, skills, opportunities and resources to live a "good life" which takes into account their particular preferences, interests and values. (Ward and Maruna, 2007, p 111)

It also assumes that, as human beings, offenders have the same basic needs as other people and will naturally seek certain goals or *primary human goods*, which have an intrinsic value and contribute to well-being. Those *goods* were outlined in Chapter One.

Within the Good Lives Model criminal justice services should aim both to promote individuals' goods *and* manage or reduce risk.

It is important to address the risks as well as promoting goods. A skewed package of intervention could result in either a happy but dangerous offender or, alternatively, a hostile and disengaged individual whose personal concerns and well-being are neglected in favour of punitive practices (Connolly and Ward, 2008). The relationship the practitioner builds with the offender is highly significant in this. McNeill comments that:

> The practitioner must balance the promotion of personal goods (for the offender) with the reduction of risk (for society) … the practitioner has to create a human relationship in which the individual offender is valued and respected and through which interventions can be properly tailored in line with particular life plans and their associated risk factors. (2009a, p 33)

As the Good Lives Model assumes that offending is caused by individuals using maladaptive or destructive ways of achieving the primary human goods that they seek, the way to reduce offending is to promote access to those goods by pro-social means and to deal with obstacles or blockages.

Several important points arise from this:

- the Good Lives Model recognises offenders' goals and can offer an incentive to engage in constructive work to achieve those goals without harming others;
- any plan of work agreed must be highly tailored to the individual so it is intrinsically sensitive to diversity;
- it is an open and collaborative approach that can make use of pro-social modelling techniques to address risk and to solve problems;
- it fits well with rights-based approaches that seek to balance the rights of offenders and others;
- it is consistent with the findings from desistance research and the literature about transformations and creating new identities.

Kemshall (2008) summarises the Good Lives Model by saying that it works with the offender to reframe goals and identify how to achieve them positively and legitimately, assisting the offender to construct a new identity and ability to work towards goals in pro-social ways.

Linking back to McNeill's three preconditions for change – motivation, opportunity and capacities (or skills) – it can readily be seen that the Good Lives Model is motivating and can provide incentives for the offender to engage in work that recognises his or her priorities as well as the risk reduction imperatives of the criminal justice practitioner. Alongside this, rounded Good Lives Model intervention would seek to enhance the offender's skills and capacities (*human capital*) and to identify and promote *good life* opportunities, in terms of access to services but also allowing the offender to try out new roles as a volunteer or in employment, for instance (thereby increasing *social capital*).

Moving beyond risk-need-responsivity

Ward and Maruna (2007) make clear distinctions between the basic orientations of the RNR model and the Good Lives Model. The former concentrates on what is missing and problematic in the conditions necessary to achieve *primary human goods*, while the Good Lives Model is more concerned with providing the conditions to obtain them, enhancing opportunities and strengths. Although both approaches have their positive uses, both are psychologically based and have been criticised for focusing on change within individuals rather than the external world and the social context of offenders' lives (McNeill, 2009a).

More recently, however, Connolly and Ward (2008) have attempted to develop a rights-based framework for work with offenders, drawing on the Good Lives Model. Their focus is clinical or therapeutic intervention with high-risk offenders. The framework nevertheless begins to sketch out how a rights-based approach might be applied in practice and how it would operationalise learning from the Good Lives Model and the focus on strengths, rather than deficits.

The following section attempts to extend this framework to the OMM, mainly relating to more complex and intensive interventions with offenders at Tiers 3 and 4 (see Chapter Two). In doing so, it starts to grapple with two major areas of debate and challenge. First, how offender management relates to the social context of offenders' lives and the communities in which they live. Offender management cannot restrict its concerns to offenders' problem solving and thinking skills and other aspects of *human capital*. It must be proactive in reaching out – and enabling offenders to reach out – to other services and organisations that may present opportunities for social integration and accumulating *social capital*. This may mean going beyond the relatively small circle of voluntary and other agencies that work in an obviously connected way with the criminal justice system, and building links with more diverse organisations.

The second area of debate and challenge relates to partnership work. Ensuring consistency and clear communication between agencies is clearly critical, but not easily achieved, particularly where a more diverse range of organisations is involved. An explicit framework and an explicit value base is helpful in establishing both, and in fostering a spirit of constructive collaboration.

Offender management re-visited

This section begins thinking about what this explicit framework might look like, based on the set of values about human rights discussed in Chapter One, and using the notions of the *good life* and *human and social capital* as key elements.

Borrowing from Connolly and Ward's (2008) framework, there are three distinct stages or phases of intervention and, within this model, four strands that cut across each of the stages. The stages can be related to the OMM ASPIRE processes (see Chapter Two):

Assessment and Sentence Planning	→	Stage 1: Engagement and assessment
Implement, Review	→	Stage 2: Changing behaviours
Implement, Review, Evaluation	→	Stage 3: Sustaining lifestyle change

Stage 1 is relatively self-explanatory as the initial processes of engagement and relationship building take place and important expectations, boundaries and the nature of the approach are established. The practitioner style should model openness, transparency and collaboration, attending to the rights of the offender within the assessment and planning processes, and encouraging active participation. It is critical to assess the offender's motivation and readiness/current capacity for change as well as what the offender values or prioritises in his or her life and his or her goals. This can then lead on to exploration of the means available to achieve these goals and the strengths that the offender possesses or can access in his or her social world.

Stage 2, here referred to as 'Changing behaviours', is essentially focused on the role that probation and other key agencies have in fostering motivation and capacities to change, assisting the offender to build key skills and to master critical internal or psychological factors that have caused him or her to seek *primary social goods* in dysfunctional ways. This stage may begin with practitioners taking a very active role, but working to allow the offender to take increasing control and to begin to imagine and then to construct new identities. In this it differs from more conventional approaches to 'help' and rehabilitation, as the power moves from the professional to the offender.

Stage 3 is concerned with social circumstances and environment, beginning with the most significant strengths or obstacles associated with living circumstances, family/friendship group and neighbourhood. Because there may be social factors that warrant immediate attention, Stage 3 does not necessarily begin chronologically after Stage 2, although it should last significantly beyond the end of Stage 2 work, which is more tightly focused and defined.

If the offender is engaged in the process of change, the focus of Stage 3 should shift over time to the enhancement of *good life* opportunities and the building of *social capital*. These opportunities may involve voluntary work and other activities that allow the offender to make good or to give something back to the community in a powerful symbolic way, as well as trying out new roles and relationships to others. Such *generative activities* are important in reinforcing and sustaining the transformation of identity involved in secondary desistance.

The four strands or themes that cut across these three stages are:

• focus on justice and accountability;
• focus on offender motivation;
• focus on strengths;
• focus on ethics and evidence base for work.

The intersections between these are represented in matrix form in Table 4.1.

It is important to note where risk features within this framework, because appropriate attention to risk is critical in establishing its legitimacy not only with other agencies and with the public but also, and significantly, with offenders. Collaborative relationships suggest openness and transparency about judgements on risk and what they are based on. Such relationships that take offenders seriously and treat them as adults can be powerful in encouraging them to adopt

Table 4.1: Engagement model

	Stage 1: Engagement and assessment	Stage 2: Changing behaviours	Stage 3: Sustaining lifestyle change
Focus on justice and accountability	*Collaboration:* assessment should be collaborative. *Transparency:* the offender should understand the aims and processes involved in assessment. *Rights:* the offender should understand his/her rights in undergoing assessment	*Rights and duties:* work should reinforce both the offender's rights and duties. *Responsibility:* the offender should be encouraged to take responsibility for the change process. *Balance:* ensure a balance between promoting the offender's pursuit of 'goods' and community interests (risks)	*Balance:* ensure a balance between promoting the offender's pursuit of 'goods' and community interests (risks). *Awareness:* work should aim to increase the offender's awareness of the needs and concerns of the community. *Environment:* identify any significant supports or obstacles to change
Focus on offender motivation	*Offender goals:* seek to identify and promote what is important to the offender. *Opportunities:* identify any 'good life' opportunities available. *Choice:* offer the offender choice within interventions where possible and be clear what areas are non-negotiable	*Offender goals:* seek to identify and promote what is important to the offender. *Promote agency:* encourage the offender to be proactive and to make positive choices about his/her life course. *Identity change:* support the identity change associated with secondary desistance	*Understanding:* ensure that the lifestyle changes identified are meaningful to the offender. *Offender buy-in:* ensure that incentives and motivation are maximised. *Opportunities:* work with the offender to expand the 'good life' opportunities available and to increase *social capital*
Focus on strengths	*Relationship:* seek to establish an alliance or collaboration with the offender, based on some degree of mutual understanding. *Recognition:* identify the offender's strengths and build these into intervention plans	*Promote agency:* encourage the offender to be proactive and to make positive choices about his/her life course. *Building skills and capacities:* help the offender enhance self-awareness and ability to deal with internal risk factors, increasing *human capital*	*Partnership:* ensure that other agencies are involved in offering 'good life' opportunities. *Brokerage:* negotiate provision of services to address needs and build capacities
Focus on ethics and evidence base for work	*Risk:* proper attention must be paid to risk, seen in the context of the offender's life. *Evidence base:* methods and tools used should be derived from a sound evidence base. *Ethics:* methods and tools should be employed in an ethical manner	*Evidence base:* methods and tools used should be derived from a sound evidence base. *Risk:* controls should be proportionate and targeted at problematic behaviours. *Review:* evaluate interventions, incorporating offender feedback	*Communication:* ensure that information is shared appropriately and effectively. *Monitor risk:* ensure that systems are in place to monitor risk. *Review:* review progress regularly, incorporating offender feedback and input from partner agencies

wider perspectives and a sense of social responsibility, effectively, in rights-based terms, to accept that they have duties in relation to the rights of other people. In this regard, pro-social modelling (Cherry, 2005; Trotter, 2006) represents a key set of technical skills needed to operationalise the model and to ensure that an appropriate balance is achieved between pursuit of the offender's social goods and the management of risk.

These principles of openness and transparency – generally but also specifically in relation to risk   are equally significant in building lasting networks involving other agencies and, potentially, communities. Within partnership structures, such as MAPPAs, decision making should be defensible and based on sound information. This model lends itself to that, because of its attention to risk assessment practices that are individualised, sensitive to the unique needs of the offender and responsive to his or her social context. It creates potential for information exchange based on real knowledge and application of professional judgement, rather than assumptions and generalisations. It also explicitly refers back to evidence – often this will be evidence gained from the offender, balanced with views from significant others involved. In addition, it incorporates knowledge gained from research and evaluation, including the emerging findings about the processes involved in desistance and the role of relationships in facilitating change.

Involving others in this rights-based approach

The management of offenders, particularly involving more complex individuals and situations, is no longer a secretive process that takes place in isolation, not least because of the accountability demanded of criminal justice agencies. In terms of effectiveness and impact, work with offenders should also draw on the skills and resources of a range of individuals and organisations in order to manage risk and to enhance prospects of reintegration and rehabilitation. However, over and above these pragmatic motivations for more joined-up approaches, this book argues that there are moral imperatives associated with promoting offenders' rights and access to social justice that are properly the concern of wider society and the institutions and organisations active within it.

In the current criminal justice context, there are clearly constraints on practitioner time and resources. But this should not be allowed to inhibit the attempt to reach out and to draw in diverse individuals, organisations and community bodies, which may each have their own contribution to make and which may enhance the efforts of (ex-)offenders to pursue *good life* opportunities and to transform identities. These contributions at different stages of the change process may involve practical help and resources, supportive social networks or access to activities that allow individuals to do good in their communities and to consolidate different types of relationships with those around them.

Above all, this book argues that offender management should be outward-looking and informed by values that are explicit to the offenders and to the other individuals and organisations involved in its processes. It should be mindful of the networks and contacts that offenders may need to sustain positive change and passionate about enabling them to build better and more fulfilling futures, rather than just lives without offending. Offender managers, offender supervisors and key workers are all in positions to enthuse others and to promote messages about positive and constructive work with offenders which is realistic about harms and risks, but which deals with these in ways that recognise their rights, their humanity and their potential for desistance.

Summary

This chapter has drawn extensively on work by Fergus McNeill, so it seems appropriate to end with a further quote that encapsulates its key messages:

My engagement with criminological research suggests clearly to me that, particularly in neo-liberal regimes, the dominance of a "risk" or "protection" discourse is very likely to frustrate its own purpose if it identifies offenders with the worst aspects of themselves, if it leads practitioners to neglect of offenders' needs, strengths, goals and aspirations and if it reinforces a social climate that creates practical and attitudinal barriers to ex-offenders' prospects of social mobility and of living differently....

My conviction, both as a citizen and as an academic, is that we will be safer in a society where ex-offenders are supported to move towards better lives, than in one where the risks that they pose are merely managed and surveilled, and where those risks are continually fixed and reinforced by their stigmatisation and exclusion as risk bearers. (McNeill, 2009a, p 36)

Further reading

Brayford, J., Cowe, F. and Deering, J. (eds.) (2010) *What Else Works? Creative Work with Offenders* Cullompton: Willan

McNeill, F., Raynor, P. and Trotter, C. (eds) (2010) *Offender Supervision: New Directions in Theory, Research and Practice* Cullompton: Willan

White, R. and Graham, H. (2010) *Working with Offenders: A Guide to Concepts and Practices* Cullompton: Willan

Part Two
Offender management: key law and policy

FIVE

Human rights

Chapter One introduced important notions relating to human rights and the duties, as well as the core elements of freedom and well-being, that they imply. The earlier discussion focused on moral rights, rather than the legal frameworks and obligations that are the subject of this chapter. Here key aspects of the previous values debate are taken further as the nature of international human rights conventions and domestic law are outlined, highlighting critical tensions for the criminal justice system and practitioners within it.

What do we mean by rights?

Debates about rights have a long history, dating from the Enlightenment period and thinkers such as John Stuart Mill and Mary Wollstonecraft, who developed liberal ideas about the rights of individuals and the social contract between individuals and the state. There are inevitably limits to the extent to which equality can be achieved in complex organised societies. Nevertheless, there has been a strong tradition of belief throughout western democracies in the power of states to work towards universal standards of freedom, justice and equality of opportunities. The apparatus of the state and its legal processes can be seen as important mechanisms for protecting the rights of citizens, and the atrocities committed in the Second World War gave huge impetus to international efforts to use them in this way.

More recently feminists and others have challenged conventional notions of rights and have ensured that thinking has moved on from a focus on individual rights to consider group and collective rights and, in doing so, to attempt to more fully recognise culture and diversity (McLaughlin, 2003), particularly in relation to indigenous populations (Connolly and Ward, 2008).

Rights, of course, can mean many different things, varying from basic rights to food and freedom to civil rights or the right to self-determination. Scott, for instance, presents one way of distinguishing different types of rights as being:

- fundamental rights, for example, freedom from torture;
- judicial rights, for example, right to a fair trial;
- social rights, for example, freedom of expression;
- personal rights, for example, protection of privacy (adapted from Scott, 2002, p 7).

All of these are of concern for criminal justice practitioners in their dealings with offenders, victims and other professionals. A further distinction might be made between negative and positive rights. The UK legal system is mainly based on negative rights, that is, the freedom to do whatever is not specifically prohibited. In contrast, a focus on positive rights, introduced in Chapter One, represents a more proactive approach, as discussed by Barbara Hudson in relation to probation practice:

> The key to the positive rights agenda is that the essence of human rights is precisely that they adhere to people merely in virtue of them being human; this means that they do not have to be earned by good citizenship and they cannot be forfeited by bad citizenship. (2001, pp 110-11)

The framework that she advocates is one where the human rights of offenders are not eradicated as a result of their behaviour but must be balanced in the process of managing any risk that they pose. Such considerations will become salient in later discussions of risk in relation to sex offenders and mentally disordered offenders (MDOs) and in looking at restorative justice. They will also be critical in thinking about equality and diversity, which is the subject of the next chapter.

International human rights

A number of international agreements and conventions have formed the legal bedrock of the rights movement, and have been significant in achieving a degree of consensus about the rights of individuals and the role of the state in protecting such rights.

Relevant international declarations and treaties include:

- Universal Declaration of Human Rights (UDHR) 1948;
- International Covenant on Civil and Political Rights 1966;
- International Covenant on Economic, Social and Cultural Rights 1966;
- United Nations (UN) Convention on the Elimination of All Forms of Racial Discrimination 1966;
- UN Convention on the Elimination of All Forms of Discrimination Against Women (CEDAW) 1979;
- UN Convention on the Rights of the Child (UNCRC) 1989.

European declarations and treaties include:

- European Convention on Human Rights (ECHR) 1950;
- European Convention for the Prevention of Torture and Inhuman or Degrading Treatment or Punishment 1987.

Articles 1 and 2 of the UDHR set out three cardinal principles of human rights which form the basis of all the more specific rights detailed in other declarations and treaties: these are freedom, equality and dignity, concepts that underpin many of the discussions throughout this book.

For the youth justice system, the UNCRC is the chief arbiter of expected standards, and this has specifically challenged the conditions under which children are held in custody in the UK.

However, for the criminal justice system as a whole, the most immediately relevant human rights instrument is the ECHR, which was signed by the UK and the other original signatories in the aftermath of the Second World War. This established the European Court of Human Rights (ECtHR) in Strasbourg where member states and, more recently and significantly, citizens of member states, as individuals or as groups, have been able to seek a remedy for a breach of rights under the ECHR (*Convention rights*). This is a lengthy, costly and cumbersome process, so it has been used on relatively rare occasions. However, before the Human Rights Act 1998 came into force in the UK, it provided an important mechanism for potential redress in situations where *Convention rights* had been breached.

An example of a case taken to the ECtHR was that of *Sutherland v UK* in 1996, when the ECtHR confirmed that the UK's age of consent for homosexual men at 18 was discriminatory and violated the right to a private life. Even in such cases where the ECtHR makes a judgment in favour of the complainant, it cannot compel the member state to amend its legislation or the practices that were found to be at fault. It does not have coercive powers, but relies on the willingness of member states to abide by the Convention. Nevertheless, it does have an enforcement mechanism in the form of a Committee of Ministers who will oversee the payment of any compensation or damages ordered and actions to redress the violation (Fenwick, 2007).

The main Articles in the ECHR are listed below and these are supported by a series of protocols or more detailed agreements on other rights-related matters, such as the right to education and freedom of movement:

Article 1: Obligation to respect human rights
Article 2: Guarantees the 'right to life'
Article 3: Freedom from torture, inhuman and degrading treatment
Article 4: Freedom from slavery, forced or compulsory labour
Article 5: Right to liberty and security
Article 6: Right to a fair trial
Article 7: No punishment without law
Article 8: Right to respect for private and family life
Article 9: Freedom of thought, conscience and religion
Article 10: Freedom of expression
Article 11: Freedom of peaceful assembly and association

Article 12: Right to marry
Article 13: Remedies – it is the duty of the member state to provide effective remedies in cases where these rights have been violated
Article 14: Prohibition of discrimination

Looking further at Convention rights

The rights covered by the ECHR are quite varied and in some cases the particular rights of an individual must be balanced with the competing or conflicting rights of others. To help make sense of this, they tend to be sub-divided into three categories.

- First tier or absolute rights, such as the right to freedom from torture, inhuman and degrading treatment (Article 3) and freedom from slavery and forced labour (Article 4). These rights apply in all circumstances and states cannot opt out of or *derogate* from these Articles.
- Second tier or limited rights, that is, rights that can be curtailed but only where specific circumstances or conditions apply. An example is the right to liberty (Article 5) that can be legitimately taken away following conviction by a competent court or after arrest for non-compliance with a court order.
- Third tier or qualified rights, such as freedom of expression (Article 10) or respect for private and family life (Article 8).

These third tier rights are contained mainly within Articles 8-11, and these Articles contain sub-clauses which allow restrictions on the rights in question, mainly relating to the state's interest in securing national security, protection of morals, the rights of others and public safety (Fenwick, 2007). In respect of these rights, states are allowed a *margin of appreciation*, effectively the ability to exercise discretion as to how far they are able to impinge upon individual rights in the pursuit of wider public benefit. This has enabled the UK government to introduce controversial items of law and policy without facing human rights challenges, particularly in relation to law and order.

Human Rights Act 1998

In opposition New Labour had committed itself to incorporating the European Convention into UK law. On assuming power in 1997, it acted on that commitment by introducing the Human Rights Act, which came fully into effect throughout the UK in October 2000. At the time, advocates were optimistic about the new dawn for civil rights that this seemed to promise. However, this was tempered by the fact that the Human Rights Act specifically omits Article 1 that requires states to secure *Convention rights* and freedoms for everyone in its jurisdiction. This means that rights are not guaranteed. The Human Rights Act also omits Article 13 which requires that states should provide a remedy in law for any breach of *Convention rights* (that is, that states should amend their law so as to 'fix the problem') (Fenwick, 2007). Although its scope is limited by these omissions, the rights under Articles 2-12 and 14 and additional rights detailed in the protocols have been received into domestic law.

The Department for Constitutional Affairs sums up the changes brought in by the Human Rights Act by saying that it is:

> A major shift in the way our political and legal system works. Before the Act, our law did not spell out in so many words that public authorities and courts had to respect ECHR rights; and the courts would only look at the ECHR in exceptional circumstances, for example, if the UK legislation was unclear. (DCA, 2006a, p 5)

The significant changes brought in by the Human Rights Act are:

- Section 2 that ensures that any court or tribunal determining a question in connection with *Convention rights* must take account of previous judgments, decisions, declarations and advisory opinions of the ECtHR. Effectively this means that courts must refer to relevant European case law as well as looking at precedents established in the UK courts.
- Section 3 which requires that as far as possible both primary and subsidiary legislation in the UK must be interpreted and implemented in ways that are compatible with Convention rights.
- Under Section 3, all new primary legislation and the subsidiary legislation that goes with it (for example, regulations, statutory orders) must be formulated so as to be compatible with *Convention rights*.
- Section 4 which operates where primary legislation cannot be construed as compatible with *Convention rights* and allows the higher UK courts (for instance, the Court of Appeal) to make a declaration of incompatibility. This does not require the government to amend the legislation, which remains valid and can still be used. However, it does create a pressure for suitable amendments to be made under a remedial order and these can be 'fast-tracked'.
- Section 6 which makes it unlawful for a public authority to act in a way that is incompatible with *Convention rights* (this is covered in a later section).

The Human Rights Act had the potential to fundamentally shift the balance of power between the Executive and the judiciary. When introduced, the media accordingly reflected debates between those who believed that Parliament was being undermined by the judiciary and those who welcomed the ability to constrain an over powerful New Labour Executive, one increasingly criticised for riding roughshod over individual rights.

Significantly, a 2006 review by the Department for Constitutional Affairs suggested that, although the courts had scrutinised the Executive and the primary legislation it produces, this shift towards judicial power had not happened to the extent that some critics had feared. In fact, the major public policy issues in national security and other areas had arisen, not from the Human Rights Act itself, but from the government's obligations under the ECHR. The review concluded that the Human Rights Act provides a helpful framework for policy formulation that leads to better outcomes and recognises the needs of a diverse population (DCA, 2006b). This is an optimistic interpretation in the light of evident tensions between the commitment to rights and ECHR obligations and other political imperatives, including the need to demonstrate strong and decisive actions in relation to crime and public protection. Recognising these tensions, the Coalition government is revisiting this legislation and the relationship with European law.

The impact of human rights for the criminal justice system

Rights are a central concern for the criminal justice system, because its core activities of crime prevention, detection, prosecution and punishment inevitably impinge upon the rights of individuals (Canton, 2007a). Sadly, the benefits of the Human Rights Act have been counteracted by other authoritarian and managerial impulses in recent criminal and youth justice policy (see for instance, Nellis, 2005; Cavadino and Dignan, 2007; Muncie, 2009).

Cavadino et al, in *Criminal justice 2000* (1999), talk about three distinct criminal justice strategies, which they characterise as authoritarian (A), managerial (B) and human rights (C). Their third strategy would promote the principles of proportionate punishment, restorative justice and due process. However, the authors comment that:

> Strategy C has never been central to governmental criminal justice policy. When pursued at all, it has always been combined with Strategies A and B in such a manner as to negate any notion that human rights and moral legitimacy are truly at the heart of the government's approach. (Cavadino et al, 1999, p 46)

Although that statement was written before the Human Rights Act came into force, it remains applicable today. In particular, a variety of concerns has arisen in relation to sentencing, and also doubts about its potential for positive impacts. The cause of such pessimism relates to two provisions: first, the fact that specific rights can be limited or qualified for particular purposes, including prevention of crime; second, the *margin of appreciation* that allows states to interpret obligations and provisions in the light of their own culture and traditions (Gelsthorpe, 2007).

These provisions have permitted items of controversial legislation to be passed and implemented, for instance, parts of the Terrorism Act 2000 that have been justified as being in the interests of national security. Similarly, in terms of sentencing processes and provisions, an arguably much harsher sentencing regime has been introduced by the Criminal Justice Act 2003 and, specifically, the increased use of indeterminate sentences of imprisonment.

Issues that raise questions over rights include: the use of anti-terrorism legislation and Section 44 stop and search powers in particular; Curfew Orders and Dispersal

Orders for young people; the pervasive use of CCTV; electronic monitoring, which may impinge unduly on privacy and family life; offenders having to wear orange jackets while performing community payback; prison conditions and facilities; and prisoners not being allowed to vote.

ASBOs also exist in a grey area in terms of rights. Individuals or communities experiencing anti-social behaviour have rights and deserve protection, but so too do the individuals subject to ASBO proceedings. Anti-social behaviour is not clearly defined in the legislation and so a wide spectrum of behaviour can result in ASBO applications, with potential for very subjective views of what is inappropriate and what is harmful to influence the process. ASBOs are also civil rather than criminal orders, although breach of an ASBO condition is a criminal offence. Civil proceedings do not have the same level of due process safeguards that criminal cases have. Case law on ASBOs has challenged the civil burden of proof, so a higher standard is now required than the *balance of probability* that would normally apply. Nevertheless, proceedings could impinge upon rights under Article 6 (the right to a fair trial), and there may also be implications for other rights, such as private and family life and freedom of movement, if inappropriate or disproportionate prohibitions are imposed. Evidence is emerging that ASBOs are being used disproportionately to regulate the behaviour of young people from working-class families (Furlong and Cartmel, 2007) and from social housing estates (Millie, 2009), populations who are increasingly finding that rights are routinely disregarded.

Duties for public authorities

In spite of the reservations expressed, the Human Rights Act does hold potential for positive impacts through the provisions of Section 6. This states that it is unlawful for a public authority to act in a way that is incompatible with a *Convention right*, unless the authority was bound to do so because of its obligations under other primary legislation. As well as definite decisions and actions, an omission or a failure to act may be viewed as incompatible.

The nature of a 'public authority' is not defined in the legislation other than to specify that it includes courts and tribunals and 'any person certain of whose functions are functions of a public nature' (excluding the Houses of Parliament and their proceedings). 'Functions of a public nature' are also not defined, which has proven to be problematic in terms of enforcement (Fenwick, 2007).

Despite these definitional weaknesses, it is clear that criminal justice agencies fall within the category of public authorities and this has two major implications. Individuals are able to bring proceedings against them for alleged violations of *Convention rights*, and employees as well as offenders or victims might bring such cases. However, over and above the threat of litigation, public authorities should take positive action to ensure that they do not breach their duties under Section 6. This requires attention at an organisational level, but individual employees also have a responsibility to ensure that their actions and decisions in practice have due regard to *Convention rights*.

Responses to the Section 6 requirements of the Human Rights Act could lie on a spectrum ranging from the entirely defensive, 'fire-watching' approach to a much more proactive development of a rights culture (Gelsthorpe, 2007). In the midst of organisational changes and economic pressures, particularly for the probation service, it is perhaps not surprising that progress has been uncertain and that the values implicit in a focus on rights are not fully embedded in day-to-day practices.

Human rights and the prison system

Prison establishments raise numerous and both general and specific dilemmas in relation to human rights. Historically, they have been closed and rather secretive institutions and it is only recently that their cultures and practices have been subjected to scrutiny. Prisoners' rights are precarious and, as Stephen Shaw, the former prison ombudsman, commented:

> Prisons are lawless places (or at least places where the law rarely impinges) and prisoners enjoy few rights, merely privileges that can be withheld at the whim of management. (Shaw, 1987, p 9)

In theory, the punishment element of imprisonment is the deprivation of liberty, and the experience of imprisonment and treatment while in prison should not be punitive in itself. Under a House of Lords ruling in 1982, more commonly known as the Wilberforce judgement, a convicted prisoner retains all civil rights 'which are not taken away expressly or by implication' in spite of imprisonment. However, Coyle points out that:

> This is all very well as a principle, but there is room for a great deal of interpretation about which civil rights are "expressly or by necessary implication" taken away by the fact of imprisonment. The coercive nature of the prison environment means that the punitive element of imprisonment extends into many features of daily life in prison. (2008, p 220)

Such features of daily life include restrictions on movement in the prison, the amount of time in cellular confinement, opportunities for work, education and recreational activities and, in certain circumstances, even access to healthcare.

Progress on human rights has been especially slow and difficult within prisons, and both Conservative and New Labour administrations have proved resistant to change (Eady, 2007). An example is the reluctance to extend voting rights to prisoners despite two ECtHR rulings against the previous government's position (*Hirst v UK (2004) ECHR 122*; *Hirst v UK (2005) ECHR 681*). The progress that has been made has been largely won through legal actions and prisoners have made use of their right under international law to bring cases to court.

However, the impacts are likely to be limited in the absence of political will to more actively promote prisoners' rights:

> Access to courts does not necessarily mean that rights or cultures will change, especially in relation to prisons, where the UK government has frequently regarded rights as "limited" or "qualified" by the very fact of imprisonment and the demands of security and order ... when rights are "qualified", the level of entitlement is always in dispute and challenges are difficult, especially for a transient population of often poorly educated short term prisoners. (Eady, 2007, p 266)

To some extent this intransigence is self-defeating. The Woolf Report (Woolf and Tumin, 1991) on the riots in HM Prison Manchester (formerly known as 'Strangeways') and elsewhere had argued for a fairer and more humane approach to the treatment of prisoners, based on the three pillars of security, control and justice. Disappointingly, progress towards this was halted by the 'prison works' stance of Michael Howard, who entered the Home Office shortly afterwards. And progress since has been piecemeal, with aspects of New Labour's political agenda for criminal justice in conflict with its own human rights legislation. This is particularly regrettable as there is always a risk that prioritising the punitive aspects of imprisonment creates a culture in which staff begin to see cruel and degrading treatment as acceptable and that such behaviours become normalised. Significantly, 'this is more likely to happen when prisoners are stripped of their humanity and treated as passive objects' (Coyle, 2008, p 223).

International law does provide a benchmark for minimum standards, effectively a safety net, in terms of the treatment of prisoners. For instance, Article 10 of the International Covenant on Civil and Political Rights, which came into force in 1976, states that:

- All persons deprived of their liberty shall be treated with humanity and respect for the inherent dignity of the person.

Such general principles are supported by more detailed international instruments, for example, the UN Standard Minimum Rules for the Treatment of Prisoners. It is unclear what exactly this human rights machinery amounts to over and above a guarantee of minimum standards. However, it is important that it is made to count because working in ways that respect the inherent dignity and worth of individuals strengthens rather than weakens prison management and is also more likely to improve public protection (Coyle, 2008).

Human rights law has been used to challenge various issues in relation to imprisonment, including:

- the powers of the Home Secretary to set 'tariffs' for life sentence prisoners;
- parole procedures and specifically indeterminate sentence prisoners held beyond their tariff date because they had not been given access to required programmes;

- the length of time taken to review the cases of offenders recalled to prison;
- conditions under which prisoners are held;
- use of bodily searches;
- removal of prisoners from cells during searches and scrutiny of correspondence;
- refusal of home leave;
- disciplinary procedures and adjudications in prison.

This last point is particularly important, as the rule of law does not stop at the prison gate (Coyle, 2008). Prisoners should have access to legal redress if assaulted, for instance, and should be dealt with in accordance with legal standards if they commit a misdemeanour themselves.

It is difficult to change cultures and practices in large and complex organisations such as prisons. Nevertheless, it is important to sustain and build on what progress has been made in promoting key rights. International human rights instruments have been particularly significant for prisoners and will continue to be so in the context of a harsh penal climate at best ambivalent to their rights and needs. The challenge now for those working in prisons is to embrace rights and to work with them to ameliorate the worst and most oppressive aspects of imprisonment. This involves recognising that:

> A rights based culture is not one that simply enables specific challenges through the courts by prisoners (a long-established right). It must also incorporate the enactment of fair and reasonable processes of maintaining order by the authorities, with effective sources of redress when this is not the case. Perhaps, above all, a rights based culture demands prison conditions that are humane, healthy and constructive, both for staff and prisoners. (Eady, 2007, p 265)

Challenges in working with offenders in the community

There are evident challenges for prisons over questions of human rights. Some of these are also concerns for probation and voluntary agencies working with prisoners. But there is a range of additional challenges in responding to offenders in the context of their communities, not least because:

> ... it is incumbent upon practitioners to see their interventions as critical to the human rights and to the responsibilities of offenders as citizens. (Scott, 2002, p 4)

This links neatly to earlier discussions about the balancing of rights and duties. There is also implicit reference here to the *social capital* of offenders and their potential to develop relationships with those around them that are characterised by trust and reciprocity. Perhaps for practitioners in the community, the legal backing for human rights is less important than the moral arguments in favour of social inclusion, equality and recognition. This is also reflected in thoughts by

Susan Wallace writing from Scotland in 2000, where the provisions of the Human Rights Act had been implemented more than a year before England. She suggests that positive approaches to supervision with a sound ethical foundation may well enhance supervision prospects with difficult and dangerous clients in particular, by providing a framework for supervision that could establish clear boundaries, obligations, duties and expectations. She further comments that:

> A flexible, honest and respectful approach has been documented as having some success with such clients and I believe this could further be enhanced within a rights-based culture. Such a transparent and ethical approach to practice, based on core values such as respect, honesty and openness will go a long way towards establishing a productive working relationship wholly in keeping with the spirit of the Convention. (Wallace, 2000, p 55)

In thinking about the areas of offender management practice where Wallace's ethical approach might be employed, these could include:

* assessment;
* management of community sentences;
* sentencing planning and goal setting;
* individualised risk management;
* communication and provision of information;
* exchange of information between agencies;
* enforcement of orders and licences;
* the way that offenders, victims and others are treated by the service;
* the quality of service and resources devoted to minority groups in the service (for instance, women on community payback).

These areas can be related to the practices and rights-based approach outlined in Chapter Four. Although those discussions do not explicitly refer to the legal requirements for compatibility with *Convention rights*, the approach outlined there would be not only compatible, but would also work within the spirit of the ECHR.

Writing in the early days of the Human Rights Act, Scott (2002) identified six possible areas where the probation service could have faced legal action. In the event, these legal challenges have not materialised. In the light of this, it is appropriate to think more broadly about some of the issues of rights that impinge upon the activities of the probation service and now, increasingly, voluntary and other agencies. Legislation and policy has focused its attention on identifying and categorising persistent or dangerous offenders and subjecting them to more stringent criminal justice processes. It is time to confront the significant questions that arise over the legitimacy of labels given by the criminal justice system and the extent to which these labels result in offender management practices that potentially infringe the human rights of individuals in ways that are unacceptable and disproportionate.

Achieving an appropriate balance

It is evident from the direction that New Labour policy took that the issue of human rights is a central – and not uncontroversial – consideration in criminal justice. The HMI Probation Serious Further Offence (SFO) review in the case of Anthony Rice, for instance, was critical of the attention paid to human rights issues at the expense of risk management, commenting that 'in particular, the human rights aspect is posing increasing levels of challenge to those charged with delivering effective public protection' (HMI Probation, 2006a, p 2).

In relation to the Rice case, it said that:

> It was also from 2001 that in our view the people managing this case started to allow its public protection considerations to be undermined by its human rights considerations, as these required increasing attention from all involved, especially as the prisoner was legally represented. (HMI Probation, 2006a, p 5)

Human rights are indeed posing a challenge for criminal justice practitioners, who are making complex judgements about the appropriate balance of offender rights and actions to protect the public. Sadly, in the Rice case, the appropriate balance was not achieved and lack of clarity in risk management allowed Rice to take legal action on human rights grounds, thereby undermining the objectives of public protection. Such cases have served to compound doubts about the legitimacy of community penalties and probation supervision (Gelsthorpe, 2007). The answer is certainly not to allow the pendulum to swing further away from the rights of offenders towards those of the victim, in what Hudson (2001) terms a 'zero-sum approach', but to try more strenuously to seek an accommodation between the rights and needs of all parties.

Summary

This chapter has outlined the most significant international human rights instruments and the incorporation of human rights obligations from the ECHR into the UK domestic law via the Human Rights Act 1998. The Human Rights Act undoubtedly represents a positive step forward. However, there are evident tensions between its emphasis on striving to ensure freedom, equality and dignity, and the ethos of criminal justice legislation that seeks to promote a security-orientated and/or communitarian agenda, that places the rights of the 'law-abiding majority' above those of offenders. Organisations may respond defensively to their human rights obligations under the Human Rights Act, seeking to guard themselves against possible litigation. However, human rights can be pursued in a more proactive way and it is argued that a rights-based approach to work with offenders is inherently compatible with *Convention rights* and also more capable of protecting the public because it recognises the humanity and dignity of offenders, rather than erasing them.

Further reading

DCA (Department for Constitutional Affairs) (2006) *A guide to the Human Rights Act 1998* (3rd edn), London: DCA.
A useful reference guide is:
Fenwick, H. (2007) *Civil liberties and human rights*, Abingdon: Routledge-Cavendish.

SIX

Equalities

Following on from the discussion of human rights, this chapter outlines the legal framework in relation to equalities and diversity, recently updated by the Equality Act 2010. This new Act seeks to harmonise discrimination law and to strengthen the legal provisions to support progress on equality. Of immediate relevance is the new public sector equality duty that applies to all criminal justice agencies. Of course, efforts to achieve greater equality of outcome for marginalised groups and to recognise diversity are not new to the criminal justice system, although they have received varying levels of attention and commitment over the past three decades. This chapter charts the development of practice and policy, focusing on 'race', ethnicity and gender, highlighting key issues and the learning that may be taken into future practice, linking to previous discussions on desistance and the adoption of a rights-based approach.

Reflecting on diversity

This chapter focuses on policy and practice responses to 'race', ethnicity and gender in the prison and probation services, because these have been the target of most activity, not because they necessarily matter more than other aspects of diversity. Striving for greater equality of treatment and of outcome for offenders is by no means easy, and the criminal justice agencies have struggled to address the complexities of diversity and social inclusion.

Lorraine Gelsthorpe (2007) highlights the difficulty in extending knowledge and understanding of experiences in the criminal justice system, even in relation to the basic areas of gender and ethnicity where data is routinely collected. Other areas impinging upon criminal justice practice – the incidence of mental ill health, the growing number of older prisoners and the impact of sexual orientation, for instance – are relatively neglected, although becoming more pressing as concerns. Nurturing a wider appreciation of diversity is a critical element in developing more open and inclusive practice, and fits with a rights-based approach that recognises that individuals who offend are precisely that – individuals – with unique experiences and perspectives and that they may well have more than one area of their lives where they face disadvantage or discrimination.

Equality Act 2010

Criminal justice practitioners – and their employing organisations – must act in ways that are compatible with obligations under the Human Rights Act 1998.

Their activities are also now regulated by the Equality Act 2010, one of the last Acts of Parliament to achieve Royal Assent before the 2010 General Election.

The Equality Act seeks to consolidate a confusing array of equalities legislation that has built up from the Race Relations Act 1965. As such it incorporates the provisions contained in previous laws and repeals legislation including the Equal Pay Act 1970, the Race Relations Act 1976, the Sex Discrimination Acts 1975 and 1986, the Disability Discrimination Act 1995, the Employment Equality (Sexual Orientation) Regulations 2003 and the Equality Act (Sexual Orientation) Regulations 2007.

The Equality Act introduces new terminology and specifically refers to the notions of *protected characteristics.* In Section 4 these are identified as:

- age
- disability
- gender reassignment
- marriage and civil partnership
- pregnancy and maternity
- race (including colour, nationality and ethnic or national origins)
- religion and belief
- sex
- sexual orientation.

The Act defines *direct discrimination* as treating a person with a protected characteristic less favourably than others would be treated. *Indirect discrimination* refers to situations where a particular provision or practice is applied to a person with a protected characteristic which is discriminatory because of that characteristic (that is, it has a different or greater impact than it would do for someone who does not have that characteristic). *Dual discrimination* can occur when an individual is discriminated against on the basis of two protected characteristics. For instance, women from a minority ethnic background may face discrimination simultaneously in relation to their gender and their ethnicity, and the combined effect can be particularly powerful. The Act also prohibits harassment or victimisation on the basis of any protected characteristic.

The requirements of this legislation apply to all criminal justice agencies as employers, and provide safeguards for employees against discrimination, harassment or victimisation on the basis of protected characteristics. In terms of disability specifically, the Act reaffirms the duty for employers to make *reasonable adjustment* to avoid a disabled employee suffering disadvantage compared to non-disabled colleagues and to take reasonable steps to provide necessary equipment and other aids.

Part 3 of the Act relates to the provision of services and public functions. Under Section 29, any provider of services must not discriminate against an individual in providing the service, or harass or victimise an individual on the basis of protected characteristics. This may present a challenge for offender management, which by its very nature must discriminate among offenders and make judgements about risk of re-offending and potential risk of harm. It is critical that such judgements are defensible and demonstrably not based on assumptions about 'race', ethnicity or any other protected characteristics. Such assumptions could potentially lead to legal challenge, but would not constitute principled or effective risk assessment practice in any event.

Public sector equality duty

The Equality Act builds on previous attempts to require public authorities to approach issues of equality and diversity in a more proactive way. It introduces a particular duty for public authorities in Section 149:

> 1) A public authority must, in the exercise of its functions, have due regard to the need to:
>   a) eliminate discrimination, harassment, victimisation and any other conduct that is prohibited by or under this Act;
>   b) advance equality of opportunity between persons who share a relevant protected characteristic and persons who do not share it;
>   c) foster good relations between persons who share a relevant protected characteristic and persons who do not share it.

In 'fostering good relations', public authorities should have due regard for the need to tackle prejudice and promote understanding. Most of the provisions of the Act came into force on 1 October 2010.

A final note on the legal framework

A previous Equality Act in 2006 established a single body to oversee progress on equalities, the Equality and Human Rights Commission. This body became operational in 2007 and replaced the previous Commission for Racial Equality, the Equal Opportunities Commission and the Disability Rights Commission, as well as taking on a remit covering other areas of potential discrimination such as sexual orientation and religious observance. The attempt to bring oversight of both human rights and equality within one body is interesting, and points to a philosophy that links equality and social justice. It is clear from press coverage that the creation of this overarching equalities organisation has been problematic and there have been criticisms of its leadership. Nevertheless, it is a useful source of information and comment, not least on the implementation of the new Equality Act.

Reflections on anti-discriminatory practice

It does not take a great deal of contact with the criminal justice system to sense that offenders experience discrimination because of their status as offenders. They may have differential experiences or suffer additional discrimination within the criminal justice system on the basis of ethnicity, disability, gender, religious belief or sexual orientation. They may also experience discrimination – or, in more radical terms, oppression – more generally, in areas such as housing, economic circumstances and education. Lack of access or opportunity may represent a criminogenic need and criminal justice interventions are often justified on those grounds. However, a rights-based perspective would argue from the other direction and say that assistance and support should be given on the basis of social justice, and that demonstrably working with offenders towards meeting their social and other needs will impact positively on the likelihood of re-offending.

Sarah Hilder insightfully comments that:

> The various manifestations of discrimination are multifarious and complex, can take direct or indirect forms and can be intentional of unwitting. The impact of a dominant group's discriminatory power over another group results in the denial of equal rights and citizenship. (2007, p 9)

In analysing individual cases and seeking to understand how this might be experienced at an individual level, a simple 'PCS' model has been developed (see Thompson, 2006). This distinguishes three layers of inequalities and discrimination that individuals may experience, these being:

- P or personal/psychological – the level of individual interactions and experiences
- C or cultural – values or patterns of thought or behaviour, social norms
- S or structural – large social or socioeconomic factors that impinge.

Personal experiences are seen as embedded within both cultural and structural layers, and this is described as the centre of the model, surrounded by the cultural and structural aspects.

The PCS model may assist in understanding and examining the multi-layered nature of social inequality and discrimination, but having gone so far, how should practitioners respond? A key notion within the 'old' debates around anti-discriminatory practice is that of empowerment. Although this is not a term heard often around the probation service in recent times, it is worth looking at in more detail and relating to more contemporary discourses around desistance and rights. Dalrymple and Burke, writing in 1995 about social work practice, identify essential principles of empowerment:

- it involves a collaborative process, with the client and the practitioner working together as partners;

- it is important for the client to see him or herself as able to effect change;
- knowledge and awareness are key elements;
- the client should define his/her own goals and the means to achieve them;
- it should be based on a view of the client as competent and capable, given access to resources and opportunity;
- the process entails accessing resources and the capacity to use those resources in an effective way;
- empowerment is achieved through the parallel structures of personal and socioeconomic development (adapted from Dalrymple and Burke, 1995, p 56).

Although the offender management context is focused on risk and enforcement, there are still some aspects of the above apparent in current thinking about desistance, particularly in relation to partnership with the offender and jointly negotiated goals. Compare McNeill's desistance paradigm which involves:

i.   Help in navigating towards desistence, to reduce harm and to make good to offenders and victims;

ii. Explicit dialogue and negotiation assessing risks, needs, strengths and resources and offering opportunities to make good;

iii. Collaboratively defined tasks which tackle risks, needs and obstacles to desistance by using and developing the offender's human and social capital. (2006, p 56)

However, there is also in this desistance paradigm implicit reference to the rights of victims and to the redemptive power of reparation, balanced with the rights of the offender. Both desistance orientations and the rights-based approach advocated in this book are much more explicit than the previous social work approaches in addressing risk and the need to be transparent with offenders in terms of the authority invested in the supervisory role. In this respect they are adopting different discourses and more open practices, while still seeking the same goals of empowerment and individualised responses.

Finally, further points from Loraine Gelsthorpe indicate why it is so centrally important for offender management to respond to diversity, at both managerial and practitioner levels. This gives pause for thought as offender management practices develop:

> Equality of treatment need not be equated with the same treatment. In other words, whilst it is important that unfair treatment is avoided, it is equally important that dimensions of diversity are appropriately accommodated as a means of promoting both *procedural* and *social* justice ... it will be important to ensure that diversity issues remain at the forefront of practice, not simply in relation to managerialist concerns (Bhui, 2006) and changing work cultures, but because of the need to do justice to difference. (2007, pp 342-3)

'Race' and criminal justice

Any discussion of 'race' and criminal justice must start with a clear distinction between 'race' and ethnicity. As Calverley et al note:

> Race is not a fact of nature. Rather, it is a social construct which may be deployed to legitimise social relations of subjugation, or used reactively in resistance to such social relations. Ethnicity, on the other hand, is about belonging to or identifying with a particular group in the population, characterised by common national, geographical or cultural origin. (2006, p xvii)

In many instances, work with white offenders should at least acknowledge their particular ethnicity and its significance to them. Attention to 'race', however, implies different dimensions of discrimination and marginalisation from mainstream structures and cultures, and can be closely linked to fears and assumptions about criminal activity.

Individuals may experience processes of *criminalisation* when it is assumed that they have connections to crime or dubious sub-cultures because of their identity or membership of a particular social group. Young people, for instance, are readily associated with anti-social behaviour in media coverage. Offending labels may also be attached to individuals who come from a travelling background or who live on particular housing estates, irrespective of their actual behaviours. This may then result in increased attention from the police and consequently more contact with the criminal justice system.

Members of black and other minority ethnic (BME) communities may face additional processes of *racialisation* whereby individuals are assigned to a particular group or category, effectively being pigeon-holed on the basis of their 'race' or culture. It is then problematic where that whole social group is ascribed negative qualities, such as criminality or aggression; any one individual has a struggle to shake off those imputed qualities. A current example would be young Muslim men who are tainted with suspicions of extremism. The effects can be powerful, particularly as 'racialisation and criminalisation are socially constructed through processes of interaction between groups and can be embodied in institutional practices' (Webster, 2007, p 3).

Criminal justice agencies are powerful instruments of the state and their practices both reflect patterns of social relations and serve to reproduce them. It is therefore not surprising that racism of many kinds, direct and indirect, individual and institutional, has been found in all the major criminal justice agencies. Conversely, it is also the case that attempts to deal honestly and positively with issues of 'race' and ethnicity in the criminal justice system, using research and available knowledge, could claim a central role in healing divisions and building a more cohesive society (Bhui, 2009a).

However, this is a considerable challenge, which is apparent from an examination of the prison system alone. Until recently, understanding of 'race' and racism behind the closed doors of prison establishments was limited, and this area is still under-researched (Bhui, 2009b). Sadly, it took the murder of a young Asian man, Zahid Mubarek, by his racist cellmate in Feltham Young Offenders Institute in 2000, to focus attention. A public inquiry followed (Keith, 2006) and the incident was also investigated by the Commission for Racial Equality (2003a, 2003b). The findings of these inquiries and successive reports from HMI Prisons reveal a complex picture.

The most recent HMI Prisons reports (2008, 2009) indicate that improvements have been made in procedures for dealing with 'race' issues and 'race' equality schemes in prisons. However, despite the commitment of prison managers and robust responses to reports of racism, it has been difficult to achieve improved outcomes. In particular, BME prisoners continue to cite discrimination, albeit now tending to be more indirect or covert. They are more likely than white prisoners to feel unsafe in the prison environment and to describe poor relationships with staff. BME prisoners report more negatively across most areas of prison life and the difference is even more marked for prisoners who are Muslim or of mixed racial heritage. This clearly points to difficulties in building and sustaining confidence amongst the BME prisoner population (Bhui, 2009b), and may be indicative of entrenched cultural and institutional processes and practices (HMI Prisons, 2009) which are resistant to change.

Prisons face additional challenges in relation to the treatment of Muslim prisoners. Training in this complex area is under-developed, leaving front-line staff ill equipped to deal with the sensitive issues that arise (HMI Prisons, 2008). Although positive progress has been made in terms of increased sensitivity to religious needs, this has been counteracted by growing policy concerns around extremism and radicalisation. Bhui (2009b) notes the degree of prison staff 'buy-in' to measures aimed at identifying Muslim prisoners who may be extremist, which he finds unsurprising in a security-driven service. He comments that it has been significantly harder to achieve the same level of understanding, legitimacy and enthusiasm in the pursuit of 'race' equality. And yet, ironically,

> Race equality must be seen as a basic and irreducible foundation for any work to tackle extremism … as general progress towards race equality has been shown to be at best faltering, it is perhaps not surprising that the evidence suggests a considerable and developing problem with tackling extremism. (Bhui, 2009b, p 91)

'Race' and anti-racism in probation

The 1981 'race' riots in Brixton, Manchester, Bristol and elsewhere reflected the breakdown in relationships between certain BME groups and the police as well as tensions caused by social and economic deprivation within specific communities. Lord Scarman's enquiry into the policing of Brixton highlighted how imperative it was not just for the police but for the whole of the criminal justice sector to attend to 'race' and 'race' relations. Accordingly, throughout the 1980s, action was taken on a number of fronts, with initiatives led by the Central Council of Probation Committees, the Association of Chief Officers of Probation and the probation officers' union, Napo. The Home Office also issued guidance and backed this with legislation. Section 95 of the Criminal Justice Act 1991 duly introduced a requirement for all criminal justice agencies to collect and publish data on gender and ethnicity.

Sadly, during the 1990s this welcome impetus for change diminished, and initiatives developed during the 1980s lost momentum. Lord Dholakia, chair of the National Association for the Care and Resettlement of Offenders (Nacro), summarised the changes in public attitudes in *Let's get it right: Race and justice 2000:*

> Somehow the real impetus for change was lost: events of the early 1980s faded from memory; criminal justice faded from public view. Crime, however, and fear of crime, became a public preoccupation. Did this fear of crime help to demonise certain groups in the public mind? We are all familiar with the image of the uncontrollable pre-teens stealing car after car on deprived estates: we are familiar with the derogatory terminology of "rat boys", the barely concealed message of "bogus asylum seekers". These messages help us identify people to blame instead of making us look for solutions … it has taken the tragic death of a young man to shock the system into action. (Nacro, 2000, p 2)

However, the impact of the murder of Stephen Lawrence and the subsequent Macpherson report (1999), with its charges of institutional racism in the police, forced criminal justice agencies to reassess their practices and approaches to diversity. HMI Probation published a thematic inspection, *Towards race equality* (2000a), which sharply criticised core areas of probation practice, particularly court reports, and clearly indicated how far the previous probation focus on anti-discriminatory practice had been eroded.

In January 2004, HMI Probation published a follow-up inspection (2004) which found that improvements had been made with regard to service delivery but showed that further action was still required. This report therefore set the agenda for change within the service alongside the broader government policy agenda which is reflected in the developing framework of equalities legislation.

In relation to service delivery, the Home Office recognised that little was known about the criminogenic needs of BME offenders, available provision and effectiveness of the approaches then in use. Its research department therefore commissioned a review to look at these areas. The results of this study by Powis and Walmsley (2002) found a dearth of strong evidence of the need for different interventions for BME offenders and little rigorous evaluation demonstrating that the few separate (mainly black empowerment) groups that had run were effective (Walmsley and Stephens, 2006). This raised important questions for practice that were explored in a later Home Office study by Adam Calverley et al, entitled *Black and Asian offenders on probation* (2004). The next sections pull out the significant messages from this research.

Black and Asian offenders' experience of probation

The study by Calverley et al (2004) involved 483 offenders over 17 probation areas and illuminated the experiences of black and Asian offenders. Their respondents reported a number of negative experiences (for example, racist abuse or frequent stop and searches) that they felt would be less likely to happen to white offenders. The probation service should be aware that such negative experiences of criminal justice agencies are likely to affect perceptions of the legitimacy of the system that, in turn can affect motivation and compliance. Practitioners should also be sensitive to the particular needs and experiences of offenders who are of mixed racial heritage.

It was striking that amongst the study sample, black, Asian and mixed heritage offenders showed less crime-prone attitudes and beliefs than comparable groups of white offenders and had fewer self-reported problems.

Additionally, there was no evidence that probationers from BME groups had distinctively different or greater criminogenic needs than white probationers. Nevertheless, the findings suggest that BME offenders had received the same community sentences as white offenders with higher levels of criminogenic need – a possible result of differential sentencing. The study also found that Asian offenders in the sample were less likely to access accredited programmes.

In relation to experiences of probation, responses were generally favourable and specifically:

- a good probation officer was seen as one who treated people under supervision fairly and with respect, and who listened to them and showed understanding;
- approximately 35 per cent wanted to be supervised by someone from the same ethnic group, whereas 56 per cent said it did not matter;
- programmes attracted favourable comments and, of those attending, 33 per cent said that the ethnic composition of the group was unimportant, with only 5 per cent expressing a wish for groups specifically for BME participants;
- the results supported mixed groups, but with some concerns about the experience of 'singleton' BME offenders in an otherwise white group (adapted from Calverley et al, 2004).

Calverley et al (2004) go on to say that their findings suggest that:

> It is important not to treat minority ethnic status as a defining identity from which personal characteristics, experiences and needs can be reliably inferred. This, however benignly intended, is itself a form of ethnic stereotyping. Effective practice requires the thorough assessment of individual offenders. Respondents in this study expected to be

treated fairly, as individuals, as a "normal person", by staff, who listened to them and respected their views. Policies and practice therefore need to be informed by awareness of diversity, but not based on untested assumptions about what diversity implies. (Calverley et al, 2004, p 59)

Although this research is a major step forward in indicating the views and experiences of BME offenders in contact with the probation service, it does have limitations, not least because the research sample was all male (Raynor and Lewis, 2006). Gelsthorpe points to the relative lack of knowledge about BME women in the criminal justice system and suggests that 'minority women offenders may well face a "double whammy" of being female in a context where women are "out of place" and "alien" because of their ethnicity, but we know far too little about the effects of these additive factors' (Gelsthorpe, 2006, p 101).

Whereas research has been conducted on 'race' and gender independently, little has been conducted on how these two factors interact and official data is collected separately. This has meant that even large-scale studies of the sentencing of women, such as that carried out for the Home Office by Hedderman and Gelsthorpe in *Understanding the sentencing of women* (1997), were unable to consider the impact of ethnicity.

In terms of the experience of BME women on probation, Chigwada-Bailey (2003) discusses previous research findings that suggested that they were less likely to be made subject to Probation or Community Rehabilitation Orders than their white counterparts. Her study involved interviewing 20 black female interviewees who reported mixed views of their experience of supervision, including feeling patronised and misunderstood (2003). Other surveys of probation service provision have revealed some developments in services for BME offenders, but not specifically BME women (Gelsthorpe, 2006). This remains an area deserving of more attention, particularly given the over-representation of black women in the female prison population.

Offenders with mixed ethnicities

One of the striking findings from the Calverley et al (2004) study was the evidence that offenders of mixed racial heritage seem to suffer particular social disadvantage compared to black and Asian offenders and to have even more negative experiences within the criminal justice system. Questions about the impact of mixed ethnicity are only just being raised by policy makers, and it was as recently as the 2001 population census that options to self-define as of mixed ethnicity was included in the ethnic categories. Individuals of mixed heritage or ethnicity tend to be demographically situated in younger age groups.

In terms of social experiences, research indicates that people of mixed heritage experience greater exclusion, are disproportionately represented in the public care system and face additional barriers in education, including the burden of low expectation (Lewis and Olumide, 2006).

A study by Feilzer and Hood (2004) highlighted higher rates of prosecution, remand, custodial sentencing and restrictive community sentences for mixed heritage young people that were still evident in spite of difficulties identifying such young people through youth justice data systems. Although the Calverley et al study included only a small sample of mixed heritage offenders (57 out of 483), their findings supported the evidence of the Feilzer and Hood research on sentencing (Calverley et al, 2004). This leads to a conclusion that:

> If steps are not taken to address the high levels of disadvantage experienced by the predominantly young and growing mixed heritage population, these factors could, over time, lead to their increased representation among the offending population ... further, those working with mixed heritage offenders should not assume they all have the same needs and experiences, but should be aware of the high levels of socio-economic deprivation among this group. (Lewis and Olumide, 2006, p 138)

Racist or racially motivated offenders

This deserves consideration, particularly as a report from HMI Probation (2000b) indicated that, although probation officers were trained in anti-discriminatory practice, they were not good at challenging racism, which frequently emerges in the course of supervision rather than being apparent at the outset (D. Smith, 2006a). This has assumed increased importance because of provisions under the Crime and Disorder Act 1998 which allow offences to be considered as more serious or 'aggravated' by the presence of racial motivation. This has meant that a greater number of offenders are entering supervision with obvious issues around 'race' to be explored. Nevertheless, research has indicated that the majority of racist offenders in contact with the probation service will tend to be 'generalists' rather than 'specialists' in violent racial crime (Ray et al, 2002).

David Smith, writing about work with racially motivated offenders (RMOs), makes some interesting observations. First, he notes the tensions that practitioners may feel in working with RMOs, which might cause them not to challenge racism:

> It would also be harder to sustain a view of the offender as "needy" and disadvantaged if overt racism entered the relationship. For such reasons, "ordinary" racism went unchallenged, while some officers almost demonised racist offenders as extremely violent political extremists. (D. Smith, 2006a, p 27)

In terms of theoretical models to understand racism, he suggests that the conventional way of defining racism as necessarily involving the presence of both prejudice and power does not work for these offenders. In contrast, he finds that:

It is likely that any effective work with racist offenders will need to be based on recognition that racism often emerges from feelings, not of power and superiority, as in the standard accounts of racist ideologies, but from a sense of weakness and subordination. (D. Smith, 2006a, p 28)

Furthermore, racism may be based in emotions rather than rationality. As such, many offenders fully recognise that racism is morally wrong at a conscious, cognitive level, but there is a disjunction between what they think and what they feel: 'Racist offending usually has its roots in powerful, but unacknowledged, emotions that are at odds with offenders' conscious rational beliefs' (D. Smith, 2006b, p 202). Effective work will therefore involve encouraging individuals to explore their feelings and to better understand how particular behaviours are connected to negative emotional states. Certainly, where individuals are uncomfortable with those behaviours and disapprove of them when in calmer frames of mind, there is room to help promote self-awareness and capacity to manage difficult feelings without focusing them on other people.

Issues of gender

Whereas 'race' has received a great deal of recent official attention, gender has rather less so, although it has continued as an academic and research preoccupation since the 1980s. This is largely due to feminist work detailing women's criminal careers, sentencing and experience of the criminal justice agencies, particularly prisons (see, for example, Carlen, 1985, 1988, 2002; Morris, 1987; Worrall, 1990; Carlen and Worrall, 2004). Feminists have also highlighted the role of masculinity in such crimes as domestic violence and rape, and this is a growing area of interest.

It is important to recognise that gender is a social construct, unlike sex, which is a biological given. Criminology as an academic discipline and criminal justice agencies have historically assumed that masculinity is unproblematic, universal and the norm. These assumptions have been challenged more recently and the essential nature of masculinity has been questioned. Offender management policies and practice have only just started to explore masculinities, but it is a relevant consideration in looking at male violence, car crime and offences such as rape, as well as racially motivated violence discussed earlier.

Probation responses to women offenders

Anne Worrall (2002b) charts the history of probation work with women offenders under the title 'Missed opportunities?', which reflects her assessment that the service has not done well by women, particularly in promoting non-custodial options. The problems of female imprisonment have been highlighted many times, most recently in an influential report by Baroness Corston (2007).

In relation to sentencing, research in 1997 found that:

- women offenders are perceived by sentencers as more 'troubled' than 'troublesome';
- there are major differences in use of non-custodial sentences for men and women;
- women are consistently more likely to be discharged than men;
- sentencers are very reluctant to fine women;
- women are more likely to receive a more severe community penalty – probation supervision (adapted from Hedderman and Gelsthorpe, 1997).

Several issues arise from this, including the low use of unpaid work for women and the more limited number of sentencing steps before they reach custody, particularly as probation has often been given more readily to women at an early stage of offending. Interestingly, this trend has continued under the Criminal Justice Act 2003 sentencing framework, with women more likely to receive supervision requirements on their community orders and suspended sentence orders than men, who are more likely to be required to complete unpaid work (Patel and Stanley, 2008).

Worryingly, Patel and Stanley's review of the use of the generic community order for women suggests that the service has not made full use of the opportunities and innovations that might be possible in putting together sentencing packages (2008). Clearly there is room for being more imaginative and responsive to women's rights and needs. And room also to shift the focus from their offending behaviour and (in)ability to comply with often onerous requirements on their orders, recognising that offending is a reflection of other deep-rooted problems, even more so for women than for men (Barry and McIvor, 2010).

Regarding sentencing, it is important to note the consistent findings of research about how women are portrayed in court by probation among other key players, as summarised by Anne Worrall:

> The female law breaker is rationally offered the opportunity to neutralise the effects of her lawbreaking activity by implicitly entering into a contract whereby she permits her life to be represented primarily in terms of its domestic, sexual and pathological dimensions. (1990, p 35)

Problems arise for women who cannot enter into this contract or will not – drug users, young women in the care system, women with violent or alcohol-related offending, black women or lesbians, for instance. They do not benefit from the leniency and paternalism often experienced by more 'conventional' women and may be subject to *double jeopardy* or *double deviance*, that is, being sentenced first for their criminal offence and second for offending against established norms for their gender (Heidensohn, 1985).

Because women have always been a minority on probation caseloads and most specifically for serious violent and sexual offending, they have historically received an inconsistent proportion of probation service resources. There is currently only one accredited programme for women and this relates to acquisitive offending (Gelsthorpe, 2007). Within a context where resources are intended to follow risk, this presents problems for developing work with women, who are more frequently in the lower tiers of risk although, perhaps, with multiple and complex needs. However, after a long period of relative inactivity, the Home Office was galvanised by evidence of a dramatic and disproportionate rise in the female prison population between the early 1990s and 2005. In 2004, it produced the Women's Offending Reduction Programme, the first major strategy focused on women offenders.

Following this, and in the wake of the Corston Report (2007), the government also published the first *National Service Framework* for women offenders with a headline aim of:

> Ensuring that women who come into contact with the criminal justice system are treated appropriately so as to protect the public and reduce re-offending, whilst also meeting their specific and individual needs. (Ministry of Justice, 2008b, p 6)

Actions required to achieve this include:

- reducing the number of women coming through the criminal justice system;
- for those women who are sentenced, ensuring their needs are met in the community wherever possible; and
- for women sentenced to custody, ensuring that the facilities are appropriate to their needs.

The intention is that this will then result in fewer women being sentenced overall and specifically fewer women being held in custody. Its objective is simultaneously to tackle re-offending, to improve the well-being of women in contact with the criminal justice system and to reduce the incidence of self-harm.

With a view to developing and implementing more appropriate services for women, in 2005 the Home Office also launched the Together Women Programme in two pilot areas in order to test out more holistic responses to women's offending. These demonstration projects became operational in 2007 and the scheme has since expanded. It is heartening to note that they are based on what academics and key players in the criminal justice system (including Baroness Corston, 2007) have been saying about the need to develop more suitable community-based resources for women.

What represents good practice with women

Writing more than 10 years ago, Lisa Wright and Hazel Kemshall identified a regrettable tendency for criminal justice agencies to pathologise women or to see them only in terms of their family and domestic roles. As a result, women were often not treated as fully competent adults and this, they felt, let so many women down, failing to engage them actively in supervisory relationships. They proposed instead a model of feminist (probation) practice with women offenders that sees them as capable and seeks to utilise their strengths:

> Woman-centred practice means acknowledging the constraints that gender roles place upon women and recognising them as whole individuals.
>
> The concept of self-determination is central: listening to women, hearing their views and assisting them to achieve the solutions they seek is important. The ultimate goal lies in empowering women to find the confidence and resources they need to lead the most constructive lives they can. A recognition that egalitarian relationships are the most empowering means that a woman-centred approach affects both the nature and content of supervision. (Wright and Kemshall, 1994, p 73)

This resonates with a rights-based approach built on a partnership between the supervisee and supervisor (or, more currently, offender manager) and is underpinned by an awareness of power relations organised on the basis of gender and of experiences of social inequality. Farrow et al (2007) offer further thoughts about sensitive and appropriate interventions for women. They stress the importance of incorporating women's perspectives and ensuring that interventions are relevant to their life experiences, to look, as Jenny Roberts (2002, p 12) suggests, 'through the women's window'. Women's experiences of socialisation are different to men's and this has an impact on the offending opportunities open to them and the choices that they make. Understanding the individual's offending behaviour and the context in which it occurs is fundamental to determining the content of any interventions.

Although much female crime is acquisitive, practitioners should be careful to avoid stereotyping women as victims of poverty and economic marginalisation because this can lead to an approach that justifies, rather than challenges, individual women's responses to their difficult life experiences. Each individual's motivation will differ according to the function that her offending fulfils (and the *primary social goods* she is seeking).

Work with women should start with steps to encourage engagement, both by paying attention to the content and methodology of programmes, and also by overcoming the barriers to involvement and continued motivation. There is some evidence that women respond more positively to collaborative ways of working which aim for change that is staged, cumulative and incremental, rather than immediate. Such work can usefully focus on beliefs supportive of offending by exploring the notion of rational choice and, alongside this, the development of skills that together create the potential to find realistic solutions to problems (Farrow et al, 2007).

Thinking more broadly about provision for women, a Fawcett Society report (Gelsthorpe et al, 2007) suggested that there are nine specific lessons that could be drawn from the body of existing knowledge. Provision designed in line with these lessons should:

1. Be women-only to foster safety and a sense of community and to enable staff to develop expertise in work with women;
2. Integrate offenders with non-offenders so as to normalise women offenders' experiences and facilitate a supportive environment for learning;
3. Foster women's empowerment so that they gain sufficient self-esteem to directly engage in problem-solving themselves, and feel motivated to seek appropriate employment;
4. Utilise ways of working with women which draw on what is known about their effective learning styles;
5. Take a holistic and practical stance to helping women to address social problems which may be linked to their offending;
6. Facilitate links to mainstream agencies, especially health, debt advice and counselling;
7. Have the capacity and flexibility to allow women to return to the centre or programme for "top up" of continued support and development where required;
8. Ensure that women have a supportive milieu or mentor to whom they can turn when they have completed any offending-related programme, since personal support is likely to be as important as any direct input addressing offending behaviour;
9. Provide women with practical help with transport and childcare so that they can maintain their involvement in the centre or programme. (Gelsthorpe et al, 2007, p 54)

The challenge for probation is developing such provision in a performance-driven climate and in a service that is historically focused on working with boys and men. The Together Women Project and other initiatives hold promise, and certainly they present an alternative to practice approaches that rule out consideration of wider social structural factors and gender-specific experiences of power relations as irrelevant to offending. However, it remains to be seen whether they will continue to attract the same level of resources in the light of severe budgetary constraints (Worrall and Gelsthorpe, 2009).

Desistance and diversity

Previous discussions of desistance have made reference to the unique pathway that each individual may take. Every offender has different resources and support networks available through which he or she may gain social capital or try out new non-offending identities. However, personal characteristics and membership of particular social groups can be highly significant in determining exactly what is available and accessible.

Calverley, for instance, writing in relation to desistance in BME offenders, comments that:

> Ethnicity is highly relevant as a dependent variable which indexes significant structural differences. These differences have implications for the operation of processes of desistance by affecting the availability of resources, opportunities and pathways out of crime, which in turn, affect the expectations and actions of desisters themselves. (2009, p 300, cited in Durrance et al, 2010, p 148)

Ethnicity and race, but also other factors such as disability, mental ill health and gender, may influence where an individual is located in social structures and the *good life* opportunities available. But availability itself is not enough; the individual must recognise that the opportunity is there and believe that it is within reach (Rumgay, 2004b). Such belief or optimism may be difficult in the light of previous experiences of insensitivity or outright discrimination.

However, that is not to say that diversity and membership of minority groups holds no positives. Research has consistently pointed to the transformative processes involved in securing secondary desistance and the need to forge an alternative self, a new identity dissociated from offending. (Re)engagement with an ethnic, cultural or religious community may provide some individuals with a means of doing this, as would political activism around disability or sexual orientation, for instance.

Calverley's (2009) unpublished study gives valuable insights into social and cultural resources among different minority ethnic groups. The research involved 33 offenders of Indian, Bangladeshi and black or mixed heritage ethnic groups, who evidenced distinct variations in their pathways to desistance. The Indian participants were more influenced by the aspirational values of their families and, through them, had greater access to economic, employment and educational resources. The Bangladeshi participants tended to experience a higher degree of acceptance and forgiveness from their families, which was connected to strongly held religious values. In contrast, the black and mixed heritage participants described their desistance experience as markedly more independent and individualised, often involving isolating themselves from previous social relationships (cited in Weaver and McNeill, 2010).

While following generally the same desistance processes as men, experiences do differ for women, particularly in relation to the transition to adulthood. Leaving home, for instance, can often be associated with an escalation in offending for young men, but not so for young women, especially if it corresponds with achieving independence or becoming a parent (McIvor et al, 2004). Relationships seem to have greater influence. In the first instance, social networks, particularly those involving drug use are strongly associated with starting to offend (Barry, 2007). In deciding to move away from offending, the women in McIvor et al's (2004) research were more likely to cite moral reasons for their decision and to emphasise the relational aspects of the process, whereas young men focused on personal choice and ability to act autonomously. Family and friendship networks also appear to be important in supporting and sustaining desistance (Rumgay, 2004b).

These are, of course, generalisations and it would be inappropriate to make assumptions about an offender on the basis of ethnicity or any other characteristic. Practitioners need to strive for a balance between responding to the individual and bringing knowledge and experience to bear, whether from previous practice or from reading and research. This requires an open and flexible approach and also requires practitioners to be secure in themselves, in their own identity and values. Where there is a limited body of knowledge – and this is particularly the case in terms of minority ethnic groups, for instance, and desistance processes – practitioners should be prepared to develop their own knowledge base, to reflect on their experiences and to challenge any taken-for-granted thinking (Farrow et al, 2007).

Summary

Responding appropriately to diversity is a challenge for the criminal justice system, whose practices and processes have to be standardised and equitable on the one hand, and sufficiently flexible to recognise individual needs and circumstances on the other. Inevitably criminal justice agencies have often struggled to find the appropriate balance. Well meaning initiatives have sometimes failed, and only too often a mixture of political imperatives and the general inertia of large and complex organisations have confounded change. However, there is a growing body of knowledge that can be used to inform practice.

Much of this knowledge relates to the experiences of minority groups in the criminal justice system and the lessons from research are critical to attempts to improve organisational and cultural practices so that they are more sensitive to difference and respectful of individual rights. However, messages from research are also starting to give some indications of what might best support desistance and enable individuals to build *social capital* and to create new identities. The implication is clearly that offender management should reach out to a variety of voluntary and other agencies and groups in the wider community to access resources and opportunities, challenging the assumption that accredited programmes and other probation or prison-delivered interventions are sufficient in themselves. This is crucial to providing properly individualised assessment and intervention that recognises and respects difference and diversity, going a long way beyond the baseline expectations of equalities legislation. Practitioner knowledge and confidence is important in this, but equally important is willingness to ask questions and to explore new knowledge and understanding.

Further reading

Bhui, H.S. (ed) (2009) *Race and criminal justice*, London: Sage Publications.

Corston, Baroness J. (2007) *A report by Baroness Jean Corston of a review of women with particular vulnerabilities in the criminal justice system*, London: Home Office.

Farrow, K., Kelly, G. and Wilkinson, B. (2007) *Offenders in focus: Risk, responsivity and diversity*, Bristol: The Policy Press.

Lewis, S., Raynor, P., Smith, D. and Wardek, A. (eds) (2005) *Race and probation*, Cullompton: Willan.

Sheehan, R., McIvor, G. and Trotter, C. (eds) (2007) *What works with women offenders*, Cullompton: Willan.

Sheehan, R., McIvoor, G. and Trotter, C. (eds) (2011) *Working with women offenders in the community*, Abingdon: Willan

Silvestri, M. and Crowther-Dowey, C. (2008) *Gender and crime*, London: Sage Publications.

Thompson, N. (2006) *Anti-discriminatory practice* (4th edn), London: Palgrave Macmillan.

SEVEN

Dealing with risk and danger

The general debates about approaches to risk assessment and management have already been introduced in the opening chapters, which identified the dominant RNR model that operates within a broader community protection framework. This chapter seeks to build on the earlier discussions, focusing on the assessment of dangerousness and serious harm. In doing so, it raises concerns about effectiveness, professional judgement and offender rights in assessment and risk management processes. It also examines multi-agency frameworks, specifically those relating to sexual and violent offenders and perpetrators of domestic abuse. Such arrangements are important developments in managing risk, but inevitably criminal justice agencies are unable to predict and prevent further offending of a serious nature in all cases. Probation services are required to review all cases where further serious offences have been committed by offenders subject to community sentences or supervision by virtue of a post-custody licence. Additionally, a small number of particularly worrying high-profile cases have been examined further by HMI Probation, and there are lessons to be drawn from these about the management of high-risk offenders. The chapter ends with a return to the discussion of general principles in risk assessment and management and how these core tasks might be fulfilled in ways that invite the participation of offenders and seek to promote their rights in balance with the imperatives of public protection.

Risk assessment in the probation service

Assessment of risk and allocation of offenders to appropriate tiers of risk underpins all work undertaken within the OMM. This section looks briefly at the history of risk assessment in the probation service, as the key agency charged with the formal assessment of risk, and how it has become increasingly structured and suited to the task of classifying or categorising offenders in this way.

First, it is necessary to explore what is meant by risk. Writing in 1995, Hazel Kemshall quotes an Oxford Dictionary definition of the components of risk as being:

> ... the (mis)chance component, the exposure to hazard or danger, and the damage or loss component. (1995, p 135)

Effectively, risk assessment in a criminal justice context is calculation of the probability that a harmful behaviour or event will occur. This involves assessing the frequency of the behaviour or event and identifying who it will affect and the likely impact (Kemshall, 1996). Kemshall goes on to outline the limits of what the probation service can be expected to do in addressing risk. It is helpful to bear this in mind in thinking about the risk–averse culture within the current criminal justice system and the tendency towards defensive rather than defensible decisions regarding risk:

> The probation service cannot guarantee to prevent risk, only to credibly identify the possibility of risk and to take adequate steps to diminish it. A risk assessment can only identify the probability of harm, assess the impact of it on key individuals, and pose intervention strategies which may diminish the risk or reduce harm. Assessments cannot prevent risk. (Kemshall, 1995, p 137)

The complexities of thinking around risk are further reflected by Gwen Robinson when she comments that the concept of risk has risen rapidly and has been confused in both official documents and in practice. This is largely due to its different meanings, particularly (but not exclusively) the fact that the notion of risk relates to both the likelihood of re-offending and the potential danger posed by the offender to others and/or to self (Robinson, 1999).

Risk, then, may refer to the likelihood of (re)offending or the possibility of harm. It may also refer to potential harm to the offender him- or herself, perhaps as a result of his or her own actions or by the actions or omissions of others (Farrow et al, 2007). Offenders may be at risk through chaotic drug use or vulnerable to self-harm in stressful situations, such as being held in police custody. Risk, however, is also specific to different contexts and, for instance, in a prison environment, the risks that are important might be risk of absconding, risk of disruption to the management of the establishment or risk towards staff. This chapter, however, focuses on the likelihood of (re)offending and, in particular, the risk of serious harm if offences do occur.

The first tools for predicting risk were developed in the probation service in the 1980s, following earlier developments in the US and responding to pressures in the UK to prove effectiveness. The most well known was a Risk of Custody Scale devised by Bale (1987) and validated on sentencing decisions in Cambridge. Further work was taking place in Manchester (Humphrey et al, 1992), which produced what the authors recognised was a crude but robust starting point for predicting reconviction in the form of an eight-banded classification system (Beaumont, 1999a). These tools were adopted by a number of services, but the use of such predictive measures was by no means systemic or widespread. Despite requirements in the first version of national standards in 1992 and strengthened in the 1995 standards, for probation officers to assess offenders in relation to risk there were no standardised means of doing so. In any case Beaumont (1999b) comments that referring to the Cambridge and Manchester scales and similar work as 'predictive scales' is a misnomer, as they are entirely based on past histories, not current behaviours.

Nevertheless, the use of such measures chimed with developments elsewhere that aimed to replace the inaccuracies of purely clinical judgements (Kemshall, 1996) with more statistical measures. Kemshall, in outlining approaches to risk, talks about an attitude to risk that treats it as an artefact:

> In the artefact approach, risk is framed as objectively knowable and amenable to probabilistic calculation ... in the penal realm this conceptualisation of risk is epitomised by the pursuit of statistically valid and predictively useful factors for recidivism and for parole violation. (Kemshall, 2003, p 50)

This is neatly summed up in Feeley and Simon's analysis in the early 1990s of what was then a new penality focused on actuarial justice, characterised by:

- "Clinical diagnosis and retributive judgement" replaced by risk calculations and risk probability assessments, hence the term "actuarialism";
- A systemic approach to justice matters, with an increasing emphasis upon managing offenders in place rather than securing rehabilitation. Crime control per se replaces attention to individual responsibility or culpability;
- The pursuit of new crime control techniques such as targeting of offenders as an aggregate group, situational crime risk management, crime prevention techniques, increased surveillance of at-risk groups such as sex offenders;
- Management replacing change as a key objective of criminal justice. (Feeley and Simon, 1992, p 450)

For the probation service, the new focus on risk following the Criminal Justice Act 1991 created interest in ways of predicting risk of dangerousness, in particular. An early response from the Association of Chief Officers of Probation, *Guidance on the management of risk and public protection*, recognised that the Criminal Justice Act 1991 and the then newly introduced national standards required a more active recognition of responsibilities for assessing risk to the public and its subsequent management (ACOP, 1994).

  However, at that point risk assessment was relatively new and certainly, as Bill Beaumont identifies, the areas most researched were around reconviction among known offenders and MDOs, leaving gaps in knowledge in terms of risk factors for more serious offences:

> One of the ironies in reconviction prediction seems to be that where accuracy matters most (where public safety from serious physical and psychological harm is at risk) the technology of statistical risk assessment is at its weakest. The over-riding difficulties of predicting rare events have not yet been overcome despite a considerable research effort. (1999b, p 95)

Beaumont issues several warnings about the over-reliance on statistical prediction tools. First, with the increase in potential ethical issues the more statistical devices influence or substitute for human decision making. Second, that even the best prediction tools – including the Offender Group Reconviction Scale (OGRS) – at that point were struggling to achieve an accuracy rate above 70-80 per cent. Finally, he concludes that prediction research is complex and does not offer easy solutions, being more accurate in relation to more routine crimes, for instance, than rare and atypical events, such as deaths linked to child abuse. Nevertheless, he goes on to say that statistical risk predictors, if introduced carefully, could provide social workers with a useful starting point in making risk judgements, 'but they will not take the uncertainty out of risk situations' (Beaumont, 1999b, p 99).

Pointing to the importance of judgement and careful use of statistical tools is significant, particularly in view of Williams' (1997) warning that such predictive instruments may be used in some criminal justice settings with a critical understanding of their limitations, and in others – for instance, prisons – seen as an objective measure.

The use of OGRS is an interesting example of a statistical tool in practice. Developed by Copas and colleagues in the mid-1990s, originally from work on recidivism risks to inform parole decisions (Kemshall, 2003), it was the first predictive tool to be endorsed by the Home Office and embedded in practice, despite opposition from professional bodies such as Napo (Kemshall, 2003). It claims the most impressive accuracy rate, but still only around 80 per cent, and therefore has not proved to be the 'magic bullet' that was originally being sought from such predictive tools.

Practice has leant towards first clinical and then actuarial models of assessing risk. However, a new formulation that mixes the two has more recently tended to gain precedence and the next section analyses the use of what are known as 'third generation' predictive tools.

Use of 'third generation' assessment or predictive tools

The need for more sophisticated tools within the probation service arose from quests for not only greater predictive accuracy, but also ways of determining how to target resources and to gain more immediate feedback about the effectiveness of probation service interventions than would be available from long-term reconviction studies (Raynor et al, 2000).

The first 'home grown' assessment tool that received relatively widespread attention in the UK was the Assessment, Case Management and Evaluation (ACE) system developed by Colin Roberts and colleagues in the Centre for Criminological Research at the University of Oxford in conjunction with Warwickshire Probation Service. The Centre was commissioned in 1993 by the Warwickshire Probation Committee to conduct a feasibility study, including a pilot research element, in order to determine whether it was possible to establish a system of data collection by staff that could inform assessments of effectiveness. After the pilot study, the same probation service asked the Centre to develop its prototype evaluation system and this is what ultimately became known and copyrighted as the ACE system (Raynor et al, 2000).

At the same time another tool, the Level of Service Inventory – Revised (LSI-R) was coming to the notice of probation services. This had been devised by two Canadian correctional psychologists, Don Andrews and Jim Bonta, from three primary sources – recidivism literature, the professional opinions of probation officers and social learning theories (Andrews and Bonta, 1995). Kemshall incisively comments that:

> In effect, these tools were developed for targeting, intervention, rationing and change measurement. However, not all needs were to be included, but only those linked to criminal behaviour ... need was reframed by the language of risk, and only certain needs were legitimised for concern and intervention. (Kemshall, 2003, p 69)

These risk prediction instruments were not value-free or entirely objective technical tools, although that was how they were promoted (Kemshall, 2003). In fact, the choice of tools and the use that is made of them in order to target services and surveillance can be extremely value-laden and potentially politicised. In particular, the popularity of ACE and LSI-R in the 1990s was due to the need for probation services at that time to demonstrate effectiveness (Burnett et al, 2007). Similarly, the commissioning in 1998 and subsequent adoption of OASys by the Home Office is identified by Kemshall (2003) as a response to a policy imperative to assess and categorise offenders' risk. It is linked more strongly to managerial imperatives than any real effort to anticipate and pre-empt serious harm (Horsefield, 2003).

Following three evaluated pilots, OASys was rolled out across the prison and probation service between 2001 and 2004. By November 2005, around 870,000 assessments had been completed on 370,000 separate offenders (Howard, 2006). In the initial stages, the probation service experienced some resistance to the requirement to complete lengthy OASys forms and concerns were expressed about de-professionalising its workforce. Interestingly, an evaluation of the use of OASys found that probation officers were not recording the full extent of their assessments and that their knowledge base in interview was far more extensive than evidenced on the forms (Crawford, 2007). This seems to suggest that practitioners were at best uncertain about how to use OASys to enhance their approach to the professional task of assessment. Assessments of motivation and responsiveness were particularly weak, and this is highly significant given the salience of responsivity within the RNR model. Sadly also, the feedback mechanisms from managers required to sign off the assessments were not being used to aid practitioner development (Crawford, 2007).

The issues around professionalism are worth exploring a little further. There has been discussion of this area in relation to the Asset tool in youth justice, which is a direct descendent of the ACE system. Rob Canton and Tina Eadie have developed a useful model to illustrate the interplay between professional discretion and accountability in YOTs, which have become subject to central regulation more recently than the probation service. Their discussion is primarily focused on working within the youth justice national standards, but also with reference to Asset completion. They contend that, within new frameworks for practice, there is still room, indeed a necessity, to employ professional values, discretion and judgement. Their model identifies four types of practice according to the extent of accountability and professional discretion involved. 'Best practice' entails high levels of both accountability and discretion, in contrast to the 'bad old days' when practitioners had considerable freedoms and were held to account very little, creating potential for inconsistent or idiosyncratic practices to develop. Practice can also be described as 'constrained' (high accountability and low discretion) or 'the worst of all worlds' (a combination of low accountability and low discretion) (Canton and Eadie, 2002). Practitioners should strive for best practice, using the room that they have to exercise discretion and judgement while still fulfilling the accountability requirements in terms of timely completion of tasks, accurate recording and evidence of work.

Both OASys and Asset invite assessors to record additional information to support their judgements. Inevitably, it is tempting in the course of a busy practice day to complete these assessments with relatively sparse information but it is important for practitioners to include sufficient relevant detail to support judgements and to evidence defensibility. Essentially, the task of risk assessment is 'speculating in an informed way' (Kropp et al, 2002, p 147, cited in Lavoie et al, 2009, p 5), and should thus involve considerable professional knowledge and understanding. Critically, the assessment should drive the process, not the form itself, which is a professional tool to be used to achieve a professional end, that is, a clear, effective and evidenced judgement on risk – sometimes referred to as a *structured professional judgement*.

Considering 'serious harm'

The most commonly used tools, such as OASys, are more suited to assessing risk of re-offending than incidence of harm (although they can be supplemented with further specialist assessments, such as Risk Matrix 2000 or SARN [Structured Assessment of Risk and Need] for sex offenders). In the practice setting, the purpose of these tools has often been unclear and they have been mistakenly assumed to be capable of predicting serious harm, whereas in fact they are designed simply to screen out those offenders who potentially present a high risk (Kemshall and Wood, 2007a). Academics would view these tools as more valuable for their assistance in determining levels of risk and identifying areas for intervention than for their predictive potentials (Lavoie et al, 2009).

Further confusions have arisen in practice where insufficient distinction is made between *risk of harm* and *risk of serious harm* (Baker, 2010). If too great a constituency of offenders is assessed as requiring intensive interventions, the resource burden becomes unmanageable, the most risky offenders do not receive the targeted attention that they warrant and potentially a whole raft of other offenders become subject to interventions which disproportionately impact on their rights. It is important therefore to be able accurately to separate out those individuals whose behaviour is of most concern, but this is a tricky task. Practitioners are asked simultaneously to be confident and certain in their assessments and also to be able to take account of variables and changes in offenders' circumstances. This context of uncertainty can be difficult and can cause a hyper-sensitive approach in which everything is seen as potentially risky, leading to overcautious assessment with too much detail and important factors not drawn out. Conversely, practitioners may become desensitised and unable to differentiate risk, or ambivalent and likely to downplay risks. These tendencies may result in limited risk assessments with too little information being considered (Kemshall, 2008). Practitioners need to find strategies for managing the anxieties that tend to be part and parcel of dealing with risk, so that they remain alert to the issues that arise but able at the same time to keep a sense of proportion. Discussion and sharing concerns with colleagues can assist in this, and line management supervision could offer a further exploratory opportunity.

Recent direction from NOMS refocusing practice on *serious harm* is helpful in clarifying where attention and resources should be targeted. Definitions of *serious harm* do differ and it is important to distinguish between the legal definitions, for instance the definitions contained in the Criminal Justice Act 2003 which are about eligibility for extended and indeterminate public protection (IPP) sentences (see Chapter Eleven), and more fluid definitions that are employed in assessing risk in practice.

The most recent NOMS risk of serious harm guidance uses the OASys definition that is:

> Serious harm: an event which is life threatening and/or traumatic, and from which recovery, whether physical or psychological, can be expected to be difficult or impossible.
>
> Risk of serious harm is the likelihood of this offence happening. (Ministry of Justice, 2009b, p 3)

Helpfully, also, the framework outlined in this document identifies three categories of relevant risk factors. Static risk factors include past convictions and history of imprisonment that are fixed and therefore unable to change. In contrast, dynamic risk factors are potentially subject to change and therefore represent appropriate targets for intervention aimed at reduction of offending. *Acute risk factors* are of most significance in high-risk cases and are defined as:

> Those factors that change quickly perhaps over days or hours and whose emergence indicates a period of critical risk in which serious offending is more likely than not to occur. Examples are increased levels of substance abuse or destabilisation of socio-economic factors, such as loss of accommodation ... while alcohol is a dynamic risk factor, intoxication would be the acute risk factor. (Ministry of Justice, 2009b, p 11)

The guidance also highlights the concept of *imminency* that implies immediate concern, that is, the offender is showing clear indications in relation to his or her risk factors (Ministry of Justice, 2009b). Determining when a risk of serious harm is imminent is subject to professional judgement. Similarly, it is not possible to present a definitive list of behaviours and circumstances that should give rise to concern although, in relation to violent offenders, these may include:

- loss of socioeconomic supports (accommodation, job, income);
- increase in drink/drug use or more chaotic use;
- crises in personal or family relationships;
- evidence of difficulties in managing stress;
- refusal to comply with psychiatric medication and/or treatment;
- poor compliance with supervision and/or concerning behaviour during contact with probation staff, partner agencies and others.

Concerns in relation to such indicators should trigger a review of the risk assessment level and risk management plan for the individual in question. In cases where there is a risk of serious harm, practitioners should go beyond assessing the individual's *risk status* to evaluating his or her *risk state*, that is, the propensity to engage in violent behaviour at that given point in time. This evaluation should focus on specific changes in psychological, biological and/or social factors in his or her life (Lavoie et al, 2009) and their likely impact on behaviours. Where risk of serious harm is judged to be present and to be imminent, immediate actions should follow to contain the risk and to protect potential victims.

Of course in many cases where there is potential for serious harm, the risk will not be judged to be imminent, and the guidance helpfully describes four levels of risk management activity corresponding to the assessed likelihood of serious harm occurring. These levels of activity are outlined in Table 7.1.

Importantly, 'monitoring' is not seen as passive and is described as involving proactive work to identify early warning signs of potential offending and any indicators of a change in risk, linked to contingency plans specifying what actions should be taken if risk does escalate (Ministry of Justice, 2009b). This highlights the ongoing nature of risk assessment and the need to be ready to respond if risk indicators change.

Table 7.1: Risk management activity

Risk level	Risk management level
Very high	Maximum
High	Enhanced
Medium	Active
Low	Monitor

Multi-Agency Public Protection Arrangements

Multi-agency initiatives focusing on dangerousness and public protection have developed alongside the growth in provision dealing with persistence in offending. There are similarities in terms of the work taking place across professional disciplines and the blurring of agency boundaries, as discussed in Chapter Three. However, the structures dealing with serious and dangerous offenders are more formalised, reflecting the tremendous responsibility that they carry (Lieb, 2003).

The origins of MAPPAs lay in previous initiatives in individual probation areas, such as the Multi-Agency Risk Panels in Greater Manchester in the late 1990s. This was institutionalised by Sections 67 and 68 of the Criminal Justice and Court Services Act 2000, which required the police and probation services to work together as 'responsible authorities' to establish a framework for risk management. This was known as Multi-Agency Public Protection Arrangements and, under these arrangements, Multi-Agency Public Protection Panels (MAPPPs) are convened to discuss individual offenders.

Guidance issued by the Home Office in 2001 outlined the role of the MAPPAs as being to:

- share relevant information about targeted offenders;
- assess the level of risk and recommend action to manage this risk; and
- monitor and review this action plan periodically.

The MAPPA framework was further strengthened by the addition of the prison service as a 'responsible authority' by the Criminal Justice Act 2003, and the imposition of a 'duty to cooperate' with the arrangements on a range of additional agencies, such as local authority children's social care, YOTs and housing departments.

MAPPAs over criminal justice areas are overseen by Strategic Management Boards (SMBs) made up of representatives of all the main criminal justice agencies and appropriate others, including a lay member of the public. Each SMB is required to publish an annual report with details of the MAPPA for their area, giving details of the volume and nature of their cases, for instance. *MAPPA Guidance 2009* requires the SMBs to 'keep the arrangements (ie MAPPA) under review with a view to monitoring their effectiveness and making any changes to them that appear necessary or expedient' (NOMS, 2009, p 215).

Three categories of offender can be referred to MAPPA, as outlined in the MAPPA guidance (NOMS, 2009). These are:

- registered sex offenders;
- violent and other sex offenders sentenced to 12 months or more in custody; and
- other offenders, not falling into Category 1 or 2, with a conviction for an offence that indicates they are a serious harm to the public.

Table 7.2: MAPPA categories 2003/04 to 2008/09

Category	2003/04	2004/05	2005/06	2006/07	2007/08	2008/09[a]
1. Registered sex offenders	24,572	28,994	29,983	30,416	31,392	32,336
2. Violent offenders/other sex offenders	12,754	12,664	14,292	14,895	16,249	11,527
3. Other offenders	2,166	2,936	3,313	3,132	2,569	898
Total	39,492	44,592	47,588	48,443	50,210	44,761

Note: [a] In 2008/09, Category 2 and 3 data changed, so data in this column represents a snapshot taken on 31 March rather than a complete account of all cases over the 12-month period.

Table 7.2 shows the growth in registrations since 2003/04 (Ministry of Justice, 2009c). Relatively few offenders are referred under Category 3, which is intended to include all those offenders who are considered by the responsible authority to pose a *risk of serious harm to the public*, under Section 352(2) of the Criminal Justice Act 2003. For instance, 2,569 or roughly 5 per cent of the total MAPPA registrations fell into this category in 2007/08 (Ministry of Justice, 2009c). To register a Category 3 offender, the responsible authority must:

1. Establish that the person has committed an offence which indicates that they are capable of causing serious harm to the public; *and*
2. Reasonably consider that the offender may cause serious harm to the public which requires a multi-agency approach at level 2 or 3 to manage the risks.

   The person must have been convicted of an offence or have received a formal caution or reprimand/warning (young offenders). The offence may have been committed in any geographical location, which means that offenders convicted abroad could quality (NOMS, 2009, p 56)

MAPPA operates at three levels of risk management:

Level 1   'Ordinary' risk management involving only one agency
Level 2   Active involvement of more than one agency
Level 3   MAPPPs to manage the 'critical few', drawing together key active partners who take joint responsibility for the management of these offenders in the community

The criteria for referring a case to a Level 3 MAPP meeting are where the offender:

- Is assessed under OASys (or other agency risk assessment tool) as being a high or very high risk of causing serious harm (however, this does not mean all cases assessed as high or very high risk will automatically require level 3 management. In addition, there may be a small number of exceptional cases with a lower risk level where, due to other factors, the case requires this level of management); *and*

- Presents risks that can only be managed by a plan which requires close cooperation at a senior level due to the complexity of the case and/or because of the unusual resource commitments it requires; *or*
- Although not assessed as a high or very high risk, there is a high likelihood of media scrutiny and/or public interest in the management of the case and there is a need to ensure that public confidence in the criminal justice system is maintained. (NOMS, 2009, p 96)

The 'critical few' really is a minority of offenders (2.06 per cent of all registrations in 2008/09). Within these there are a smaller number identified as Critical Public Protection Cases (CPPCs) where registration with the Public Protection Unit in NOMS is required. These are cases that attract or are likely to attract significant media interest.

Although relatively short-lived in criminal justice terms, evaluation and research evidence on MAPPAs is now coming into the public domain. The main report to note is *Strengthening Multi-Agency Public Protection Arrangements (MAPPAs)* (Kemshall et al, 2005). This found that partnerships had developed since an earlier evaluation in 2001 and there had been specific improvements in the involvement of the 'duty to cooperate' agencies. Concerns were expressed, however, at the patchy integration of mental health services, which are so important for many of the offenders being dealt with at Level 3 (Kemshall et al, 2005; Wood and Kemshall, 2010).

In terms of risk assessment and MAPPAs, evidence from observations by Kemshall and others indicates that practitioners involved in MAPPPs are tending to use a mixture of clinical and actuarial knowledge to inform their judgements on risk, reflecting perhaps the complexity and contingent nature of some of the risks under consideration.

A thematic inspection report, *Putting risk of harm in context* (HMI Probation, 2006b), raised important issues about preparation of prisoners for release and the fact that risk of harm reviews were not being conducted with the required frequency. More positively, it did find that most areas now had MAPPA coordinators and that this was helpful in promoting good practice and greater awareness of human rights in MAPPA processes. It also noted a debate about the extent to which offenders should be invited to be present at MAPPA meetings, although not appearing itself to be in favour of this development and calling for national guidance (HMI Probation, 2006b).

MAPPAs sit firmly within a community protection model of risk management. Interestingly, Kemshall and Wood have compared MAPPAs with a more public health-orientated model of managing sex offenders in the UK and Ireland under an organisation called Stop It Now! This study felt that the public health mode was less exclusionary and was able to promote community involvement in managing risk, rather than seeing it as the sole preserve of the professionals (Kemshall and Wood, 2007b). This is significant in terms of the rights and the freedoms of the small but growing number of offenders being managed at Level 3 (see Chapter Seventeen, this volume).

Such comparisons beg questions of how the effectiveness of MAPPAs might be measured. Reconvictions might be one measure, but it is always difficult to judge exactly how many offences have been prevented. Proactive enforcement might be another indicator, but increased enforcement could be viewed as either positive, prompt action in response to non-compliance or supervisory practices that fail to engage offenders and secure their cooperation. More qualitative assessment might consider the nature of relationships between agencies, communication and agency contributions to risk assessments. Wood and Kemshall's (2007) evaluation found that staff were positive about the contribution of MAPPAs and highlighted the following:

- effective communication among the police, probation and prisons;
- the systematic exchange of information;
- access to housing and particularly specialist supervised accommodation;
- links to social services;
- victim liaison, particularly where victim workers attend panels;
- MAPPA-approved discretionary disclosure (risk-related information released to key individuals on a need-to-know basis);
- rapid response to escalating risk;
- option to facilitate supervision of high-risk offenders beyond the end of licence;
- ability to facilitate access to additional resources (adapted from Wood and Kemshall, 2007, p 8).

Feedback was also sought from offenders and this was generally positive, specifically where the requirements of supervision and the role of MAPPAs had been fully explained and they were able to recognise their legitimacy. They also appreciated attention to their personal and social problems, consistent with the approach advocated in the Good Lives Model (Wood and Kemshall, 2010). Responsiveness to offenders is important as MAPPAs should be accountable to them, just as accountability exists between agencies and to victims and to the wider public (Wood and Kemshall, 2008).

Multi-Agency Risk Assessment Conferences

Multi-Agency Risk Assessment Conferences (MARACs) are a more recent development allied to MAPPAs but not established on the same sort of statutory footing. These multi-agency meetings were first used in Cardiff but have become more widespread after evaluations showed reductions in re-victimisation, particularly for high-risk families. Initially they were adopted in areas with a specialist domestic violence court, but the government has also provided funding for other areas, so they are rapidly becoming part of the multi-agency risk landscape.

MARACs fill a key gap, as the domestic violence perpetrators they focus on may not be currently within the MAPPA or PPO frameworks. However, there is clearly some overlap and, where this does occur, MAPPA supervision takes precedence.

Although MARACs have been broadly welcomed by the domestic violence sector, there have been criticisms of a model of work centred round professional assessment and intervention, particularly from feminist groups who have been very important historically in the domestic violence field and who espouse a more empowering way of working with the domestic violence survivor at the centre. There have also been criticisms because of the focus on cases assessed as high risk (using both clinical and actuarial methods), which leaves perpetrators and victims at lower risk levels without adequate support. It is encouraging, despite this, to see domestic violence being taken seriously and coordinated efforts made to reduce its incidence and impact.

Serious Further Offence reviews

One further set of practices relating to risk is the review of SFOs, which apply when offenders under probation supervision commit a serious offence.

The origins of SFO procedures lie in PC 41/1995 that required the then probation services to inform the Home Office when offenders or defendants under supervision committed murder. The following year PC 79/1996 increased the range of offences that probation services should notify to include: murder; attempted murder; arson with intent to endanger life; manslaughter; and rape. Other offences, such as armed robbery, should also be reported but the services had more discretion with these additional offences whether or not to report. PC 71/1998 required that the local probation committee should always receive a copy of what were then known as Serious Incident Reviews (SIRs). The purpose of the reviews – from March 2004 known as SFO reviews – is to concentrate on gaps in provision or failures or weaknesses in procedures that mean that opportunities to prevent an offence have been neglected, with a view to identifying what the probation service might learn for the future (Merrington and Stanley, 2007).

An HMI Probation inspection in 2000 found inconsistencies in the practice of the then SIRs, with some problems of communication between services and the Probation Unit in the Home Office – particularly in a number of cases where initially serious charges had been dropped or replaced with a lesser charge (2000b). Practice has since tightened up considerably and a later review of SIRs in the London Probation Area raised interesting points about risk prediction: the study showed that, while probation officers were predicting potential for harm quite accurately, SFO cases came from all three of the risk bands – low, medium and high – then being used (this study pre-dates the OMM). Ansbro comments that:

> The fact that 22% of the serious incidents emanated from a group of high risk offenders comprising only 4.3% of the London Probation

Area (LPA) caseload demonstrates considerable accuracy in identifying the high risk of harm group. Notwithstanding this, the majority of serious incidents were triggered by offenders outside the high risk/ MAPPA band. (2006, p 53)

She goes on to reflect observations from both Bill Beaumont (1999a) and Hazel Kemshall (2003) about the limits to predictive accuracy, although her study did indicate that previous violent offences were a more certain predictor of further serious offences than sexual offences. She notes that this lack of precision has implications for the tiering structure of the OMM that concentrates so many resources on Tiers 3 and 4 when in fact serious offences might arise from offenders in all tiers (Ansbro, 2006).

Reflection and critical learning must take place when cases go badly wrong in an effort to ensure that mistakes and deficiencies in practice are not repeated. The reviews of the Anthony Rice and the Damien Hanson and Elliot White cases (HMI Probation 2006a, 2006c) indicate the importance of being clear about responsibilities in managing cases, impartiality in assessment, ensuring compliance with the conditions of supervision and maintaining a focus on public protection.

Final reflections on dealing with dangerousness

It is interesting to look at the research on offenders' view of the assessments they have undergone. Small-scale studies of high-risk sex offenders (Attrill and Liell, 2007; Wood and Kemshall, 2007) have shown that they share most of the professionals' concerns about predicting likelihood of re-offending and relevant risk factors. In the Attrill and Liell study the offenders were also concerned about what information was collected, how it was used and the skills and competence of the assessor. They concluded that:

> What they often wanted was probably much the same as we do, as professionals involved in risk assessment and decision-making. They wanted accuracy, fairness and a chance to be involved in decisions about their future. In this, and many other things, we have common ground. (2007, p 201)

Wood and Kemshall (2007) found that their sample of sex offenders subject to MAPPA supervision were more likely to comply and engage with supervision if informed about and involved in the risk assessment process by supervising officers. Kemshall later comments that these small-scale studies indicate that many offenders may understand the purpose of risk assessment and management, accepting the focus on risk as both legitimate and sensible (2008).

It is important to establish legitimacy and this is best done through open and transparent processes, where the rights of the offender are respected, starting with the right to know how the assessment process will be conducted and how information about him or her will be gathered, used and communicated to others.

The research above also indicates the possibilities in terms of joint working around problem areas and promoting self-management of risk. This means being explicit about risks and agreeing how they could be reduced by strengthening positive factors and using controls and constraints in proportionate and targeted ways. Of course, not all offenders will be willing or able to embark on this joint enterprise, but, where potential does exist, it makes eminent sense to work with it.

Summary

Risk is a complex area and the management of high-risk situations and individuals even more so because it is imbued with uncertainty. Procedures are in place, now more explicitly targeted on individuals who present a risk of serious harm. Some would say that all offences cause harm, but that may be unhelpful in trying to separate out where the public protection activities of criminal justice agencies can be most effective. A focus on potential to cause serious harm allied to awareness of acute risk factors and assessment of how imminent an event or action might be is needed to enable agencies to intervene to prevent harm in an informed and timely way. Of course, even the best practice will not eradicate serious offences entirely, particularly as a significant proportion of these are committed by individuals with few prior indicators. However, the lessons that can be learned from instances where offenders subject to probation supervision have committed serious further offences indicate that clarity and consistency in practices and procedures and effective inter-agency collaboration are critical in reducing the chances of such events happening again.

Conceptions of risk and approaches to risk are highly influential in achieving the aim of public protection. Structures such as MAPPA operate within a community protection framework, with extensive use of restrictions and controls. However, even within MAPPA the potential for building relationships and supporting offenders in positive ways is being exploited. This can be taken much further within a collaborative, rights-based approach that seeks to involve offenders, wherever possible, as active participants in assessing and managing their own risk and creating a better life.

Further reading

Kemshall, H. (2008) *Understanding the community management of high risk offenders*, Maidenhead: Open University Press.
Robinson, G. and Crow, I. (2009) *Offender rehabilitation: Theory, research and practice*, London: Sage Publications.

More specific discussion can be found in:
Harrison, K. (ed) (2010) *Managing high risk sex offenders in the community: Risk management, treatment and social responsibility*, Cullompton: Willan.
Ireland, J.L., Ireland, C.A. and Birch, P. (2008) *Violent and sexual offenders: Assessment, treatment and management*, Cullompton: Willan.

EIGHT

Safeguarding children

Safeguarding children – and within that child protection – is a complex and demanding area of practice. Again, there are critical concerns about rights, those of the parent(s) and those of the child. In particular, social work treads difficult ground around Article 8 of the ECHR – the right to privacy and family life – in making judgements about what levels of intrusion into family life are warranted.

Inter-agency communication and decision making are key elements in safeguarding practice. In order to contribute in a timely and effective way, criminal justice practitioners need to be aware of the main structures in place and the legal framework for child protection, and to understand their own and their agency's responsibilities. This chapter sets these out, providing a brief context for the development of the child protection and safeguarding arrangements in England and Wales. Naturally working within those arrangements presents practitioners with challenges in terms of personal values and beliefs and may also raise ethical dilemmas about what is 'the right thing to do' in any given situation. There are no easy answers, but a sound knowledge base and ability to reflect on emotional and other responses that may come into play are important in maintaining clarity of purpose and dealing confidently with other professionals.

Supporting and protecting children

> The support and protection of children cannot be achieved by a single agency ... every service has to play its part. All staff must have placed upon them the clear expectation that their primary responsibility is the child and his or her family. (Laming, 2003, paras 17.92, 17.93)

With the advent of YOTs, the probation service no longer works directly with children, except for small munbers on community payback or as victims of crime. However, child protection remains a central concern for the service not least in terms of adult offenders who may pose a risk to children and in working with offenders who are parents or carers. It is also a central concern for the prison service, particularly those establishments accommodating young people under the age of 18, and for the voluntary sector as it assumes a more substantial role in delivering criminal justice services.

Practitioners need to be clear about the core aspects of the child protection system and their responsibilities within it. Offender managers within probation should also be aware of the wider responsibilities of the service in contributing to the multi-agency structures that help safeguard and promote the welfare of children. The key guidance document, *Working together to safeguard children*, defines safeguarding and promoting welfare as:

- Protecting children from maltreatment
- Preventing impairment of children's health or development
- Ensuring that children are growing up in circumstances consistent with the provision of safe and consistent care. (DCSF, 2010, p 34)

It goes on to locate child protection within safeguarding and promoting welfare, and identifies it as the activity that is undertaken to protect specific children who are suffering, or are at risk of suffering, *significant harm*.

Underlying child protection work is a number of issues that are challenging to practitioners in terms of personal values and attitudes. Significantly, there is no definitive view of what constitutes abusive behaviour and what is considered abusive is 'ambiguous, contested and shifting' (Munro, 2008, p 47).

Some writers (for instance, Metcalfe and Kennison, 2008) have described child abuse as socially constructed, and this raises questions about power relations and where authority to label behaviour as abusive might lie. Certainly, it is the case that societal beliefs and values are critical in determining what is treated as abuse:

> Definitions of abuse, therefore, embody beliefs about what child-rearing behaviour is unacceptable or dangerous and values about people; the relative rights of adults and children; the relative values of males and females. Hence there is considerable variation over time and cultures in what is deemed abusive. (Munro, 2008, p 46)

An example of this might be the change in attitudes towards smacking children, as exemplified by the prohibitions enacted in Scottish law.

Background to the child protection system

As with other areas of policy, the child protection system that exists today has not been constructed in a vacuum, but has been a response to political concerns and specifically the publicity around key public inquiries into child deaths (Beckett, 2007), among these, Maria Colwell in 1973 and Jasmine Beckford in 1984. It is also a product of wider social attitudes towards childhood and the role of the state in protecting and nurturing children, as indicated by Eileen Munro:

> Societies vary in their basic concepts of childhood and family, in their beliefs about the relationship between children and parents, and in the relative duties and powers of parents and the state … the current form of any child protection system is a product of its culture and history. It also needs to be understood in relation to the state's attitude to families and children more generally and the type of help states offer all parents, not just abusive ones, in caring for their children. (2008, p 29)

This might lead us to reflection on the attitudes towards children – and adolescents, particularly – represented in the media and elsewhere.

Historically, child abuse has not always been readily recognised and articulated, although the Victorians, for instance, evidenced concern for 'moral contamination', and it was during this period that such bodies as the NSPCC were established. Following the Second World War, two major reports led to the development of more specific statutory services, with support and intervention being provided through the old local authority children's departments, established under the Children Act 1948 as part of the developing welfare state (Munro, 2008). The Children and Young Persons Act 1963 gave further responsibilities to local authorities, empowering them to act to prevent family breakdown. In 1971, the children's departments were reorganised into the generic social services departments that operated until the recent round of structural changes, with the intention of providing a more effective and professional means of highlighting and preventing serious harm to children.

During the 1960s, there was a growing awareness of physical abuse of children, exemplified by the 'discovery' of the 'battered baby syndrome' by C. Henry Kempe and colleagues in 1962 (Munro, 2008). By the 1980s, however, attention had turned to child sexual abuse, at that stage often referred to as 'incest', and this was most dramatically brought to public attention at the end of the decade by events in Cleveland. The inquiry into the practices of two doctors at Middlesbrough General Hospital and the social services department was also significant in shaping the child protection system and specifically the measures in the Children Act 1989 which were an attempt to provide a balance between the rights of parents and the need for compulsory intervention.

The impact of highly publicised cases of both individual children and groups of children (Cleveland and the Islands of Orkney) has resulted in most resources within the child welfare system being devoted to investigation and protection services (Audit Commission, 1994). This situation is similar in other English-speaking countries, such as the US, Australia and New Zealand, whereas European countries have developed systems with greater emphasis on family support (Munro, 2008).

Previous chapters have highlighted the pre-eminence of risk prediction in criminal justice, and this same tendency has been evident in the child protection system, although practice is still more concentrated on clinical prediction methods. Clearly some of the same tensions exist between advocates of more structured and more intuitive methods of assessment and decision-making (Munro, 2008) and concerns have been voiced about the impact of bureaucratic processes and set timescales on professional judgement. Beckett notes critically that

- The child protection system is too much about monitoring and policing and not enough about helping and supporting
- Trying to predict child deaths is like trying to find a needle in a haystack. Arguably, the whole system has been shaped by a goal which will never be reached. (2007, p 7)

The system, then, can be seen as overly defensive and concentrated on risk of significant harm rather than focusing on earlier interventions to prevent risky situations developing around children and young people. This was recognised in the recent round of changes in the organisation of children's services, influenced by the findings of the report of the public inquiry by Lord Laming into the death of Victoria Climbié. These pointed to a lack of co-ordination and communication of key information between agencies, as a result of which the *Every Child Matters* programme and the Children Act 2004 required major structural changes in children's services and a commitment both from organisations working directly with children and others, such as the probation service, to have regard to the need to safeguard and to promote the welfare of children.

However, what is interesting in looking at recent developments in integrating children's services is how marginal local authority children's social care services have become (Frost and Parton, 2009). Early intervention and services aimed at lower levels of need are being delivered by other agencies – health, youth offending services, voluntary agencies and Connexions – whilst local authority children's social care has become more insular and focused on increasingly bureaucratic child protection activities. The impact of standardised assessments driven by electronic systems has reduced practitioner discretion and, certainly, at least one study has questioned whether formalised processes and timescales actually reduce quality and create risk (Peckover et al, 2009).

So the changes in children's services have not necessarily been positive for the social work profession, which has found itself caught between the imperatives of a managerial culture and the societal demands for certainty in a highly uncertain area of practice. Professor Munro in her current review of child protection comments that

> Many of the problems in current practice seem to arise from the defensive ways in which professionals are expected to manage that uncertainty. For some, following rules and being compliant can appear less risky than carrying the personal responsibility for exercising judgement. (Munro, 2010, p 6)

The review identified that the child protection system has been shaped by

- the importance of the safety and welfare of children and young people and the understandable strong reaction when a child is killed or seriously harmed;
- a commonly held belief that the complexity and associated uncertainty of child protection work can be eradicated;
- a readiness, in high profile public enquiries into the death of a child, to focus on professional error without looking deeply enough into its causes; and
- the undue importance given to performance indicators and targets which provide only part of the picture of practice, and which have

skewed attention to process over the quality and effectiveness of help given. (Munro, 2011, p 6)

Her final report which has just been published, establishes a vision for a new system that values and supports quality of relationships, is child-centred, is proactive in early intervention and allows social workers to use their professional discretion without undue prescription (Munro, 2011). This requires social care services to be open, learning organisations, rather than approaching practice in a defensive way as many are currently doing. It therefore represents a major change, but one that could be hugely positive if the best of New Labour's reforms are kept, alongside a renewal of social work skills and professionalism.

Children Act 1989

This Children Act brought together all previous child protection measures within one over-arching piece of legislation, which took effect from October 1991. In terms of its key principles, Section 1 of the Act makes clear that the child's welfare should be the paramount consideration in all court proceedings, and this should apply to criminal court proceedings as well as care and protection matters within the family court system that was established under this Act.

Section 1(5) of the Act states that a court may not make an order 'unless it considers doing so would be better for the child than making no order at all', thereby creating a legal presumption that means that the local authority has to prove that a court order will be necessary to enable them better to protect the child.

The key principles of the Act are:

1. Children are generally best cared for within the family, with both parents playing a full part in their upbringing, helped, when necessary, by the local authority providing social services on a voluntary basis.
2. Children's voices should be listened to.
3. Court proceedings should be a last resort.
4. In any court proceedings the child's welfare is the court's paramount consideration.
5. Delay by courts in reaching decisions is likely to be damaging to the child.
6. In most proceedings, courts should consider the whole range of available orders and not only those applied for.
7. Courts should only make orders which are likely to be of positive benefit to the child.

These principles clearly emphasise that the welfare of the child should be paramount within the decision making and practices of all those involved in working with children. There is also a clear enunciation of the fact that the court process is potentially damaging to a child's interests and from a criminal justice/youth justice perspective this raises the issue of offenders who are still children. As noted above, the welfare principle should still apply when sentencing young offenders, although it is arguable whether this remains the case.

A further practice promoted by this Act is that of working in partnership with parents, underpinned by the notion that the local authority should only resort to seeking a court order when parents have not been willing to cooperate on a 'voluntary' basis (the quotation marks recognising that there is likely always to be a degree of coercion on parents when child protection concerns have been raised).

Three sections of the Act are significant and are outlined in the following sections. The term 'children' is used to refer to all children and young people under the age of 18, irrespective of whether these children at 16 or 17 are living independently of family.

Children in need

Section 17(1) of the Children Act 1989 states that:

> It shall be the general duty of every local authority:
>
> - To safeguard and promote the welfare of children within their area
> - So far as is consistent with that duty, to promote the up-bringing of such children by their families, by providing a range and level of services appropriate to those children's needs.

This emphasises that the local authority's primary role is supporting children and families, not child protection per se. Child protection provisions form a safety net when the family and support services have failed (Davis, 2009).

Furthermore, Section 17(10) states that:

> A child shall be taken to be in need if:
>
> a) He is unlikely to achieve or maintain, or to have the opportunity of achieving or maintaining, a reasonable standard of health or development without the provision for him of services by a local authority under this Part
> b) His health or development is likely to be significantly impaired, or further impaired, without the provision for him of such services, or
> c) He is disabled.

Interpretations of this legal definition do seem to vary considerably, with sometimes inappropriately high thresholds being applied by local authorities in terms of access to services. However, this section still places a responsibility on the local authority, primarily social care services for children, to provide support and, where required, appropriate resources. This may include accommodating the child on a voluntary basis.

Beckett (2007) furthermore notes that there is a considerable grey area between 'children in need' (Section 17) and 'children in need of protection', but that is preferable to work with families on a voluntary basis under Section 17, rather than the heavier child protection section, where possible.

Children in need of protection

Section 47(1) of the Children Act 1989 states that:

> Where a local authority
>
> a) Are informed that a child who lives, or is found, in their area (i) is the subject of an emergency protection order, or (ii) is in police protection, or (iii) has contravened a ban imposed by a curfew notice imposed within the meaning of Chapter 1 of Part 1 of the Crime and Disorder Act 1998; or
> b) Have reasonable cause to suspect that a child who lives, or is found, in their area is suffering, or is likely to suffer significant harm;
>
> The authority shall make, or cause to be made, such enquiries as they consider necessary to enable them to decide whether they should take any action to safeguard or promote the child's welfare.
>
> In the case of a child falling within paragraph A (iii) above, the enquiries shall be commenced as soon as practicable and, in any event, within 48 hours of the authority receiving the information.

The legislation requires that the local authority:

- should make sufficient enquiries to allow it to determine what actions need to be taken to protect the child;
- should arrange for the child to be seen, unless sufficient information can be obtained without doing so;
- if denied access to a child, or refused information about the child's whereabouts, should apply for a court order (an Emergency Protection Order [EPO], a Child Assessment Order, a Care Order or a Supervision Order);
- more generally, should decide whether it is in the interests of the child to initiate court proceedings.

It is important to note that the concept of *significant harm* is not defined in the Act and is a matter of judgement and the weighing up of complex considerations by the social workers and others involved.

Emergency protection

There is a range of powers available to allow agencies to take emergency action to safeguard children. Where possible the local authority should apply to the court for an EPO under Section 44 of the Act, which gives authority to remove a child and places the child under the protection of the applicant. The court will be able to grant such an order if it is satisfied that there is reasonable cause to believe a child is likely to suffer *significant harm* if:

- he or she is not removed to different accommodation; or
- he or she does not remain in the place in which he or she is then being accommodated.

An EPO can also be made if Section 47 enquiries are being frustrated because the authorised person is being refused access and the applicant has reason to believe that access is needed as a matter of urgency.

In more urgent situations, Section 46 empowers a police officer to remove a child and retain him or her in police protection for up to 72 hours. The alleged perpetrator may also be removed rather than the child by exclusion requirements in interim Care Orders or EPOs, subject to legal requirements being met.

Children Act 2004

The subsequent Children Act 2004 focuses less on child protection and more on reshaping the landscape of children's services and the responsibilities of agencies, including those in the criminal justice sector, that have contact with children or their carers. Section 10(2) of the Act sets out the five outcomes to which children's services should have regard in establishing multi-agency arrangements:

- physical and mental health and emotional well being;
- protection from harm and neglect;
- education, training and recreation;
- making a positive contribution to society; and
- social and economic well being.

These are expressed in more simple terms in the *Every Child Matters* documentation that explains the rationale for change and the direction of travel as:

- be healthy
- stay safe
- enjoy and achieve
- make a positive contribution
- achieve economic well-being.

Briefly, the provisions of the Act are as follows:

- creation of a Children's Commissioner (at the time of writing in 2011 this is Maggie Atkinson in England and Keith Towler in Wales)
- all county and unitary authorities to appoint one director responsible for children's services, so combining previous directorates of education, social services and other children's services;
- all county and unitary authorities to appoint a lead member (elected councillor) for children's services;

- Section 10 requires each local authority to make arrangements to promote cooperation between the authority, relevant partners and others working with children in the area. The probation service is considered a 'relevant partner';
- Section 11 requires a range of organisations, which include the probation service, to make arrangements for ensuring that their functions and services provided on their behalf are discharged with regard to the need to safeguard and promote the welfare of children;
- Sections 13–16 set out requirements for Safeguarding Children's Boards (SCBs).

These latter three points will be expanded in subsequent sections. The significant point to note here is that, under New Labour, children's services were changing dramatically, and that serious attempts were made to break down barriers between agencies working directly with children, so that they worked more closely together. At the same time, other agencies with roles in relation to children were being held more accountable for their contributions to the strategic development of children's services, through new partnership arrangements.

Each county or unitary authority area was required to establish a Children's Trust by April 2008 – these take many different forms, but certainly at pilot stage New Labour's intention was to try out a range of delivery models to see whether arrangements could be established at a local level that were better than the previous separate local authority, health service and voluntary sector structures. The creation of children's services, in whatever form they take locally, involves the separation of the local authorities' social care functions for children from those for adults – thereby breaking up the social services departments that were in existence for approximately 30 years.

The blurring of professional boundaries is apparent in attempts to introduce one common assessment process, the Common Assessment Framework (CAF) across all children's services, to help reduce the number of different assessments that individual children's services had developed. There are distinct parallels here with the standardisation of assessments in criminal justice agencies, as discussed in Chapter Seven.

Sections 10 and 11 of the Children Act 2004

Section 10 of the Act came into force on 1 April 2005 and required the probation service to become a 'relevant partner' in work with other children's services. PC 22/2005 offered guidance to services and said that:

> This Act provides the framework for a whole system programme of reform in children's services to both safeguard children (as now) AND promote their welfare (from now onwards).

It then went on to comment that:

The Children Act 2004 makes it clear that in addition to direct work with children, there is now, significant, indirect work to be completed with adults who are the parents or carers of children in order to promote the welfare of children. In this respect, it links into the national framework being developed as part of NOMS, for work with children and families of offenders as part of the Reducing Re-offending Action Plan, which forms the basis of each region's resettlement strategy. (PC 22/2005, p 2)

The guidance suggested that the probation service's contribution to inter-agency arrangements would most appropriately be at a managerial level, as members of the board of a Children's Trust and representation on the SCB, for instance.

Section 11 is of more relevance to those at a practitioner level. The NOMS Public Protection Manual, Chapter 2 (Ministry of Justice, 2009e), explains the duty on key persons and bodies, in this case the probation service, to ensure that in discharging their functions, and in contracting services, they have regard to the need to safeguard and promote the welfare of children. The guidance recognises the contribution of the probation service to safeguarding and promoting the welfare of children as being:

- the management of adult offenders in ways that that will reduce the risk of harm they may present to children through skilful assessment, the delivery of well targeted and quality interventions and risk management planning;
- delivery of services to adult offenders, who may be parents or carers, that addresses the factors that influenced their reasons to offend, for example, poor thinking skills, poor moral reasoning, drug/alcohol dependency;
- recognition of factors which pose a risk to children's safety and welfare, and the implementation of agency procedures to protect children from harm (through appropriate information sharing and collaborative multi-agency risk management planning);
- seconding staff to work in YOTs;
- providing a service to child victims of serious sexual or violent offences;
- providing a service for female victims of male perpetrators of domestic abuse participating in accredited domestic violence programmes. In practice this will mean having regard to the needs of any dependent children in the family. (adapted from Ministry of Justice, 2009e, p 10)

In terms of accountability, probation trusts (and presumably in due course other agencies involved in offender management) have clear responsibilities for training and enabling their staff to work within safeguarding and child protection procedures. Specifically they are required to ensure that all staff who work with offenders:

- are familiar with guidance on the recognition of children in need, particularly those who have been abused or neglected;
- know what to do if they have concerns about the welfare of children, are aware of the CAF and know how to refer a child about whom they have concerns to the local authority children's social care for their locality; and
- recognise the role they can play in working with offenders that can improve their skills as parents and carers as well as reduce the likelihood of re-offending .(adapted from Ministry of Justice, 2009e, p 11)

Elsewhere in the guidance, a point is made about practitioners preparing sentence plans needing to consider how planned interventions might impact on parental responsibilities and whether the planned interventions could contribute to improved outcomes for children known to be in an existing relationship with the offender.

Practitioners may also come into contact with children who are brought to an office or in the context of home visits, for instance, and it is important that they respond appropriately if a child appears to be at risk or there are concerns that come to light. Subsequent sections highlight what national guidance stipulates by way of actions, but it is also important to be aware of local guidance.

The provisions of Sections 10 and 11 are welcome particularly in view of a 2002 thematic inspection by the HMI Probation, *Safeguarding children: The National Probation Service role in the assessment and management of child protection issues* (2002), which highlighted commitment among staff to child protection, but weaknesses in practice (identification, recording, lack of attention to diversity, poor understanding of the CAF) and in managerial oversight at operational and strategic level. The new emphasis on involvement with LSCBs and new interagency guidance, *Working together to safeguard children* (DCSF, 2010) will hopefully provide a fresh impetus to this area of work.

Local Safeguarding Children's Boards

LSCBs are the key statutory mechanism for agreeing how the 'relevant organisations' in each area will cooperate to safeguard and promote the welfare of children in that locality. They superseded the previous Area Child Protection Committees in 2006, covering many of the same areas of responsibility but broadening the remit to include a more preventative approach.

The scope of the LSCB role falls into three areas of activity:

- Activity that affects all children and aims to identify and prevent maltreatment, or impairment of health or development, and ensure children are growing up in circumstances consistent with safe and effective care. This might involve monitoring HR (human resources) practices or promoting levels of awareness of safeguarding in organisations in contact with children.

- Proactive work that aims to target particular groups, for instance, work with children living away from home or in custody.
- Responsive work to protect children who are suffering, or at risk of suffering, harm. (Adapted from DCSF, 2010, p 88.)

The LSCB is responsible for developing policies and procedures for use across its area, and this may include setting thresholds for referrals for children's social care under Sections 17 and 47 of the Children Act 1989, as well as specific local protocols relating to:

- children abused through prostitution;
- children living with domestic violence, substance abuse or parental mental illness;
- female genital mutilation;
- forced marriage;
- children missing from school;
- children who may have been trafficked; and
- safeguarding looked after children who are away from home.

Generally, the LSCB should have oversight of procedures for investigations under Section 47 of the 1989 Act and child protection arrangements, intervening whether there are disputes between agencies or where agencies are not engaging with duties under Section 11 of the Children Act 2004. They also have a function in relation to investigating child deaths and serious case reviews, in some respects not dissimilar to the SFO reviews discussed in Chapter Seven. Statutory membership of the LSCB includes the police, the probation service, YOTs and the governors of any juvenile secure establishments in the area.

Two joint inspections of safeguarding arrangements have been conducted. The first, in 2002, was critical of the lack of priority given to safeguarding work, but the more recent inspection in 2005 was positive about the improved commitment of agencies. Nevertheless, a number of concerns remain, especially about the position of disabled and of looked after children, the inconsistencies in thresholds for services being applied by local authority children's social care, some of which are inappropriately high, and the uncertainty in agencies outside social care about recognising signs of abuse or neglect and knowing how to respond appropriately (CSCI, 2005). This last point is a challenge for all criminal justice agencies in equipping staff with appropriate skills and knowledge to contribute positively to safeguarding and to child protection work.

Working together to safeguard children

The inter-agency guidance, which was updated in 2010, is called *Working together to safeguard children*, and a link to the document is included at the end of this chapter. (It is a weighty tome, but it is useful to know where to find it for reference purposes.) The following sections and diagrams are taken from this document.

The guidance identifies that all agencies and practitioners in contact with children should:

- be alert to potential indicators of abuse or neglect;
- be alert to the risks of harm that individual abusers, or potential abusers, may pose to children;
- prioritise direct communication and positive and respectful relationships with children, ensuring the child's wishes and feelings underpin assessments and any safeguarding activities;
- share and help to analyse information so that an assessment can be made of whether the child is suffering or is likely to suffer harm, their needs and circumstances;
- contribute to whatever actions are needed to safeguard and promote the child's welfare;
- take part in regularly reviewing the outcomes for the child against specific plans; and
- work cooperatively with parents, unless this is inconsistent with ensuring the child's safety. (DCSF, 2010, p 32)

Concerns for a child may relate to physical, emotional or sexual abuse, which for under-18s includes prostitution activity. They may also relate to neglect, which could manifest itself, for instance, as failure of parents or carers to provide adequate food or shelter, failure to protect a child from physical or other harm, or unresponsiveness to emotional needs. Definitions of each of these is given in the guidance, although, as with any attempts to define such sensitive areas, they are not fully comprehensive and do not spell out questions of degree (Beckett, 2007).

Referrals to the local authority

There is a clear procedure for practitioners who meet circumstances that warrant referral to the local authority children's social care (this is the term used in the documentation to refer to what in agencies is still known as social services). It is good practice to seek to discuss concerns with the family and to try to secure their agreement, but this should not be done where it is likely to place the child at increased risk of *significant harm*.

Initially it is the responsibility of the social worker to clarify with the referrer:

- the nature of the concerns;
- how and why they have arisen; and
- what appear to be the needs of the child and family.

The social worker should then liaise with the police if the referral indicates that a crime may have been committed.

If the initial referral is made by telephone, it should be followed up in writing within 48 hours. Both the referrer and local authority children's social care should record discussions and agreed actions. The written referral should be acknowledged within one working day of receipt. Local authority children's social care should decide and record the next steps of action within one working day, having discussed the case with the referrer and sought additional information from agency records or other professionals, as necessary.

If no further action is to be taken, this should be communicated to the referrer. If, on the other hand, it appears that urgent action may be needed as the child is at risk of *significant harm*, there should be an immediate strategy discussion involving the police, local authority children's social care and other agencies as appropriate.

In other cases, an initial assessment will be undertaken within seven days by local authority children's social care, in order to identify needs and appropriate services and also to indicate whether a full assessment, known as a Core Assessment, will be required. This initial assessment should involve seeing and speaking to the child and family members, as appropriate, drawing together existing information from a range of sources and involving and obtaining information from other professionals in contact with the child and family.

Following the initial assessment, local authority children's social care should decide on the next course of action, involving the parents in discussion, unless this increases the risk for the child. It may be that the child is not considered to be at risk but is a child in need under Section 17 of the 1989 Act, in which case services may be offered either immediately or after a more in-depth assessment (see Figure 8.1).

Where a child is in need and there is risk of significant harm

Where a child is suspected to be suffering, or likely to suffer, *significant harm*, the local authority is required by Section 47 of the 1989 Act to make enquiries. The level of risk may become apparent in the course of the initial assessment or may have been sufficient to warrant emergency protection from the outset, either immediately or, more routinely, following an urgent strategy discussion between key professionals.

In most cases where *significant harm* is suspected, a strategy discussion will be held soon after the initial assessment in order to determine whether to proceed with a full Section 47 enquiry and what measures are needed in the interim to protect the child. The discussion should give direction about how to progress with the enquiry – access issues, whether interpreters are required and so on. Strategy discussions may also address whether to press ahead with a criminal investigation and the timing of such investigations, and will determine if the situation is such that parental consent should be waived in relation to communication with relevant agencies.

Offender managers may be part of the small group of professionals involved in strategy discussions where they have initiated the referral to local authority children's social care or where they have a significant role in relation to key figures

Figure 8.1: Referral

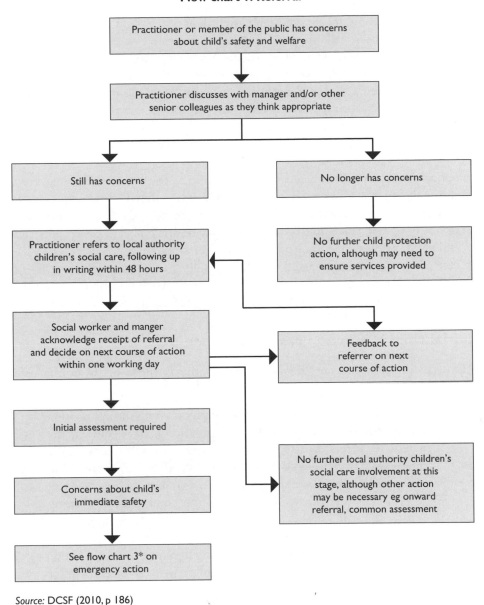

Flow chart 1: Referral

Source: DCSF (2010, p 186)

around the child – as offender manager for the child's parent, who may be on a substance misuse programme, for instance.

The Section 47 enquiry by a qualified and experienced social worker will follow the format of the Core Assessment. The *Framework for the assessment of children in need and their families* (DH, 2000a) provides the structure for collecting and analysing information. Agencies such as health, education and probation have a statutory duty under Section 47 to assist the local authority in its enquiries, not least by provision of relevant information. A Section 47 enquiry may involve medical examination or other specialist assessment of the child, and of course the child him- or herself will be a key source of information – with some allegations the only source of information about what has taken place.

If parents do not cooperate with local authority children's social care in the Section 47 enquiry, the local authority may apply to the court for a Child Assessment Order, through which the court can direct the parents to comply with the requests of social workers.

Broadly speaking, the Section 47 enquiry can have three outcomes:

- concerns are not substantiated, so child protection measures are not necessary, although other support or onward referral may be offered;
- concerns are substantiated but the child is not considered to be at continuing risk of *significant harm* – in this case a plan may be agreed between key agencies and child/parents without need for a full case conference; or
- concerns are substantiated and the child is judged to be at continuing risk of *significant harm* – in this instance a full case conference will be convened by local authority social care within 15 days of the strategy discussion.

Initial child protection case conference

Working together to safeguard children identifies the purpose of the initial case conference as being:

- to bring together and analyse, in an interagency setting, the information that has been obtained about the child's developmental needs, and the parents' or carers' capacity to respond to those needs to ensure the child's safety and promote the child's health and development within the context of their wider family and environment;
- to consider the evidence presented to the conference and taking into account the child's present situation and information about his or her present and past family functioning, make judgements about the likelihood of the child suffering significant harm in future, and decide whether the child is continuing to, or is likely to, suffer significant harm; and
- to decide what future action is required to safeguard and promote the welfare of the child, including the child becoming the subject of a child protection plan, what the planned developmental outcomes are for the child and how best to achieve these. (DCSF, 2010, p 161)

While earlier strategy discussions will involve professionals only, the child or the child's representative may be invited to the case conference and family members, including wider family, will almost certainly be involved. This should be carefully planned and should take account of dynamics within the family, such as significant conflict or potential intimidation, or situations where one family member is the alleged abuser.

In terms of other attendees, a legal adviser from the local authority is likely to be present. The meeting will be chaired by a manager from local authority social care who is independent of operational or line management responsibilities for the case in question. A written report should be available from the social worker who conducted the Section 47 enquiry, and where appropriate, this should have been shared with the parents and child in advance of the meeting. Other professionals attending should bring with them details of their involvement with the child or family members, and it is helpful if this is submitted in writing in advance (local protocols will usually include a format for a case conference submission).

Quality of information is critical, and it is important to be clear about the basis of the information presented and

> Whether statements are of fact, observation, allegation or opinion. Rigorous discipline as to these matters at this stage will help to avoid problems later, especially if the case proceeds to court, and it will help to avoid the failures highlighted in cases falling foul of ECHR requirements as to due process. (Williams, 2008, p 163)

The key question for the conference will be, *is the child at continuing risk of significant harm?* If the collective opinion is that the child is at continuing risk, a formal child protection plan will need to be formulated, and it is the job of the case conference to put together the outline child protection plan in as much detail as possible. While the child and parents or carers may participate in the meeting, they will not be party to this decision-making process.

If a child protection plan is required, the chair should determine what category of abuse warrants the plan, that is, physical, emotional, sexual abuse or neglect. This is the point where previously a decision would have been made as to whether to place the child on the Child Protection Register or not, but from April 2008 such registers no longer exist in the form that has been familiar to professionals for many years. The fact that a child protection plan has been agreed and the category of abuse – neglect, emotional, physical, sexual or a combination of these – is currently the indicator that will appear on the child's social care record, and this alternative method of flagging up a child protection case has taken over from the old registers.

If it is agreed that a child protection plan is needed, the conference has a number of other tasks to complete:

- appointing the lead statutory body (either local authority children's social care or the NSPCC) and a lead social worker (who is the lead professional), who should be a qualified, experienced social worker and an employee of the lead statutory body;
- identifying the membership of a core group of professionals

and family members who will develop and implement the child protection plan as a detailed working tool;

- establishing how the child, their parents (including all those with parental responsibility) and wider family members should be involved in the ongoing assessment, planning and implementation process, and the support, advice and advocacy available to them;
- establishing timescales for meetings of the core group, production of a child protection plan, and for child protection review meetings;
- identifying in outline what further action is required to complete the core assessment and what other specialist assessments of the child and family are required to make sound judgements on how best to safeguard and promote the welfare of the child;
- outlining the child protection plan, especially, identifying what needs to change in order to achieve the planned outcomes to safeguard and promote the welfare of the child;
- ensuring a contingency plan is in place if agreed actions are not completed and/or circumstances change, for example, if a caregiver fails to achieve what has been agreed, a court application is not successful or a parent removes the child from a place of safety;
- clarifying the different purposes and remit of the initial conference, the core group, and the child protection review conference; and
- agreeing a date for the first child protection review conference and under what circumstances it might be necessary to convene the conference before that date. (DCSF, 2010, p 169)

The outline child protection plan should seek to strike a balance between securing the child's safety and well-being and respecting the principle of family unity (Williams, 2008). The plan should make clear what responsibilities each professional in the conference has taken on and what tasks have been allocated at the meeting, with timescales. It is part of the professional role to seek clarity about what is expected if the meeting has not made this sufficiently clear.

There will be case conferences that do not identify ongoing risk of *significant harm*, and in these cases the role of the conference is to discuss and agree relevant work or support packages with the child and/or family, based on the assessment in the Section 47 enquiry.

What next?

Where an outline child protection plan has been agreed, it is the responsibility of the lead social worker identified at the conference to make sure that plan is developed into a more detailed inter-agency plan, acting as the lead professional and coordinating the contributions of professionals working with the child and family.

Figure 8.2: What happens after the child protection conference, including the review process?

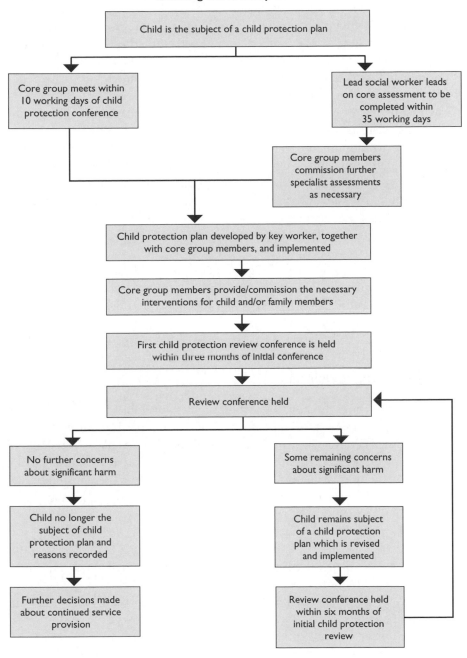

Flow chart 5: What happens after the child protection conference, including the review process?

Source: DCSF (2010, p 190)

The first meeting of the core group should take place within 10 working days of the initial case conference, in order to flesh out the outline child protection plan and progress the core assessment, which should be completed within 35 days. Thereafter, core groups will meet at whatever frequency is deemed necessary to conduct its monitoring role.

Communication with the child is a key element of the process and the child protection plan should be explained and agreed with the child in a manner appropriate to age and understanding. Similarly, parents should be involved as much as possible and work should take place in a spirit of openness and transparency about the perceived risks and reasons for actions to be taken.

The first review case conference should take place within three months of the initial conference, and thereafter at intervals of not more than six months. Reviews are designed to monitor progress against outcomes set in the child protection plan and to determine any changes to the plan that might be needed, as well as to ensure that the child continues to be safeguarded from harm. Written reports may be required for review meetings from relevant professionals, which may include offender managers.

The child protection plan may be discontinued if:

- it is judged that the child is no longer at continuing risk of significant harm – this decision can only be taken at a child protection review conference;
- the child and family have moved to another local authority area, in which instance the case is transferred; or
- the child has reached 18 years of age, has died or has permanently left the UK.

Further legal provisions

As well as protecting children, the state has a responsibility for their care and welfare in situations where the child or children may not be able to live with birth parents or other family members. Section 31 of the Children Act 1989 contains provisions for local authorities to take over the role of parent by means of care orders. By virtue of this, the local authority assumes 'parental responsibility' and is able to act in loco parentis for the duration of the order or until the young person reaches the age of majority.

Other relevant orders can be made under Section 8 of the Act, specifically:

- Contact Orders – detailing what contact a non-resident parent or other specified individual is permitted;
- Residence Orders – detailing where a child should live and under whose care. The designated person assumes parental responsibility by virtue of this order;
- Prohibited Steps Orders – prohibiting specified actions;
- Specific Issues Orders – provides for safeguards in other circumstances.

The notion of 'parental responsibility' is key within Children Act 1989 provisions. If both parents are married at the time of the child's birth, both assume responsibility. The father's name on a child's birth certificate will also confer parental responsibility, if the birth has been registered on or after 1 December 2003. Otherwise the father may gain parental responsibility through an agreement between the parents or through a court order.

Parental responsibility bestows rights as well as responsibilities and enables the individual to exercise choice and influence over what happens to the child. This is defined in Section 3(1) of the Act as giving the individual or individuals with parental responsibility 'all the rights, duties, powers, responsibilities and authority which by law a parent of a child has in relation to a child and his property'.

For those children who have been in care, either long term or intermittently, growing up can be a painful process. It has rather belatedly been recognised that young people leaving care may need additional support in the transition to independent living and adulthood, which for them may be a more brutal and abrupt transition than for other young people. The Children (Leaving Care) Act 2000 therefore requires local authorities to provide transitional support for young people in preparation for leaving care and also to provide advice and assistance up to the age of 21 for young people who have been *looked after* when aged 16 or 17 but who have since moved out of care.

Important considerations

Much of the previous discussion has focused on legislative provisions and policies, but there is a great deal more to child welfare and protection services than simply following step-by-step guides: the procedures and flow charts given in *Working together to safeguard children* may seem very logical, yet they mask the very real complexity of communication and decision making in child protection cases. Furthermore, the definitions and understandings of abuse may vary considerably:

> Definitions of child abuse depend on our beliefs about acceptable and unacceptable ways of treating children … it is not just the changing nature of the concept of abuse that causes problems for research and practice. There is also the difficulty of defining it so precisely that agreement is reached on what actions are abusive and how serious they are. (Munro, 2008, p 56)

A further and major challenge is seeking to engage parents and working in partnership, particularly as practitioners may have strong feelings about the way a child is being treated or the relationships within a family. However, promoting partnership with parents, where possible, and recognising their rights, are key principles in child protection work, and can be important strategies in motivating behavioural change. As with offending behaviour, collaborative and problem-solving approaches can prove effective, but it is necessary as a professional to know when to step in or at what point to pass information to the social worker. Olive Stevenson, an influential writer in this field, asks:

> What then are the ingredients of good professional judgements in child protection work? Earlier discussion suggests that it involves the capacity to manage within oneself the inherent and essential ambivalence engendered by the (at times) conflicting needs and rights of parents and children. There is no place for dogma; the unending challenge (and, let it be said, fascination) of the work lies in the attempt to balance these sets of needs and rights in a way that does least harm to all parties, whilst accepting a first duty to protect children. (1989, p 171)

The emotional impact of this balancing act can be considerable, and this is noted by Chris Beckett in commenting that:

> Child protection work is difficult because it involves dealing with human pain, and because it involves operating at a point where two of society's most strongly held beliefs meet and clash: the belief that children should be protected from harm, and the belief that outsiders and strangers should not intrude into intimate, personal relationships. (2007, p 46)

It is, then, necessarily intrusive work, and the critical judgement is what degree of potential harm warrants public intervention into private family or domestic situations and what level of intervention is proportionate. In considering this question, practitioners need to reflect on the life experiences and attitudes that might shape their judgements. What is 'good enough parenting' for one professional will not be for another, whose life has brought different experiences of family life and parenting.

Summary

Child protection work is possibly the area of practice where critical reflection is most telling. Knowledge of professional procedures and responsibilities is important but understanding and awareness should extend a long way beyond that:

> In child protection work it is important to reflect upon your personal style, your approach, your priorities, and to consider how these are linked to your own experience. You need to be aware, for instance, of which kinds of poor parenting you find most unforgivable and which kinds you find it easiest to understand. You need to know which kinds of situations arouse in you the desire to "rescue" and what kinds of people make you feel punitive. You need to have some sense of how your own needs may get in the way of your judgement of the needs of others ... we cannot necessarily change our feelings, but professional priorities should not necessarily be based on them, and this means that we need to know what those feelings are. (Beckett, 2007, p 47)

Further reading

Beckett, C. (2007) *Child protection: An introduction*, London: Sage Publications.

DCSF (Department for Children, Schools and Families) (2010) *Working together to safeguard children*, London: DCSF (www.publications.education.gov.uk/eOrderingDownload/DCSF-00304-2010.PDF).

Frost, N. and Parton, N. (2009) *Understanding children's social care: politics, policy and practice*, London: Sage Publications.

Munro, E. (2008) *Effective child protection*, London: Sage Publications.

Williams, J. (2008) *Child law for social work*, London: Sage Publications.

It is also worth reading the reports arising from Professor Eileen Munro's Review of the Child Protection system, available on the Department of Education website (www.education.gov.uk/munroreview).

NINE

Procedures at court

This chapter aims to demystify what sometimes seem rather over-complicated court processes and to explore the issues for defendants in the court arena. The justice system operates with reference to ideals or principles of justice but, in practice, judicial processes do not always result in just or fair outcomes. The court system contains significant due process safeguards in relation to defendants' rights and must act in ways that are compatible with *Convention rights* and the general equality duty. Nevertheless, questions remain about where the balance of power lies and the potential for differential or discriminatory treatment of individuals.

Probation and other agencies involved in delivering community penalties are primarily interested in court proceedings once they approach sentence, but practitioners should be aware of the way that trials are conducted and the various stages they travel through. The probation service and voluntary agencies may also be involved in terms of bail advice or information to the courts during the period leading up to sentence or trial and probation will certainly be involved in breach cases where it is itself bringing the prosecution. Court work is a core element of probation practice and it is important that all those in offender management roles have knowledge and confidence in working within the court setting.

Brief outline of the court system

Figure 9.1 shows the current court system in England and Wales, which deals with both criminal and civil matters. It is a hierarchical system, in that decisions made at one level can be challenged or 'appealed' and will then be looked at again by a higher court. However, for criminal matters, in England and Wales there are essentially two levels of court – the Magistrates' Court and the Crown Court. Summary offences such as driving infringements or soliciting for the purposes of prostitution can only be dealt with at the Magistrates' Court level. More serious or indictable offences, such as rape or murder, can only be heard at Crown Courts. Other offences, for example, theft, criminal damage or assault, can vary considerably in seriousness and so are termed 'triable either way' offences, which can be brought before either court depending on the circumstances of the particular offence(s).

The vast majority of offences are dealt with at the Magistrates' Court, with proceedings being taken against an estimated 1.92 million defendants in 2008. Of these, 8 per cent were youth court cases, and 69 per cent related to summary offences, of which 37 per cent involved motoring. The remainder were for 'triable either way' offences (Ministry of Justice, 2009d).

Figure 9.1: Court system in England and Wales

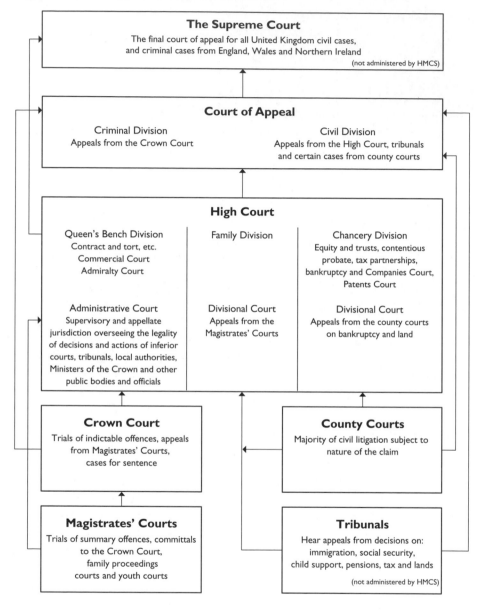

The Supreme Court
The final court of appeal for all United Kingdom civil cases,
and criminal cases from England, Wales and Northern Ireland
(not administered by HMCS)

Court of Appeal

Criminal Division
Appeals from the Crown Court

Civil Division
Appeals from the High Court, tribunals
and certain cases from county courts

High Court

Queen's Bench Division
Contract and tort, etc.
Commercial Court
Admiralty Court

Family Division

Chancery Division
Equity and trusts, contentious
probate, tax partnerships,
bankruptcy and Companies Court,
Patents Court

Administrative Court
Supervisory and appellate
jurisdiction overseeing the legality
of decisions and actions of inferior
courts, tribunals, local authorities,
Ministers of the Crown and other
public bodies and officials

Divisional Court
Appeals from the
Magistrates' Courts

Divisional Court
Appeals from the county courts
on bankruptcy and land

Crown Court
Trials of indictable offences, appeals
from Magistrates' Courts,
cases for sentence

County Courts
Majority of civil litigation subject to
nature of the claim

Magistrates' Courts
Trials of summary offences, committals
to the Crown Court,
family proceedings
courts and youth courts

Tribunals
Hear appeals from decisions on:
immigration, social security,
child support, pensions, tax and lands
(not administered by HMCS)

Note: HMCS = Her Majesty's Courts Service.
Source: www.hmcourts-service.gov.uk

Magistrates do conduct trials, although the popular image of the trial is that of
the full jury trial at Crown Court, with all its associated pomp and drama. In
2008, 90,040 cases were committed to Crown Court for trial across England and
Wales, and 87,735 cases were disposed of in the course of the year. In contrast,
the magistrates had more than 180,000 trials listed for that same year. Of these,

18 per cent were 'ineffective', that is, they were adjourned, and a further 38 per cent were 'cracked', which means the trial did not go ahead (Ministry of Justice, 2009d). Trials often 'crack' because the defendant pleads guilty at the last minute, but this can also happen where the court makes a determination that the defendant is unfit to stand trial or where the prosecution offers no evidence.

The notion of the trial holds a central place in the court systems in the UK jurisdictions, even though a relatively small proportion of defendants experience the full trial process and increasing numbers are dealt with in summary proceedings. In contrast to European countries that tend to adopt a more inquisitorial approach, the UK system has developed along adversarial lines. Essentially, this means that the focus of the trial is not to search for truth, but rather to test the version of the truth put forward by the prosecution. In terms of competing narratives, Johnstone and Ward comment that:

> If there is one, and only one, coherent narrative that fits the evidence, and it also fits the legal categorisation of an offence, that is what the jury will usually accept as "beyond reasonable doubt". Where there is a coherent, plausible story consistent with innocence, there will be a reasonable doubt. (2010, p 136)

However, they also note that this can be a rather unequal contest from the defendant's perspective, as the prosecution may have considerably more resources to deploy in constructing and putting forward a version of events (Johnstone and Ward, 2010).

First appearance in court and bail

The police are able to grant bail either at the police station or on the street, under Section 4 of the Criminal Justice Act 2003 ('street bail'). In these instances, once charged, a defendant will be summonsed to appear in court on a specific date. In cases where the police view immediate bail as inappropriate, the defendant will be brought before the first available court for the magistrates' consideration. A defendant may also appear in court as a result of a warrant being executed.

Before a summons can be issued, in the majority of cases the Crown Prosecutor will outline the basis of the case to the magistrates, a process referred to as 'laying an information'. Where the probation service is the prosecutor in breach proceedings, this will be done by the probation service.

Many cases cannot be dealt with on first appearance, often because the defence solicitor has still to receive full information about the charge or 'disclosure'. In these instances, the magistrates have to determine what should happen to the defendant during any period of adjournment.

Ashworth and Redmayne (2005, p 207) comment that:

> The bail/custody decision raises some of the most acute conflicts in the whole criminal process. On the one hand there is the individual's right

to liberty, safeguarded by Article 5 of the Convention, and the interest of the person arrested and charged with an offence in remaining at liberty until a trial has taken place. On the other hand, there is a public interest in security and in securing protection from crime.

They go on to say that:

> No judgement of balance can be properly reached until there is a clear appreciation of what rights defendants (and potential or actual victims) have at this stage, and fuller analysis of the content and legitimacy of the claimed public interests and of the evidential foundations for prediction of risk. (2005, p 207)

The role of the probation service, YOTs or voluntary agencies attached to the court may, then, be critical in providing information to assist decisions on bail.

The key legislation in relation to bail is the Bail Act 1976, although this has been subject to a number of subsequent amendments. Young people aged 17 are treated as adults for the purposes of this Act. Section 4 creates a presumption in favour of bail but provides for exceptions to this right as follows in Schedule 1, para 2:

> The defendant shall not be granted bail if the court is satisfied that there are substantial grounds for believing that the defendant, if released on bail (whether subject to conditions or not), would –
>
> a) Fail to surrender to custody or
> b) Commit an offence whilst on bail or
> c) Interfere with witnesses or otherwise obstruct the course of justice, whether in relation to himself or some other person.

Bail may also be withheld under that same paragraph:

- if the court is satisfied that the defendant should be kept in custody for his own protection or, if he is a child or young person, for his own welfare;
- if the defendant is already serving a custodial sentence;
- if the defendant, having been released on bail, has been arrested for absconding or breaking the conditions of his bail;
- if the offence is indictable or triable either way and the defendant was on bail in criminal proceedings on the date of the offence (Section 26 of the Criminal Justice and Public Order Act 1994). This has been further amended by Section 14 of the Criminal Justice Act 2003 to create a presumption that a person should not be granted bail if it appears that he has committed an offence while on bail for another charge 'unless the court is satisfied that there is no significant risk of his committing an offence' if granted bail.

Where bail is refused, under the Magistrates' Court Act 1980, this is usually for a maximum of eight days in the first instance, although if the defendant is present in court he or she may consent to a longer period, providing a fixed date for a return to court is established. Thereafter remand status must be reviewed at intervals of not more than 28 days. The defendant has the right to apply twice to the magistrates to have the bail decision re-examined, and can only make further applications where there is a new argument to advance. There is a limited right of appeal to the Crown Court against Magistrates' Court decisions in summary cases. In other cases, applications can be made to the Queen's Bench division of the High Court and a judge can then grant bail or vary conditions of bail. This will not be done in front of an open court and the process is often referred to as a 'judge in chambers' application. In certain circumstances, the prosecution may appeal against bail that has been granted by the Magistrates' Court for indictable or either way offences.

If a person who has been released on bail fails without reasonable cause to surrender to custody (effectively, to turn up at court), he or she is liable to be charged under Section 6(1) of the Bail Act 1976.

The bail decision is not just about whether or not to grant bail or to remand in custody: Section 3 of the Act allows for conditions to be attached to bail. The range of conditions and use of conditions has changed over time and the next section looks at this in more detail.

Conditional bail

The Bail Act 1976 was enacted at a time when there was widespread recognition that the number of defendants released on bail should be increased and optimism that it was safe to do so. However, the penal climate has since progressively hardened, and the Act has been amended to mean that bail is effectively restricted for more serious offenders although still widely in use without conditions for more routine cases.

Custodial remands rose from 48,000 in 1990 (10 per cent of defendants) to 84,000 in 2000 (14 per cent of defendants). In 2000, the average remand population in prisons was 11,270 and almost two thirds of these were unconvicted rather than awaiting sentence (McConville and Wilson, 2002). Unfortunately, clear information about the proportion of defendants granted bail unconditionally and those made subject to conditions is less readily available.

Conditional bail was introduced with the intention of reducing the need for custodial remands; it is doubtful whether it has done so and research suggests that, despite enabling some defendants to be diverted from custody, in general it has had a net-widening and up-tariffing effect (Dhami, 2004). Conditional bail may be suggested by defence solicitors where the Crown Prosecution Service have raised an objection or opposed bail.

Section 4 of the Bail Act 1976 sets out the factors to which sentencers should have regard when considering bail. These include:

- the nature and seriousness of the offence;

- the defendant's character, previous convictions, employment record, associations and community ties;
- the defendant's previous record as regards past grants of bail;
- the strength of the case against the defendant;
- any other factor that appears to be relevant. (White, 1999, p142)

Dhami (2004) cites previous research which suggests that magistrates have complex reasons for imposing conditional bail that go beyond the purposes stipulated in the Bail Act, and may include deterrence, punishment and the intention to add structure to the defendant's life. Her own research indicated that magistrates' decisions about whether and which conditions to use were influenced by non-legal factors such as gender, ethnicity, age and strength of community ties.

Section 6 of the Bail Act allows the court to impose any conditions it considers necessary where there would otherwise be an exception to bail or to make defendants available for enquiries or reports. It is not therefore unusual for magistrates to require a defendant to attend a specified appointment for a pre-sentence report (PSR), for example. The most commonly used conditions include:

- residence;
- curfew;
- reporting to the police station; and
- non-contact with witnesses. (Adapted McConville and Wilson, 2002, p 128)

In general, research has shown that magistrates are not particularly creative in their use of conditions, and the Dhami study shows that their decision making and level of confidence is more consistent with unconditional bail and with custodial remand cases than it is in relation to conditional bail.

Nevertheless, the use of conditions has continued to grow and, in October 2005, electronic monitoring became available to help enforce curfew conditions. Additionally, Section 19 of the Criminal Justice Act 2003 provided for Restrictions on Bail (RoB) for substance misusing offenders and RoB schemes were piloted during 2005. The legal criteria for these schemes applies where:

- the defendant is over 18; and
- has tested positive for a Class A drug either in connection with the offence (Section 63B of the Police and Criminal Evidence Act 1984) or after conviction but before sentence (Section 161 of the Criminal Justice Act 2003); or
- has been charged with an offence of possession or intent to supply a specified Class A drug (Section 5 of the Misuse of Drugs Act 1971); or
- the court is satisfied that there are substantial grounds for believing that the defendant's misuse of a specified Class A drug caused or contributed to an offence or was motivated, wholly or partly, by intended use of such a drug.

The court may grant bail with a condition to follow through assessment or treatment with the defendant's agreement. If a defendant refuses assessment or treatment following assessment, the court must remand in custody unless it is satisfied there is no significant risk of him or her committing an offence while on bail – a significant overturning of the usual presumption in favour of bail.

RoB schemes are located within DIPs and are part of the government's initiative to reduce drug-related offending. They aim to use a carrot and stick approach with a previously hard to reach group – the 'carrot' being an offer of rapid treatment for those who want to comply, the 'stick' obviously being the threat of custodial remand for refusers. Although there has been reported success from the trials in encouraging offenders to undergo assessment and/or enter treatment, maintaining a treatment programme is obviously a different challenge (Hucklesby et al, 2007).

Clearly the use of conditions such as RoB schemes and electronic curfews is highly intrusive and does raise issues about rights and whether responses are proportionate to the risk involved. This has moved a long way from the due process concerns with defendants' rights that motivated the original Bail Act 1976:

> While in theory, all defendants have a right to unconditional bail, in practice an increasing number are denied that right ... it seems clear that in the current climate remand policy will continue to focus on restricting the use of bail, by either remanding more defendants in custody or restricting their liberty whilst in the community by increasing the number of defendants subject to conditional bail and/or strengthening the conditions imposed. (McConville and Wilson, 2002, p 135)

Probation service and bail

There are clearly opportunities for the probation service to offer appropriate information to the courts to assist bail decisions and to provide programmes of support for defendants on bail in order to reduce custodial remands, either directly or by contracting with other agencies. However, the service has traditionally displayed an ambivalent attitude to this area of work (Haines and Morgan, 2007).

Historically, the provision of bail information in courts has been patchy, partly because there were no dedicated funds for such work until the rising prison population caused the Home Office, in 1992-94, to offer probation services ring-fenced pots of money to develop bail work. Most did apply for the hypothecated grants and pre-trial work reached its peak during that period of the early 1990s, declining again when the ring-fenced monies were absorbed into mainstream funding, under the pressure of other spending priorities (Haines and Morgan, 2007).

Interest in bail information schemes (although not bail support programmes) has resurfaced in the light of the prison over-crowding crisis and a report from the National Audit Office, *Facing justice: Tackling defendants' non-attendance at court*

(2005). This report highlighted the reduction in the number of bail information reports prepared by the probation service from a peak of 24,779 in 1997 to 5,677 in 2003. This was judged to be due to a redirection of resources to areas of statutory work and as a response to national guidance that designated bail information work as a medium priority for services.

PC 19/2005 subsequently sought to highlight the need to provide bail information, not as a blanket service in the light of resource constraints, but targeted at:

- vulnerable defendants;
- defendants likely to cause harm or to re-offend;
- those who have a disproportionately high risk of being remanded in custody such as female, BME and 18- to 21-year-old offenders;
- PPOs;
- those likely to fail to attend court based on their past record of attendance.

Services were also asked to conduct a cost and benefits review of their bail services to provide a better evidence base for making future decisions about resource allocation and development.

Ongoing concerns about high rates of custodial remands has since prompted NOMS to commission an accommodation and support service for defendants on bail and Home Detention Curfew that from June 2010 has been run by Stonham Housing.

Committal to Crown Courts and jury trials

Magistrates' Courts may commit cases to Crown Court for trial or send them there for sentence where they feel that their sentencing powers are inadequate to reflect the seriousness of the offence.

A summary offence cannot be committed to Crown Court, whereas an indictable offence can only be tried at Crown Court and will be sent there 'forthwith' by virtue of Section 51(1) of the Crime and Disorder Act 1998. This is a considerable speeding up of the previous processes under the Magistrates' Courts Act 1980 which required more examination of the evidence and sometimes a full rehearsal of the oral evidence before committing to Crown Court (this was known as an 'old fashioned' committal). If there are additional charges for triable either way offences alongside the main indictable charge, these will also be dealt with at Crown Court.

The situation regarding either way offences is more complex and requires the magistrates to make a decision about the most appropriate court for a trial to be heard. This will often be referred to as a determination of venue or mode of trial. Because this can be a lengthy procedure, Section 49 of the Criminal Procedure and Investigation Act 1996 requires the magistrates to ask the defendant to enter an early plea, in order to reduce the number of unnecessary mode of trial deliberations.

Where the defendant gives no indication or gives an indication of a likely not guilty plea, there are a range of factors which the magistrates should consider under Section 19 of the Magistrates' Courts Act 1980 (as amended by the Criminal Justice Act 2003):

- the nature of the offence
- whether the circumstances of the offence make the offence one of a serious character
- whether the punishment which a Magistrates' Court would have power to inflict for it would be adequate
- any other circumstances which appear to the court to make it more suitable for the offence to be tried in one way rather than the other *(complexity or difficult questions of law may be a relevant consideration)*
- any representations made by the prosecution or the defence.

Under the Criminal Justice Act 2003, the magistrates are now informed of the defendant's previous convictions, if any, before making their decision as to venue.

A defendant may also elect to go to Crown Court to face jury trial, even where the magistrates' view is that summary trial would be appropriate. Once magistrates have stated this view, under Section 20 of the Criminal Justice Act 2003 the defendant may then request an indication of whether a custodial or community sentence might be imposed if he or she were to plead guilty and to be dealt with as a summary case. If the magistrates indicate that the outcome would not be a custodial sentence, they cannot subsequently impose custody. This change was clearly an attempt to provide an incentive for defendants not to elect to go to Crown Court trial (Ashworth and Redmayne, 2005).

Jury trials are expensive, require a great deal of effort and a proportion of defendants, after extensive preparation by the professionals involved, enter late guilty pleas. In the light of perceived inefficiencies, the right to jury trial was questioned by the Conservative government in the early 1990s, but they quickly backed away in the face of determined opposition. The issue was raised again by New Labour, who put forward two versions of a Criminal Justice (Mode of Trial) Bill in 1999 that would have severely curtailed this right. The Bills were defeated in the face of strong arguments that the measures they contained would have a negative effect, particularly on the confidence of BME groups in the criminal justice process. As it is, issues of confidence are thought to underlie the fact that BME defendants are significantly more likely than white defendants to enter not guilty pleas and to exercise their right to elect for jury trial (Gelsthorpe, 2002; Redmayne and Ashworth, 2005).

Hearings before the trial

Because trials can be complicated affairs, the practice of having either plea and direction (P&DH) or preliminary hearings has developed. These allow for the progress of the case to be reviewed as it proceeds towards trial and are used where:

- there are case management issues that call for such a hearing;
- the case is likely to last more than four weeks;
- it would be desirable to set an early trial date;
- the defendant is a child or young person;
- there is likely to be a guilty plea and the defendant could be sentenced at the preliminary hearing; or
- it seems to the court that this is a suitable case for a preparatory hearing at Crown Court.

Such hearings assess the readiness of all parties to proceed, confirm the robustness of prosecution evidence and give opportunity for practical issues about participation of defendants and witnesses to be discussed. They also provide a way of gaining a sounding about whether the trial will actually go ahead.

One of the major concerns in preparation for trials is that of disclosure – effectively the information that the prosecution has to share with the defence about the basis of its case and the information that in turn the defence has to pass on to the prosecution about the defence case, for instance, what witnesses will be called. In general, defendants will have the right to see materials such as witness statements, although in relation to sexual offences this is restricted by the Sexual Offences (Protected Material) Act 1997. The legal framework around disclosure is contained in the Criminal Procedure and Investigation Act 1996, with some amendments in the Criminal Justice Act 2003.

The defendant's rights at trial

One fundamental right is that of access to justice and to a fair trial. The defendant should have appropriate advice throughout the process and should be able to put forward his or her side of the story. In practice, relatively disempowered individuals may have difficulty doing this, particularly in the intimidating formal environment of the Crown Court.

The relevant Practice Direction states a strong principle that:

> All possible steps should be taken to assist a vulnerable defendant to understand and participate in those proceedings. The ordinary trial process should, so far as necessary, be adapted to meet those ends.

This will be particularly salient for young people or individuals with a mental health disorder. Conduct of the trial may well have been discussed at a P&DH, including whether it is appropriate to deal with an individual separately from co-defendants. Where a case against a vulnerable defendant has attracted adverse public or media interest, the court should seek to protect against exposure to intimidation, vilification or abuse. For instance, in cases involving young people, reporting restrictions may be imposed under Section 39 of the Children and Young Persons Act 1933.

Another important right at trial is the right for the defendant, vulnerable or otherwise, to remain silent. In the past, defendants have been able to remain silent without any implications. However, the Criminal Justice and Public Order Act 1994 allows 'such inferences as may appear proper' to be drawn by a jury from a defendant's refusal to answer questions under oath and/or to put forward evidence. In these instances, the judge must satisfy him- or herself that the defendant has received appropriate advice or, if not represented, is aware of the implications of remaining silent. This provision does not apply to under-14-year-olds or other defendants who may be considered vulnerable.

The conduct of a trial

Within an adversarial system, the onus is on the prosecution to provide sufficient evidence to convince that the defendant is guilty *beyond all reasonable doubt*. This is known as the *burden of proof* and requires a high standard of evidence, in contrast to civil cases where hearsay and third party evidence is admissible at court.

The trial will start with the prosecution outlining its case against the accused and then calling its witnesses, who are questioned by the prosecution (the Crown Prosecution Service at Magistrates' Court, a barrister at Crown Court in the majority of cases). The defence can then question or cross-examine the prosecution witnesses, after which the prosecution has opportunity to pick up issues with the witnesses that were raised in cross-examination. This emphasis on the ability to test oral evidence is a key feature of a criminal trial and requires the physical presence of witnesses in court (Johnstone and Ward, 2010).

At this stage, the prosecution can submit to the court that there is no case to answer and, if that is accepted, the defendant will be acquitted. Otherwise the trial proceeds to the defence case, calling its own witnesses and presenting its evidence.

The Youth Justice and Criminal Evidence Act 1999 contains a range of measures to facilitate young, disabled or otherwise vulnerable witnesses giving evidence and these are covered later in Chapter Thirteen.

When both sides have put their case and examined each other's evidence, each has opportunity to make a closing statement. In Crown Court cases this will be followed by the judge's summing up, which draws the jury's attention to important points or gives direction on law.

These same procedures are followed in contested breach trials where the probation service is the prosecutor. Case records, correspondence with the defendant and proof of instructions given, for instance, will be used as evidence, so the completeness and accuracy of these is critical. Witnesses from the service may be called, including the offender manager or perhaps an unpaid work supervisor, but in breach proceedings court attendance can be minimised by the use of written statements, known as Section 9 Statements (Section 9 of the Criminal Justice Act 1967).

Retrials

There is a longstanding principle in the English legal system that once tried and acquitted for an offence, a person cannot be retried for the same offence – a principle known as 'double jeopardy'. This has more recently been questioned in the light of technological advances, such as DNA testing. The first exception to the double jeopardy principle was provided in Section 54 of the Criminal Procedure and Investigations Act 1996, in respect of cases where there has been suspected interference or intimidation of a juror or witness.

Following a recommendation from the Stephen Lawrence report and a review from the Law Commission, more substantial provisions were enacted in the Criminal Justice Act 2003. Part 10 of the Act deals with retrials for serious offences and allows a prosecutor, with the consent of the Director of Public Prosecutions, to apply to the Court of Appeal for a retrial. An application can be made in respect of a case acquitted at trial first time round or on appeal. A Court of Appeal can only order a retrial if there is 'new and compelling evidence' that was not used in the previous hearings. Section 79 also requires that a retrial should be in the interests of justice, and relevant considerations here are the length of time since the original offence was committed and whether or not the 'new' evidence was available for previous hearings but was not put forward because of a 'failure by an officer or prosecutor to act with due diligence or expedition'.

The first case to be tried and convicted under this new provision was that of Billy Dunlop, who had faced two jury trials in 1991 for the murder of his former lover, with both juries being unable to reach a verdict. Although he had made a confession to the police in 1999, he could not be put before a third jury until this change in the law.

Courts: a shop window for the probation service?

The probation service arose from the work of the police court missionaries in the late 1800s. For many years, following its formal inception in 1907, its most important relationships were with the courts. More recently, with the prominence of concerns about public protection, working practices with the police and with prisons have competed with the dominance of the courts for probation. Nevertheless, the interface with courts is critical for the probation service, whose contribution at key decision-making points in relation to bail and sentencing is often greatly valued. In many respects, the court arena can be seen as the 'shop window' for the service, where it can advertise the range of services and interventions that it offers and ensure that it gains an appropriate 'market share' of sentencing disposals.

Gaining and maintaining the confidence of sentencers is one of the most important facets of probation service (and youth justice) work, in both the higher and lower courts. In part this arises from the presence of probation in the court setting and its interventions at appropriate points (providing information, interviewing defendants, making enquiries of other agencies on the court's behalf). This can be a proactive, rather than a passive role, particularly where experienced court officers are able to anticipate what the court may need to know in given circumstances. The courts will also respond to the quality of PSRs, whether fast or standard delivery, in terms of their thoroughness and the way that information and assessments are presented. Although the service has moved away from reports that give a narrative of offenders' lives, their content should still be well structured, persuasive and evidenced.

Finally, the courts are able to take an intimate view of the probation service's enforcement practices, most particularly in contested breach trials. However, even in more routine breach cases, aspects of offender management are publicly aired. It is, for instance, an issue of credibility for the service where it is apparent that a case is brought to court later than it should have been because earlier instances of non-compliance cannot be cited due to poor record-keeping or lack of clarity in instructions given. More positively, breach reports provide an opportunity for the probation service to present itself at its best, with clear assessments of the extent that the offender has complied and is motivated to comply in future, and constructive suggestions as to how the court may deal with the breach. The tone of such reports is a powerful indicator of the service's approach to engaging and working with offenders.

Summary

Knowledge and understanding of the court system is essential for all probation practitioners, and particularly for offender managers. It is also important for the increasing number of voluntary agencies active in the court setting. All offenders in contact with NOMS have experience of court proceedings and many will have strong feelings about the way they were treated and the outcomes of sentencing. Unfair or insensitive treatment can impact on belief in the legitimacy of criminal justice processes and therefore of criminal justice agencies. As a key player in the court arena, the probation service can offer positive assistance to the court through providing good quality and timely information, as well as assessments presented orally and in written formats. PSRs guiding the court's decisions about sentencing are a core task for the probation service and are critical in ensuring that sentences passed are proportionate and suitable for the individual offender, with attention to individual risks, needs and circumstances. Breach proceedings are similarly critical in terms of the service's credibility with the courts and the offender's belief in the fair and appropriate exercise of the service's authority.

Further reading

Johnstone, G. and Ward, T. (2010) *Law and crime*, London: Sage Publications.

Smartt, U. (2009) *Law for criminologists*, London: Sage Publications.

TEN

Community sentencing

This chapter covers a breadth of discussion, but also contains the specific detail about community sentencing needed for effective offender management. The questions of rights, proportionate criminal justice responses and differential impacts on particular categories of offenders are critical in considering these legal provisions and how they are implemented. The generic community order allows flexibility in putting together sentencing packages and creates potential for innovative and highly individualised interventions. Sadly, evidence suggests that offender managers are not fully exploiting this potential (Mair et al, 2008). This is a wasted opportunity for the probation service, as confident and assertive practice in making sentencing proposals to the courts can only improve the probation service's standing with sentencers. It also brings benefits in work with offenders, where sentences are responsive to risks and needs, and where the elements of punishment or constraint are targeted and proportionate.

Historical perspectives

As outlined in previous chapters, the 1980s was a challenging time for the probation service and a period when it was pushed into accepting significant change. The White Paper, *Crime, justice and protecting the public* (Home Office, 1990), proposed a new sentencing framework with a strong anti-custodial stance for the majority of non-violent offenders. This purported to bring the probation service 'centre stage' but more definitely cast it in a correctional mode and talked for the first time about penalties in the community:

> It redefined alternatives to custody as community penalties, placed protection of the public and prevention of offending on a par with rehabilitation as an aim of the probation order and introduced the combination order … the Home Office line was that the probation service had been too preoccupied with the "identity and values" of the past and that it should have moved on from the days when social work skills and values embodied its whole purpose. (Gelsthorpe, 2007, p 487)

The Criminal Justice Act 1991 that followed proved a watershed not just for the probation service, but also for the relationship between the legislature and the judiciary. For the first time, there were clear limits set by government on the circumstances in which a custodial sentence could be imposed, although the discretion of sentencers in individual cases was maintained.

The principles enshrined in the Act were:

- the length of a sentence should be in proportion to the main (index) offence or combination of the two most serious offences;
- the use of custody should be restricted, with the majority of cases being dealt with in the community; and
- serious or dangerous violent and sexual cases should be separated out from more routine cases – this could be described as a twin-track or bifurcatory approach, in which proportionality in sentencing was the predominant principle for most offenders, but where incapacitation would be the overriding principle for those offenders considered more serious or dangerous.

Nigel Stone described the Act as 'a major initiative to provide a comprehensive statutory framework for sentencing, based primarily on the seriousness of the offence, while providing some scope for longer custodial sentences for public protection' (2007a, p 70).

The 'broad statutory architecture for sentencing' (Stone, 2007a) introduced by the Act created three bands of sentences and associated terminology. While creating criteria for sentencing within the three bands is a due process measure aimed at establishing consistency and limiting discretion, in essence this was a retributionist sentencing framework, paying back for the harm that had been done.

Custodial sentences	'So serious' that only such a sentence can be justified or to protect the public from serious harm
Community sentences	'Serious enough' to warrant such a sentence
First tier penalties	'Not serious enough' to justify a community sentence

Key terms: seriousness, proportionality, restriction of liberty, public protection, serious harm

The Criminal Justice Act 1991 was the first Act where public protection was paramount and, alongside its attempts to reduce the prison population, it began to refocus the probation service on work with more serious offenders and risk of dangerousness. It hugely increased the probation service's responsibilities for supervising adult offenders on release from custody and therefore prompted a shift in resources towards custodial work (discussed in later chapters).

The Act also had ramifications for Probation and Community Service Orders, as well as other sentences bracketed together as community sentences or community penalties, although as George Mair (2007) notes, the term is deliberately vague and it is unclear exactly what is meant by 'community'. The following section discusses these changes in more detail.

Community sentences or penalties under the Criminal Justice Act 1991

Community sentences in the Act were identified as being:

- Probation Orders
- Community Service Orders
- Combination Orders – newly introduced by Section 11 of the Act
- Supervision Orders – for young offenders up to 18 years
- Attendance Centre Orders – for young offenders up to 21 years
- Curfew Orders.

The significance of Section 8 for the probation service was that, for the first time, Probation Orders became a sentence of the court for offenders over 16 years old, rather than a stay of sentencing. This fundamentally changed their status and made it possible for them to be put together with community service in the new Combination Orders.

As with custodial sentences, there were restrictions on the use of community penalties related to proportionality and seriousness, but also suitability for the offender, who had to give consent to all orders.

The purposes of a Probation Order were spelt out in Section 2(1) as being rehabilitation of the offender, protecting the public and preventing commission of further offences, again an important reshaping of the probation role. Probation Orders could run for between six months and three years and a variety of conditions could be added by virtue of Schedule 1A, including:

- residence
- refraining from particular activities
- presenting at a particular place for a period up to 60 days
- attendance at a probation centre for up to 60 days
- treatment for mental health
- treatment for drug dependency.

This last condition was controversial for drug agencies at the time, as their work was premised on voluntarism and they were unused to working in partnership with criminal justice agencies – a very different scenario to the current context where a significant proportion of funding for drug treatment and rehabilitation is channelled through the criminal justice system (see Chapter Fifteen).

These conditions, particularly where community service was also part of an order, meant that probation supervision could be extremely structured and restrictive. In part this was to convince sentencers that probation interventions could form a viable and substantial alternative to custody, but it also fed into the developing punitiveness in the criminal justice world.

Section 12 of the Criminal Justice Act 1991 created the Curfew Order and Section 13 provided for this to be electronically monitored, although this was vigorously opposed by probation officers and their union at the time and the technology was still at an early stage of development. It was only some years later, with the introduction of Home Detention Curfews, that the probation service began to accept and to work positively with electronic monitoring, in instances where it represented an opportunity to keep offenders out of custody.

Other provisions of the Criminal Justice Act 1991

As a large piece of criminal justice legislation, there were a number of other facets of the Criminal Justice Act that have been significant, and these include:

- substituting PSRs for the previous social enquiry reports, requiring a focus on the offence and assessment of offence seriousness, including aggravating and mitigating factors, rather than the social circumstances of the offender;
- stipulating where a court is required to consider a PSR before passing a custodial or community sentence;
- allowing the contracting out of prisons;
- introducing requirements in Section 95 for criminal justice agencies to collect and publish information relating to 'race' and gender in order to monitor their performance and to ensure they are not unfairly discriminating in terms of 'race' or sex or any other improper grounds – Section 95 publications are a fascinating source of information about the workings of the criminal justice system and a useful source of reference; and
- requiring the Home Office to publish standards for the probation service – the first national standards were issued in 1992.

One further aspect of the Criminal Justice Act 1991 is significant and that is Section 29 – in line with 'just deserts' thinking, this prevented the courts from sentencing on the basis of the offender's previous convictions rather than the current offence(s) before the court. This scrupulousness can be contrasted with the current over-emphasis on previous history as a predictor of future behaviours. It focused probation officers' attention on assessment of the current offence and circumstances surrounding it, and required more nuanced judgements about relevance and the amount of previous history to discuss where it revealed patterns of behaviour.

Section 29 was soon repealed, however, largely because the penal climate that had produced the Criminal Justice Act 1991 had rapidly dissolved in the early 1990s. With Michael Howard rather than the more patrician Conservative, Douglas Hurd, as Home Secretary, the tone and nature of criminal justice thinking turned from 'just deserts' to punishment:

> Immediately following the implementation of key sections of the Act, there followed a series of crises which led to a backlash against the legislation. Rising crime figures, public and police concern about

youth crime … combined with concern about car crime and offending whilst on bail, all played their part in this. Almost at once, fuelled by sentencers' dislike of the legislation, the Government back-tracked. (Gelsthorpe, 2007, p 488)

Other criminal justice legislation pre-Criminal Justice Act 2003

Although the two major Acts to be considered in relation to sentencing are the Criminal Justice Acts of 1991 and 2003, there has been much other legislation, some of which has had an impact on sentencing. The overall thrust of this legislation has been to move further away from the principle of 'just deserts' towards deterrence, incapacitation and punishment. Significant measures to note are as follows.

Crime (Sentences) Act 1997

Section 38(2) abolished the need to obtain offender consent before making a Probation or Community Service Order. This was a critical change for the probation service who no longer needed to establish offender agreement to the supervisory process and who were therefore in a position of working with higher proportions of offenders unwilling or uncommitted to change.

Crime and Disorder Act 1998

- Introduced Drug Treatment and Testing Orders and Sex Offender Orders.
- Created ASBOs.
- Reformed the youth justice system, taking away the statutory work with young people that probation and social services had traditionally performed.
- Established a range of new orders for young people (see Chapter Fourteen).
- Required local agencies to work together in CDRPs (now CSPs).
- Provided for offences to be identified as racially aggravated.

Criminal Justice and Court Services Act 2000

This is the Act that created the National Probation Service and separated the criminal and the children and families work of the service, creating a new agency (Cafcass). The functions of probation are outlined in Section 2:

- the protection of the public;
- the reduction of re-offending;
- the proper punishment of offenders;
- ensuring offenders' awareness of the effects of crime on the victims of crime and the public;
- the rehabilitation of offenders.

This consolidated the shift towards prioritising protection of the public which had developed since the Criminal Justice Act 1991, and it is also significant to note the inclusion of the victim perspective.

Under this Act, various community orders were renamed, so that:

Probation Orders	➔	Community Rehabilitation Orders
Community Service Orders	➔	Community Punishment Orders
Combination Orders	➔	Community Punishment and Rehabilitation Orders

The Act also introduced two new community sentences, the Drug Abstinence Order (Section 47) relating to Class A drugs, and the Exclusion Order (Section 46) which could operate for up to two years.

Background to the Criminal Justice Act 2003

With increasing concerns about persistence and the serious nature of particular offences, the proportionality framework of the Criminal Justice Act 1991 became increasingly viewed as inappropriate and limiting. The Home Office commissioned two reports, one from John Halliday on sentencing and one from Patrick Carter on the implementation and management of sentences. The introduction of the Halliday report (2001), *Making punishments work: Report of a review of the sentencing framework for England and Wales*, summed up the concerns in the following terms:

> The review was born out of a belief that the present sentencing framework suffers from serious deficiencies that reduce its contributions to crime reduction and public confidence. The report finds that belief to be well-founded, although the framework has strengths on which to build. The case for improvement is strong; but following a period of incessant change, practitioners fear that further reform may not be for the better. They need and deserve a framework that is not only better and easier to understand, but also one that works and will last. (Halliday, 2001, p 1)

The report was published in July 2001 and contained a series of 55 recommendations, many of which featured in the subsequent White Paper, *Justice for all* (Home Office, 2002a). As identified by Hancock (2007a) the principal issues that the review team had been grappling with were how to sentence persistent offenders, how to respond to dangerousness and how to make sentences more effective by bringing prison and probation work more closely together. – not a simple task by any means. Published two years later, *Managing offenders, reducing crime* (Carter, 2003) addressed the structural changes necessary to bring about the 'seamless sentence' envisaged for those serving period in custody followed by licence supervision. This resulted in the creation of NOMS and the OMM.

In terms of community sentences, Halliday advocated the creation of a generic sentence with a variety of conditions or 'ingredients' that could be attached to reflect seriousness and need. He re-established the principle that the severity of the sentence should increase to reflect previous convictions, recognising that this would have an impact on the number of offenders in custody and on restrictive community sentences.

Recommendation 3

The existing "just deserts" philosophy should be modified by incorporating a new presumption that severity of sentence should increase when an offender has sufficiently recent and relevant previous convictions. (Halliday, 2001)

He further recommended the codification of guidelines and the establishment of mechanisms to produce guidelines in a more systematic way than the previous practice of receiving guideline judgments from the Court of Appeal. The Sentencing Guidelines Council was initially created by the Criminal Justice Act 2003, but has since been superceded by the Sentencing Council to fulfil this function.

Halliday argued for principles in sentencing:

Recommendation 4

The principles governing severity of sentencing should be:

- Severity of sentencing should reflect the seriousness of the offence (or offences as a whole) and the offender's relevant criminal history
- The seriousness of the offence should reflect its degree of harmfulness or risked harmfulness and the offender's culpability in committing the offence
- In considering criminal history, the severity of sentence should increase to reflect a persistent course of criminal conduct, as shown by previous convictions and sentences. (Halliday, 2001)

This marked a significant departure from the focus on proportionality that was the cornerstone of the Criminal Justice Act 1991; the sentencing provisions in the Criminal Justice Act 2003 represented a major change for the probation service, but in some respects also tended to enact the trend towards more restrictive and bifurcated sentences that had developed over more than a decade. This continues to have potential implications for the rights and fair treatment of offenders.

Contrasting Nigel Stone's relatively optimistic view of the Criminal Justice Act 1991 with his opinion of the 2003 Act, the tone is markedly less positive when he describes the latter as:

A wide-ranging, labyrinthine and controversial initiative to win public confidence in criminal justice, attempting to embrace crime prevention and public protection in sentencing in tandem with proportionate punishment. It revises "early release" and expands the use of confinement and extended regulation of violent and sexual offenders. (2007b, p 71)

Sentencing under the Criminal Justice Act 2003

The provisions relating to community sentences are contained in Chapters 2 and 4 of Part 12 of the Act, while Chapter 8 deals with deferment of sentence (this is not a community sentence but, for the sake of completeness, will also be covered here). There are also provisions that apply across the board and for the first time, in Section 142, the Criminal Justice Act 2003 spells out the purposes of sentencing for adults over the age of 18 (except for certain mental health cases):

> Section 142: Purposes of sentencing
> 1) Any court dealing with an offender in respect of his offence must have regard to the following purposes of sentencing:
>   a) the punishment of offenders,
>   b) the reduction of crime (including its reduction by deterrence),
>   c) the reform and rehabilitation of offenders,
>   d) the protection of the public, and
>   e) the making of reparation by offenders to persons affected by their offences.

Although this gives some clarity to sentencing, there are potential conflicts between these principles and they have been subject to criticism from Nigel Stone, among others:

> The CJA [Criminal Justice Act] 2003 requires courts to "have regard to" a raft of sentencing purposes ranging from "punishment" to "reparation" and specifically refers to "deterrence" and "reform". No ranking of priority or other guidance is given to sentencers in resolving tensions between these objectives or in weighing the merits of competing values ... the return of the "smorgasbord" approach begs questions about the capacity of sentencing to prevent crime and suggests that consistency will be undermined as sentencers seek to give dubious simultaneous effect to deterrence, incapacitation and rehabilitation. (2007b, p 71)

The generic community order was introduced by Section 177 for offences committed by over-18-year-olds on or after 4 April 2005. Significantly, Section 11(1) of the Criminal Justice and Immigration Act 2008 restricts the making of a community order to cases involving an imprisonable offence, underlining the need to target these orders at appropriate levels of offence seriousness.

Under Section 197, the *responsible officer* is an officer of the local probation trust or member of a YOT except where the only condition on the order is for a curfew or for a period at an attendance centre. In these cases the *responsible officer* will be an employee of an approved electronic monitoring contractor or the manager of the attendance centre respectively.

All community orders have at least one condition out of a range of a possible 12, and conditions can be combined to respond to risk of harm or offender need. However, the decision-making process is potentially rather more complicated than for the previous range of sentences and the conditions can be combined in a variety of ways (see Table 10.1).

The national implementation guidance (PC 25/2005) suggests that there are five groupings of combinations:

- restriction
- practical support
- personal change
- treatment
- control.

The guidance gives examples of model combinations that form coherent packages of intervention or support, but these in themselves have no legal status. Report writers should note that in making proposals they should refer to the specific requirements as outlined in the Act.

In terms of risk and seriousness the following applies:

Low   = maximum 1 requirement
Medium = maximum 1–3 requirements
High   — maximum 1–3 requirements, depending on the combination, but this may be exceeded where intensive control or a long period of treatment is required

The accurate assessment of seriousness is clearly critical to this framework and the Sentencing Guidelines Council's comments on culpability are especially relevant:

> Four levels of criminal culpability can be identified for sentencing purposes:
>
> Where the offender:
>
> i) has the *intention* to cause harm, with the highest culpability when an offence is planned. The worse the harm intended, the greater the seriousness.
> ii) is *reckless* as to whether harm is caused, that is, where the offender appreciates at least some harm would be caused but proceeds giving no thought to the consequences even though the extent of the risk would be obvious to most people.

iii) has *knowledge* of the specific risks entailed by his actions even though he does not intend to cause the harm that results.

iv) is guilty of *negligence*. (2004, p 4)

Table 10.1 of the 12 present Criminal Justice Act 2003 requirements has been taken from the NPS national implementation guide (PC 25/2005), and the suggested lengths of orders are cross-referenced with the guidance from the Sentencing Guidelines Council.

Table 10.1: Requirements under the Criminal Justice Act 2003

Requirement	Level of seriousness	Consent needed?	Length	Type of report	Main purpose
Sections 199/200 **Unpaid work**	Low Medium High	No	40-80 hours 80-150 hours 150-300 hours	FDR FDR FDR	Punishment Reparation Rehabilitation
Section 213 **Supervision**	Low Medium High	No	Up to 12 months 12-18 months 12-36 months	FDR Standard Standard	Rehabilitation
Section 202 **Programme (Accredited)**	Medium High	No	Stated number or range of sessions	Depends on programme	Rehabilitation
Section 209 **Drug rehabilitation**	Low Medium High	Yes	6 months 6-12 months 12-36 months	FDR/SDR Standard Standard	Rehabilitation
Section 212 **Alcohol treatment**	Low Medium High	Yes	6 months 6-12 months 12-36 months	FDR/SDR Standard Standard	Rehabilitation
Sections 207/208 **Mental health treatment**	Medium High	Yes	Up to 36 months	Standard	Rehabilitation
Section 206 **Residence**	Medium High	No	Up to 36 months	Standard	Rehabilitation Protection
Section 201 **Specified activity**	Medium High	No	20-30 days Up to 60 days	FDR	Rehabilitation Reparation
Section 203 **Prohibited activity**	Medium High	No	Up to 24 months	FDR	Punishment Protection
Section 205 **Exclusion**	Low Medium High	No	Up to 2 months Up to 6 months Up to 12 months	FDR	Punishment Protection
Section 204 **Curfew**	Low Medium High	No	Up to 2 months 2-3 months 4-6 months	FDR FDR FDR	Punishment Protection
Section 215 **Attendance centre**	Low	No	12-36 hours	FDR	Punishment

Note: Attendance centre requirements are only available for offenders under the age of 25 where such a centre operates in the local justice area.

FDR = full disclosure report; SDR = standard delivery report.

Supervision under the Criminal Justice Act 2003

The supervision requirement on a community order effectively represents what was previously the Probation Order, requiring the offender to keep in touch with the responsible officer and to attend appointments. Such contact must be conducted within the national standards but there is no stipulation about what the content of supervision sessions might contain, other than an expectation that they remain relevant to the goals of rehabilitation and reduction of offending.

The supervision requirement, however, is the mechanism by which the OMM will be delivered for many community orders so, although this appears to be just another in a list of requirements, supervision and the supervisory relationship are still central to the process. This is particularly so where there are complex risk management issues or the need for personal support to promote change. The offender manager oversees community orders with a supervision requirement, paying attention to sequencing of components of the order, brokerage of services and coordination of the other professionals involved in the order. This means that the offender management is central both to securing engagement and compliance and to enhancing the process of desistance.

PC 56/2005 details expectations of the implementation of intensive community orders. These are not separate orders in any legislative sense, but are orders where level of risk or need indicates that a number of requirements may be constructively utilised. The guidance states that:

> When proposing an intensive community order, the court must be satisfied that the offender can comply with the requirements. In the case of an intensive community order, PSR authors *must* ensure that the overall punitive weight of the combination of requirements is proportionate to the seriousness of the current offence(s) and that the individual requirements are likely to meet the identified offending related needs ... the PSR author must also ensure that the requirements are compatible and do not interfere with the offender's religious beliefs or times of work and education. (PC 56/2005, p 3)

Drug Rehabilitation Requirement

The Drug Rehabilitation Requirement (DRR) replaces the Drug Treatment and Testing Order that was introduced by the Crime and Disorder Act 1998, but differs from that order in that it can be used at all levels of seriousness. PC 57/2005 contains guidance on the implementation of the DRR and Alcohol Treatment Requirement (ATR) in which it stipulates that:

> The target group for the DRR is broader than for the drug treatment and testing order, as it encompasses all the community sentencing bands from low to high seriousness ... the amount of drug treatment

> delivered under a DRR can be tailored to individual treatment needs,
> providing the overall restriction on liberty reflects the seriousness of
> the offence. (PC 57/2005, p 4)

The minimum period for a DRR is six months and the offender's consent is needed before such an order is made. Potential DRR cases may involve quite sophisticated work at the assessment stage, particularly where there are associated mental health concerns ('dual diagnosis'). For complex treatment needs a specialist assessment is required and this is particularly so where the prescribing of a drug substitute, such as methadone, is being considered. In many cases a full adjournment period for a standard PSR will therefore be necessary but, if the need and proposed intervention is relatively straightforward and the offence falls into the low seriousness band, a fast delivery report can be used.

The legal conditions to be met before a DRR can be imposed are contained in Section 209(2). The court must be satisfied that the offender is dependent on or has a propensity to misuse drugs. It must also be satisfied that the dependency or drug misuse requires and may be susceptible to treatment, that appropriate treatment arrangements are in place and that the treatment proposed is suitable for the offender.

For the purposes of Section 209 'drugs' refer to controlled substances under Section 2 of the Misuse of Drugs Act 1971 (see Chapter Fifteen).

The order requires the offender to provide urine samples at specified periods and must detail other requirements of treatment, in terms of attendance at relevant agencies, following particular structured daycare programmes or residential rehabilitation. Most services are commissioned by the local multi-agency Drug and Alcohol Action Team from a centrally allocated pooled budget, and the range of options available varies between areas. DRRs can also be combined with a requirement to participate in an accredited substance misuse programme or other activity requirements to deal with, for instance housing, ETE (education, training and employment) or other issues where these are not dealt with as part of the holistic treatment plan. At the other end of the seriousness spectrum, a DRR can be a stand-alone requirement, but in cases where there is no additional supervision requirement, an offender manager will be allocated to monitor and to enforce the order.

In 2000, the Home Office initiated the Drugs Intervention Programme in order to provide speedier access to treatment services for drug-using individuals who come into contact with the criminal justice system. Services under the DIP include arrest referral schemes and other programmes, often operating at a pre-sentence stage. The Criminal Justice Intervention Teams (CJITs) who are the operational arm of the DIP may well already have established contact with an offender before assessment, and the guidance notes that it is important to work alongside the Team in order to prepare an offender for the work that may subsequently take place as part of a DRR under probation service management.

A PSR proposing a community order with a DRR should give specific details of the treatment provider and specify where the treatment required will be residential. Sufficient detail of the pattern of drug use should be included to enable the sentencers to determine the appropriate-length community order, and to indicate suitability for treatment. The report author should also suggest the length of the treatment requirement needed.

DRRs may be subject to review as Drug Treatment and Testing Orders were previously, but the requirements around reviews are tighter. Legally, reviews are only required when the DRR runs for over 12 months, whereas national standards specify that they should take place for every DRR of 12 months or longer. National standards also require that the offender manager submits a written progress report to the court once every four weeks for the first 16 weeks and a minimum of 16 weeks thereafter where reviews are mandatory or requested by the court. Further guidance about reviews and powers to amend DRRs is given in PC 57/2005.

Alcohol Treatment Requirement

The ATR is contained in Section 212 of the Criminal Justice Act 2003 and, similar to the DRR, can be made for periods of between six months and three years. The court must be satisfied that the offender is dependent on alcohol, that the dependency may be susceptible to treatment and that arrangements have been for treatment, residential or otherwise. However, it does not have to be satisfied that the dependency on alcohol caused or contributed to the offences before the court, and in this differs from the DRR.

As with the DRR, the offender's consent is required. The amount and type of treatment offered must be tailored to the individual's assessed need and should also be proportionate to the offences in question. Briefly, the services available operate at four levels or tiers:

- Tier 1: Screening, brief advice and referral, often delivered by non-specialists
- Tier 2: Open access support to reduce alcohol-related harm, assessment and referral services, for example, counselling, support groups
- Tier 3: Community-based treatment typically involving structured packages of care
- Tier 4: Residential or in-patient treatment

The ATR requirement is not subject to court review where it is a requirement of a community order, but it may be if used as part of a Suspended Sentence Order.

Community order in practice

Although there are 12 conditions that may be included in community orders, research on earlier implementation suggests that not all are being used to full effect. Table 10.2 presents sentencing information from the Ministry of Justice relating to all four quarters of 2007.

A study by the Centre for Crime and Justice Studies, King's College (Mair et al, 2008), indicated that six requirements were rarely used: alcohol treatment; mental health treatment; residence; exclusion; prohibited activity; and attendance centre. Together these represented only 3 per cent of all requirements. This research, covering the period up until September 2007, also found that the way that the new community orders were being used showed little sign of innovation. They frequently mirrored the old style community penalties in the type of conditions that were included, although it was unclear at that early stage of implementation whether this was due to the sentencers' lack of confidence/ knowledge or offender managers tending to propose familiar and obvious combinations. In any event, it is clear that there is further room for creativity and innovation that could be exploited by officers in court reports to benefit offenders.

While the Coalition government has announced plans for sentencing reform, the community order will remain in place (Ministry of Justice, 2010a). Aspects of implementation may change, however, specifically the range of agencies involved in service delivery and oversight of orders. Indeed, the Coalition's eagerness to encourage new organisations and new approaches may reflect impatience with the lack of innovation highlighted above as much as its own ideological leanings.

Table 10.2: Requirements on community orders made in 2007

Element 1	Element 2	Element 3	Jan-Mar	April-June	July-Sept	Oct-Dec
Unpaid work			10,371	10,251	10,274	10,031
Supervision			4,368	4,509	4,665	4,355
Supervision	Acc Prog		4,053	3,696	3,811	3,569
Supervision	Unpaid work		2,478	2,661	2,467	2,383
Supervision	DRR		1,608	1,672	1,705	1,686
Supervision	Unpaid work	Acc Prog	1,611	1,463	1,366	1,241
Curfew			960	939	977	1,172
Unpaid work	Unpaid work		805	763	849	832
Supervision	Specified activity		712	602	688	605
Supervision	Acc Prog	DRR	764	650	661	586
All other combinations			5,435	5,183	5,569	5,537
Total			**33,165**	**32,389**	**33,032**	**31,998**

Note: Acc Prog = accredited programme.

Source: Ministry of Justice (2008c)

Deferred sentences

The guidance from the Sentencing Guidelines Council in 2005 envisaged that the range of sentencing options available under the Criminal Justice Act 2003 should mean that deferment of sentence would be used less often. However, the guidance acknowledges that this practice still has a role:

> The use of deferred sentences should be predominantly for a small group of cases close to a significant threshold where, should the defendant be prepared to adapt his behaviour in a way clearly specified by the sentencer, the court may be prepared to impose a lesser sentence. (2005, p 15)

It suggests that the offender may have some influence on the eventual sentence because the deferment:

a. tests the commitment of the offender not to offend;
b. gives the offender an opportunity to do something where progress can be made over a short period (for example, engaging with drug treatment); and
c. provides the offender with an opportunity to behave or refrain from behaving in a particular way that might be relevant to sentence. (Sentencing Guidelines Council, 2005)

Schedule 23 of the Criminal Justice Act 2003 contains the relevant provisions and requires the offender to comply with any conditions set by the court. Good practice would be for the court to outline a clear set of objectives for the offender to work towards during the period of adjournment, which may be anything up to six months. Where an offender manager has prepared a report for the court hearing where the deferment was made, whether or not the author of the report suggested the deferment, it will normally be expected that he or she will prepare an update report for the adjourned date, detailing progress in relation to the conditions stipulated by the court.

Summary

Sentencing arrangements are complex and it is a challenging job to manage community sentences and to work with offenders post-custody. In all of this, there are considerations of rights and how best to enable offenders to enjoy key rights that promote their inclusion and participation in society, while still having regard for public protection and the rights and interests of victims. Creative use of community sentencing may assist with this, and within this, the relationship between the offender manager and offender should represent the fulcrum, bringing together and levering the other elements of intervention so that they take best effect. Involving appropriate partner agencies and the timing of interventions is critical, but so is the outward-looking approach that seeks to enhance networks and create opportunities for building *human and social capital*.

Further reading

Bottoms, A., Gelsthorpe, L. and Rex, S. (2002) *Community penalties: Change and challenges*, Cullompton: Willan.

Gelsthorpe, L. and Morgan, R. (eds) (2007) *Handbook of probation*, Cullompton: Willan.

ELEVEN

Custodial sentencing

As the focus on both risk of serious harm and persistence of offending has grown, the probation service has concentrated increasingly more resources and efforts on more intensive and restrictive sentences in the community and work with offenders in custody. This has been hastened by the creation of NOMS and the bringing together of the prison and probation services, although this has not been a straightforward process: there are cultural differences between the services, separate histories and, in many respects, a stark contrast between the institutional setting of prisons and the work of probation in the community. Nevertheless, both services have an interest in the welfare and rehabilitation of offenders while in custody, and in protecting the public and reducing risk of re-offending on release. This chapter examines the positives of working together as well as the tensions created by the new framework for custodial sentencing, which blurs some of the distinctions between community and custodial sentencing. Brief details of custodial sentences for young people are covered, but are discussed in more detail in Chapter Fourteen.

A synopsis of probation work with prisoners

There are two aspects to probation work with prisoners. The first relates to work that takes place within the institution, and the second relates to the support and oversight of prisoners after release. These areas of work originated from the activities of charitable organisations, such as the Discharged Prisoners Aid Societies, and the prison gate missionaries in the late Victorian period. During the first half of the 20th century, prisoners continued to be supported by charities and by the newly established probation service on a voluntary basis.

The probation service's first statutory involvement with ex-prisoners was the supervision of boys and young men released from Borstals and Approved Schools. This was followed shortly after by provisions in the Criminal Justice Act 1948 which required the service to become officially responsible for the aftercare of longer-term prisoners released from preventive detention and corrective training. In the 1960s, it assumed primary responsibility for all statutory and voluntary aftercare.

In the mid-1960s, probation officers also began to work in teams inside prisons, initially allocated to institutions through a national formula, but from the mid-1990s through contracts between the prisons and the local chief probation officer, thus ensuring a degree of ownership on both sides (Hancock, 2007b).

Meanwhile, the Parole Board was established under the Criminal Justice Act 1967, and this allowed for the release from prison of certain long-term prisoners 'on parole', that is, with requirements to keep in contact with a probation officer, not to re-offend and to adhere to any other specified conditions. This increased the probation work with prisoners considerably and, as the parole system became embedded, by 1980, half of those eligible were being released early (Maguire, 2007). The balance of work throughout the 1980s was shifting away from voluntary to statutory aftercare and the Criminal Justice Act 1991 moved the probation service much further in that direction, along with the articulation of concerns about public protection.

Criminal Justice Act 1991

The previous chapter discussed the 'just deserts' emphasis of this legislation, and the introduction of the principle of proportionality and the 'so serious' criterion for custodial sentencing. It also introduced three new categories for determinate periods of custody, depending on the length of sentence:

- automatic unconditional release (AUR) – under 12 months
- automatic conditional release (ACR)   – 12–48 months
- discretionary conditional release (DCR) – 4 years and over

The concept and practice of early release – previously operated under the system of discretionary remission of sentence – had been deployed by the Home Office to greater or lesser degrees over time as a means of managing the prison population (Cavadino and Dignan, 2006), but was institutionalised more firmly by the Criminal Justice Act 1991, with explicit requirements relating to probation supervision. Although released early, prisoners who re-offended before the sentence expiry date would be subject to recall. The time between the end of licence supervision and the sentence expiry date was known as the 'at risk' period.

Section 33 required that short-term prisoners (those serving under four years) should be automatically released at the halfway point of the sentence. Although sentences under 12 months had no requirements for supervision on licence, prisoners serving over 12 months were on licence after release until three quarters of the way through the total sentence period. Long-term prisoners (those serving four years or more) had to be released after two thirds of their sentence, but could be released earlier on parole at the halfway point.

There are still longer-term prisoners within the system who have been sentenced under the DCR arrangements, although they are now automatically released halfway through their sentence. There are also still prisoners serving less than 12 months who are subject to Section 33 automatic unconditional release because the 'custody plus' sentences under the Criminal Justice Act 2003 have never been implemented.

Other relevant legislation

Although the Criminal Justice Act 1991 remained the primary piece of legislation relating to custody, the following Acts were indicative of the increased focus on risk and public protection building up to the next significant piece of legislation, the Criminal Justice Act 2003.

Criminal Justice and Public Order Act 1994

This Act was passed in the context of increasing concern about PYOs and in the aftermath of the abduction and murder of the toddler, James Bulger. It is therefore not surprising to see a toughening up of measures relating to children and young people:

- Creation of secure training centres and secure training orders for 12- to 14-year-olds – a hugely controversial measure!
- The maximum period that could be served in a young offender institution by a 15- to 17-year-old was increased from 12 to 24 months.

Crime (Sentences) Act 1997

This again was a contested piece of legislation that started its passage through Parliament under the Conservative administration but eventually achieved Royal Assent under New Labour. The Act strengthened measures focused on serious, dangerous and persistent offenders. Specifically, it introduced:

- Section 2, which requires mandatory life sentences to be passed for offenders over 18 years old convicted for the second time of a 'serious offence' (which includes attempted murder, conspiracy or incitement to murder, rape/attempted rape and manslaughter) unless the judge considers that there are 'exceptional circumstances';
- Section 3, which requires a minimum seven-year sentence to be imposed for a third conviction for trafficking a Class A drug; and
- Section 4, which requires a minimum three-year sentence for a third conviction for domestic burglary.

These mandatory sentences clearly impinged on judicial discretion, but chimed with what was felt to be the public mood. However, there is some room for judges to take into account exceptional circumstances or particular factors relevant to the case that would make these mandatory sentences unjust. Clearly use was made of these 'get out clauses'.

Crime and Disorder Act 1998

Many of the provisions in the Act relate to young offenders, and Section 73 created a new custodial sentence for offenders up to the age of 18. The Detention and Training Order increased the supervision requirement for young offenders as half the sentence is spent in a closed institution and the other half under notice of supervision to the YOTs.

Section 58 (now Section 85 of the Powers of the Criminal Court [Sentencing] Act 2000) also contained measures relating to extended licence provisions for sexual and violent offences, so that a licence period could be set that extended beyond what would otherwise be the sentence expiry date.

Section 99 allows prisoners in certain categories to be released conditionally before their usual release date. This section is the legal backing for the Home Detention Curfew scheme.

Criminal Justice and Court Services Act 2000

This Act permits post-custody licences to contain requirements for electronic monitoring and drug testing.

Criminal Justice Act 2003

By the turn of the century the principles of proportionality enshrined in the Criminal Justice Act 1991 had lost credibility and favour with politicians and the public. The Halliday report in 2001 was extremely critical of the way that custodial sanctions were being used. Halliday particularly singled out 'the lack of utility in prison sentences of less than 12 months' (2001, p iv), and the practice of releasing short-term prisoners halfway through their sentences (or earlier on Home Detention Curfew) which restricted scope to offer rehabilitative intervention in custody to a group of offenders highly likely to re-offend. In terms of longer-term sentences, he commented that the last quarter of the sentence (the post-supervision period) lacked any real purpose, and that impacts on offenders' behaviours were minimal, despite the commitment and best re-settlement efforts of the agencies involved. He therefore proposed a new approach to the use of custodial sentences, with a closer relationship between work conducted in the prison environment and post-release in the community. David Hancock offers a useful summary:

> Community supervision was seen as an essential component of custodial sentences, and the recommended framework of prison sentences ensured that supervision in the community followed every period of incarceration. The notion that custodial sentences were served partly in the prison and partly in the community would see a closer partnership between prison and probation and was an

expression of the intention that custodial sentences should become more rehabilitative. (2007a, p 133)

The principal recommendations from the Halliday report were subject to consultation with the White Paper, *Justice for all* (Home Office, 2002a), and were subsequently enacted in the Criminal Justice Act 2003. Apart from extending the powers of the magistrates to enable them to impose custodial sentences of up to 12 months (Section 154 but still not implemented), the following new short-term sentences were introduced:

• custody minus – enacted as suspended sentences
• custody plus
• intermittent custody.

These were major changes in relation to short sentences and, in the words of Jenny Roberts, 'in effect these provisions make any prison sentence of less than a year an additional requirement of a community order' (2007, p 82). She expresses some serious reservations about this merging of community and custodial categories and the potential implications in sentencing practice:

> Wrapping shorter periods of custody in community orders tailored to the needs and circumstances of individual offenders might render short prison sentences less destructive, but making them (or making them appear to be) more "effective" seems very likely to encourage their use, enabling courts to "have it both ways" by combining the perceived benefits of a community sentence with the punishment of custody. In the great majority of criminal cases, courts would no longer need to choose between a prison sentence and a community penalty, or between one community penalty and another. (Roberts, 2007, p 82)

The Criminal Justice Act 2003 also concentrated on clarifying and rationalising sentences of over 12 months and those specifically for more serious offenders/offences. The relevant provisions are:

• the standard determinate sentence;
• extended sentences for public protection; and
• indeterminate IPP sentences.

The following sections look at the short-term custodial provisions, followed by the provisions for over 12 months, then a discussion of the 'seamless sentence' and re-settlement in operation.

Custody plus

Essentially the proposed new sentences – custody plus and custody minus – were intended to be complementary and to bolster support and intervention for short-term prisoners. In brief, custody plus, introduced in Section 81 of the Act, was conceived as a short period in custody, followed by a longer period in the community on licence. The licence period could include all the requirements available for the community orders discussed in Chapter Ten, except for the DRR, ATR and mental health treatment requirements, all of which need offender consent. The court would be able to stipulate at the point of sentence the licence requirements that it wished to impose, but additional requirements could also be added by the prison before release.

It was intended that the custodial element of the sentence for one offence would be between 2 and 13 weeks, before deducting any time spent on custodial remand. The supervision or licence period would be a minimum of 26 weeks up to a maximum of 49 weeks (or up to 65 weeks for multiple offences).

Writing in 2003 as the then Criminal Justice Bill was awaiting Royal Assent, Julian Roberts predicted that 'a sanction of this nature, combining custody followed by a more protracted period of probation supervision (with significant conditions) may well prove attractive to judges and be widely imposed' (2003, p 242). This perceived attractiveness has three associated problems. First, the possibility of a rise of the use of custody and, second, the risk that, with an influx of new cases, the probation service would be inundated and would adopt a 'tick box' form of supervision, thereby undermining its potential benefits (Maguire, 2007). Third, implementation has significant resource implications.

Precisely for these reasons, custody plus was never implemented, although custody minus has been brought into practice as the Suspended Sentence Order. That change of name is significant in terms of public perception of the sentence and reflecting the fact that this sentence could, in fact, be tougher and longer than the proposed custody plus (Roberts, 2003).

Suspended Sentence Order

The provisions for the Suspended Sentence Order are contained in Section 189 of the Act. Effectively, when making a custodial sentence of 28-51 weeks, the court can choose to suspend the period of imprisonment and to impose a set of requirements that the offender must comply with in the community. These are the same requirements that are available for the community order outlined in Chapter Ten, and superficially it may seem that these orders are very similar, particularly where the offender complies and never actually goes to prison. However, there are three significant differences: first, because the Suspended Sentence Order is a custodial sentence, the court is restricted to making an order in situations where it judges that the offence or offences before it are 'so serious' that only a custodial sentence can be justified; second, if a Suspended Sentence Order is breached, there is a presumption that the offender will go to custody; and, third, commission of a further offence while subject to a Suspended Sentence Order constitutes a breach of the order, which is not the case with the community order.

Three terms are significant here:

- *the custodial period* is the maximum period that will be served in prison if the sentence is activated;
- *the operational* period refers to the length of time that the sentence is suspended;
- *the supervision period* refers to the time for the requirements stipulated by the court to be completed. This must be shorter than the operational period.

When sentencing, the courts must detail both the operational and supervision periods, which may run from 26 weeks to two years. It will be expected that report authors would give guidance to sentencers wherever relevant. The full range of requirements available for community orders can be used for Suspended Sentence Orders, including those relating to drug, alcohol and mental health treatment. However, it is not automatic that a supervision requirement per se will be part of the order and it should also be noted that, whereas a community order may contain requirements running for up to three years, for a Suspended Sentence Order, the maximum period is two years.

Suitability is a key consideration for this sentence. Although it is similar to a community order in many respects, but with an almost automatic custodial penalty for breach, it is nevertheless a custodial sentence and is treated as such for the purpose of the Rehabilitation of Offenders Act 1984. This means that there is a longer period before the conviction becomes 'spent' than would be the case if a community sentence had been given.

PC 25/2005 additionally notes that, if a substantial programme of rehabilitative work is required, then a community sentence should be considered instead, pointing out that community sentences can still be imposed even where a court has judged that an offence is above the custody threshold. The guidelines from the Sentencing Guidelines Council further state that:

> Because of the very clear deterrent threat involved in a suspended sentence, requirements imposed as part of that sentence should generally be less onerous than those imposed as part of a community sentence. A court wishing to impose onerous or intensive requirements on an offender should reconsider its decision to suspend sentence and consider whether a community sentence would be more appropriate. (2005, p 25, para 2.2.14)

The situation regarding breach of a Suspended Sentence Order is rather compromised by the non-implementation of custody plus. It had been envisaged that if the custodial element had to be activated, this would involve revoking the order and replacing it with a custody plus order, stipulating a new and potentially different range of requirements on its licence component. In the interim, custodial periods are being imposed with no licence supervision on release, except for offenders under 21 who still have a statutory three months on notice of supervision (Section 65 of the Criminal Justice Act 1991).

The Suspended Sentence Order is nevertheless proving relatively popular, with 41,005 being made in 2008, 5,959 of these on women (Ministry of Justice, 2010b). Concerns around their use centres on the low completion rates at only 37 per cent in 2006 (Ministry of Justice, 2007a) and, again, the lack of variety and innovation in the requirements added to the order (Mair et al, 2008).

Intermittent custody

This was implemented in pilot areas after January 2004 but hit a range of practical problems and, with the current pressure created by prison overcrowding, it has again been shelved. Nevertheless, it was an interesting proposition and borrowed extensively from custodial practices in other jurisdictions, the Netherlands in particular. Indeed, different models of intermittent or 'part-time' custody are so embedded elsewhere that Roberts (2003) comments that it is surprising that it had previously been considered as an option.

The concept of intermittent custody is that a number of days would be served in custody over a stipulated period, but that these need not be served consecutively. In theory, an offender could maintain a job in the community and return to custody for a 48-hour period at weekends. In practice, this creates challenges for managing bed spaces, particularly as the intention is that intermittent offenders should not serve their custodial time alongside 'full-time' prisoners, as it was felt that mixing would undermine the goal of enabling the intermittent prisoner to maintain community links and to promote rehabilitation.

The provisions relating to intermittent custody are contained in Sections 183–186 of the Criminal Justice Act 2003. The number of days in custody must be a minimum of 14 up to a maximum of 90, to be served over a period of between 28 and 51 weeks for a single offence. The same licence conditions are available as for custody plus and in general it is advised that this sentence would be unsuitable for drug or alcohol misusing offenders, and also for sexual or other violent offenders.

Standard determinate sentence

This has replaced the automatic conditional and discretionary conditional release (ACR and DCR) arrangements of the Criminal Justice Act 1991 for all offences committed on or after 4 April 2005. The new provisions in Section 249 are more demanding than the previous ones, because the offender, having served half the sentence in custody, must be supervised for the entirety of the other half in the community. This obviously involves a greater restriction of liberty, and the Sentencing Guidelines Council suggested that the courts should recognise this by reducing all fixed term custodial sentences by a factor of 15 per cent. Section 234 allows courts to suggest requirements that might be appropriate for the licence period, but generally these will be set while in custody, taking account of work undertaken in the prison. The role of the Parole Board has changed and they are no longer involved in decisions about release of these determinate sentenced prisoners, as they were in the DCR arrangements.

Extended sentences for public protection

Extended and indeterminate sentences for public protection are in many senses the most explicit renunciation of the 'just deserts' principles of the Criminal Justice Act 1991, which sought to get rid of previous provisions dating from 1967 that allowed longer sentences than would otherwise be warranted for certain offenders in the name of public protection.

The term 'extended sentence' was recycled by the Crime and Disorder Act 1998 in relation to 'extended licence periods' (Stone, 2007b) and has been expanded in the provisions contained in Section 227.

Extended sentences are available for offenders over 18 who are convicted of a violent or sexual offence where

- The offence is a 'specified offence' as identified by Schedule 15 of the Act
- The offence is *not* a 'serious offence' ie one that carries a maximum penalty of 10 years imprisonment or more
- The offender represents a *significant risk* to members of the public of *serious harm* by committing further 'specified offences'.

In these circumstances, the court was originally required to impose an extended period of licence supervision, up to a maximum of five years for violent offenders and eight years for sexual offenders. The Criminal Justice and Immigration Act, however, amended Section 227(2) so that the court 'may' rather than 'must' pass an extended sentence.

The offender is eligible for release from the halfway point of the basic sentence, disregarding the extension period. Although this was initially subject to Parole Board approval, following the Criminal Justice and Immigration Act 2008, release is now automatic.

There are provisions for licences relating to extended sentences to be revoked after review by the Parole Board (Schedule 18).

Indeterminate sentences of imprisonment for public protection

Section 225 contains provisions allowing for the indeterminate imprisonment of offenders where:

- the offence is a *specified offence* as identified by Schedule 15;

- the offence is also a *serious offence* carrying a maximum penalty of 10 years imprisonment or more (detailed in Schedule 15A); and
- the offender represents a *significant risk* to members of the public of *serious harm* by committing further *specified offences*.

Both this and the extended sentence provisions are focused on possible future behaviours, rather than past offences. *Serious harm* is defined in Section 224(3) as *death or serious personal injury, whether physical or psychological.*

The original 2003 legislation required that the court should make an indeterminate sentence of imprisonment for public protection in every case where a life sentence was not appropriate but where the court considered that the three criteria above relating to specified offences, serious offences and risk and serious harm were met. This has been relaxed for sentencing occasions after 14 July 2008 under Section 13 of the Criminal Justice and Immigration Act 2008, which allows the courts greater discretion and imposes a seriousness threshold. This requires that the offence must merit at least two years of actual custodial time before a sentence of imprisonment for public protection can be passed. In addition, the court is no longer bound to presume dangerousness in all cases where the offender has a previous conviction for a specified offence.

Significantly, national standards guidance suggests that court reports should not contain specific proposals for IPP sentences, and that the court must make its own determination of the type of custody most appropriate for the case before it.

Although the court would not set an end date for an IPP sentence, it should identify a minimum period that it would expect the offender to serve in custody. This tends to be colloquially referred to as 'the tariff' and is based on the sentence that would have been passed had the offender not been considered to be at risk of causing *serious harm*, taking into account aggravating and mitigating factors and discounts for guilty pleas.

Release is dependent on the Parole Board and the offender must be subject to licence, which can be revoked after a 10-year period by the Secretary of State on the Parole Board's recommendation. From January 2008, Phase III of the implementation plan for the OMM extended it to the growing number of prisoners in this category (approximately 3,400 at that point; Ministry of Justice, 2007b).

The Prison Reform Trust has been an outspoken critic of sentences of imprisonment for public protection, arguing that early statistics showed that these sentences were being used for relatively minor offences and for younger people rather than the concerning recidivists for whom they were intended. The average (median) tariff was initially as little as 30 months, which does not suggest the level of seriousness that would be appropriate for such sentences (Prison Reform Trust, 2007). Furthermore, there were – and continue to be – concerns about the efficient release of prisoners on such indeterminate sentences. The Prison Reform Trust has commented that:

This warehousing of IPP prisoners, stuck in bureaucratic tailbacks, is crucial. It strikes at the heart of what makes prisons run smoothly and what promotes rehabilitation: fairness. People going into prison need to be offered an implicit bargain that goes along these lines: if you behave yourself and work towards rehabilitation, you will progress through your sentence, earn more privileges and eventually win your release more quickly than otherwise. Instead of a clear, responsible bargain like that being offered to IPP prisoners, they are waiting in limbo, waiting out endless years on the packed and transitory landings of Victorian local prisons. (2007, p 6)

Although there is a degree of flowery rhetoric in that statement, it is useful to reflect on the Woolf and Tumin report on the Strangeways riot in 1991, which argued that a stable prison system should be built on the three pillars of security, control and justice (Woolf and Tumin, 1991). What is effectively 'bed-blocking', with large numbers of prisoners serving indeterminate sentences is deeply problematic for an overcrowded prison estate which is already under extreme stress and which will have increasing problems establishing the foundations that will ensure stability in the system.

Recognising the criticisms and concerns of campaigners, judiciary and criminal justice professionals, in July 2007, Jack Straw, then Minister for Justice, announced a review of these sentences. The amendments to these sentences contained in the Criminal Justice and Immigration Act 2008 are a response to some of these concerns and, in particular, the overuse of public protection sentences. Unsurprisingly, further amendments can be expected as part of the Coalition's sentencing reforms (Ministry of Justice, 2010a).

Re-settlement of prisoners

Re-settlement has become an increasingly important element of probation service and voluntary sector activity, but is not without its challenges, particularly given the difficulties in engaging and sustaining contact with offenders in custody. Moreover, although the term is widely used in criminal justice circles, it is not always clear what is meant (Maguire, 2007). However, a useful definition of re-settlement is presented in the *Dictionary of probation and offender management*, and this seems a helpful starting point:

> Beginning inside the prison – some would say even from the first day of sentence – "resettlement" is the process of reintegration back into the community in a positive and managed way. It continues after release and is the core component of a period of supervision on licence, because it targets the criminogenic risks of an offender and aims to reduce them. Good resettlement should decrease the risk of re-offending and, in the case of dangerous offenders, limit the risks posed. (Mead, 2007, p 268)

What, then, constitutes 'good re-settlement'? Certainly attention to the insights of the Social Exclusion Unit and the seven pathways arising from *Reducing re-offending by ex-prisoners* (2002) and featuring in the regional Reducing Re-Offending Action Plans:

- accommodation
- education, training and employment
- mental and physical health
- drugs and alcohol
- finance, benefit and debt
- maintaining relationships with children and families
- attitudes, thinking and behaviour.

Offenders in prison typically have multiple and complex needs. This may be particularly so for women who tend to be held further from their home areas and are more likely to have sole responsibility for dependent children. Yet, whereas re-settlement work has historically adopted a welfare model and has offered interventions around the areas outlined above, Maguire notes a different emphasis in the NOMS version of re-settlement, which is characterised by:

- A strong focus on offending behaviour and its reduction;
- Systematic assessment of offenders' needs and risks by professional staff;
- A focus on the "needs" thought to be "criminogenic" or to heighten risk;
- A degree of compulsion to co-operate in rehabilitative activities;
- Work on attitudes, thinking skills and/or motivation; and
- Increasingly strict enforcement of attendance requirements and other conditions of release. (2007, p 407)

This throws much of the responsibility back onto the offender, and a critical voice could argue that help and assistance is given because of its utility in reducing risk of offending rather than as a social good in itself. Maguire discusses a more empathetic and collaborative way of working with prisoners, based on desistance models, although the theoretical underpinnings of such an approach are still relatively undeveloped (2007).

Individual relationships and engagement is one aspect of re-settlement, but equally important are the managerial and structural arrangements to support it. The sentencing provisions outlined in this chapter broadly speaking promote re-settlement for short-term prisoners, although this has been limited for those serving under 12 months by the moratorium on implementing custody plus. Greater emphasis is also being placed on longer-term prisoners and, under the principle of *resources follow risk*, at least in theory they will receive more sustained attention while in custody and greater intervention on release. Whether this is experienced as assistance or intrusion by the majority of offenders subject to more rigorous conditions is debatable, and there must be questions in the current resourcing climate about the probation service's ability to 'make supervision meaningful' rather than focused on enforcement.

That said, the creation of NOMS was largely motivated by the perceived need to coordinate the work of the prison and probation services and to make sentences more coherent. The Carter review in 2003 found the penal system dominated by the need to manage both services, rather than focusing on offenders and reducing re-offending, and advocated a more strategic 'end to end approach' (2003).

NOMS is clearly still developing as an organisation, and there are challenges in relation to change and staff morale in both the major services involved, as well as in relation to public opinion and confidence. Yet despite risk associated with potential political backlash and other as yet untried innovations, such as contracting out of offender management services and greater voluntary sector involvement, Maguire is broadly optimistic, on the one hand:

> In comparison with the bleak situation of less than a decade ago, when the problems of people coming out of prison were virtually ignored (or worse, ex-prisoners were deliberately excluded from services for people in need), the current prospects for resettlement are encouraging. The level of government interest is unprecedented, as is the attention the issue is receiving from non-criminal justice agencies. (2007, p 416)

Yet, on the other hand, he is very aware of the enormity of making progress in this area because of the sheer scale of the social and personal problems afflicting prisoners and ex-prisoners (2007).

Work with offenders in custody

As indicated above, for most prisoners work towards re-settlement should begin at an early stage of the sentence so they are given assistance with immediate personal problems and so that longer-term strategies to improve the social circumstances into which they will be released can be established. This necessarily requires communication and cooperation between the offender manager back in the home community and the offender supervisor and key workers in the prison setting. This is where the OMM's concept of the *team around the offender* is most salient – a lack of teamwork and joint understanding may have negative impacts on the prisoner's experience and chances of 'doing things differently' on release.

Currently, the OMM is in place for specific offender groups in custody, rather than all prisoners. These groups include PPOs, offenders assessed as posing a high risk of serious harm and those sentenced to an indeterminate sentence of imprisonment for public protection under the Criminal Justice Act 2003. In these cases, the offender manager is expected to take the lead role in the assessment process and to chair sentence planning meetings, bringing together the contributions of practitioners from both the prison and the community. It may be a challenge for the offender manager to be authoritative and to be in control of the process when not on his or her own territory and where the offender supervisor and key workers in the prison may have more knowledge of the prisoner based on greater levels of contact. Nevertheless, the offender manager's task is to promote a collaborative process and to ensure clarity about roles, responsibilities and allocated tasks taken on by the different professionals involved and, indeed, the prisoner.

The written sentence plan should be completed within eight weeks of sentence where the prisoner has less than two years to serve in custody before release or tariff date, and 16 weeks in all other cases. This should be integrated with any other individual plans in place for the offender, for instance, relating to learning needs, mental health or multi-agency risk management plans. The sentence plan and associated risk assessment should be kept under review in line with national standards requirements.

Summary

The provisions for custodial sentencing are complex and they have been made even more so by the sentences for public protection (extended and IPP sentences) introduced by the Criminal Justice Act 2003. Over the past two decades, the balance of the probation service's work has swung decisively towards custody and working with prisoners, pre- and post-release. This requires the prison and probation services to develop closer relationships, particularly concerning prisoners assessed as high risk of harm and/or re-offending. Prison establishments are starting to look outwards and to consider how to prepare prisoners for life outside the prison gate, while offender managers are in a better position to more fully appreciate the patterns and processes of prison life and the psychological impact of the closed environment on both prisoners and prison staff. This is a major shift for both services, and relationships at strategic and at practitioner level are still often uncomfortable, which is exacerbated where lack of resources mean that probation visits to prisons are restricted. Nevertheless, practice has developed in a positive direction, assisted by policies and statutory requirements, so that some progress – albeit stumbling and imperfect – has been made towards the aspiration of *end-to-end offender management.*

Further reading

Carlen, P. and Worrall, A. (2004) *Analysing women's imprisonment*, Cullompton: Willan.

Maguire, M. (2007) 'The resettlement of ex-prisoners', in L. Gelsthorpe and R. Morgan (eds) *Handbook of probation*, Cullompton: Willan, Chapter 14.

Scott, D. and Codd, H. (2010) *Controversial issues in prisons*, Maidenhead: Open University Press.

TWELVE

Engagement and enforcement

Having outlined the key legislation relating to both community and custodial sentences in the previous two chapters, this chapter turns to the management of sentences. The first area of discussion relates to the introduction and the development of guidance for the probation service over the past 15 years, in the form of national standards, with associated debates about accountability, professional autonomy, consistency and managerialism. The current standards now apply to all agencies involved in offender management, underlining the importance of collective efforts to secure compliance and to enforce statutory orders and licences with rigour.

The chapter then considers enforcement practice and the role of discretion, which is still present in that process although more constrained than previously. Finally, a broader discussion considers the extent to which there is room to concentrate upon engagement, motivation and compliance rather than punitive actions.

So what is enforcement?

Nicholls' definition is helpful and succinct, pointing to the changes in the probation service's practices and approach explored in this chapter:

> Action taken by the probation service in response to non-compliance, either through the courts in relation to community orders, or through executive recall to prison in the case of the vast majority of post-release licences.
>
> Few areas of probation practice illustrate the changes in function, culture and activity that have taken place in the probation service as emblematically as enforcement. (2007, p 120)

It is evident that enforcement has been highly significant for the probation service and it will assume increasing importance for those voluntary agencies assuming roles in either the management or delivery of community sentences.

Development of national standards

Although national guidance and standards had been published in 1989 for community service (as it was then known), the legal basis for a comprehensive set of national standards covering most aspects of probation service activity came in the Criminal Justice Act 1991. Section 15 allowed the Secretary of State to issue regulations in respect of probation supervision and community service. The

Criminal Justice Act also established the probation inspectorate on a statutory footing to monitor the work of the probation service, with reference to the first set of standards published in 1992. These developments evidenced the managerialism, the demand for greater accountability and the challenge to unfettered professional autonomy characteristic of that period (Morgan, 2007).

Despite reservations expressed by probation officers and their union, national standards quickly became a relatively routine part of practice and did have a role in clarifying expectations and minimum quality standards:

> National Standards were intended to enhance quality, constituting an essential assurance to courts about how orders would be implemented and what they might expect from the probation service; they increased consistency, so that the character and frequency of dealings with the service no longer depended on the judgement (and perhaps idiosyncrasies) of the supervising officer; and they also made it very clear to offenders what was expected and what would follow in the event of non-compliance. (Canton and Eadie, 2007, p 186)

National standards undoubtedly promoted more consistency and could be said to have improved probation supervision during the 1990s in the sense that offenders were much more aware of contact requirements, for instance. One view is that, as a consequence of this, offenders might be potentially more empowered within a supervisory relationship where the issues of authority were more overt and less arbitrary. Alternatively, critics have argued that consistency does not necessarily equate with fairness (Eadie, 2007), and that the standards have reduced the ability of officers to respond to the diverse and often unique characteristics of offenders, contributing also to a process of deprofessionalisation. As progressive versions of national standards became harsher and more focused on enforcement (Gelsthorpe and Morgan, 2007), these concerns grew.

The 2007 version of national standards was issued by the Ministry of Justice, rather than the National Probation Service and applied to all providers of offender management services commissioned by NOMS. In relation to the above comments, it is interesting to note in the introduction to the standards the NOMS expectation that offender management, interventions and activities will be carried out:

> With due regard to the human rights, dignity and safety of offenders, victims and partners, and that services will be responsive to the diverse needs and circumstances encountered in correctional work. (Ministry of Justice, 2007b, p 3)

There was also a new section in the standards addressing the experience of the offender, which partly focuses on transparency of processes, information and expectations but, in addition, identifies that offenders should be active participants in assessments, planning and reviews 'wherever possible'. Furthermore, Standard 3.6 expressed an ambitious expectation that:

Offenders experience their relationships with staff as being characterised by:

- Courtesy, respect and the valuing of diversity
- Enthusiasm and commitment
- The encouragement of compliance and co-operation
- Recognition and reward for achievement and progress
- The firm, fair and legitimate use of authority
- Behaviour that models pro-social and anti-criminal attitudes, cognitions and behaviours
- The teaching of problem-solving skills
- Help to access wider community-based resources and facilities
- Encouragement to take responsibility for behaviour and its consequences. (Ministry of Justice, 2007b, p 52)

Interesting tensions could be found here between these expectations and other aspects of the standards, such as enforcement, that are more easily measured and translated into performance targets. It is also significant to note that rehabilitation was placed fifth out of the five aims for offender management stated in these standards.

The contents of Standard 3.6 applied to all offender management activity, not just those explicitly aimed at rehabilitation, but the way the probation service and other criminal justice agencies conduct their business, establish relationships with offenders and follow processes that respect diversity and rights, are important in rehabilitation, reintegration and, ultimately, reduction of offending. The critical question is how far it was possible to exercise 'firm, fair, legitimate authority' within this particular enforcement regime and what that might actually mean in terms of supervisory relationships.

Focus on enforcement

It is useful to chart the historical development of enforcement work in the probation service, before looking at the actual legal provisions. Until the first version of national standards, there was no clarity of expectation about when and how swiftly offenders might be breached for non-compliance. The tightening up of regulations for enforcement after the Criminal Justice Act 1991 was an evident part of the government's intention to present the probation service as a credible and demanding 'punishment in the community'. However, this did not have immediate effect on practice on the ground. The following quote from George Mair and Rob Canton illustrates the difference between current attitudes and:

> The situation ten years ago, when enforcement of community penalties tended to be seen as one of the more distasteful tasks of a probation officer and to be avoided if at all possible. Lax and inconsistent practice with regard to enforcement is indefensible and the introduction of

National Standards began the process of tightening up the enforcement of community penalties.

> No matter how onerous the requirements of a community sentence, it comes to little if it is not enforced ... a passive or recalcitrant prisoner is still being punished; an unenforced community penalty, by contrast, is indistinguishable from impunity. (2007, p 270)

Successive Quality and Effectiveness reports from HMI Probation in the 1990s continued to show poor rates of enforcement and, in 1997, data from HMI Probation indicated that breach rates were as low as 30 per cent for Probation Orders. This meant that only 30 per cent of offenders who should have been subject to breach proceedings actually had actions taken against them in line with national standards (Home Office, 1999). Responding to this, a Key Performance Indicator for the service was introduced in 1998, which stipulated a stringent enforcement target of 90 per cent. Guidance from the Home Office (PC 3/99) detailed the actions that services should be taking to help sharpen their practice. The Association of Chief Officers of Probation also committed itself to two enforcement audits to provide further impetus for improvement (Hedderman and Hearden, 2000).

While enforcement rates have improved and the target of 90 per cent has since been achieved, concerns have been raised about the focus on this target:

> Welcoming the findings of the second audit in April 2000, ACOP's [Association of Chief Officers of Probation] chair said, "Enforcement is for probation what waiting lists are for hospitals, detection rates are for the police and exam results are for schools" (*Guardian*, 12 April 2006: 6). The comparison is almost too apt: all such headline statistics invite scepticism about whether the right things are being measured in the right way and suspicions of sleights of hand in counting rules, the introduction of perverse incentives and distorting effects on practice. (Mair and Canton, 2007, p 207)

Furthermore:

> In the particular matter of enforcement, is the public to expect high or low rates of breach? Would a high rate demonstrate the probation service's robust response to non-compliance – or failure to engage offenders in the process of supervision? Would a low rate show the service's success in gaining compliance and giving effect to the orders of the court – or that officers were negligent in their response to breach? (Mair and Canton, 2007, p 207)

These are truly pertinent questions, and it is interesting to note that a renewed interest in securing engagement and compliance was evident in the extracts from the 2007 national standards quoted earlier and is supported by the growing literature on desistance. Interestingly, the new framework for National Standards issued under the Coalition government in April 2011 shows a strikingly different approach, with a focus on outcomes, not enforcement processes, and willingness to explore use of practitioner discretion. As Mair and Canton identify, two future challenges for the service – and offender management generally – are:

- the need to take (and to be seen to take) enforcement seriously, without breaching too many offenders; and
- the need to shift the balance from enforcement to compliance without compromising credibility. (adapted from Mair and Canton 2007)

This subject is explored further in the later parts of this chapter, while the following sections detail the changes in legal provisions relating to enforcement.

Enforcement under the Criminal Justice Act 1991

Enforcement powers in relation to community sentences (Probation, Community Service, Combination and Curfew Orders) were contained in Schedule 2 of the Criminal Justice Act 1991. Once information had been laid before the magistrates relating to an alleged breach, the magistrates could issue a summons to court or a warrant. At the court appearance, if the offender admitted or was found to be in breach, the magistrates could impose a fine, a Community Service Order or Attendance Centre Order, and allow the original community sentence to continue. It could also choose to revoke and resentence for the original offences, provided that the community sentence had been made in the Magistrates' Court.

There are several important features that differ from the current enforcement powers contained in the Criminal Justice Act 2003 community order:

- the legislation used the term 'may impose' in relation to penalties for breach – this meant the court could simply warn or admonish the offender and allow the order to continue without amendment. This was a course of action frequently proposed by probation officers and referred to as a 'disciplinary breach', that is, used primarily to secure future compliance;
- the Magistrates' Court could only revoke and resentence orders made in the Magistrates' Court and had to commit to Crown Court cases involving orders made in the Crown Court where there was a denial of breach or a recommendation to revoke and resentence;
- the Magistrates' Court had the power to amend orders and could remove requirements where this was considered appropriate and, sometimes, pragmatic, for instance, where an offender's circumstances had changed;
- until 1997, an offender still had to give consent before a community order could be made although persistent refusal to comply with reporting and other instructions was considered a de facto withdrawal of consent; and
- magistrates were required to consider the extent of compliance in determining an appropriate penalty, in line with the principle of proportionality.

This framework allowed for a reasonable degree of flexibility in dealing with breaches and it should also be noted that the initial versions of national standards allowed for three missed probation appointments before breach and were also more lenient in terms of community service absences than has been the case in later versions. In addition, court proceedings were less speedy than is currently the case, and probation would often continue to offer offenders appointments pending their court appearance, with the intention of giving them the opportunity to demonstrate renewed commitment to supervision.

The basic requirements of a Probation Order were for the offender to keep in touch with the supervising officer and to inform of any change of address. As outlined in Chapter Ten on community sentences, various conditions could be added, such as residence, activities, attendance at a day centre or drugs interventions. In legal terms, any breach action had to be specific about the grounds for breach, the particular allegations of non-compliance and the requirement of the order that had been breached. For Combination Orders, which were new under the 1991 Act, if the offender failed to comply with one element of the order, the whole order was deemed to be in breach.

Under the Criminal Justice Act 1991 provisions, the courts were also responsible for breach matters relating to post-custody licences for offenders serving less than four years. Their powers were restricted to a fine and suspension of licence, effectively a recall. Section 38, which contained these provisions, was subsequently revoked by Section 103 of the Crime and Disorder Act 1998, which required that breach of all custodial licences relating to offences committed on or after 1 January 1999 be referred to the Parole Unit – a move away from deliberations in the court arena and towards the extensive recall arrangements currently in place.

Changes in 2000

Two important developments occurred in 2000, the first of which was the publication of a new set of national standards for adult orders. A separate set of standards was issued alongside this by the Youth Justice Board (YJB) governing the activities of the reformed youth justice system, as orders for young people were transferred from the probation service and local authority social services departments to the new YOTs.

The revised adult standards increased the severity of enforcement by requiring that, for community sentences, offenders would be returned to court after the second unexplained or unacceptable failure to comply within a 12-month period. The previous standards had allowed two failures before a third was returned to court and there had been no specific time frame attached. Deviation from the new standard would require line management authorisation. Practitioner discretion was thus limited in relation to breach actions and also in terms of setting levels of contact less than the national standards minimum.

There was also a tightening up in relation to licence supervision, with the requirement for approval at assistant chief officer level or equivalent if the offender was not to be breached after the third unacceptable failure.

Second, new provisions in the Criminal Justice and Court Services Act 2000 created a presumption in favour of a custodial penalty for breach. Significantly, the custody threshold (the *so serious* criterion) did not apply in breach proceedings as it would have done on the original sentencing occasion, thus widening the scope for imposing imprisonment in cases where the original offence was relatively minor.

The combination of new legal provisions and new national standards significantly raised the stakes in terms of penalties for the offender's non-compliance, particularly coupled with the trend towards more restrictions and requirements on orders, making it ever easier to breach (Mair and Canton, 2007). These changes also raised the stakes for the probation service, because the 90 per cent enforcement target was now being measured against these more rigorous standards.

The Halliday report, *Making punishments work* (2001), described the then enforcement framework as:

> An unnecessarily complicated patchwork of "enforcement" activity, with no consistent principles underlying the current legislation, structures and practices – and, worse. Real risks of inequity of treatment of a similar act of non-compliance, depending on the type of licence and the procedures that apply. (2001, p 45)

Community sentences under the Criminal Justice Act 2003

The Criminal Justice Act 2003 provisions for the generic community sentence were intended to respond to the suggestions of the Halliday report and to rationalise the community sentencing landscape, including the enforcement of sentences. Schedule 8 of the Act details the provisions relating to revocation, amendment and breach of community orders, including procedures for warnings in paragraph 5.

Alleged breaches of orders made in the Magistrates' Court must be returned to the Magistrates' Court. Crown Court orders should be returned to the Crown Court, unless a direction has been made at the time of sentencing that the Magistrates' Court has the power to deal with breach matters. Even where a direction of this kind has been made, the magistrates may still choose to send the order back to Crown Court for sentencing.

If the offender admits or is found to be in breach, five items are of note:

- The court cannot allow the order to continue without amendment.
- The court must impose more onerous requirements if it wishes the order to continue, but can only choose from those available at the time of the original sentence.

- An unpaid work requirement may be imposed for 20 hours or more where unpaid work was not one of the original requirements.
- The court can impose a custodial sentence of up to 51 weeks for persistent and wilful non-compliance even where the order in question was made in respect of a non-imprisonable offence.
- The presumption in favour of custody has been removed.

The powers of the Crown Court are comparable to those of the Magistrates' Court although, if the offender is resentenced to a custodial sentence for an imprisonable offence, the powers of the Crown Court are obviously greater.

The National Implementation Guide for the Criminal Justice Act 2003 sentences (PC 25/2005) clarifies the powers in relation to paragraph 9:1(a) above:

> 5.4.2 Following a breach of a Community Order, the court must:
>
> - amend the Order so as to impose more onerous requirements which the court could include if it were making the Order, that is:
>   - amend any of the existing requirements to make them more onerous (provided it does not extend them beyond the maximum length available), and/or
>   - substitute any of the existing requirements with another of a different type and length which is more onerous, and/or add one or more further requirements
>
> In amending the Order, the court cannot extend the original length of the Order by which all the requirements must be completed. (PC 25/2005, p 85)

The Guidance goes on to say that the court is not able to:

- take no action
- issue a warning or
- impose a fine

and still to allow the order to continue. Although this would seem to represent a significant escalation in the penalties for breach, it is worth noting the guidance from the Sentencing Guidelines Council:

> Having decided that a community sentence is commensurate with the seriousness of the offence, the *primary* objective when sentencing for breach of requirements is to ensure that those requirements are completed. (2005, p 13)

The purpose of sentencing for breach in the court is not therefore primarily punishment, and the principle of proportionality is still strongly present. The guidance further goes on to state that:

- Custody should be a last resort and reserved for cases of deliberate and repeated breach.
- Before increasing the onerousness of requirements, sentencers should take account of the offender's ability to comply and should avoid precipitating breach by overloading the offender with too many or conflicting requirements.
- There may be cases where the court will need to consider resentencing to a differently constructed community sentence in order to secure compliance with the purposes of the original sentence.

This is in many respects a tougher regime for sentencing breaches than the one in place under the Criminal Justice Act 1991. Nevertheless, there is room for offender managers to think creatively about changing and amending orders and ensuring their suitability for the offender, bearing in mind proportionality and justice.

Treatment requirements

A separate note about treatment requirements is needed here. Schedule 8, paragraph 11(1), states that an offender with a DRR, ATR or mental health treatment requirement should not be considered to have breached by virtue of refusing to undergo surgical, electrical or other procedures, if this is deemed reasonable in the circumstances by the court. This is an important safeguard in terms of coerced treatment and considerations of bodily integrity.

An offender on a DRR, however, can be breached for failure to provide a urine or other required sample, but not for testing positively for Class A drugs (although this may be viewed as a failure to participate in treatment).

Treatment requirements may only be amended with the consent of the offender.

Suspended Sentence Orders

The enforcement of Suspended Sentence Orders is dealt with in Schedule 12 of the Act and relates to both non-compliance with the requirements of the order and further offending within the period of suspension (the operational period). In this respect, Suspended Sentence Orders differ from the community sentence where a further conviction does not represent a breach.

If the offender admits or is found to be in breach, the court may:

- order the offender to serve the whole of the custodial period that had been suspended; or
- order the offender to serve a custodial period shorter than the one originally suspended.

The presumption is that a custodial period will be imposed. However, under paragraph 8(3), if the court considers this would be unjust in view of all the circumstances, it must do one of the following:

- impose more onerous community requirements;
- extend the operational period; or
- extend the supervision period.

The total operational period once extended cannot be more than the maximum two years, and the supervision period, if extended, must still be either the same or shorter than the operational period.

The Sentencing Guidelines Council suggests that:

> Where the court decides to amend a suspended sentence order rather than activate the custodial sentence, it should give serious consideration to extending the supervision or operational periods (within statutory limits) rather than making the requirements more onerous. (2005, p 26)

Again, advice from the probation service may be critical in influencing outcomes and determining what might be most constructive for the offender, while still acknowledging the breach. Because of the nature of the order, the custodial period for a Suspended Sentence Order must be 51 weeks or less and this means that, without implementation of custody plus, any offender aged over 22 will be released without further supervision.

A Suspended Sentence Order cannot be revoked and resentenced, except where custody is imposed, so the only non-custodial outcome is an amended order.

Custodial licences

There are standard sets of conditions on all post-custody licences to which additional requirements can be imposed according to the case in question. Some prisoners are released early under Home Detention Curfew and will have special licences for that additional period at liberty.

Conditions for young offender notices of supervision and licences on standard determinate and extended sentences

- To keep in touch with your supervising officer in accordance with any instructions you may be given.
- If required, to receive visits from your supervising officer at your home/place of residence (eg approved premises).
- Permanently to reside at an address approved by your supervising officer and notify him or her in advance of any proposed changes of address or any propose stay (even for one night) away from that approved address.
- Undertake only such work (including voluntary work) approved by your supervising officer and notify him or her in advance of any change.
- Not to travel outside the UK unless otherwise directed by your supervising officer (permission for which will be given in exceptional circumstances only) or for the purposes of complying with immigration deportation/removal.

- To be well behaved, not to commit any offence and not to do anything that could undermine the purpose of your supervision, which is to protect the public, prevent you from re-offending and help you re-settle successfully into the community.

Conditions on licences for indeterminate sentence prisoners

- He/she shall place himself/herself under the supervision of whichever supervising officer is nominated for the purpose from time to time.
- He/she shall on release report to the supervising officer so nominated and shall keep in touch with that officer in accordance with that officer's instructions.
- He/she shall, if his/her supervising officer so requires, receive visits from that officer where the licence holder is living.
- He/she shall reside only where approved by his/her supervising officer.
- He/she shall undertake work, including voluntary work, only where approved by his/her supervising officer and shall inform that officer of any change in or loss of such employment.
- He/she shall not travel outside the UK without the prior permission of his/her supervising officer.
- He/she shall be well behaved and not do anything which could undermine the purposes of supervision on licence which are to protect the public, by ensuring that their safety would not be placed at risk, and to secure his/her successful reintegration into the community.

A note on young offenders

Whereas adults released from a sentence of 12 months have no statutory supervision, special arrangements exist for young offenders up to the age of 22. Young people in this category will be released on a notice of supervision for three months unless the young person reaches his or her 22nd birthday during that period, when the notice will cease to have effect. This will contain the same conditions as a standard determinate sentence licence but cannot have extra conditions added. It also differs from the standard determinate sentence in that breaches are dealt with in court, rather than through recall procedures, which reflects the origins of this provision in Section 65 of the Criminal Justice Act 1991.

About conditions

All licences contain a 'good behaviour' condition which is described by PC 29/2007 as a catch-all clause. This would cover incidents of abusive conduct or racist harassment, for instance, while on probation premises, but also such conduct in the community where there is sufficient evidence available through surveillance or other sources. In terms of court processes, it is much easier to prove the former, particularly where offenders have been given explicit guidance or instructions as to what constitutes inappropriate behaviour while engaged in activities with the probation service or on service premises.

The issues of proportionality and enforceability of conditions come to the fore when additional conditions are considered, particularly in exceptional circumstances where 'bespoke' conditions are being suggested. Requests for additional conditions will be made in most cases within the PD1 form completed before the offender's release. For certain long-term and indeterminate sentence prisoners, the request should be made in the Parole Assessment Report (PAROM1) for consideration by the Parole Board.

The responsibility for identifying appropriate additional conditions lies with the offender manager, although the need for special conditions may originally have been identified by an inter-agency risk meeting, such as a MAPPP. Annex A of PC 29/2007 contains a list of permitted licence conditions which must be justified in terms of:

- ensuring protection of the public;
- preventing re-offending; and/or
- securing the successful reintegration of the offender into the community.

They must also be lawful, that is, authorised by Statutory Instrument 648 of 2005 and compliant with Article 8 of the ECHR (right to respect for private and family life). PC 29/2007 further states that:

> … a condition must be a necessary and proportionate measure for the purposes of ensuring public safety and/or prevention of crime.

Before requesting additional conditions, offender managers should consider whether the 'good behaviour' condition would be sufficient to meet the purposes outlined above or whether more specific directions would help make expectations clearer and assist enforcement, where required.

In terms of more unusual 'bespoke' conditions, it would be useful to bear in mind the comments from Mair and Canton (2007) about community sentences being meaningless if not enforced. This can relate to the practicability of enforcement as well as willingness to enforce. It is necessary to consider whether conditions are being suggested where evidence of breach would be impractical to collect and/or prove at court. An example would be a curfew without electronic monitoring imposed on an offender living in supported accommodation where no staff are present at night.

Recall procedures

For determinate sentenced prisoners the powers of recall are contained in Section 254 of the Criminal Justice Act 2003. If an offender misses an appointment or fails to comply with another condition of his or her licence without acceptable explanation, the offender manager can issue up to two warnings before instigating recall. However, this is dependent on judgement of risk and if there are felt to be sufficient concerns about public safety, enforcement action (recall) can be initiated with the relevant regional team within the Public Protection Casework Section of NOMS of the Ministry of Justice immediately. Recall, of course, may also take place if further offences are committed triggering a SFO review, as discussed in Chapter Seven.

Procedures for recall are outlined in PC 14/2008. Further details of licences and recall can be found in Prison Service Order 6000 *Parole release and recall*.

A fuller discussion of imprisonment for public protection sentences and life licences is also covered in Chapter Eighteen.

Re-release following recall

Section 29 of the Criminal Justice and Immigration Act 200 has introduced changes in arrangements for the re-release of prisoners. The Act distinguishes three categories of prisoners who will be treated differently under these provisions:

- Prisoners serving a determinate sentence for offences which are not violent or sexual in nature (except where the recall took place during the period of Home Detention Curfew) – these prisoners will now be released automatically after 28 days rather than being referred to the Parole Board. This is known as a 'fixed term recall' (FTR).
- Prisoners serving a determinate sentence for violent or sexual crimes or who have been assessed as unsuitable or ineligible for FTR – the Secretary of State has discretion to release prisoners in this category if the probation service assessment suggests it is safe to do so. These cases will be referred to the Parole Board on their return to custody after 28 days. If kept in custody, the cases will now automatically be subject to Parole Board review every 12 months.
- Prisoners serving an extended sentence – these prisoners will only be re-released if recommended by the Parole Board.

Use of discretion

Use of discretion is a key element in striving for just and fair treatment within the criminal justice system, but it involves challenges and dilemmas for offender managers as neatly encapsulated in the words of Tina Eadie:

> The central conundrum around discretion is that justice requires sufficient regulation and predictability to guard against arbitrariness, while also needing to allow for exceptions to the rule. Linking this to offender management includes the question of when to return an individual to court for breach of a community sentence. While a probation officer might use his or her discretion in an arbitrary or

discriminatory way, a set of rules risks achieving bureaucratic sameness at the cost of ignoring relevant differences. (2007, p 94)

She describes the balance to be struck between consistency and flexibility as more of an art than a science, a potentially tricky series of judgements for practitioners.

Within the enforcement process there are points where professional discretion and judgement have important parts to play. These may include:

- whether to exceed minimum contact requirements in a particular case, as a response to risk or offender needs;
- the acceptability or otherwise of reasons that are given for non-compliance, and therefore whether warnings are given;
- whether an offender's risk is such that he or she should be returned to court or recalled after only one instance of non-compliance;
- whether to seek managerial authorisation not to breach on the second failure (community sentences) or third failure to comply (post-custody licences);
- whether to apply to the court for an order to be amended, rather than prosecuting breach, in cases where the offender is not judged to be at fault;
- preparation of breach reports, and particularly assessment of the extent to which the offender has complied and of motivation for future compliance;
- advice to the court on dealing with breaches, including appropriate amendments to orders;
- advice to the court about whether or not to activate the custodial element of a Suspended Sentence Order, in part or in full;
- information at the point of recall about an offender's suitability for fixed term recall.

This list is not exhaustive and, considering also the room for manoeuvre in offender management processes – arrangements for supervision, the timing and sequencing of requirements, for instance – it is evident that there is still considerable scope for professional judgement to be exercised in practice. Indeed, responding in a fair and just manner to the instances cited above requires resort to considerable professional understanding, knowledge and experience.

Compliance not punishment

Official attention is now turning from a punitive view of enforcement to looking more broadly at compliance and what might influence ability and willingness to comply. This has exercised the academic world for some time, as evidenced by Rob Canton:

There are no doubt many reasons why offenders fail to comply or comply variably with the legal requirements of supervision. "Can't comply" and "won't comply" are probably better seen as ends of a spectrum on which an instance of non-compliance can be plotted. Unless supervisors consider the reasons behind non-compliance, it is possible that their response will simply miss the point or make matters worse: their duty may be met by returning the offender to the court, but not enough will have been done to effect the required change in the offender. (2007b, p 58)

It is also significant that research studies have failed to find a positive link between tougher enforcement and lower reconviction rates (Hearnden and Millie, 2004), or have been based on such small samples that the results cannot be considered convincing (May and Wadwell, 2001). The renewed interest in engagement and securing compliance is therefore not surprising, as it represents an approach that is more respectful of offenders and their needs and rights (a moral good) and may at the same time be more effective in ensuring offenders' benefit from interventions and are enabled to reduce re-offending (an instrumental good).

A strong argument for this shift is presented in *Community penalties: Change and challenges,* as follows:

> Current practice relies predominantly on deterrent-based approaches for securing short-term compliance (compliance with requirements of orders). Such approaches do not necessarily get an offender out of bed or on the right bus to attend a programme in the community. A more imaginative, incentives based and encouragement-based approach might be more effective. This would rely on realistic incentives beyond the early discharge of an order. It might be fruitful to focus on the offender as citizen, based on an understanding of what motivates people to adopt law-abiding choices and lifestyles. (Bottoms et al, 2001, p 248)

The concluding sentence begins to refer to the psychology of compliance and, by extension, desistance, understanding of which may assist officers in the management of orders and the exercise of their authority. The model developed by Anthony Bottoms (2001, p 90) gives further insights into compliance which can be:

• instrumental/prudential	based on calculation of cost/benefits
• normative	acceptance of norm, linked to attachment and belief in legitimacy
• based on constraint	physical and other restrictions
• based on habit or routine	

A punishment-based version of enforcement is predicated on the assumption that threat of court action or recall is sufficient deterrent to cause reluctant offenders to comply, but many in contact with the probation service may already be de-sensitised to such threats. It is certainly more useful to consider normative compliance and the potential power of the supervisory relationship in keeping offenders engaged, giving incentives to participate and imparting or enhancing pro-social attitudes, behaviours and values. This is not to deny that incapacitation or deterrent threat may have roles with some offenders, as part of a broad strategy, but that longer-term compliance is likely to be more dependent on relationships and the social context around offenders.

If offender management is about promoting behavioural change, then securing compliance could well be an interim goal in that change process, as an offender learns to accept, negotiate and ultimately work with the authority of the probation service, used legitimately and with demonstrable fairness. Relatedly, McNeill and Weaver argue that 'securing and maintaining engagement, particularly in the project of change, is likely to depend on developing and sustaining relational legitimacy' (2010, p 43).

Returning to compliance, Hazel Kemshall, Rob Canton and colleagues conducted a study of programme attrition in the Welsh region of the probation service and, in that study, discussed the key characteristics of motivational work and pro-social modelling which they identified as:

- being clear about the supervisory role, including purpose and expectations of supervision, the appropriate use of authority, and the role of enforcement;
- pro-social modelling and reinforcement, involving clear expectations about required values and behaviours and their reinforcement through the use of rewards. Challenge and confrontation of undesirable behaviours and the discouragement of pro-criminal attitudes and values;
- negotiated problem-solving, clear objective setting, monitoring and accountability of the offender's progress; and
- honest, empathic relationship with an emphasis on persistence and belief in the offender's capacity to change. (Kemshall et al, 2002, p 24)

What seems noteworthy here is that the approach to authority/enforcement and the way that it is communicated is an integral part of the whole set of working relationships that help an offender make progress. Again, collaborative, problem-solving styles of working have been indicated as most effective in promoting desistance (for example, Rex, 1999) and in keeping sometimes very difficult offenders engaged. The chasing of compliance and sentence completion targets risks subverting the welcome focus on engagement and compliance, and creating inconsistencies in practice, undermining attempts to work in pro-social ways. The new approach indicated in the introduction of the April 2011 National Standards may be more helpful and allow more scope for professional judgement and creativity, so long as what emerges is more sensitive to the growing understanding of the psychology of compliance behaviours.

Summary

The recent approach to engagement and enforcement is indeed indicative of the changes that have taken place in the probation service over the past two decades and clearly the direction is about to change again. The enforcement regime has been stricter, but is also more transparent and accountable. This may have benefits for offenders, where it brings greater clarity about expectations and consistency in responses to non-compliance. However, enforcement is more than a mechanical and bureaucratic application of procedures; fair and just enforcement involves a sophisticated understanding of motivations to comply and ability to deal with offenders honestly and openly. Offender managers should seek to re-engage offenders wherever possible, re-stating rules and expectations and paying attention to internal and external barriers to compliance. Much of this will depend on the quality of relationships between the offender and the offender manager, and often with offender supervisors and others delivering interventions as well. As discussed in Chapter Four, such relationships can promote and facilitate the process of desistance, but this must start with the basics of compliance and engagement and then build from there.

Further reading

Robinson, A. (2010) *Stone's companion guide to enforcement* (4th edn), Andover: Sweet and Maxwell.

There is a useful collection of chapters also in
McNeill, F., Raynor, P. and Trotter, C. (eds) (2010) *Offender Supervision: New Directions in Theory, Research and Practice*, Cullompton: Willan.

Issues around engagement and legitimate use of authority are covered in:
Cherry, S. (2010) *Handbook for practitioners and managers transforming behaviour: Pro-social modelling in practice*, Cullompton: Willan.
Trotter, C. (2006) *Working with involuntary clients: A guide to practice*, London: Sage Publications.

Part Three
Offender management:
key areas of practice

THIRTEEN

Work with victims

This chapter focuses on the developing legal and policy frameworks with regard to the victims and witnesses agenda. This is a highly topical area within criminal justice as the primary focus of recent legislation has been to 're-balance the scales of justice' towards protecting the interests and needs of victims and witnesses and away from a concern for the rights of defendants.

The discussion explores explanations of the impetus for a shift in perspective in relation to victims, details the main legal and policy changes and looks at the current and still developing agenda, as well as identifying key issues for work with both victims and offenders. The chapter also introduces restorative justice as an alternative paradigm for criminal justice, and considers the difficulties of moving towards this more inclusive approach in the light of current penal thinking.

Victims coming in from the margins

The rhetoric around re-orientating the criminal justice system away from its concerns with defendants/offenders and towards a fuller appreciation of the needs of victims has been developing over a number of years. The victim perspective has been moving increasingly centre stage and, 'where once victims were best described as the "forgotten party" within criminal justice, now ... it has "become difficult politically to deny victims"' (Crawford and Enterkin, 2001, p 707). This is reflected in new responsibilities for all criminal justice agencies in relation to victims and particularly in the growing victim awareness agenda within the probation service. However, foregrounding victims brings its own challenges and raises dilemmas for the criminal justice system:

> As victims' access to justice has increased in recent decades in response to their real and perceived needs, so the question of victims' rights has emerged. When and if victims' needs should be redefined as rights is a debate that touches on underlying principles of justice. To put the victim at the heart of the criminal justice system is to reinterpret centuries of practice where the role between the State and offender has been central to the resolution of crime and the administration of justice in common law systems, and the victim has been relegated to the role of witness. (Goodey, 2005, p 127)

Concerns about victims have become more salient for the criminal justice system during the last 20 years. This change is underpinned by scepticism about the ability of the criminal justice system to support victims from the point of offence to eventual sentence, and the perceived tendency of the criminal justice system to protect the defendant/offender to the detriment of the victim. Ian Edwards (2004) notes that victims have emerged as a focus for attention because of concern (and anger) at the perceived privileges given to defendants, and points to a significant overlap between those calling for improvements in the position of victims and those demanding curbs on defendants' rights and protections.

In terms of public confidence, the British Crime Survey (BCS) – a large-scale victimisation survey now conducted annually – has consistently highlighted a large discrepancy between offences experienced and numbers of offences reported to the police and therefore featuring in official statistics. For instance, in 2009/10, the BCS estimated that 9.6 million crimes had taken place whereas only 4.3 million crimes had been recorded by the police (Flatley et al, 2010).

Regarding perceptions about rates of crime, the 2009/10 BCS revealed a significant 'perception gap' between perceived and actual levels of crime and also between national and local crime trends. Thirty-one per cent of survey respondents thought that crime levels had increased locally and 66 per cent nationally, whereas in fact overall crime levels have fallen successively since 1995. The differences were particularly marked with reference to knife crime and gun crime, possibly due to their media profile, and generally the largest perceptions gaps relate to more serious violent (and therefore rarer) crime types (Parfrement-Hopkins and Green, 2010).

There is, then, a high level of anxiety about crime but, when it does happen, there is an apparent reluctance amongst some members of the public to present to the police, at least partly due to lack of faith in the workings of the criminal justice system: this sense of disempowerment and disillusionment has largely fuelled the politicisation of victim issues over the past two decades.

James Dignan identifies six key reasons for the increase in 'victim visibility', which has grown, not in a vacuum, but in a particular social climate:

- the work of penal reformers;
- the role of the media, particularly in relation to the victims of high profile cases such as the Moors Murders;
- the sensitisation during the 1970s and onwards towards the victims of particular crimes such as domestic violence, partly as a result of feminist campaigning;
- a number of highly publicised incidents of politically inspired criminal violence;
- the growing use of victim surveys – including the BCS and research projects, but also very localised surveys; and
- the work of academic criminologists in the field of victimology (adapted from Dignan, 2005, pp 15-16).

As victims have become more prominent in criminal justice thinking and debate, critical issues about their rights have quite rightly come to the fore, but framed in specific ways that have tended to set their rights against those of offenders:

> The language of balance has immense rhetorical power and popular appeal, and has been harnessed to great effect by politicians and campaigning groups, yet is deceptively simple ... the rhetorical force of the metaphor makes it hard to refute the argument that "defendants have rights, so why shouldn't victims?" (Edwards, 2004, p 968)

The following sections explore what victim rights have been promoted, how effective the measures introduced have been and the extent to which an appropriate balance has been achieved in practice.

Views of victims

Reviewing the range of policy and practice initiatives that have developed, Dignan (2005) pinpoints how victims are looked on and talked about in very selective ways, with sharp distinctions between victims and offenders – two categories that the discourse suggests can never overlap, although in reality they clearly do (Williams, 1999b).

   The notion of the *ideal victim* presented by Nils Christie is helpful in thinking about the characteristics frequently ascribed to victims. These attributes are:

1. The victim is weak in relation to the offender – the "ideal victim" is likely to be either female, sick, very old or very young (or a combination of these)
2. The victim is, if not acting virtuously, then at least going about their legitimate, everyday business
3. The victim is blameless for what happened
4. The victim is unrelated to and does not know the "stranger" who has committed the offence (which also implies the offender is a person rather than a corporation and that the offence is a single one-off incident)
5. The offender is unambiguously big and bad
6. The victim has the right combination of power, influence or sympathy to successfully elicit victim status without threatening (and thus risking opposition from) strong countervailing vested interests. (Christie, 1986, cited in Dignan, 2005, p 17)

Dignan identifies a connection between this stereotypical view of the *ideal victim* and the factors used by the media to judge the 'newsworthiness' of specific crime stories, which in turn influence campaigners and politicians as they seek to promote the interests of victims. An example of this can be seen in the case of Madeleine McCann, which received widespread international media interest. A second example, on the other hand, is apparent in the words of politicians, and particularly in the exclusionary rhetoric of the 'law-abiding majority'. This has implications in instances where the victim does not fit the stereotype, as a member of a BME group or as a 30-year-old male, for example, or – possibly most damagingly – in the case of rape where a young woman knew her attacker ('date rape') or was drunk at the time of the incident. This social construction of victimhood also has implications for offenders as victims and the extent to which their victimisation is acknowledged (Williams, 1999b). Again, Dignan says that:

> To the extent that much legal, media and political discourse represents vulnerable and innocent victims as the very anti-thesis of dangerous and wicked offenders, it is failing to engage with a far less predictable world in which much crime is committed in the context of highly complex social interactions between victims, offenders and possibly others. Real victims and offenders – like most human beings – rarely conform to such stereotypes. (2005, p 20)

In thinking about victims, as well as recognising diversity, different types of victimisation should be considered, including direct/indirect and repeat victimisation, and also collective victimisation, as in the defrauding of pension funds. According to the BCS, 14 per cent of victims of burglary in 2009/10 were burgled more than once in the year. More than a quarter of victims of violent crime were victimised again in the year, rising to 47 per cent in the case of domestic violence (Osborne, 2010). Continued repeated victimisation causes disproportionate suffering and can be extremely damaging, even though the individual offences may be relatively trivial. Certainly, criminal justice agencies have struggled to respond adequately to persistent racism or domestic violence, for instance, because they are geared up to deal with incidents, rather than the cumulative impact of an ongoing and corrosive dynamic (Francis, 2007).

Victims as witnesses

Within the criminal justice system, one of the most significant roles for victims is that of witness, where the alleged perpetrator is facing trial. The experiences of witnesses throughout this process have frequently been extremely negative to the extent that their treatment at the hands of criminal justice agencies has been described as *secondary victimisation*, making many victims reluctant to come forward or to follow through complaints.

An ICM poll for the Institute for Public Policy Research (IPPR) revealed that 12 per cent of adults would not report a murder, 59 per cent would not report screaming from their neighbours and 70 per cent would not report a street brawl; 4.5 times more crimes are committed than are reported to the police; and only 14 per cent of those witnessing an assault actually report it (Spencer and Stern, 2001).

Drawing on consultations with criminal justice professionals and members of the public, the IPPR found that the public were deterred by fear of retribution, anxiety about their treatment in the justice system, lack of confidence in the outcome, differing views on the seriousness of offences, and the general inconvenience. Those witnesses who did attend court were dissatisfied with the length of time they were kept waiting and with not being told what was happening. Only

54 per cent gave evidence on the day they were called to court and 17 per cent had to wait longer than four hours. Under questioning, they felt as though they were in the dock themselves, added to which, at the end of the process, 40 per cent had not been informed of the outcome of the trial.

The report authors noted that reluctance to report property crime reflected a lack of confidence in the police response: there were performance management issues within the police in terms of recording offences and particular concerns about clear-up rates which had been dropping. With violent and sexual crime the issues are likely to be more complex and may include fear of further violence from the perpetrator, concern about public reaction and blame in 'going public', and also lack of confidence in the system in terms of findings of guilt and appropriate sentencing (Spencer and Stern, 2001).

Intimidation in the aftermath of an offence is a key concern and, in that regard, *Victim and witness intimidation: Key findings from the British Crime Survey* (Tarling et al, 2000) revealed that:

- In the 1998 BCS, 8 per cent of all incidents led to victim intimidation. This rose to 15 per cent for incidents where there was potential for intimidation (that is, where the victim had some knowledge of the offender).
- Intimidation was more likely to follow offences of violence and vandalism. Women were particularly likely to experience intimidation following a violent offence (26 per cent). Many of these incidents involved domestic violence.
- The harasser was the original offender in most cases (85 per cent). In others it was the offender's family or friends. Where the harasser was the original offender, 41 per cent of women who experienced intimidation did so from a partner or ex-partner.
- Nearly three quarters of intimidatory incidents involved verbal abuse, 16 per cent physical assaults and 9 per cent damage to property.
- Victim intimidation occurs for many reasons. Only a minority (8 per cent) of those intimidated said it was to deter them from giving evidence to the police or in court.

Clearly concern about victims and witnesses goes beyond the group that have conventionally been seen as 'vulnerable'.

Early development of victims' policy

The first substantial policy response to victims was the establishment of the Criminal Injuries Compensation Scheme in 1964. It still remains limited to victims of violence and arson, but its major benefit is that it is able to pay financial compensation to the victim whether or not the offender is identified, apprehended or convicted (Dignan, 2005). However, it has strong eligibility criteria and these have tended to favour victims corresponding to Christie's *ideal victim*, with its original criteria making a sharp distinction between 'deserving' and 'undeserving', such that sex workers who had experienced assault, for instance, would have been excluded, as would the claims of those with a criminal record.

It took some time subsequently for a head of steam to build but, with the first Victim Support scheme established in Bristol in 1974, the victims and witnesses lobby began to grow. In response, the government introduced the Victims' Charter in 1990, and then issued a revised and extended Charter in 1996. This played a key role in changing the ways that criminal justice agencies engage with victims and witnesses, although it was replaced in 2006 by the Victims' Code of Practice.

While clearly the Charter was a major step forward, it was recognised that this was the start of a process of change rather than the final outcome. Both versions of the Charter have been criticised for an approach which sees the victim as a consumer – albeit a reluctant one – of criminal justice services (Williams, 1999a; Crawford and Enterkin, 2001; Mawby, 2007), and for portraying victims in terms of Christie's *ideal victim* (Dignan, 2005). Nevertheless, it broke new ground by establishing that victims could have expectations and entitlements by virtue of that status as victims, and also by recognising that victims should be provided with information, even though it identified few binding actions for criminal justice agencies. Indeed, Fenwick (1995) suggests that under the Charter, victims had moral rather than legal rights and therefore no access to legal redress. One significant requirement, however, was placed on the probation service to seek the 'wishes and interests' of victims of certain offenders, initially only those serving life sentences, to be considered as part of the decision-making process before release.

Vulnerable witnesses

At the same time as the victims' lobby was making progress, the government was also developing policy with regard to vulnerable witnesses. *Speaking up for justice: A report of the Interdepartmental Working Group on the treatment of vulnerable or intimidated witnesses in the criminal justice system* (Home Office, 1998c) reflected concerns about children but also many adult victims and witnesses who may find the criminal justice process daunting and stressful. This is particularly so for those who are vulnerable because of personal circumstances, including their relationship to the defendant or because of the nature of certain serious crimes, such as rape.

The document recommended a raft of improvements to the criminal justice system, including the reporting of crime, identification of vulnerable or intimidated witnesses and measures to assist witnesses before, during and after trial. One specific recommendation was the ending of the right for a defendant to cross-examine the complainant in a rape trial, because of its potential to compound the experience of victimisation, and also to discourage other women to report rape.

The development of policy for victims and witnesses eventually culminated in the key strategic document called *Criminal justice: The way ahead* (Home Office, 2001). This announced a review of the Victim's Charter, recognising the debate about rights versus standards, and for the first time talked about a victims' ombudsman. Focusing specifically on the victim/witness perspectives, the policy initiatives following from this included:

- stronger requirements to keep victims informed throughout the progress of their case;
- Victim Personal Statements which allow the victim to describe to the courts and other criminal justice agencies how the crime has affected his or her life;
- requirements for every victim of a violent or sex offence to be consulted and notified about relevant licence conditions when an offender sentenced to more than 12 months in prison is about to be released;
- initiatives to improve witnesses' experiences of appearing at court – reducing delays and collapsed trials;
- improving information regarding the progress of cases through the courts and information from the Crown Prosecution Service regarding prosecution decisions;
- increased protection against witness intimidation.

Witness care units have been established, with police, the Crown Prosecution Service and others informing and supporting victims. Clearly there are humanitarian and deeply moral concerns in dealing sensitively with all witnesses and particularly vulnerable witnesses, but there are also pragmatic reasons for improving services, because of the reduction in the number of trials that fail or 'crack' because a witness pulls out and the consequent increase in successful convictions.

With regard to court proceedings, the Youth Justice and Criminal Evidence Act 1999 had already established a definition of vulnerable witnesses that included all witnesses under 17 years of age, those with a mental disorder or a significant impairment of intelligence and social functioning, or with a physical disability or disorder. It greatly increased the scope of provision for vulnerable and intimidated adults and children, allowing for a range of 'special measures' including:

- Screening the witness from the accused (Section 23)
- Evidence by live video link (Section 24)
- Evidence given in private (no members of the public in court) (Section 25)
- Removal of wigs and gowns (Section 26)
- Visually recorded interviews as evidence in chief (Section 27)
- Visually recorded cross-examination or re-examination (Section 28)
- Examination of a witness through an intermediary (Section 29)
- Aids to communication for vulnerable witnesses (Section 30)

This represents a large investment in effort and resources. However, there may be a significant gap between the intended use of 'special measures' and actual implementation (Goodey, 2005), which is dependent on the ability of the police to identify vulnerable witnesses appropriately.

In 2003, just as the Criminal Justice Act was about to receive Royal Assent, New Labour detailed its future plans to further enhance the rights of victims and witnesses in *A new deal for victims and witnesses* (Home Office, 2003a). The Domestic Violence, Crime and Victims Act 2004, following from this, gave statutory footing to the Victim's Code of Practice and established a post of Commissioner for Victims (Louise Casey took up this position in 2010).

Support for victims

The previous section focused on measures for witnesses, but the support network for victims more generally has also been growing, such that in 2003, there were 389 Victim Support schemes in England and Wales. During the financial year 2002-03, they employed between them 1,155 people and coordinated a total of almost 12,000 volunteers. In 2008, Victim Support became a single registered charity, rather than an association or federation of smaller schemes, thus consolidating its position as the main representative organisation for victims in the criminal justice arena.

The success of Victim Support has been remarkable, and this has been partly attributed to the scrupulously non-political stance it adopted until 1995 (Williams and Goodman, 2007b) and its ability to work alongside statutory agencies (Mawby, 2007). This has meant that it has received a much greater official endorsement and government funding than more political and often feminist-inspired organisations such as Women's Aid and Rape Crisis (Williams, 1999a; Dignan, 2005). Williams and Goodman (2007b) further point to its ability to extend its activities and its 'strategy of domain expansion' as contributing to its current position of power. Meanwhile, Dignan (2005) attributes much of its status to its relatively uncontroversial and service-led approach, but also notes a growing willingness to adopt more proactive and partisan approaches, using the language of rights to argue for victims.

Victim Support is important in strategic terms and has been the government's preferred organisation to represent the victim and witness perspective in consultation and on policy-making bodies. It also tends to be represented on LCJBs. It has therefore moved into a strange hybrid position, half in and half out of the official criminal justice system.

The voluntary sector has played a major role in developing services for victims, but statutory agencies have also increased their responsibilities as a result of successive policy moves and specific requirements in the Victims' Code of Practice. Compared to other criminal justice agencies, however, victim work within the probation service has been described as more 'tangential' (Mawby, 2007) and mainly takes place post-sentence.

Victim Personal Statements

One of the key items in the 1996 Victims' Charter was that victims should be given the opportunity to say how the crime had affected them. Evaluated pilot projects, held from 1996 to 1999, confirmed the demand for a victim statement scheme and highlighted lessons to be learned. Among other things, the research counselled against raising victims' expectations inappropriately and spoke of the need for a mechanism to update a Victim Personal Statement.

The resulting scheme, available nationally from October 2001, has tried to address these and other points. This includes the opportunity presented through the Victim Personal Statement to identify whether the victim needs support. The scheme is a two-stage process. At stage one, the victim is given the chance to make a Victim Personal Statement when the police take a witness statement. Stage two allows the victim to provide a further statement later on describing any longer-term effects the crime has had on them (which might not have been apparent when the first Victim Personal Statement was taken).

Victim Personal Statements are intended to provide information about the impact of crime rather than personal opinions about sentencing (B. Williams, 2002). In the US Victim Impact Statements have a greater significance in the sentencing process than in the UK, although even here the physical, emotional and psychological consequences of an offence may impact on the assessment of offence seriousness. For example, an offence of ABH (actual bodily harm) that resulted in only minor physical injuries could become more serious if the victim indicated more serious psychological consequences.

In a comparative study of victim participation, Ian Edwards (2001) identified four different rationales for involving victims in providing information to feed into the decision-making process:

- to promote accurate or effective sentencing outcomes;
- to promote efficiency and responsiveness in the internal workings of the criminal justice system;
- to allow for therapeutic or cathartic benefits to victims; and
- because it is a good in and of itself independent of any instrumental value.

Whereas in Australia, notions of welfare have predominated, no one rationale in the UK has assumed precedence, leaving a lack of clarity about the purpose of Victim Personal Statements. Edwards comments that:

> The failure to articulate a theoretical basis for victim participation has a significant impact on the criteria used to assess the effectiveness of such schemes, but it also has considerable effects on victims themselves, who may be unclear just why they are being asked, or entitled, to participate. (2001, p 50)

He notes that reform of sentencing to include victims has only limited potential to give therapeutic benefits to victims, and that if their position is to be improved, this should be done through changing practice and procedures at an earlier stage in the criminal justice process.

In a later article, Edwards explores further the nature of victim participation, devising a typology of varying levels of involvement in sentencing: control over the process; consultation; providing information; and expressing emotion.

Reflecting on these forms of participation, the ambiguities inherent in the victim's role in the Victim Personal Statement scheme become apparent. While there is no sense in which a victim completing a Victim Personal Statement has a controlling or decision-making role, there is evidence of the other three types of participation (Edwards, 2004). The lack of clarity he identified earlier was still present and is compounded by key tensions:

> The lack of clarity stems not only from opacity at the political level. The victim's place within criminal justice is equivocal. The victim qua witness is needed in criminal justice as an information provider … for the State, the need to have particular information on which to prosecute or sentence may be compromised if victims want and are able to participate in a more extensive way, through expressive condemnation of the offender and the inclusion of subjective and impassioned information and opinions. (Edwards, 2004, p 978)

There are, then, significant issues in the well-meaning introduction of Victim Personal Statements that may mean they are less empowering than intended and can raise false expectations of the extent to which the statement can influence sentencing.

Probation service's victim work

Probation work has historically been directed towards offenders and it is true to say that 'inconsistency has bedevilled the probation service's work with victims from the beginning' (Williams and Goodman, 2007a, p 536). The beginnings were the new requirements under the Victims' Charter to contact the victim or relatives of the victim of life sentenced prisoners to provide information and to seek their views and wishes in relation to release plans for the offender. This requirement was implemented without increased resources (Nettleton et al, 1997; Crawford and Enterkin, 2004) and put probation services in the position of having to choose between competing demands. Although this requirement represented a significant cultural shift for the probation service, the actual number of victims involved was relatively small. The focus was definitely shifting towards victims, however, as is evidenced by the requirement in the 1995 national standards for probation officers to discuss impact on victims in PSRs.

Subsequently, the revised Victims' Charter in 1996 increased the victim contact remit to all prisoners with violent and sexual offences serving four years or more. Some probation services chose to work generically, with probation officers contacting victims alongside other duties; some created specialist posts; others established contracts with voluntary agencies (Nettleton et al, 1997). Section 69 of the Criminal Justice and Court Services Act 2000 further increased the range of victim contact work by requiring services to contact the victims of all offenders serving over 12 months for violent or sexual crimes.

As Section 69 was being implemented, Adam Crawford and Jill Enterkin (2001) studied two probation areas, one with a long history of contracting out victim work and one with a specialist worker model. The victims they interviewed had been unclear about what benefits they might gain from the victim contact scheme, but had wanted information more than anything else. Some victims also appreciated the emotional support that was offered to them. Importantly, the authors point to a strategic lack of synergy and coordination in victim services provided by the probation service and elsewhere, such that they form:

> A tangle of overlapping competencies all seeking potentially to integrate the victim in different ways, at different stages and for different ends in the criminal justice process ... on occasions it appears almost as if diverse agencies are vying for the soul of the victim, pulling him or her in competing directions. (Crawford and Enterkin, 2001, p 721)

This indicates significant difficulties for the probation service in making its victim work effective and ensuring it is not isolated from other victim services. However, despite these difficulties, the emphasis on victim work was growing and was subsequently highlighted in the strategy for the new National Probation Service. The key objectives for the new National Probation Service included more involvement with victims of serious sexual and other violent crime. In addition, PC 62/2001 included a Statement of Purpose with regard to this area of work, which was supported by a requirement in national standards that contact is made with victims within two months of the sentence date.

Statement of Purpose

The purpose of the National Probation Service's work with victims is to provide a victim-focused service to victims of sexual and violent offenders sentenced to a custodial sentence of 12 months or more. The role of local areas is:

- to provide information to victims about the criminal justice process on an ongoing basis once an offender has been sentenced to a term of imprisonment of 12 months or more for a sexual or violent offence;
- to provide the opportunity for victims to give their views on proposed conditions surrounding the offender's release;
- to inform the victims of any conditions of release which relate to contact with the victim;
- to inform and seek the victim's agreement to any special victim protection arrangements which are proposed;
- to receive and act on information from victims and their families about breaches of release conditions.

The second inspection on victim contact work by HMI Probation, *Valuing the victim* (2003), recognised significant progress and was satisfied that victim work had been adopted as a priority within the strategic framework of the service, building on guidance from the NPD (National Probation Directorate). However, it was (and still is) unclear what impact the creation of NOMS and major structural changes might have for marginal groups, such as victims, in the probation service's work (Williams and Goodman, 2007a). Nevertheless, this area of work has continued to grow, and recent developments include support for the female partners of men undertaking domestic violence programmes and an extension of work in relation to the victims of mentally disordered offenders.

Changes to the Domestic Violence, Crime and Victims Act 2004

The Mental Health Act 2007 amends the Domestic Violence, Crime and Victims Act 2004 to extend the rights of victims of sexual or violent offenders where the offender is subject to a Hospital Order with no Restriction Order currently in place (see Chapter Sixteen). The probation service has no remit for non-restricted offenders in hospital, but these provisions require the service to establish whether the victim would wish to make representations in relation to any conditions of discharge and requests for information. If the victim does express a wish, the probation service should liaise appropriately with the hospital manager. If a Community Treatment Order is proposed for the offender after discharge, the victim should then be informed and given opportunity to make representations accordingly. PC 23/2008 gives details of these provisions.

Principles of restorative justice

Reference has already been made to the way that 'traditional' criminal justice tends to pit victim and offender against each other. Restorative justice has developed in the UK independently of the victims' lobby as a movement that seeks to deal with crime in a different and less adversarial way. There is far greater synergy between the restorative justice and victims' movements in the US, and it is interesting that they have remained very separate and perhaps to a degree antagonistic to each other's aims in the UK.

This final section introduces some of the debate around restorative justice as a counterpoint to some of the more conventional ways of thinking about victims and offenders. It was also significant in New Labour Third Way philosophies, which, as they entered office in 1997, sought to find a discourse and a new way of dealing with disputes other than the retributive or rehabilitative orientations that have historically dominated criminal justice policy.

While there are various strands of restorative justice thinking, a useful definition is provided by the Restorative Justice Council (www.restorativejustice.org.uk):

> Restorative justice works to resolve conflict and repair harm. It encourages those who have caused harm to acknowledge what they have done and gives them opportunity to make reparation. It offers those who have suffered the harm opportunity to have their harm or loss acknowledged and amends made. Conflict between people is inevitable, but where it occurs restorative justice can "restore" the balance in a just and fair way. In resolving the harm done, it works to stop it happening again.

This definition can be amplified:

> RJ [restorative justice] involves restoring responsibility to offenders for their offending and its consequences, certainly, but it is also about taking charge of the need to make amends for what has been done and restoring a belief in them that the process in which they are involved, and the outcomes reached, are fair and just. The offender's inclusion in the process and in determining the outcome, therefore, is crucial. This means that, in restorative processes, offenders themselves speak about their offending and matters associated with it, rather than through some third party. (Gelsthorpe and Morris, 2002, p 243)

Restorative justice, then, aims to be an inclusive approach that upholds the rights of victims, offenders and community. An important underpinning notion is that of *reintegrative shaming*, whereby the offender is made to face up to his or her actions but is then offered an opportunity for redemption (Braithwaite, 1989). Proponents of restorative justice have been critical of conventional justice and their major arguments are presented in Table 13.1.

There are three important parties that may be involved in restorative interventions – the offender, the direct victim and the community – although it is not necessary to have all three involved, depending on the nature of the intervention. Restorative justice is a small element of our attempts to deal with disputes in the UK, but appears typically in four areas of activity:

- victim–offender mediation/restorative conferencing (essentially, a meeting between the victim and offender);
- reparation activities;
- sentencing circles (see Chapter Seventeen, this volume); and
- family group conferences.

Table 13.1: Conventional versus restorative forms of justice

Retributive justice	Restorative justice
– Blame	– Balance responsibility and actions to repair
– Stigma	– Fewer legal rules and procedural safeguards
– Guilt, not moral responsibility	– Condemnation + empathy
– Assumption of rational, individualistic choice	– Educative and reintegrative
– Pain/punishment	– Complex moral judgements

Source: Adapted from Zehr (1990)

Opinion differs on whether restorative justice measures should be entirely voluntary and separate from the criminal justice system or whether they can exist within it without compromising their 'restorativeness', but in the UK official policy has tended to develop restorative justice as part of the system. This rather underplays the potential of restorative justice for promoting inclusion and an appropriate balancing of interests, with typically a low rate of victim involvement (McIvor, 2007). Naturally, restorative justice is more in line with a rights-based approach than the divisive policies explored in this chapter which have tended to characterise the victim debate and to see the rights of victims and offenders as separate and mutually exclusive.

There is clearly potential to find different ways of resolving conflict at both individual and community level. The proposed new Neighbourhood Justice Centres may provide one impetus for change, while restorative cautioning and other initiatives could represent other avenues. The essential question is the extent to which new ventures might transform the current system and the extent to which they themselves become absorbed into the overwhelmingly retributive framework.

Summary

Victims create problems for criminal justice agencies, particularly those more accustomed to dealing with offenders. The recent rise of victims in criminal justice policy has challenged many aspects of traditional practice. This has brought benefits for victims themselves, although some initiatives such as victim contact services and Victim Personal Statements actually promise more than they deliver and, in fact, may unhelpfully raise expectations. The key conundrum is that, despite political rhetoric, victims are still marginal to the criminal justice system. The rhetoric, however, of victims' rights, has a powerful impact on offenders where rights are seen in opposition. This need not be the case as restorative justice practices demonstrate and as argued in the rights-based approach in this book. The categories of victim and offender are not mutually exclusive, and many offenders have experience of victimisation themselves, which may indeed be a contributory factor in their offending. A more sophisticated approach to victimisation and to resolving harm is overdue, but movement towards this, if it has happened at all, has been piecemeal.

Further reading

Davies, P., Francis, P. and Greer, C. (eds) (2007) *Victims, crime and society*, London: Sage Publications.

Davies, P. (2011) *Gender, Crime and Victimisation*, London: Sage.

Dignan, J. (2005) *Understanding victims and restorative justice*, Maidenhead: Open University Press.

Goodey, J. (2005) *Victims and victimology: Research, policy and practice*, Edinburgh: Pearson Education Ltd.

FOURTEEN

Youth justice

The way that the criminal justice system is now organised means that many criminal justice practitioners do no direct work with children and young people under the age of 18. However, the probation service and a small number of committed agencies in the voluntary sector have long and honourable histories of support and intervention for young people. This work has been critical to the development of important underpinning values in work with offenders, specifically, those emphasising welfare considerations, the belief in the capacity of the individual to change and the salience of social context for offender-based work.

This chapter outlines the major reforms in the youth justice system and discusses its divergence from the adult criminal justice system as well as parallel developments evident in the growing emphasis on effectiveness, performance management and multi-agency working. Indeed, YOTs are the most developed examples of New Labour's vision of 'joined-up justice', which 10 years on can be seen as successful in certain areas and markedly less so in others. 'Youth' as a life stage is more regulated and controlled than ever before; the legal framework around youth justice and the anti-social behaviour agenda includes significant measures encouraging intervention in young people's lives. These are helpful in some instances, but highly controversial in others, impacting on rights and freedoms.

Connecting probation and youth justice

The main elements of the reformed youth justice system were put in place in 2000. Since then, the probation service has been charged with a responsibility to contribute to these new multi-disciplinary arrangements, in terms of strategic management, resources and seconded staff. Yet despite the separation of youth and adult justice systems at operational level, practitioners still need a basic understanding of the legal framework for young offenders and the broad issues about the nature and tone of the new system. Rod Morgan, former Chair of the YJB, and Tim Newburn (2007) emphasise how important the connections between the probation service and the youth justice system are because, sadly, so many adult offenders were first convicted under the age of 18. Close cooperation is needed to ensure that there is continuity and consistency between adult and youth justice services that together help ease young people's transitions into adulthood.

Policy development in youth justice

Youth justice policy is a huge area to summarise, but John Muncie provides a useful starting point:

> Youth Justice in the twenty-first century has evolved into a particularly complex state of affairs. It is designed to punish the offender whilst keeping their welfare paramount. It is at one and the same time about crime prevention and retribution. It makes claims for restoration and reintegration whilst seeking some of the most punitive measures of surveillance and containment in custodial and community settings....
>
> But the "new" never replaces the old. In the twenty-first century discourses of protection, restoration, punishment, responsibility, rehabilitation, welfare, retribution, diversion, human rights and so on exist alongside each other in some perpetually uneasy and contradictory manner. (Muncie, 2009, p 309)

The ideas and aspirations underpinning the present youth justice system are very mixed, as Muncie notes, and have become increasingly complex as the fundamental and longstanding aims of punishment and welfare/rehabilitation have been joined by restoration, early intervention and social control – not to mention the impact of the debate about children's rights.

In tracing historical development, the first major piece of criminal justice legislation to recognise and promote the welfare of young people was the Children Act 1908. This created juvenile courts, which attempted to combine welfare and justice by dealing with the socially needy alongside the delinquent (Hendrick, 2006). However, the fact that the court was expected to 'rescue' as well as to punish children has created inherent conflict and ambivalence in its workings from the outset (Gelsthorpe and Morris, 1994). These contradictions have been reflected in the youth justice system as it has grown and developed over the years, with the 1960s seeing particular concerns about how to respond to young people in trouble.

In Scotland, the Kilbrandon Report in 1964 strongly advocated a welfare-orientated system of dealing with young offenders in the community rather than in custody. The Children's Hearing system was instituted by the Social Work (Scotland) Act 1968, which replaced youth courts for under-16-year-olds with what were effectively welfare tribunals.

The Scottish Hearing system is still in place today with its original welfare approach in place, and it is only recently that the centrality of welfare has been questioned in Scotland. The situation in England and Wales has been very different, although starting in the 1960s from a strong welfare base. The 1968 White Paper, *Children in trouble,* introduced by the Labour Party (Home Office, 1968), argued that in all probability only a minority of children would grow up without ever having broken the law, and that often such behaviour represents little more than an incident in the pattern of a child's normal development (Home Office, 1968, cited in Muncie, 2009).

The White Paper was followed by the controversial Children and Young Persons Act 1969 which contained, among other measures, radical proposals to drastically reduce the use of custody in favour of community disposals and residential provision, to raise the age of criminal responsibility from 10 to 14, and also to shift the locus of decision making decidedly away from courts towards social services departments. However, with an election bringing in a change of administration in 1970, key parts of the Act were not implemented, and the net result throughout the 1970s was an increase in both custody and in welfare options, such as Intermediate Treatment programmes:

> The retreat from welfare had begun before it had arrived. Even those portions of the CYPA [Children and Young Persons Act] 1969 which were retained were soon attacked vociferously by police and magistrates, who argued that it left them powerless to deal adequately with young offenders. (Sheila Brown, 2005, p 80)

Welfarism was also increasingly criticised from more liberal perspectives during the 1970s, partly because of what some would argue is its primary virtue, which is the ability to respond to individual need. The key conundrum is that the definition of what constitutes 'need' was, and still is, highly problematic. Welfare approaches did afford young people care and protection, but they could also have much less positive effects in drawing more young people into the ambit of youth justice (Muncie, 2009). In addition, its apparently progressive nature actually contained a critical contradiction because it was social workers rather than young people themselves who were charged with deciding what was in their 'best interests', a further erosion of their rights (Brown, 2005a).

The backlash resulted in the justice movement, which was concerned at the rise in young people being sent to custody and was critically influenced by the 'nothing works' conclusions of Robert Martinson (1974) and others. Moreover, proponents of the justice movement considered that welfare itself, rather than being benevolent, had historically operated as a form of social control. As the 'just deserts' model became the dominant approach in the 1980s, it therefore sought to put limits on both the use of punishment and welfare interventions according to the principle of proportionality, curbing the discretion of sentencers and the use of indeterminate treatment-based disposals.

The grassroots momentum around 'just deserts', culminating in the Criminal Justice Act 1991, came predominantly from the youth justice system. The practices of gate-keeping, diversion and systems management were developed and embedded much more in work with young people than with adults, designed to keep young people out of the criminal justice system wherever possible.

In terms of government direction, from 1983, 110 alternative to custody projects were established through the Department of Health and Social Service's Intermediate Treatment Initiative, focusing the work on more serious young offenders close to the custody threshold. At the other end of the spectrum, cautioning schemes burgeoned, with Home Office Circular 14/1985 encouraging the police to use informal warnings or to take no further action against young people for minor misdemeanours. By the 1990s, approximately 60 per cent of young offenders were dealt with by cautions (Muncie, 2004). The Criminal Justice Act 1991, aiming to reduce the use of custody, subsequently shortened the maximum period that the court could impose in a young offender institution to 12 months, and simultaneously introduced an expectation of local multi-agency cooperation, thus mixing the justice thinking with elements of the new public management that was beginning to pervade public services (Morgan and Newburn, 2007).

The effect of the above, coming into the 1990s, was a decrease in custody and in young people being processed through the youth courts, although at the same time some harsher responses to more entrenched offending. However, the justice model had its own critics, some from more radical perspectives, such as Barbara Hudson, who felt that it ignored social problems and, rather than challenging, tended to collude with an oppressive legal system (1987).

There were criticisms also from the political right wing and, with Michael Howard in situ at the Home Office, by 1993, the principle of proportionality and promotion of community sentencing contained in the Criminal Justice Act 1991 were being undermined by a stated belief that 'prison works'. In terms of young offenders, a number of public concerns had been raised about, for instance, repeated offending, truancy, drug use and urban unrest (Muncie, 2004). These concerns became sharply focused during the moral panic that followed the murder of the toddler, James Bulger, in February 1993:

> The Bulger case had at least three related consequences. First, it initiated a reconsideration of the social construction of 10 year olds as "demons" rather than as "innocents". Second, it coalesced with, and helped to mobilise, adult fear and moral panic about "youth" in general. Third, it legitimised a series of tough law and order responses to young offenders, which came to characterise the following decade. (Muncie, 2004, p 3)

The justice movement, which had thrived in a more rational and sympathetic climate, had no real response to these more punitive attitudes and the increasing politicisation of youth justice. Furthermore, it had become associated with a lack of faith that any form of preventative or developmental intervention could be effective (Smith, 2003). The climate in the mid-1990s was becoming increasingly hostile to 'hands-off' approaches and clearly there was a political will for something demonstrably to be 'done' about young offenders. Both left and right parties were espousing a tough rhetoric about youth offending and both picked up the messages from a key report from the Audit Commission, *Misspent youth* (Audit Commission, 1996). This was highly critical of the youth justice system as existed at that time and the practice of probation officers, social workers and others.

Before looking at this report and its influence on the policies that New Labour introduced, the next section discusses welfare concerns in the youth justice system and some of the tensions therein during the 'just deserts' period and since.

Welfare in youth justice

As stated previously, the Children Act of 1908 created the juvenile court within a social context where there were new and developing beliefs in reforming, socialising and treating individuals (Muncie, 2009). During the interwar period, the psycho-social understanding of delinquency developed further, assuming a significant overlap between offending and welfare concerns, assumptions that were ultimately embodied in the Children and Young Persons Act 1933:

> ... which provided for juvenile courts to act in loco parentis as a closer link was forged between delinquent and neglected children in the belief that "there is little or no difference in character and needs between the delinquent and the neglected child". (Hendrick, 2006, p 9)

This approach, which advocated the wider use of probation, approved schools and other forms of social care for young people was not necessarily popular with sentencers and the police, but nevertheless key provisions of the 1933 Act still operate today, most importantly the welfare principle contained in Section 44 and the provisions relating to reporting restrictions of cases in youth court:

> Section 44: Every court in dealing with a child or young person who is brought before it either as an offender or otherwise, shall have regard to the welfare of the child or young person and shall in proper cases take steps for removing him from undesirable surroundings and for securing that proper provision is made for his education and training.

The primacy of welfare continued after the Second World War, as the new welfare state was being constructed and the social work profession was further establishing itself, although there were glimpses of a harder penal edge appearing simultaneously (Morgan and Newburn, 2007). An additional element of tension was introduced to the mix as youth or teen cultures began to develop and distinguish themselves from adults:

> In general, the post war period up until the 1970s was unquestionably that of "youth" (not so much of children) and this cultural "moment", with all its unforeseen tensions, together with consensual, if limited, acceptance of "welfare" as a political principle, profoundly influenced all manner of attitudes and policies. (Hendrick, 2006, p 10)

This, then, was the context in which the Children and Young Persons Act 1969 was introduced, and it is not difficult to understand why the welfare consensus, which had become increasingly fragile, finally shattered. Nevertheless, several important provisions of the 1969 Act were enacted and these include:

- Supervision Orders which remained the most important sentencing disposal for young people until as recently as 2009; and
- Criminal Care Orders – these enabled the courts to make a Care Order as a response to offending rather than imposing a punitive sentence.

Although the fundamental welfare principle remained in place, other changes shifted the welfare focus in the youth justice system. The first of these was the Children Act 1989 which created the family court and removed care matters from the juvenile court, leaving it to deal with criminal offences only.

Second, the welfare of children was also given a position of primacy by the 1989 UNCRC to which the UK is a signatory. There are key sections that relate to children – defined as any person under the age of 18 – in the justice systems. UK legislation and youth justice agencies are required to comply with the principles of the Convention, not an easy or uncontroversial task, particularly in relation to young people held in custody.

The third set of changes came with the Criminal Justice Act 1991: this abolished Criminal Care Orders and raised the age range for the juvenile court to encompass 17-year-olds, with the court being rebranded as the youth court. The 'just deserts' sentencing rationales introduced considerations of proportionality, so sentencing became based on 'deeds, rather than needs', but with a requirement still to have regard to welfare considerations in sentencing decisions.

Finding an appropriate balance has been difficult for practitioners and there has been confusion about where welfare sits alongside other competing aims of the system. To some extent, New Labour, coming to power in 1997, tried to resolve these perceived contradictions in the White Paper, *No more excuses* (Home Office, 1997b), which preceded the Crime and Disorder Act 1997, as the following extract illustrates:

> The Government believes that there has been confusion about the purpose of the youth justice system and the principles that should govern the way in which young people are dealt with by youth justice agencies. Concerns about the welfare of the child have too often been seen as in conflict with the aims of protecting the public, punishing offences and preventing offending. This confusion causes practical difficulties for practitioners and has contributed to the loss of public confidence in the youth justice system.
>
> Children need protection as appropriate from the full rigours of the criminal law. Under the UN Convention on the Rights of the Child and the European Convention on Human Rights, the United Kingdom is committed to protecting the welfare of children and young people who come into contact with the criminal justice process. The Government does not accept that there is any conflict between protecting the welfare of a young offender and preventing that individual from offending again. Preventing offending promotes the welfare of the individual young offender and protects the public.
>
> *Source:* Home Office (1997b, p 6)

This is a rather different way of thinking about welfare needs and it is unclear what measures to prevent offending might at the same time promote welfare. Nevertheless, it acknowledges the need to have regard to welfare and the obligations of state agencies to meet the standards of key human rights instruments, although the overall tone sounds, if anything, impatient with the welfare lobby.

The tensions around welfare have been returned to again in official documents. It was significant that when the Department for Education and Skills was preparing the *Every Child Matters* Green Paper that heralded the changes brought in by the Children Act 2004 (see Chapter Eight), this did not cover children who offend, who were considered in a separate document issued by the Home Office.

Youth justice: Next steps (Home Office, 2003b) looked at the implications – and benefits – of the wider changes proposed in the *Every Child Matters* programme for children and young people who offend, and also discussed a range of youth justice specific matters. One of these was the continued confusion in the aim of sentencing and, at that point, the stated intention was to legislate so as to define the prevention of offending as the principal aim of sentencing, reflecting the principal aim of the reformed youth justice system. However, when the legislation received Royal Assent in May 2008, the relevant section, Section 9 of the Criminal Justice and Immigration Act, still retains the welfare provision of Section 44 of the 1933 Act, alongside the other aims of sentencing – so hardly clarifying the position and importance of welfare relative to other system priorities.

Background to reform

The Audit Commission was established to analyse the performance of public service against the key concerns of managerialists – economy, efficiency and effectiveness (the three 'Es'). When, in 1996, it investigated the youth justice system as it then existed, the findings were critical both overall and specifically in relation to the three 'E' tests (Morgan and Newburn, 2007).

Its report, *Misspent youth* (Audit Commission, 1996), concluded that the system was expensive, slow and inefficient and, most damningly, had minimal impact on offenders. It was particularly critical of the fact that three out of five young offenders apprehended were given a warning or caution and received little, if any, intervention to change their behaviour. At the other end of the spectrum, it criticised the delays in dealing with PYOs in court and the lack of intensive and focused work with them once sentenced. It authoritatively and comprehensively challenged the focus of youth justice in the 1980s on minimum intervention, diversion and welfare as concerns grew about the prevalence of youth crime.

The report also recognised that youth crime was a community-based problem and highlighted the need to focus on crime prevention strategies informed by the findings of the major longitudinal Cambridge Study in Delinquent Development (Farrington, 1989, 1994) and the work of Graham and Bowling (1995) among others. These identified risk factors including: inadequate parenting; truancy and exclusion from school; peer group pressure to offend; early involvement in anti-social behaviour; and drug/alcohol use.

This report effectively set the agenda for youth justice and the development of YOTs, and signalled a more interventionist approach to young people's offending. After the 1997 General Election, the government White Paper, *No more excuses* (Home Office, 1997b), reflected the Audit Commission's recommendations and sought to bring more coherence to what it viewed as a fragmented system, with no unifying aim or purpose.

The emphasis was shifting from a primary concern for the individual young offender to a new focus on preventing offending, which in itself was being described as in the best interests of young people. The other key change was the multi-agency approach in which different agencies would be expected to work to common objectives within the crime reduction agenda. These common objectives included:

- the swift administration of justice so that every young person accused of breaking the law had the matter resolved without delay;
- confronting young offenders with the consequences of their offending, for themselves and their family, their victims and their community;
- punishment proportionate to the seriousness and persistence of offending;
- encouraging reparation to victims by young offenders;
- reinforcing the responsibilities of parents; and
- helping young offenders to tackle problems associated with their offending and to develop a sense of personal responsibility.

Reforms to the youth justice system: the Crime and Disorder Act 1998

Section 37 of the Act refers to the youth justice system and identifies a primary aim:

> Section 37: (1) It shall be the principal aim of the youth justice system to prevent offending by children and young persons.

Youth justice services

Section 38 places a duty on local authorities with responsibilities for social care and education to ensure that appropriate youth justice services are available in their area. Chief officers of police, police authorities, boards of probation trusts and health authorities are required to cooperate with the local authority in arrangements to provide:

- individuals able to act as appropriate adults during police interviews;
- assessment and rehabilitation programmes associated with a final warning;
- bail support;

- access to placements for children and young people on remand in local authority accommodation;
- reports or other information required by the courts in criminal proceedings;
- supervision of community sentences and other court orders;
- supervision following the release from custody.

Youth offending teams

The delivery mechanism for all this is the multi-disciplinary YOT. Section 39 places a duty on local authorities to establish one or more YOTs which are then responsible for coordinating the provision of youth justice services in their area and for carrying out tasks and functions identified in the local youth justice plan (Section 40). Chief officers of police, probation trusts and health authorities must cooperate with the local authority in establishing YOTs which must contain staff from:

- the police
- probation
- local authority children's social care
- health
- education.

The team may also include individuals from other organisations, which could include voluntary agencies, depending on the local youth justice landscape, and in most cases, Connexions. The multi-agency management or steering groups for YOTs are accountable to the CSPs in local areas, but also report to children's services strategic groups.

Governance

Section 41 established the Youth Justice Board for England and Wales with a facilitating and overseeing role, which was expanded in 2000 to include the commissioning of all placements in the secure estate for under-18s (Morgan and Newburn, 2007). The YJB – now abolished by the Coalition government – was a non-departmental public body, attached to the Ministry of Justice but independent of it.

YOTs hold two key tensions. First, they have been line-managed and steered at local authority level, but with accountability in terms of performance, quality assurance and annual planning to the YJB at the centre. They have been funded by both partner agencies and central government through the YJB while it existed. Second, they sit between children's services and the criminal justice agencies and, if located correctly, can powerfully negotiate and mediate between the two but, when weighted unduly to one side or the other, may be less effective.

During its lifetime, the YJB greatly influenced the way that YOTs developed and was responsible for introducing a high degree of managerialism into the system, while at the same time producing benefits in terms of consistency and improved standards of practice. Although it was criticised for encouraging approaches that could routinise practice and stifle innovation (Smith, 2003), it did have capacity to support creativity and voiced scepticism about New Labour policy (although outspoken, if accurate criticisms, may have been one reason why the contract of Rod Morgan, a highly respected Chair of the Board, was not renewed).

Summary of the reforms

The Crime and Disorder Act constituted a huge shift in the philosophy, structure and practice within youth justice and directed a new approach underpinned by:

- a primary focus on preventing and reducing offending;
- a belief in early intervention with offenders;
- a reduction in significance for existing welfare considerations with regard to young people;
- a determination to build an inter-agency community-based approach to youth crime;
- more demanding and restrictive community sentences;
- a shift toward restorative justice and a watering down of proportionality principles; and
- a particular focus on PYOs, in terms of court processing and effective intervention.

It is unclear at the time of writing how this framework will change under the Coalition government and what future arrangements will be made to provide oversight and determine the strategic direction of the youth justice system. Although open to criticism, the YJB did at least raise the profile of young offenders and ensured that their needs were included in important strategic agendas and service plans.

Impact of Crime and Disorder Act provisions for children

In addition to the structural changes in the youth justice system, the New Labour legislation contained a number of other key measures relating to children and young people, some of which were extremely controversial. Section 1 of the Crime and Disorder Act created the ASBO, and Section 8 Parenting Orders (see later). Sections 11 and 14 provided for Child Safety Orders for under-10s and local child curfew schemes, although these have been used very little.

The other significant effect of the Act was the abolition of *doli incapax*, a legal presumption dating from the 14th century that children between the ages of 10 and 13 do not know right from wrong, and are therefore incapable of criminal intent. This meant that prosecutors had to rebut the presumption and prove that the young person in question could make that moral distinction. Its abolition has put England and Wales further out of step with the majority of Europe and has attracted criticisms, domestically and internationally (Morgan and Newburn, 2007). And, ironically, this move came at a point where the UK government was being exhorted by the UN to raise the age of criminal responsibility so that it was more in line with the rest of Europe (Muncie, 2004).

Pre-court interventions

The final warning scheme established under Section 65 of the Crime and Disorder Act 1998 replaced the previous system of juvenile cautioning which had attracted so much criticism from the Audit Commission (1996). A first offence can be met with a reprimand, a final warning or criminal charges depending on its seriousness. Young people are allowed one reprimand after which the second offending episode will lead to a warning or a charge. Any further offending following a final warning should automatically result in a charge being brought. There are very limited circumstances in which a second warning may be given.

Reprimands and warnings can be issued at a police station or a YOT office, by either a uniformed officer or one of the YOT police secondees. Section 66 requires that after receiving a warning a young person is referred to a YOT who will then assess him or her for a programme of intervention. Any reprimand or warning will be citable in court in the same way as previous convictions. Although the intervention offered is voluntary, if a young person subsequently goes to court, the YOT will report on his or her compliance.

There are a number of issues associated with the final warning system that has been credited with speeding young people's entry into the formal court system, because it limits the discretion that can be used before a young person has to appear in court. Research conducted on final warnings as operated in YOTs also raised questions about the quality of interventions and whether they are appropriate and effective (Smith, 2003). Despite these reservations, the YJB was keen to expand pre-court initiatives and piloted a more extensive intervention in the form of the youth conditional caution. The Coalition government appears less keen and in the Green Paper, *Breaking the cycle* (Ministry of Justice, 2010a), suggests it intends to reintroduce more flexibility.

First tier penalties

First tier penalties include fines, discharges and the Referral Order. A Reparation Order, made available under Sections 67 and 68 of the Crime and Disorder Act 1998, is also a first tier penalty. This requires the young person to make reparation to the victim of his or her offence, where the victim wishes it, or to the community at large. It can be made as a penalty in its own right or, more rarely in practice, combined with certain other disposals. The reparation must be commensurate with the seriousness of the offence(s) and the order will specify a number of hours up to a maximum of 24 to be undertaken within three months.

The intention of both this order and the Referral Order was to introduce a greater degree of restorative justice into the system. On the one hand, *No more excuses* (Home Office, 1997b) describes reparation activities as a potential catalyst for reform and rehabilitation of the offender as well as benefiting victims. On the other hand, sceptics such as John Muncie have pointed to the narrow definitions of restorative justice that have appeared in practice, which tend to responsibilise the young person rather than unlocking the potential of community empowerment, social inclusion and restorative social justice (Muncie, 2009).

Youth Justice and Criminal Evidence Act 1999

Referral Orders

The new youth justice arrangements from the Crime and Disorder Act 1998 were not yet in place when the next piece of legislation was passed, establishing Referral Orders and youth offender panels. As well as attempting to bolster restorative justice within the system, Referral Orders were intended to have more of a community focus than the 'traditional' social work casework methods used by youth justice practitioners.

Referral Orders were designed to become the standard sentence imposed by the youth court or other Magistrates' Court for young people convicted for the first time when under the age of 18. This means that, for first time offenders pleading guilty or found guilty in youth court, the magistrates are restricted to a choice of absolute discharge, Referral Order or Detention and Training Order. The order will last between 3 and 12 months and requires the young person to attend meetings of a young offender panel in a designated YOT area.

The court may impose more than one Referral Order for two or more associated offences to run concurrently or consecutively providing that the total length does not exceed 12 months. The court can also impose a discretionary Referral Order where mixed pleas have been entered to the court or where a young person subject to a Referral Order is convicted of a second offence, usually occurring before the Referral Order was made. In these circumstances, the court may extend the original order or make a second order, up to a combined maximum of 12 months. Recent changes introduced by the Criminal Justice and Immigration Act 2008 have further expanded availability of Referral Orders on second or subsequent convictions.

Youth offender panels

The YOT specified in the Referral Order must establish a youth offender panel for the case and arrange for it to meet. The panel must consist of at least one YOT member and two trained volunteers. Community venues are used with the intention that the panel should be held in the young person's local area and involve local community members, although in reality the extent to which this is the case depends on practicalities. Panel volunteers do tend to be more representative – and certainly younger – than magistrates, but most YOTs face difficulties in recruiting from minority ethnic communities and from more socially disadvantaged areas.

Identified victims are usually invited to panels, and in this sense the panel process does attempt to incorporate a restorative justice approach, although early research suggested that victims only attended in approximately 10-15 per cent of cases (Crawford and Newburn, 2003). The panel will agree a contract with the young person (and carers, if appropriate), which will operate like a supervision plan and which should contain at least one element of restorative work. Significantly, and unlike any other court order, the order does not run from the date that it is made in court, but starts on the date that the contract is signed.

Panels will meet at regular intervals to review progress on the order and may amend the contract at these follow-up meetings. The panels themselves have no legal powers, so they must refer the young person back to court in instances of non-compliance either with the contract or the panel process itself. Again, this differs from other court orders, in that it is the panel that must make the referral back, not the responsible officer.

An early evaluation of Referral Order schemes found that contracts were not as creative as might have been anticipated, and that this was partly due to practical concerns about supervision of activities, health and safety and insurance. The report authors describe the Referral Order as representing 'a particular and rather peculiar hybrid attempt to integrate restorative justice ideas and values into youth justice practice' (Crawford and Newburn, 2003, p 239). Yet they also acknowledge that it is an attempt to institutionalise restorative practices in youth justice and conclude that:

> A careful reading of the early experience of the introduction of referral orders requires ... an acknowledgement of mixed success – certainly if one is judging by the standards of what we might think of as "restorative justice ideals" ... we have nonetheless sought to show that there is much that is positive in these developments. From the recruitment, training and involvement of community volunteers to the establishment of relatively informal, deliberative panel meeting, the introduction of referral orders intimates that it might just be possible to do youth justice differently. (Crawford and Newburn, 2003, p 242)

Community penalties

Community sentencing for young people has changed dramatically, with the Youth Rehabilitation Order becoming available on 30 November 2009. This is essentially a youth justice equivalent to the adult community order and has the same range of potential requirements and some additional requirements relevant to young people (education, intensive fostering, for example). The Youth Rehabilitation Order, established by Section 1 of the Criminal Justice and Immigration Act 2008, is managed under new *National standards for youth justice services* (YJB, 2009) that allow more flexibility than the adult standards but still represent a rigorous framework for the supervision of offenders. The range of potential requirements is set out in Figure 14.1, along with the other sentencing options for young people.

Figure 14.1: Youth justice disposals

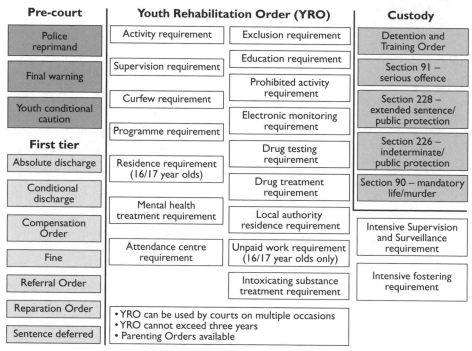

Intensive supervision and surveillance

A significant development for YOTs has been the introduction of intensive supervision and surveillance (ISS) schemes from 2001 in selected areas and now across all YOTs. These draw on examples from the US and earlier UK models, including those scattered projects working with prolific offenders that fed into the requirements of the PPO scheme. It is unsurprising that such developments aimed at diversion from custody coincide with extreme pressure on over-stretched prison accommodation (Moore et al, 2006).

Until the Youth Rehabilitation Order became available, ISS had no separate legal status, but could be delivered as a requirement of:

• a Supervision or Community Rehabilitation Order;

- a bail support programme; or
- a post-custody licence.

There are criteria relating to either persistence or seriousness of offending, and young people can only be subject to a ISS requirement on a Youth Rehabilitation Order where the 'so serious' criterion for custody is met, reflecting its intended use as an alternative to custody. However, increasing numbers of young offenders are finding themselves on these highly restrictive programmes, going straight from Referral Orders and almost bypassing the other potential steps in the sentencing ladder.

ISS programmes can be very flexible, with different programme lengths and intensities according to where the young person is allocated within the Scaled Approach, which is the youth justice equivalent of the tiering framework in the OMM. The baseline requirement starts with a minimum 25 hours per week intervention, with the YJB stipulating that each individual programme should contain elements of:

- education and training
- changing offending behaviour
- interpersonal skills
- family support
- restorative justice.

There should be arrangements for both face to face contact and monitoring of young people outside conventional office hours (usually by means of an electronic curfew). In theory, the majority of the hours should be provided through training schemes or school/alternative education placements for under-16s, but this can be a difficult group of young people to engage or maintain in structured activities and, in some instances, youth justice workers face a real challenge in putting together sufficient elements to create a coherent 25-hour programme.

Clearly these high levels of contact have the potential to allow for imaginative and highly supportive responses to young people's needs, but the overall effect of these intensive packages tends rather to be restrictive and incapacitative. Interestingly, Moore et al (2006), discussing the national evaluation of ISS schemes, remark that:

> A simple conceptual test shows that these interventions, while potentially rehabilitative are used because they are punitive. More specifically, the programmes can help ensure that the offender receives his or her "just deserts" by enabling courts to tailor the punishment to the current offence. (2006, p 25)

Moreover, in terms of interventions, the national evaluation perceived differences between the PYOs who might have multiple and complex needs and offenders on ISS with more serious offences but typically fewer criminogenic needs and pro-criminal attitudes. The evaluators suggested that ISS may be less suited to the latter group, which they identified may contain higher proportions of female and minority ethnic offenders (Moore et al, 2006).

It is still early in the life of ISS schemes and the evidence of effectiveness is not established. However, it would appear that overall they do reduce the frequency and seriousness of re-offending, although re-offending rates remain stubbornly high for what is admittedly a high-risk group. Breach rates are also high, as might be expected with such an intensive level of contact, because with more appointments and activities there are obviously more opportunities to fail. Nevertheless, where breach action results in custody, this must impact on the potential of the ongoing work to effect change, so there is clearly a balance needed between strict and prompt enforcement and flexibility to respond to this offender group.

A number of critics have pointed to the increasingly intrusive nature of youth justice interventions and the conflicts in youth policy that, on the one hand, seek to advocate inclusion, and on the other, seek to separate out, control and exclude (see, for example, Smith, 2003). It is also questionable, with custody rates for young people still worryingly high, the extent to which ISS is keeping young people who would otherwise be in custody in the community or whether it may actually serve to hasten some young people to custody for failure on their programme.

Young people and custody

Wider discussions of youth justice and societal attitudes to young people tend to be reflected in the more specific debates and the practices associated with the use of custody for young people. Indeed, Barry Goldson comments that:

> Mapping the historical trajectory of youth justice policy and practice in England and Wales exposes a curious affinity with custodial institutions ... in other words, penal custody in its various forms, has retained a foothold in the youth justice system since the "invention" of "juvenile delinquency" in the early nineteenth century. (2006, p 139)

Space does not allow a full examination of the history of custodial arrangements from the first Borstals in 1908, but it is worth noting the historical tensions found in secure establishments over the years between punishment, containment and rehabilitation.

Young people (including a significant number on remand) are currently held in three types of establishment:

* young offender institutions – for boys 15–17 years old; for girls there are four small units within adult prisons for 17-year-olds only;
* secure training centres, run by the private sector; and
* local authority secure children's homes.

On 30 June 2010, the numbers in these establishments were as shown, in Table 14.1.

Table 14.1: Young people in custody 30 June 2010

Type of custody	Young offender institution	Secure training centre	Local authority secure children's homes	Total
Males	1,632	212	148	2,774
Females	28	55	21	104
Total	**1,660**	**267**	**169**	**2,096**

Source: Ministry of Justice (2010c)

Detention and Training Orders (Sections 73-79 of the Crime and Disorder Act 1998)

The Act provides for a single custodial sentence for 10- to 17-year-olds to replace the previous sentences of a Secure Training Order and detention in a young offender institution for under-18s. Detention and Training Orders are available for:

- 15- to 17-year-olds, for any imprisonable offence 'so serious' as to justify custody under Section 1 of the Criminal Justice Act 1991;
- 12- to 14-year-olds, who are, in the opinion of the court, persistent offenders, for offences 'so serious' that they justify custody under the 1991 Act; and
- legal powers allow for Detention and Training Orders to be made on 10- to 11-year-olds for persistent offending and when the court considers that only custody is sufficient to protect the public from further offending. However, this has never been implemented.

Detention and Training Orders are for periods of 4, 6, 8, 10, 12, 18 or 24 months. In determining the length of the order, the court is required to take into account any period where the young person has been remanded to custody or in secure accommodation. Such periods are not deducted from the sentence.

The maximum period of detention available to magistrates at 24 months is significantly higher than the maximum in the adult Magistrates' Court, and this was specifically with the intention of reducing the number of young people being committed to Crown Court.

Section 76 states that the second half of the order will be a period of community supervision that will build on the work undertaken during the custodial period. The legislation provides for late release on the basis of poor behaviour but in practice this has been rarely used. An early release scheme not dissimilar to Home Detention Curfew has been introduced and most young people serving eight months or longer are considered for this.

The responsible officer, in most instances, will be a member of the YOT (depending on protocols in place with the local probation trust). He or she will be appointed at the start of the sentence and will also be responsible for post-release supervision. A range of conditions can be added to the Detention and Training Order notice of supervision, similar to an adult post-custody or young offender institute licence, and these include requirements for electronic monitoring and participation in an ISS programme

Breach of a notice of supervision will be dealt with in court and the young person may be fined or further detained for a period of three months or the remainder of the order – whichever is the shorter. New offences committed while the order is in force may result in a return to custody irrespective of the sentence for the new offence.

Long-term sentences

Short-term custodial sentences, as outlined above, have been rolled into the Detention and Training Order, and this represents the majority of custodial sentences for under–18s. The provisions for longer-term sentencing date back to Section 53 of the Children and Young Persons Act 1933, as updated by Sections 90 and 91 of the Powers of the Criminal Court (Sentencing) Act 2000. These sections allow the Crown Court to make what for adults would be life sentences, mandatory and discretionary – here termed detention at Her Majesty's Pleasure and detention for life respectively. Section 91 also provides for determinate sentences of longer than two years (the maximum length of the Detention and Training Order).

Sections 226 and 228 of the Criminal Justice Act 2003 add to the Section 91 provisions and allow for indeterminate sentences (detention for public protection) and extended sentences for cases which:

- could be liable for detention for life (Section 226) or involve a specified offence (Section 228), referring to Schedule 15 of the Act;
- are not judged to be sufficiently serious to warrant detention for life under Section 91 but involve a significant risk of *serious harm*.

These parallel the imprisonment for public protection and extended sentence provisions for adults, and have the same licence arrangements and recall procedures in place.

Rights and standards

Custodial sentences for young people have increased in frequency and length in the last 15 years, although the Ministry of Justice figures presented earlier record a recent drop. In contrast, 2,999 young people were in custody in June 2009 compared to figures of 1,419 and 1,564 for 1992 and 1994 respectively (Howard League for Penal Reform, 1995). This trend is likely to be enhanced by the provisions for longer sentences in a sentencing climate that is on an inflationary trajectory.

There are a whole host of concerns about young people being held in custody in the UK, particularly in relation to their rights. These include:

- the number of young people (primarily 15- to 17-year-old males) being held in prison rather than childcare establishments;
- the distance that that some young people are held away from home areas;
- physical conditions in some establishments;
- available facilities and services;
- inadequate regimes;
- discipline and restraint;
- bullying and harassment; and
- rates of self-harm and suicide.

There are particular and longstanding concerns surrounding young women in prison, as they have historically been held in establishments also containing adult women in contravention of Article 37 on the UNCRC. A long campaign by the Howard League for Penal Reform has ensured that 15- and 16-year-old females are no longer held in prisons. However, rather than also removing 17-year-old young women from prisons, in 2004 the YJB announced that they would be housed in special dedicated units within four prison establishments (Howard League for Penal Reform, 2005).

The YJB as commissioner of placements in the secure estate was instrumental in trying to drive up standards and used contractual arrangements as leverage in doing so. However, the demand for places in an overcrowded system is such that managing accommodation and basic security needs may well divert attention from quality of service and the resettlement needs of young offenders.

Parenting Orders

The Parenting Order, created by Sections 8-10 of the Crime and Disorder Act 1998, imposes requirements on parents or guardians to help them support their child in addressing his or her anti-social/offending behaviour. It is available in criminal, civil and family proceedings courts:

- when a court makes a Child Safety Order;
- when a court makes an ASBO or a Sexual Offence Prevention Order;
- where a child or young person has been convicted of an offence; or
- where a person has been convicted of an offence under the Education Act 1996, failure to comply with a school attendance order or failure of a registered pupil to secure regular attendance at school.

The Parenting Order can consist of two elements:

- a requirement on the parent or guardian to attend counselling or guidance sessions, a maximum of once a week, for up to three months; and

- requirements encouraging the parent or guardian to exercise a measure of control over the child, for example, attending school regularly or avoiding certain places and people, which can last for up to 12 months.

The order is overseen by a responsible officer, who will usually be a member of a YOT but could be within a probation trust or from local authority children's social care. In most areas, the Education Department will take responsibility for those orders made as a result of school non-attendance. Further provisions and extensions of Parenting Orders were contained in the Anti-Social Behaviour Act 2003, and these allow for Parenting Orders to be made in independent proceedings, that is, without an order being made on a young person at the same time.

Anti-social behaviour

If the use of custody for young people is one area of youth justice that is emotive and contentious, anti-social behaviour is clearly another. The irony is that the focus before 1995 was decidedly on crime, and it was only as the crime rates peaked and then reduced that the issues associated with anti-social behaviour came to the fore:

> For us the problematisation of ASB [anti-social behaviour] marks the arrival of an increasingly insecure, divided and intolerant culture. Likewise, the policing of ASB suggest an increasingly disciplinary society and, contrary to contemporary political rhetoric regarding social inclusion, a markedly more exclusive one. (Squires and Stephen, 2005, p 8)

Although initially anti-social behaviour measures were intended to deal with nuisance neighbour and other aspects of adult behaviour, ASBOs quickly became associated with young people and, along with other measures, used as a means of control. Part of the problem has been the lack of clarity about the dividing line between anti-social behaviour and criminal acts, defined in Section 1 of the Crime and Disorder Act 1998 as behaviour that *has caused or is likely to cause harassment alarm or distress* to persons beyond the perpetrator's immediate household. From these beginnings in 1998 the legal provisions and the structures to deal with anti-social behaviour have mushroomed.

Anti-Social Behaviour Orders

Section 1 of the Crime and Disorder Act permits a 'relevant authority' to apply for an ASBO in respect of an individual or individuals whose behaviour is anti-social. 'Relevant authorities' include the local authority, the police, British Transport Police and registered social landlords. An ASBO has effect for a minimum of two years and imposes prohibitions that the court considers necessary to prevent further anti-social acts. Although an ASBO is a civil order, breach is a criminal offence punishable by imprisonment.

The Police Reform Act 2002 significantly expanded the provisions for ASBOs by:

- allowing courts to make an ASBO on conviction of a criminal offence, (these orders are often referred to as 'CRASBOs');
- creating 'interim' ASBOs so that restrictions can be in place before a full hearing;
- allowing ASBOs to be made in county courts in, for example, possession proceedings involving anti-social behaviour; and
- allowing ASBOs to be made with conditions that cover any area within, or all of, England and Wales.

Although the take-up of ASBOs was initially slow, they have been increasingly used by local authorities and the police as a response to community concerns about anti-social behaviour and particularly 'youth nuisance', reinforcing the conflation of young people and crime in the collective public consciousness. In 2007, 920 young people were made subject to ASBOs, 40 per cent of the total number of ASBOs for that year (Home Office, 2009).

The Anti-Social Behaviour Act 2003

This Act extends penalty notices for disorderly behaviour to 16- and 17-year-olds (and potentially to younger ages by order of the Home Secretary) and controversially introduced powers of group dispersal. While a Dispersal Order is in force, it enables constables and police community support officers to break up groups of people and to require any person who does not live in the area covered by the order to leave and not to return within 24 hours.

This is a worrying development in terms of the freedom for young people to congregate in public spaces, added to which the Act contains provisions that enable a constable or police community support officer to remove a young person under 16 years and take him or her home, unless they believe that he or she may suffer significant harm there.

Prevention activities

Alongside the measures focused on enforcement and disruption, local areas have developed support and intervention projects, such as youth inclusion and support panels, mentoring schemes and voluntary parenting projects. These are positive initiatives, but availability varies across geographical areas and research has shown significant inconsistencies in the use of these measures and the balance of enforcement and support/diversion employed (Hughes and Follett, 2006; Matthews and Briggs, 2008). There are also strongly voiced and legitimate concerns about support and mentoring being available through a criminal justice route, rather than generic children's services, and the net-widening effect that might follow.

The Coalition government's plans to tackle anti-social behaviour

Tackling anti-social behaviour remains central in Home Office thinking, although the Coalition has been critical of the patchwork of provisions made available by New Labour to respond to anti-social behaviour and ASBOs in particular. The Coalition consultation document, *More effective responses to anti-social behaviour* (Home Office, 2011), states the intention to simplify the range of measures available and, specifically, to deal with bureaucratic delays. The proposed elements of this are

- a criminal behaviour order that will be available on conviction for any criminal offence, containing prohibitions but also required elements of support;
- a crime prevention injunction which will be a civil order with a civil burden of proof, making it easier to obtain than an ASBO. Such orders will have elements of prohibition and support;
- community protection orders, replacing a range of provisions such as noise abatement notices, dispersal orders and crack house closure orders

So what do the reforms add up to?

It is 10 years since YOTs came into being and the whole apparatus of youth justice began its growth spurt. It is now a developed system of its own, with real positives in the way that it strives to ensure that planning processes in mainstream services take account of the needs of hard-to-reach young offenders. However, many policies have had unintended impacts and, as often is the case, there is disjunction between the ideals enshrined in legislation and policy and how they are implemented on the ground. In particular, the anti-social behaviour measures and the generally interventionist nature of youth justice provision contain a considerable potential for controlling and criminalising young people at the margins of society.

Inevitably, specific aspects of these reforms were motivated by concerns about PYOs and those young people with complex and entrenched patterns of problematic behaviours. Sadly, New Labour's youth justice system does not seem to have risen to the challenges that these young people present. In a biting evaluation of the reforms, Solomon and Garside conclude that:

> The overall picture is of a YJS [youth justice system] that was designed with the best intentions of providing effective multi-agency provision, but that in practice is struggling to meet the needs of a group of vulnerable children and young people who require carefully co-ordinated specialist support. (2008, p 11)

As indicated earlier, YOTs need to connect and build relationships with the full range of children's services as well as with criminal justice agencies, and it is hard to maintain all those links at both strategic and operational levels. Perhaps in some respects, what YOTs have been tasked with is just too ambitious, particularly in a social climate where young people are not viewed sympathetically and are the focus of so much adult anxiety and distrust. It is not surprising, then, that youth justice reforms have amounted to a mixed bag of successes and failures, and that often the efforts of YOTs have been characterised by a bureaucratic processing of young people, rather than consistent and positive responses to their (often complex) needs.

A summing up by Rob Allen, former member of the YJB, indicates that:

> There are aspects of Labour's reforms that have had a positive impact....
>
> There are other elements that are deeply disappointing: the increasing criminalisation of young people involved in minor delinquency and the stubbornly high use of custodial remands and sentencing. Finally, there are some developments of which we really should be ashamed – in particular aspects of the way we lock up children, the demonisation of young people engaged in ASB [anti-social behaviour], and the coarsening of the public debate about how to deal with young people in trouble. The state of the youth justice system can perhaps best be described as the good, the bad and the ugly. (2005, p 9)

Summary

The reforms of the youth justice system began with the Crime and Disorder Act 1998, have continued since and will move into yet another phase as the Coalition government reveals its plans. Youth justice services have already coped with a spate of new initiatives in working with offenders and in anti-social behaviour and prevention projects. This is challenging work and inevitably some of the enterprising spirit found in the early YOTs has eroded in the face of stringent expectations of performance and managerial pressures. This chapter has identified developments and trends in punishment and control that are regrettable and open to criticism. Nevertheless, at a practice level youth justice still holds elements of the 'traditional' focus of earlier probation and social services intervention, working with young people towards change in the context of their families and communities.

In many respects, youth justice case management is similar to adult offender management, based on sound assessment of risks and needs. Maturity, personal development and social/family support networks should be carefully considered, so that interventions are age-appropriate and able to engage young people. Enabling young people to access positive sources of *social capital*, as discussed in Chapter Four, is also important in easing the transition to adulthood. As with adult work, there is potential for practitioners to avoid the pressures to work in routinised and bureaucratic ways, and to develop an approach that values young people and their experiences and respects their rights and social needs.

Further reading

Brown, S. (2005) *Understanding youth and crime: Listening to youth?*, Maidenhead: Open University Press.

Muncie, J. (2009) *Youth and crime* (3rd edn), London: Sage Publications.

Wood, J. and Hine, J. (eds) (2009) *Work with young people*, London: Sage Publications.

FIFTEEN

Substance use and misuse

The criminal justice system has a long history of involvement with offenders experiencing problems with alcohol. From the 1980s, with heroin widely available on the streets, drug-using offenders have also featured prominently. Both present dilemmas in determining whether the balance should be in favour of care or control, treatment or punishment and restraint. In policy terms, the emotive pull of the 'war on drugs' and, more recently, inter-agency developments, have occupied the agenda. In contrast, alcohol and its impacts have received relatively little attention and few resources, perhaps reflecting ambivalence about its place within western culture and the commercial power of producers and retailers.

The discussion in this chapter makes clear distinctions between (illegal) drugs and (legal) alcohol. Psychological and many social aspects of problematic or dependent use are similar for drugs and alcohol, and many individuals are involved with both. However, they are treated differently in criminal justice terms and adult treatment services for drugs and alcohol are separate (young people's services are more likely to deal with both).

Crime and substance misuse

Currently adult drug users coming into contact with the criminal justice system may access services from the point of arrest through to sentence, by virtue of prison-based services and the DRR on community orders. Over the past two decades, policy makers have explicitly required treatment services and criminal justice agencies to come together, although historically they have not sat comfortably alongside each other, and tensions still exist around the concept and practice of treatment under coercion. Policy has been driven by an underlying belief that drugs and crime are linked and, specifically, that drug use causes crime (Heath, 2010). Such assumptions are worth exploring and testing against the evidence.

There are three main explanatory models for the relationship between drugs and crime (Bean, 2008):

- Drugs cause crime – most obviously where dealing or possession of a substance is a criminal offence in itself or in connection with the operation of the drugs market. This explanation also covers situations where crime is committed to fund drugs or results from the effects of drugs, such as inhibition or intoxication.
- Crime leads to drug use – perhaps because criminal subcultures are supportive of drug use, or where environmental conditions provide access and opportunities.

- Drug use and crime have a common aetiology or origin – this suggests that the links between drugs and crime are not necessarily direct and certainly one does not cause the other. It does suggest, however, that they arise from common causes, such as poverty, social isolation and individual psychological factors.

There are further but less developed arguments to the effect that drugs and crime may have a reciprocal relationship (Bennett and Holloway, 2005): in other words, drugs cause crime *and* crime causes drug use, so the causal connection can work in either direction and there may be a mutually reinforcing effect, although as yet little is known about how that might work (Bean, 2008).

Bennett and Holloway's (2005) summary of the research evidence on the links between drugs and crime found that high-rate drug users are more likely to be offenders than other drug users or non-users, and that they offend more frequently. Similarly high-rate offenders are more likely to be drug users than non-offenders or less prolific offenders. This provides strong evidence that drug use in general and crime in general are associated, but does not prove that one necessarily causes the other.

Looking more closely at the relationship between offending and drug use studies suggest that the connection varies according to drug type, with heroin, crack and cocaine most strongly connected. There is a weaker association between offending and recreational drugs, such as amphetamine and cannabis (Bennett et al, 2008). However, less is known about the nature of the relationship, particularly where drugs are being used in combination, for instance, heroin and crack together (Bennett and Holloway, 2005).

The offending patterns most strongly associated with drug use involve acquisitive crime or drug dealing. However patterns may vary, with women seemingly more likely to resort to sex work, drug dealing and shoplifting than to burglaries and robberies to support their drug use (Bennett and Holloway, 2005).

In the 1990s, official policy in relation to young people was predicated on the assumption that 'soft' drugs and alcohol act as a 'gateway' to further drug use and a criminal career. Again, Bennett and Holloway's (2005) review of the available research is revealing. Studies suggest that young people had typically experienced their first drug use before the time they had committed their first offence. However, this pattern was reversed when 'hard' drugs such as heroin were concerned, as the start of Class A drug use tended to occur after the onset of criminal activity. These contradictory findings point to complicated relationships and possible causal connections between drugs and offending. In each individual case, situational and personal factors also play a part. Further research adds to the complexity by suggesting that the drugs–crime connection may be stronger for adults than it is for young people (Bennett et al, 2008). As a result, Gateway theories are now largely discredited, and official messages have had to adapt to respond to the reality of cannabis use in mainstream youth culture.

The associations between drug use and criminality, then, are subtle and complex, and both are connected to the social and economic conditions that shape the lives of disadvantaged groups and communities. However, this complexity has received little official recognition in the face of dominant assumptions about a causal link between the two. Drugs and crime exist within deeply embedded cultures and structures that reinforce social deprivation, and 'it is this nettle – of social inequality – that is hard for policy-makers to grasp' (Hughes and Anthony, 2006, p 88).

Transformations in drug policy

The definition of drug use as a social problem is a relatively recent phenomenon, although the practice of taking substances for their palliative or mind-altering properties is not new in itself. The framing of drug (and alcohol) use as a problem has political dimensions and responses based on:

> A distinction between the drug use of the unrespectable poor, who have been understood as weak, inadequate and immoral and susceptible to vice, and drug usage by the respectable, professional and middle class, who are more likely to be understood as suffering from a disease. (Scott and Codd, 2010, p 129)

Historically, there is evidence of cannabis, opium poppies and coca leaves being used by ancient civilisations with little or no moral condemnation and few social controls (Bennett and Holloway, 2005). In the UK, opium products were familiar household items during the 1800s, and cocaine and other drugs were available for purchase, mainly for medical purposes. However, rising awareness of public health, child deaths from opiates administered as a sedative or cough suppressant, and moral panics over Chinese 'opium dens' combined to produce a change in previously permissive social attitudes (Bennett and Holloway, 2005).

The control of drugs began in earnest in the late Victorian period. Two approaches to regulation soon became apparent, focusing on the law and criminal justice on the one hand, and medicalisation and treatment on the other (Shiner, 2006). UK policy has tended to feature a mixture of the two. The medical view, underpinned by a view of drug use as a disease, initially held sway. However, at the same time, the Dangerous Drugs Acts of 1920 and 1923 criminalised possession of controlled drugs unless under prescription from a doctor. The earlier Defence of the Realms Acts during the First World War had already restricted possession of cocaine and introduced regulation of alcohol sales, thus establishing the Home Office in a central role. Nevertheless, the Rolleston Committee in 1926 reaffirmed the disease model of addiction and the practice of prescribing heroin and morphine to dependent individuals in what became known as the 'British System' (Bean, 2008).

This medical approach dominated for almost four decades and was further endorsed by the first report of the Brain Committee in 1961. However, by that time, drug use was no longer restricted to a small and stable group of middle-class (often medical) professionals dependent on opiates. More substances were available – now including cannabis, LSD and amphetamines – and they were being taken by increasingly younger and more socially varied users. Noting this, and seeking to tighten up lax prescribing practices, in the late 1960s the government introduced a raft of new legislation and implemented the recommendations of the second Brain Committee report. This restricted prescribing to licensed doctors only and required them to notify details of each addicted patient to the Home Office, resulting in the development of specialist clinics or units and, over time, a preference for prescribing oral methadone rather than heroin (Bennett and Holloway, 2005).

The high point of the medical dominance of the drugs field was reached in the 1960s. Thereafter, prevention and criminalisation have increasingly characterised official responses as the debate has been intensively politicised (Shiner, 2006), although in the 1980s, harm reduction approaches also became important with the explosion in heroin users and the emergence of the human immuno-deficiency virus (HIV) (Hughes and Anthony, 2006).

In May 1995, the Conservative government published *Tackling drugs together: A strategy for England and Wales 1995-98* (Home Office, 1995), which promised further action on tackling drug supplies, but also a renewed focus on strong actions to reduce demand (Bennett and Holloway, 2005). The strategy also proposed bringing agencies together in Drug Action Teams (DATs), a partnership approach implemented by New Labour as it assumed power (Heath, 2010). Their own strategy *Tackling drugs to build a better Britain* (Home Office, 1998b) contained four elements:

- to help young people resist drug use in order to achieve their full potential in society;
- to protect our communities from drug-related anti-social and criminal behaviour;
- to enable people with drug problems to overcome them and to live crime-free lives;
- to stifle the availability of illegal drugs on our streets.

Importantly, this signalled a move from voluntary provision to coerced treatment as part of a court order (Bennett and Holloway, 2005), and the explicit mention of public health and health risk that had featured in the 1995 strategy was dropped (Lart, 2006). Alongside this, the post of national drugs coordinator (the 'drugs tsar') was created to spear head the fight against drugs, significant in setting the combative tone of policy and establishing the Home Office, rather than the Department of Health as lead agency (Heath, 2010). This is reflected in the later *Updated drugs strategy* (Home Office, 2002c) and a quantity of criminal justice legislation containing new powers to expand drug testing and treatment delivered through criminal justice routes. Aspects of these developments are problematic and may well be self-defeating in neglecting the psychological, social and economic factors that shape drug use and the behaviours of drug users:

> Hostility towards illegal substances has become synonymous with hostility towards illegal substance users, making it harder for those recovering to socially reintegrate. With a growing commitment by the UK government to use the criminal justice system to deliver drug treatment combined with rigorous drug testing and regular reviews, there is a risk that the physical aspects of addiction may be mistakenly over-emphasised. (Buchanan, 2008, p 246)

The language of the last New Labour strategy covering 2008-18 is largely consistent with the above, and robustly pledged to:

> Reduce drug-related offending through more effective targeting and offender management, continuing to identify and grip drug-misusing offenders, so that we drive down anti-social behaviour and crimes such as burglary and robbery. (HM Government, 2008, p 11)

Interestingly, much of this is continued in the Coalition's Drug Strategy issued in December 2010, although with an emphasis on voluntary sector support and treatment provision and the introduction of PBR (see Chapter Four).

Regulatory framework

The focus of UK legislation in relation to drugs is prohibition, contrasting with the approach to alcohol, although this is also associated with physical and social harms. Despite calls for drugs to be decriminalised, the Coalition government has confirmed its commitment to maintaining current legal sanctions.

The main Act of significance is the Misuse of Drugs Act 1971 which is based on the principle that the state has a duty to protect its members from causing harm to others as well as to themselves. The Act classifies drugs according to their potential for harm as A, B or C, with each class attracting different levels of punishment (Shiner, 2006). Currently, the legal penalties are as laid out in Table 15.1.

The criteria on which harmfulness is judged is not straightforward or based on consistent evidence. Interestingly, Nutt et al (2007), in *The Lancet*, propose a different and more transparent system of assessing harm based on physical, social and dependency-related factors. Table 15.2 outlines the substances as classified by the 1971 Act, with an indication of relative harmfulness as rated through the system devised by Nutt and colleagues, 1 being the most harmful and 20 the least. This reveals significant and interesting divergences within these 'hierarchies

Table 15.1: Misuse of Drugs Act 1971 penalties

	Possession	Supply
Class A	7 years' imprisonment and/or fine	Life imprisonment and/or fine
Class B	5 years' imprisonment and/or fine	14 years' imprisonment and/or fine
Class C	2 years' imprisonment and/or fine	14 years' imprisonment and/or fine

Table 15.2: Classification of substances under the Misuse of Drugs Act 1971

Substance	Class A	Class B	Class C	None	Nutt et al (2007) harm rating
Heroin	X				1
Cocaine/crack cocaine	X				2
Barbiturates		X			3
Street methadone	X				4
Alcohol				X	5
Ketamine			X		6
Benzodiazepines (eg Valium, Librium)			X		7
Amphetamine		X			8
Tobacco				X	9
Buphrenorphine (eg Tamgesic, Subutex)			X		10
Cannabis		X			11
Solvents				X	12
4 -metahylioamphetamine	X				13
LSD	X				14
Methylphenidate (eg Ritalin)		X			15
Anabolic steroids			X		16
GHB			X		17
Ecstasy	X				18
Alkyl nitrates				X	19
Khat				X	20

Note: Class B drugs such as amphetamines prepared for injection are treated as Class A. Methadone and related substances have recently been included in Class B.

Source: Adapted from Nutt et al (2007, pp 1049-50)

of harm'. Certainly Professor Nutt, as a former chair of the Advisory Council on the Misuse of Drugs, tried strenuously to raise debate about the existing approach to regulation, although sadly without success.

There is clearly some convergence in the two classification systems, with heroin and crack being in the top bracket of both. The discrepancies particularly relate to the level of harm associated with alcohol, tobacco and solvents which are not covered by the Act but which rated as highly harmful in Nutt et al's (2007) system. An earlier Inquiry by the Police Federation also found that most controlled drugs were no more harmful than alcohol and tobacco, and that cannabis was less harmful than either of these. It had further concluded that the Misuse of Drugs Act overstates the harmfulness of particular drugs (Shiner, 2006), especially LSD and ecstasy.

Putting aside the debates about the classification of particular substances, policy over the past decade has focused the efforts of correctional agencies more specifically on users of heroin and crack cocaine, where there is less controversy about harm (although still significant debates about what social responses are most appropriate). Alongside this, the New Labour administration adopted a more strategic approach to alcohol, linked to both the public health and crime and disorder agendas.

Effects and patterns of use

The previous discussion outlined the legal categories applied to various substances but they can also be grouped according to their psycho-pharmacological effects:

- stimulants speed up the central nervous system to increase neural activity in the brain. Stimulant substances include amphetamine, cocaine/crack cocaine, ecstasy and, interestingly, caffeine;
- depressants slow down the central nervous system and may cause drowsiness. Substances with depressant effects include alcohol, heroin and other opiates, and tranquillisers such as Valium;
- hallucinogens alter perceptions and sensory experiences. Examples of hallucinogenic drugs are LSD, magic mushrooms and some strong forms of cannabis.

Whereas individuals who use substances regularly will tend to have a preferred drug – or drug of first choice – in practice, many will use a variety of substances, sometimes depending on availability or cost. Other combinations are more deliberate, as in 'speed-balling' with the use of heroin and cocaine. It may be that multiple drug use reflects a chaotic and problematic lifestyle, but this cannot be assumed; for other individuals it will represent a consumer choice, and is about exercising control rather than lack of control.

Patterns of substance use vary tremendously, with the majority of adults in the UK drinking alcohol and a significant minority of respondents to surveys such as the BCS reporting having used controlled drugs within the previous year (25 per cent of 16- to 25-year-olds and 11 per cent of 16- to 59-year-olds in the 2005/06 BCS; cited in Bean, 2008). A simple typology suggests that substance use can be:

- experimental
- recreational
- problematic
- dependent.

The first two of these are likely to attract little official attention except in relation to young people. Alcohol and drug use of any kind at a young age has been treated as a risk factor in terms of developing more problematic patterns of drug use and criminality, causing concern for some that this produces too much intervention that does not sufficiently distinguish between these different levels of use (Melrose, 2006).

In medical terms, a diagnosis of dependence may be made when:

- there is an increased tolerance for the drug;
- there are signs of physical and/or psychological dependence; and
- there are signs of withdrawal symptoms if drug use is stopped. (Bennett and Holloway, 2005, p 9)

Individuals who are dependent may need medical intervention to relieve physical or psychological symptoms, alongside assistance to deal with social and other conditions. However, an entirely medical approach based on assumptions about biological compulsion may not be helpful in terms of engaging an offender actively in treatment because it limits the extent to which he or she can be encouraged to take responsibility for his or her problems and actions to address them. Seeing dependent behaviour as located within a social and cultural context helps understand it as a response to environmental circumstances, influenced by personal factors (Farrow et al, 2007).

Problematic substance use may manifest itself in different ways and may not even involve a pattern of regular use. Many of the crime and disorder concerns associated with alcohol relate to problematic rather than dependent use, and may involve rowdiness or aggression, for instance, after binge drinking. The frequency of drug use or alcohol use may not be the primary concern, but the pattern or nature of use may cause legal, financial, psychological, physical or family problems.

Women and drug use

A separate note on women in relation to drug use is important, because it should not be assumed that their motivations for using/continuing to use drugs are entirely the same as for men or that their experiences equate. Women's problematic drug use tends to be more strongly linked to violence, sexual abuse, exploitation, intimidation and poverty (DrugScope, 2005), both in their personal histories and in their current life circumstances. Research suggests that, compared to men, women typically move more quickly from the point of first use to dependent use and that their initiation into drug use is more often associated with their intimate relationships (Anglin and Hser, 1987). Moreover, the world of drug use is male-dominated and women tend not to occupy powerful positions within drug-dealing hierarchies, reflecting their structural position in society.

The question of power is significant in relation to women drug users, with some arguing that women users, with few exceptions, are restricted to passive and victimised roles (Morgan and Joe, 1996). Rosenbaum refers to the narrowing range of options available to women as they become more involved in drug use, which are even more limited than those open to male users (1981). Other feminist voices have challenged views of women drug users as socially inadequate and pathological. Trish Harding, for instance, cites Taylor's ethnographic study of women sex workers in Glasgow that found women drug users to be 'rational, active people making decisions based on the contingencies of both their drug-using careers and their roles and status in society' (Taylor, 1993, p 8).

Women who use drugs are often of child-bearing age, and this may be significant in terms of:

- the impact of drug use during pregnancy and child birth;
- relationships with child welfare agencies;
- reluctance to disclose drug use or present for treatment because of fear that children may be taken away;
- the difficulties of regaining custody of children once they have been removed and the emotional impact of this (Bean, 2008);
- their role as primary carers for dependent children (Harding, 2006).

More positively, pregnancy and parenthood may motivate some women to cease drug use, where they experience a conflict between their identities as drug users and as mothers. In terms of assuming new non-offending identities, the role of mother may provide an available, if conventional, alternative identity and purpose (Bean, 2008). However, for some women that is simply not achievable, and they experience the double stigma associated first with offending against the law and second against the social norms expected of women, in terms of sobriety but also in terms of the sexual stereotype that demands they should be capable of keeping men in order (Broom and Stevens, 1991). Considering desistance and moving on from drug use,

> The point is that male drug users can more easily reclaim their status; women find it harder to do so, especially where the label was that of a junkie. (Bean, 2008, p 224)

All the above indicates why women's needs from treatment tend to differ from men's and why a more broad-based holistic approach is appropriate. This sort of provision is not consistently available and women often find themselves shoehorned into treatment options designed for men (Bean, 2008). Moreover, recent policy in relation to street sex workers has focused on coercing them into entering treatment, assuming a simplistic (and inaccurate) causal link between drug use and involvement in sex work and ignoring the wider social and economic context of their lives (Melrose, 2009). Nevertheless, examples of good practice have developed, one being the 218 Project in Glasgow, which demonstrates the benefits of a woman-centred approach that offers flexible and varied sources of support (Malloch and Louckes, 2007).

Strategic multi-agency partnerships

Discussion now turns to a more explicit focus on the policy context, outlining the strategies in place and the operational structures beneath them. The strategic framework around drugs interventions was established in the late 1990s with the setting up of DATs and CDRPs (now CSPs). Neither are legal entities, but both provide structures that bring statutory and voluntary sector partners together to agree on shared aims and actions. The interests of CSPs are primarily in crime reduction, but this includes actions to address drug-related offending and problems arising from the misuse of alcohol in the night-time economy. CSPs have therefore worked closely with DATs and in unitary authority areas many have combined to become one body.

DATs (or DAATs, where alcohol is included in their remit) are not service providers, but provide a commissioning structure for drug and alcohol services for adults and, separately, for young people. They allocate resources from a pooled budget of money granted currently from the National Treatment Agency (but this will change under the Coalition government) and from other sources such as the Home Office, intended for specific initiatives such as the DIP. At present, primary care trusts hold the money and take care of the operational side of commissioning, but again this will be subject to change under Coalition plans.

Commissioning currently follows the Models of Care framework established by the National Treatment Agency that identifies services at four levels or tiers:

> Tier 1: Information and advice, screening and referral to specialised drug treatments
> Tier 2: Information and advice, assessment, referral to structured drug treatment, brief psycho-social interventions, harm reduction interventions and aftercare following specialised treatment
> Tier 3: Community-based specialised drug assessment and coordinated treatment supported by care planning, drug specialist liaison
> Tier 4: Residential specialised drug treatment, with care planning and coordination to ensure continuity of care and aftercare. (adapted from NTA, 2006)

As with other partnerships, DATs represent a mixture of local flexibility to deal with the needs and circumstances of the area, and nationally set objectives and standards (in this case by the Home Office and the National Treatment Agency). The challenges that they face include:

- a complex set of accountabilities, with members of the DAT board collectively accountable to the Home Office and each individually accountable to his or her own agency and to the other members of the board;
- ensuring that commissioning is evidence-based and informed by service providers, service users/ex-users and carers;
- achieving a balance between criminal justice and health interests so that there is equity for those individuals accessing treatment through non-criminal justice routes;
- ensuring that the local delivery structure is able to handle data sensitively so as to fulfil the dual requirements of confidentiality around clinical information and

of passing information about compliance to courts and enforcement agencies (adapted from Woodin, 2007).

Moreover, DATs and CSPs have been tied into relevant targets set in Public Service Agreements, which make explicit links between drug use and criminal activity and identify treatment as a means of reducing the harm caused by drugs and alcohol. The instrumental crime reduction rationale is apparent in the organisation of services and targeting of resources, with health and well-being being secondary drivers in recent service development.

Drugs Intervention Programme

The DIP was established in 2003 and since 2005 has been fully operational across England and Wales. It has received considerable investment and political impetus for its stated aims of improving through-care and aftercare for drug-misusing offenders. Delivered locally by CJITs, it employs a case management approach in order to provide continuity of approach from arrest to sentence and beyond (Turnbull and Skinns, 2010).

DIP services are primarily located within Tier 2 of the Models of Care framework and include:

* arrest referral schemes, where DIP workers make contact with individuals in custody suites with a view to assessment and referral to treatment services;
* drug testing in the police station (either on arrest or charge);
* restrictions on bail (see Chapter Nine);
* support for offenders in prison and on release from prison.

From 2006, the 'Tough Choices' regime was introduced in specified 'intensive DIP' areas. The Drugs Act 2005 permits police officers in these areas to require an offender who has tested positive for a Class A drug to undertake an initial assessment with a drugs workers and a mandatory follow-up appointment with the CJIT. This significantly increases the element of coercion and raises concerns in relation to rights in those cases where the offender is not charged or is acquitted at court. The choice referred to is the choice to attend as directed and to stay for the duration of appointments or to accept the consequences in terms of a court appearance and possible sanctions.

Messages about the effects and the effectiveness of DIP are mixed, partly because schemes vary considerably from one area to another in terms of the services commissioned and the case management approach employed (Turnbull and Skinns, 2010). Concerns have been expressed in relation to sex workers and whether the treatment options available are sufficiently responsive to their complex and diverse needs. These women are already penalised but risk further penalisation if they choose not to access or to stay in inappropriate treatment (Sanders et al, 2009).

Nevertheless, the main evaluation research on DIP (Skodbo et al, 2007) produced positive findings. A cohort of 7,727 offenders dealt with through test on arrest or charge schemes reduced their offending by 26 per cent, although, with no comparison group in place, it is unclear how much of this reduction was due to DIP interventions. Entry into treatment and retention treatment levels were also better than for previous types of arrest referral schemes, both for the standard DIP clients and those subject to Tough Choices (Skodbo et al, 2007).

A further study of the workings of CJITs (ICPR, 2007) also showed that they enabled offenders to make significant reductions in both drug use and offending. However, attrition rates at the early assessment stage were high, in common with other types of arrest referral schemes. Areas for improvement were highlighted as coordination of services, information exchange and closer integration. These are highly pertinent given subsequent developments in bringing DIPs and CJITs within the ambit of Integrated Offender Management and the challenges of achieving a level of inter-agency integration never previously experienced (Turnbull and Skinns, 2010).

Sentencing and treatment

The question of treatment within a sentencing framework is a sensitive one, and fundamentally hinges on the debate about the ethicality and viability of treatment under coercion. The different attitudes to voluntarism and coercion are at the crux of historical and cultural differences between criminal justice agencies and treatment providers, often from the voluntary sector. Within a partnership arena dominated by commissioning arrangements, agencies do not necessarily meet as equals and contracting agencies can use their power to ensure that their perspectives and purposes override the professional autonomy of partners (Heath, 2010). In this regard, criminal justice interests may often 'trump' clinical priorities and autonomy.

The first specific sentencing provision relating to treatment allied to probation supervision came in Schedule 1A(6) of the Criminal Justice Act 1991, which permitted a condition to be attached to a Probation Order requiring the offender to comply with treatment. Extended powers were subsequently introduced by the Crime and Disorder Act 1998, which created the Drug Treatment and Testing Order, and by the Criminal Justice Act 2003, which provides for a DRR to be included as part of a community order. The DRR allows for more flexibility than the previous Drug Treatment and Testing Order, and is able to include a greater variety of interventions in terms of treatment types and intensities.

In all three cases the offender must consent to treatment before the requirement can be imposed and this defines the treatment as 'coerced' rather than compulsory, because the offender has an element of choice in whether or not to comply (Heath, 2010). However, coercion is not straightforward, and Philip Bean comments that:

> Much confusion centres on the term "coercion", as if there were something sinister about the fact that offenders are coerced ... it is not whether coercion is acceptable for, by definition, coercion is part of criminal justice. The questions are, or should be: what is an acceptable level of coercion and what should be the powers of those able to coerce? What should the boundaries be of a coercive regime? (2008, p 87)

The extent and form of drug testing is one area of tension, as is the level of contact required and whether this should reflect clinical need or the seriousness of offending (Stevens, 2010). These points have been, and will no doubt continue to be, debated within partnerships and between professionals concerned to find an appropriate balance between managing risks and respecting the rights and choices of offenders.

Interestingly, Bean (2008) cites research evidence from the US suggesting that, in terms of treatment outcomes, it is more important that individuals enter treatment and stay in treatment than whether they found their way there voluntarily or under coercion. Maintaining motivation and retention in treatment are critically dependent on relationships of trust between professionals and those in treatment (Stevens, 2010).

Aside from these wider debates, there are concerns about implementation of the current arrangements in the UK and whether they meet appropriate ethical standards. Quality and reliability of testing is one significant issue (Bean, 2008), as was the rush to implement Drug Treatment and Testing Orders before the evaluation results from the pilots were available, with consequent impacts on national rollout (Stevens, 2010). The push for the DIP and for Drug Treatment and Testing Orders and DRRs is politically inspired, not based on evidence of effectiveness and carefully crafted inter-agency arrangements (Bean, 2008). Overall, through these measures, New Labour's targets of directing at least 1,000 offenders per week into treatment by March 2008 were exceeded. Nevertheless, this increased activity has not resulted in a reduction in the numbers of those sent to prison and seems instead to have expanded the reach of correctional control. Although many have benefited from supportive relationships and access to services that help them deal with dependency,

> This does not mean we should unthinkingly corral ever-increasing numbers of drug users into treatment. To do so would not only threaten the human rights to which all of us are entitled, but also damage the principles of successful treatment which appear to apply equally to the increasingly large number of people who enter it through the criminal justice system. (Stevens, 2010, p 183)

The role of the courts in drug treatment

The role of the courts has expanded with the development of Drug Treatment and Testing Orders and then DRRs as sentencing options, because of the requirement to bring offenders back to court periodically to review progress. However, examples of a fuller and more involved role for sentencers have grown in the US and have been established in sheriff courts in Fife and Glasgow and also in Dublin (Bean, 2008). From 2006, drug courts have operated in a more modified fashion in West London and Leeds and will be extended to other sites (McIvor, 2010).

Two main features distinguish drug courts from more traditional court settings, including the framework for Drug Treatment and Testing Order and DRR reviews (which is conventional in terms of criminal justice process). First, the judge or sheriff is more centrally involved in supervision of the offender and, second, the process itself is intended to contribute to the therapeutic aims of the treatment intervention:

> Under traditional court models, rehabilitation may be an aim of criminal justice processing, but within a model of therapeutic jurisprudence, it is intrinsic to the process. (McIvor, 2010, p 135)

Essentially, it is a different way of delivering justice, with a closer integration of criminal justice and treatment goals, and attention to the process rather than the procedures involved (McIvor, 2009). Further distinguishing features of the US drug courts are summarised by Philip Bean (2008, p 125) and contrasted with practice on Drug Treatment and Testing Orders (which have not changed significantly with the introduction of DRRs) (see Table 15.3).

The contribution of the probation service within the drug court model is reduced in the light of a stronger alliance between the courts and treatment

Table 15.3: Comparing drugs courts and DTTO review courts

Drugs courts	Drug Treatment and Testing Orders review courts
Aim is abstinence. That may include alcohol	Aim is harm reduction, especially heroin or cocaine
Treatment providers are employed by the court	Treatment providers work for the probation service
Judge conducts the supervision	Probation service conducts the supervision
Adversarial system replaced by team approach	Adversarial system remains intact
Judge can impose multiple sanctions	Court restricted in breach proceedings defined by legislation
Drug test results sent to the judge immediately	Drug test results take up to five days before arriving at court
Courtroom procedure is less formal	Formal procedures remain
Offender may be required to pay for treatment	Treatment a part of NHS provision
Drugs court judge concentrates on drug offenders	Judges retain full range of offenders
Probation service has only a minor part to play	Probation service is central to the workings of the Drug Treatment and Testing Order

providers – effectively cutting out the mediating and monitoring function that the service performs. The effect is to create a more direct link between the judge or sheriff and the offender, and a greater degree of informed interest. Studies in Scotland found that participants identified the most important characteristics of drug court sheriffs as being their willingness to listen and to understand, their discretion, insight and tact and their knowledge about the issues that they face as drug users (McIvor, 2009).

Furthermore, drugs courts are not only associated with reduced recidivism (McIvor, 2010); they have other positive benefits:

> The exchanges that take place between sentencers and offenders can be a critical element in encouraging compliance both during an order and in the longer term. Elements of procedural justice were clearly manifested in the Scottish drugs courts and this, ...is likely to confer greater legitimacy to sentencers and to increase the responsiveness of participants to exhortations that they should change. (McIvor, 2009, p 47)

Judicial involvement may assist rehabilitation by recognising where an offender is changing ways of thinking and being, and is engaged in the process of creating a new life narrative and an identity dissociated from drug use and offending (McIvor, 2010). In this sense, there is potential to empower and enable offenders in their change. This is highly significant for drug-using offenders, because they are typically excluded, marginalised and stigmatised socially and economically. But these sorts of judicial processes and problem-solving orientations may be appropriate for wider use in relation to different types of offending behaviours and situations (for instance, to respond to offenders engaged in domestic violence or with mental ill health or learning disabilities).

Drug interventions in prisons

The discussion so far has focused on the courts and treatment in the community, but these are not the only areas where policy has changed and developed in response to political and social pressures. Historically prisons have not worked to any explicit policy statement in relation to drugs although, by the 1980s and the appearance of HIV, it was becoming clear that the Home Office advocated an abstinence approach (Scott and Codd, 2010). This stance has proved problematic in terms of dealing with the numbers of drug-using offenders entering prisons and coping with the reality of drug use within prison establishments. Prisoners may use drugs such as cannabis and heroin to help survive the boredom and mundanity of prison life, but also for relaxation and escapism (Paylor et al, 2010). Illegal drugs in these respects can assist in maintaining order within prisons, but they may also present points of conflict in terms of the internal illicit economy and the problems of violence and intimidation associated with prisoner debt (Scott and Codd, 2010). Additionally, there are concerns about the medical use of drugs in prison, particularly the over-prescription of heavy tranquillisers such as Largactil for women prisoners (Bean, 2008).

The first prison drugs policy was published in 1995 and it has been since updated in line with successive Home Office drug strategies. The most recent version in 2008 continues the emphasis on:

- reducing the supply of drugs into prisons, through improved security and surveillance;
- reducing the demand through provision of rehabilitation; and
- effective through-care, aiming to improve continuity of care as prisoners are released back into the community.

Incorporating the prison service drugs strategy into the wider NOMS strategy should in theory promote consistency and coordination of prison and community-based services and improve through-care, which has previously suffered from not being the primary responsibility of any one single agency (Paylor et al, 2010).

Treatment options within prison have expanded as resources have grown, although they still remain overly focused on opiate use and struggle to cope with the diversity of drug users and drug use (Paylor et al, 2010). As well as methadone prescribing, current provision includes:

- CARAT services (Counselling, Assessment, Referral, Advice and Through-care) – available in every prison, workers provide case management as well as assessment and both individual and group intervention.
- Integrated Drug Treatment Services – an expansion and enhancement of CARAT, this was launched in 2008 to improve both clinical and psycho-social interventions and coordination of services.
- Medical interventions – including detoxification and maintenance prescribing for prisoners in receipt of methadone before their imprisonment.
- Drug-free voluntary testing units and voluntary testing programmes.
- 12-step treatment programmes – this includes programmes provided by Alcoholics Anonymous and the Rehabilitation of Addicted Prisoners Trust;
- Cognitive Behavioural Therapy – both high and low intensity programmes are available and these may take a harm reduction approach.
- Prison – Addressing Substance-Related Offending programme (P-ASRO) – an accredited programme of low to medium intensity.
- Therapeutic communities – these provided 300 bed spaces in the prison system in 2006/07 (adapted from UK Drugs Policy Commission, 2008, p 10).

In addition, DIP workers support short-term prisoners during their sentences and attempt to ensure that they are linked in to community treatment services on release. This adds up to a complex patchwork of multi-agency provision that is not necessarily consistent and comprehensive (Paylor et al, 2010). Rehabilitation in prison remains difficult, both in practical terms and in terms of the prison environment and regimes which are not conducive to abstinence and treatment (Scott and Codd, 2010). Nevertheless, there is more support available for drug-using offenders if they are in prison and recognition that support and intervention should be continued in the community, even if the mechanisms to deliver this are imperfect.

Approaches to alcohol

Policy approaches to alcohol are necessarily different because of its legal status and the commercial interests involved. They are significantly less underpinned by notions of a simple causal connection between use and offending, despite the evident crime and disorder concerns surrounding the night-time economy and public drunkenness. The treatment aspects of drugs policy are focused on routes into treatment through the criminal justice system, with the ultimate aim of promoting abstinence. Policy in relation to alcohol has developed differently with more emphasis on prevention and management.

In an attempt to bring together all the various actions to tackle the harm caused by alcohol, New Labour published the *Alcohol harm reduction strategy for England* in 2004, which was updated in 2008 in *Safe, sensible, social: The next steps in the national alcohol strategy* (HM Government, 2008). Key to its success is the Licensing Act 2003 which will shortly be subject to review. The Act contained a range of new powers to regulate the sale of alcohol and to increase the penalties for licensees acting irresponsibly (for instance, selling alcohol to children). It also expanded police powers to close down disorderly and noisy premises and these were further extended by the Violent Crime Reduction Act 2006. CSPs are now required to audit and to address alcohol-related offending in their areas, while other agencies are pursuing public health and safer drinking campaigns. In this way, the cross-departmental cooperation at national level is reflected in local actions.

The role of correctional agencies within the strategy focuses on the identification and assessment of offenders experiencing problems through their use of alcohol and delivery of appropriate intervention, which may involve health and harm reduction goals. The renewed emphasis on work around alcohol is welcome, and to some extent redresses the balance that had tipped so significantly towards responding to the use of illegal drugs, preventing a proper attention to the harms caused by alcohol.

Notes on working with drink/drug-using offenders

It is important that offender managers retain involvement and an interest in offenders even where the intervention element of court orders is being delivered by a specialist agency. This is particularly because:

- individuals may need support and encouragement to enter or to maintain their motivation to engage in treatment;

- there may be practical or relationship issues that will impact on treatment if not addressed;
- social needs may be as significant as medical and psychological needs, particularly towards the latter stages of treatment. Drink and drug-using offenders are typically depleted in *social capital* and offender management should be proactively assisting individuals in building social networks and new identities;
- an offender manager can be an anchoring point in the midst of a process of change and can encourage and validate progress.

Fundamental to all this is a principled approach that responds to the individual and seeks to explore the reality of the individual's life with drink or drugs, avoiding making assumptions about patterns of use or what use might mean to the individual.

Summary

This chapter has focused on the use of drugs, because the strategic emphasis and the resources made available have been so much more than for alcohol. Nevertheless, attention has now turned to alcohol and the associated harms, in terms of health and criminal behaviours, which are no less by virtue of its legal status. Indeed, the question of which substances are approved or tolerated and which are banned is highly political and reflects wider societal attitudes and values. Much has been made of the 'war on drugs' which some identify as translating into a 'war on drug users' (Buchanan, 2008). Certainly the response to drug-using behaviours now criminalises the user, and the criminal justice system and criminal justice processes are being seen as a means to channel and indeed to coerce users into treatment. This clearly raises ethical questions, but also issues about whether individuals are motivated to engage with treatment and processes of change. Working with degrees of choice and seeking to empower individuals in the context of court-ordered treatment may be tricky but not entirely ruled out by the partnership arrangements and the treatment options on offer.

Further reading

Bean, P. (2008) *Drugs and crime* (3rd edn), Cullompton: Willan.
Bennett, T. and Holloway, K. (2005) *Understanding drugs, alcohol and crime*, Maidenhead: Open University Press.
Hucklesby, A. and Wincup, E. (eds) (2010) *Drugs interventions in criminal justice*, Maidenhead: Open University Press.

SIXTEEN

Mentally disordered offenders

It is widely recognised – almost a truism – that mental illness is more prevalent in the offender population than among the public at large (Canton, 2008), and also that the criminal justice system struggles to recognise and to respond appropriately to mental health need. A subset of offenders with mental health problems are the focus of particular concerns and may find themselves detained or receiving treatment under specific legal powers. This chapter focuses on these individuals categorised as 'mentally disordered offenders' – including those subject to the provisions of the Mental Health Act 1983 – and the challenge of engaging with them and the network of other professionals who may be involved.

As with sex offenders, this work is full of dilemmas for practitioners around personal values, individual freedoms and proportionate responses to risk. The presence of severe and longstanding mental disorder makes assessment of risk an especially tricky business and subtle judgements may be needed about degrees of care and control, often in conjunction with mental health professionals. Work with MDOs is 'a quintessentially multi-agency matter' (Pakes and Winstone, 2010, p 169), with potential interactions with health and social care at various points from arrest to long-term care planning. This chapter asks what constructive inter-agency practice might look like and how it can respect the needs and rights of individuals with mental disorders while responding realistically to risk. This is not to make light of the challenges of work with MDOs, but to demystify work in this area and to highlight the potential for practice that is sensitive to social and personal needs.

Mentally disordered offenders in context

MDOs present real dilemmas for society, falling as they do so awkwardly between the control mechanism of the criminal justice and mental health systems. And society's response is deeply conflicted and ambivalent, reflecting the significant – and largely unanswered – questions about where key responsibilities and accountabilities should lie. MDOs are difficult to categorise, particularly where there are complex combinations of mental health vulnerabilities and moral culpability. It is often arguable whether the appropriate response should be from health or social care or from the criminal justice system and who should take lead responsibility (Peay, 2007). Rob Canton suggests that:

> Mentally disordered offenders are doubly censured. They are "other" both among offenders and among the mentally disordered. Unpredictable, deluded and uncontrolled offenders, they cannot be

managed in the criminal justice system: untrustworthy and delinquent, they are less deserving of healthcare. (2002, p 239)

More recently, he has identified that practice with offenders who have mental health problems can involve positive and complementary endeavours from both criminal justice and mental health agencies working well together. But there are also instances where there is an uneasy interface between the two major systems with their different priorities, policies and understandings of mental health, leading to neglect and even rejection of this very needy group (Canton, 2008).

Medical models tend to dominate the writing and thinking about offenders who experience problems with mental health and MDOs specifically. However, social contexts and circumstances are highly relevant and may shed light on the experience of offenders. Offending lifestyles typically involve significant levels of stress and anxiety that could act to exacerbate mental health problems. Indeed, exposure to criminal justice processes may themselves add to the pressures and the social isolation and stigma that might cause an individual's mental state to deteriorate. Criminal justice workers at various stages can help ease the passage through the criminal justice system and divert where appropriate from further processing or from punishment.

Practitioners in criminal justice may also have a significant role, not directly in a treatment sense, but in assisting defendants/offenders to deal with social issues, to access services and to improve skills and ability to resolve problems, thereby alleviating the factors that might increase vulnerability to mental ill health (Canton, 2008). It is therefore important that practitioners should not allow a mental health diagnosis to dominate to the extent that social and other needs are neglected, because there is a valuable – occasionally a vital – contribution to be made there.

What do we mean by 'mental disorder'?

It is frequently observed that there is no one agreed definition of mental disorder and that the criminal justice system and mental health systems refer to different definitions (see, for example, Winstone and Pakes, 2005; CJJI, 2010a). The latter uses systems of clinical classifications relating to forms of, for example, psychoses and neuroses (the Diagnostic and Statistical Manual of Mental Disorder Version 4 [DSM IV] being one). The criminal justice system is more likely to employ a legal definition and it is the definition contained in the Mental Health Act 2007 that will be used in this chapter. However, it is also worth noting Nacro's definition of offenders with mental health problems that is used in Lord Bradley's recent and influential review:

Those who come into contact with the mental health system because they have committed, or are suspected of committing, a criminal offence, and who may be acutely or chronically mentally ill ... it also includes those in whom a degree of mental disturbance is recognised, even though it may not be severe enough to bring it within the criteria laid down by the Mental Health Act 1983 (now 2007). (Bradley, 2009, p 17)

The original Mental Health Act 1983 identified four categories of mental disorder, which were intended to be comprehensive but, in practice, were problematic to use (Crow, 2001) and were further complicated when considered in relation to individuals in the criminal justice system and the exercise of the specific legal powers relating to MDOs.

The Mental Health Act 2007 abolishes the four categories of mental disorder outlined in the previous legislation in favour of a single, simplified definition. Section 1(2) states that:

> … "mental disorder" means any disorder or disability of the mind and "mentally disordered" shall be construed accordingly.

This therefore covers psychological conditions, such as personality disorders, as well as psychiatric illnesses. Section 2 ensures that individuals with learning disabilities are not considered to come within this definition unless their disability results in abnormally aggressive or seriously irresponsible behaviours. The amended Act also states that drug or alcohol dependency is not considered to be a mental disorder within the meaning of the 1983 Act, even where clinically it may be regarded as such.

Despite these specific exclusions, this is still a broad definition, and Jill Peay questions what behaviours and mental states might fall within what she describes as:

> A term of acute terminological inexactitude … the term "mental disorder" acts like a concertina, expanding and contracting depending on the context in which it is applied in order to accommodate difficult client groups with little or no coherence. (2007, p 503)

The 2007 Act amends and updates the Mental Health Act 1983 rather than replacing it as originally proposed, and the following sections consider the controversy about revising this legislation, before detailing the key provisions of each Act.

Reforming mental health legislation

Reform of the mental health law dealing with compulsory detention and compulsory treatment in England and Wales has been a lengthy and controversial process (Roll, 2007). That process began as long ago as July 1998 when Frank Dobson, the then Health Secretary, announced a review of the 1983 Act. This review was published the following year at the same time as the government Green Paper, *Reform of the Mental Health Act 1983* (DH, 1999) and a further consultation document, *Managing dangerous people with severe personality disorder: Proposals for policy development* (Home Office/DH, 1999). Already the conflation of mental health with dangerousness was apparent and the public protection agenda was made explicit. This was in stark contrast to the previous approaches towards MDOs, which had been orientated on diversion from the criminal justice system into treatment under the direction of Home Office Circular 66/90 (Crow, 2001; Peay, 2007).

Winstone and Pakes (2005) note the concentration on rights and compulsion in the proposals for reform, suggesting that the measures initially put forward could further exacerbate the exclusion and marginalisation of individuals with a mental disorder, whether offenders or non-offenders. Interestingly, there were two strands of government policy, these being, first, a general reform of mental health legislation and, second, a concentration on MDOs who were seen as potentially dangerous. The White Paper was accordingly published in two separate volumes.

Both these strands of proposals proved contentious, and campaigning bodies such as Mind and the Mental Health Alliance, were highly critical. In 2007, after the third version of the Mental Health Bill eventually received Royal Assent, they commented that:

> The debate over the Mental Health Bill has been a difficult one, not least for the people most affected by it. During that process, it has become clear that this has been as much a conflict of values as of the legal framework needed for effective mental health treatment in England and Wales.....
>
> Overall, the 2007 Mental Health Act will go down in history as a missed opportunity. While other countries, often with less well developed mental health services, are fundamentally modernising their mental health laws, our already outdated law has at best been mildly improved. (Mental Health Alliance, 2007, p 9)

In relation to MDOs, Winstone and Pakes (2005) also referred to a missed opportunity, and felt that the MH Bill as it then was threatened to focus on control and repression, to the detriment of treatment and rehabilitation. They reflect the opinions of professional campaigners against the Bill, that equating mental illness and dangerousness is a profoundly unhelpful message to send out publicly. Furthermore, they had concerns that the Bill was attempting to eliminate risk altogether – which they saw as a futile venture – rather than trying to balance risk and rights.

Guiding principles

The Code of Practice for the amended Mental Health Act establishes a series of guiding principles for implementation that may have an impact in safeguarding offenders' rights and freedoms and to some extent may counteract the critical concerns outlined above. Decisions under the Act must be taken with a view to minimising the undesirable effects of mental disorder, by maximising the safety and well-being (mental and physical) of patients, promoting their recovery and protecting other people from harm. Restrictions on a patient's liberty should be the minimum necessary to achieve the intended purpose. Participation in planning, developing and reviewing treatment should be encouraged.

These principles relate to the civil aspects of the legislation, which allow for compulsory hospitalisation of individuals for assessment and treatment – effectively the 'deserving' end of the spectrum of people suffering from mental illnesses or disorders, rather than offenders sentenced in the criminal courts through the mental health legislation. Nevertheless, these principles should be borne in mind in relation to patient participation in treatment and respect for the individual, even where questions of liberty are overridden by sentencing.

Mental Health Act 1983 Part II, as amended by the Mental Health Act 2007

Part II contains civil provisions for the compulsory admission to hospital or guardianship for individuals not involved in criminal proceedings. The new Act allows for a wider group of practitioners to have powers under the legislation, on the medical side referred to as the responsible clinician and on the social care side an approved mental health practitioner.

The 'nearest relative' referred to in the 1983 legislation is a specific person, such as a spouse or a parent, with responsibility for the care of the individual and therefore a defined legal status. The new Act includes civil partners in the list of relatives who can take on this role and allows patients to apply to the court to change the nominated nearest relative.

Under the 1983 Act, compulsory treatment was only available in a hospital setting and this is one of the issues that the Mental Health Act 2007 set out to address. Another problematic aspect of the earlier legislation was that certain parts of the Act were only applicable where the mental disorder was assessed as being 'susceptible to treatment', so key provisions could not be used for cases of personality disorders, for instance, which were considered untreatable.

The amended Act therefore allows for supervised community treatment for offenders who have already been detained for assessment or treatment. It also abolishes the need to prove that the illness will be susceptible to treatment before an individual can be detained, and replaces this with a more flexible criterion that stipulates only that 'appropriate medical treatment' should be available. Such treatment may now include nursing, psychological intervention and specialist mental health habilitation, rehabilitation and care – allowing for more psychological and social as well as strictly medical interventions.

Admission for assessment

Applications for assessment in a hospital setting can be made either by the individual's nearest relative or an approved mental health practitioner. The approved mental health practitioner must have interviewed the individual and on the basis of that be satisfied both that the statutory criteria for detention are met and that detention in hospital is the most appropriate way to assess the individual's need for care and medical treatment. The application should be made within 14 days of the initial assessment interview to the manager of a particular named hospital.

It is obviously preferable for the patient to enter hospital voluntarily, assuming he or she is able to give informed consent, but, if this is not possible, Section 2 of the Act allows for compulsory detention providing there are two medical recommendations, which confirm that:

- the patient is suffering from a mental disorder of a nature or degree that warrants detention in hospital for assessment (or assessment followed by medical treatment) for at least a limited period; and
- he or she ought to be detained in the interests of her or his own health or safety or with a view to the protection of others.

The 'section' can last for up to 28 days, but the patient can be discharged earlier by the responsible clinician or hospital managers or at the request of the nearest relative, subject to 72 hours' notice. The patient has the right to apply to a First Tier Tribunal – Mental Health (previously a Mental Health Review Tribunal and from here onwards referred to just as tribunal) within the first 14 days and this also has the power to authorise discharge. The 28-day period is not renewable.

Admission for assessment in cases of emergency

Section 4 provides for a fast track version of the above for urgent cases. The approved mental health practitioner or nearest relative must have seen the patient within the previous 24 hours. Only one doctor is needed to confirm that it is of 'urgent necessity' for the patient to be admitted and detained under Section 2, and that waiting for a second doctor would cause 'undesirable delay'. The patient must be admitted within 24 hours of examination otherwise the 'section' becomes invalid. The maximum period for which an individual can be held under Section 4 is 72 hours, during which time a second medical opinion should be sought.

Admission for treatment

Section 3 allows for compulsory detention for up to six months (renewable by the responsible clinician under Section 20) if two doctors confirm that:

- the patient is suffering from a mental disorder of a nature or degree that makes it appropriate for her or him to receive medical treatment in hospital; and
- it is necessary for her or his own health and safety or for the protection of others that she or he receives such treatment and it cannot be provided unless she or he is detained under this section; and
- appropriate medical treatment is available.

The patient can be discharged by the responsible clinician or hospital managers or at the request of the nearest relative subject to 72 hours' notice. The patient has the right to apply to a tribunal once during the first six months of detention (including time detained under Section 2 for assessment) and then once every subsequent year. If no application to the tribunal is made within the first six months, the case will be referred automatically.

Section 5 also permits a voluntary patient already in hospital to be detained for up to 72 hours if it is felt that an application for compulsory admission should be made.

Guardianship Orders

Sections 7–10 deal with Guardianship Orders which, for over-16s, allow the social care section of the local authority or a person approved by that section to specify where the patient should live and where he or she goes to access employment, training or medical treatment, and also to facilitate doctors, social workers and so on being able to see the patient at home.

Guardianship Orders are only available where it is necessary for the welfare of the patient or protection of others as confirmed by two doctors. These orders last for up to six months, but are renewable under Section 20 of the Act. Guardianship Orders are also available for MDOs under Section 37 through the criminal courts.

Supervised community treatment

Supervised community treatment was introduced by the 2007 Act, which inserts a new Section 17A into the Mental Health Act 1983. This was a controversial proposal: heated debate about rights and freedoms have resulted in more limited provision in the Act than was originally envisaged, whereby such treatment can only be ordered for individuals who have previously been detained for assessment or treatment. Before a patient can be discharged, the responsible clinician and an approved mental health practitioner must both agree that a Community Treatment Order would be appropriate and that:

- the patient is suffering from a mental disorder of a nature or degree that makes it appropriate for her or him to have medical treatment;
- treatment is necessary for his or her health and safety or for the protection of other persons;
- the treatment can be provided without the need for the individual to be detained in hospital, although she or he will remain liable for recall for the duration of the order;
- the responsible clinician is able to exercise the power to recall to hospital; and
- appropriate medical treatment is available.

Conditions can be added to the Community Treatment Order if the responsible clinician and approved mental health practitioner agree they are necessary to ensure that the patient receives medical treatment and/or to prevent risk of harm to the patient or to others. Under the order, the patient will be required to make her- or himself available for medical examination. The order will last for six months initially and is renewable for the further six months and yearly thereafter.

The order is not enforceable in a legal sense, but the patient can be recalled to hospital for breaking the condition of the order to present for medical examination and also on the judgement of the responsible clinician about his or her mental state. If the Community Treatment Order is revoked, the patient must stay in hospital, but otherwise should be discharged still subject to the order within 72 hours.

Other civil powers

In addition, elsewhere in the Act, Section 136 permits a police officer or an approved mental health practitioner to take a person who appears to be 'suffering from a mental disorder' and 'is in immediate need of care or control' from a public area to a place of safety. This is usually a hospital but can be a police station. Section 136 orders last for up to 72 hours to allow for a doctor and approved mental health practitioner to see the individual and arrange for any necessary treatment or care.

Section 135 permits the police or an approved mental health practitioner to seek a warrant from a magistrate empowering them to search for and remove an individual where there is reasonable cause to suspect that a person suffering from a mental disorder is being ill-treated or neglected, or lives alone and is unable to care for her- or himself. The warrant will last for 72 hours and is intended to allow for appropriate assessment of need in a place of safety, rather than admission to hospital.

Mental Health Act 1983 Part III, as amended by the Mental Health Act 2007

Part III of the Act contains measures for patients involved in criminal proceedings and these are the provisions that relate to MDOs, that is, individuals before the court who experience illness or other mental disorder. Significantly, the legislation does not require an identified causal link between the offending and the mental disorder.

Remand to hospital for medical report

Under Section 35, an individual can be remanded to hospital by either Crown Court or Magistrates' Court for up to 28 days where a single doctor approved under Section 12 has given evidence that:

• there is 'reason to suspect' that she or he is suffering from a mental disorder; and

- it would be 'impracticable' for a report on her or his mental state to be made if she or he were on bail

and where

- the court is advised by the relevant responsible clinician or his/her representative that hospital admission can take place within seven days.

The 28-day period can be renewed by the court for up to a maximum of 12 weeks. Section 36 also permits for an offender to be remanded to hospital for treatment.

Hospital Orders

Hospital Orders under Section 37 are an alternative to any other sentence, so cannot be combined with fines, imprisonment or any community disposal. They can last for an initial six months and are then renewable for a further six months and at yearly intervals thereafter. They are made by the Crown Court or Magistrates' Court in the case of offenders convicted of imprisonable offences. They can also be used by Magistrates' Courts for unconvicted offenders suffering from a mental illness or severe mental impairment if the court is satisfied that the offender committed the alleged act.

Interim Hospital Orders can also be made for an initial period of 12 weeks up to a maximum of six months (Section 38).

Evidence, presented orally or in writing, is required from two doctors, one of whom must be approved under Section 12, that:

- the offender is suffering from a mental disorder of a nature or degree that makes it appropriate for the defendant to be detained in hospital for medical treatment; and
- appropriate medical treatment is available; and
- the court is advised by the responsible clinician or a representative of him or her that arrangements have been made for admission to hospital within 28 days.

The Hospital Order can be discharged by the responsible clinician, hospital manager or tribunal. The patient can apply to the tribunal once in the period 6-12 months after the Hospital Order is made and once yearly thereafter. The case is automatically referred to the tribunal if a three-year period has passed since the last review.

Restriction Orders

A Crown Court in making a Hospital Order may at the same time impose a Restriction Order (Section 41), if:

- this is necessary to protect the public from *serious harm*; and
- at least one of the doctors who made recommendations for the hospital order has given evidence orally.

The court should have regard to:

- the nature of the offence;
- the antecedents of the offender; and
- the risk of the offender committing further offences if set at large.

Restriction Orders can only be discharged by the Secretary of State for Justice or a tribunal, which in this case can be a First Tier Tribunal or an Upper Tribunal. As with Hospital Orders, the patient can apply to the tribunal once in the period 6-12 months after the Restriction Order is made and once yearly thereafter. The case is automatically referred to the tribunal if a three-year period has passed since the last tribunal.

Transfer to hospital from prison

Section 47 allows for offenders to be transferred from prison to hospital by order of the Secretary of State for Justice where evidence from two doctors confirms that:

- the prisoner is suffering from a mental disorder;
- the mental disorder is of a nature or degree which makes it appropriate for the prisoner to be detained in hospital for medical treatment; and
- appropriate medical treatment is available.

The transfer direction lasts for 14 days, by which time the prisoner should have been transferred to the specified hospital. Beyond this time, the transfer direction ceases to have effect.

The period of detention is up to six months, renewable for a further six months and yearly thereafter. As long as the Secretary of State for Justice has not imposed a Restriction Order (Section 49), the patient can be discharged by a responsible clinician, hospital manager or tribunal. Where a Restriction Order is in place, the prisoner could be returned to prison if treatment is no longer appropriate or effective. If this is not the case, the Restriction Order and the 'section' will cease at the point where the sentence expires.

Hospital and limitation direction

It starts to get complicated with this amendment to the original 1983 Act inserted by the Crime (Sentences) Act 1997: Section 45A applies where a Crown Court, rather than making a Hospital Order, imposes a fixed term sentence of imprisonment but orders the offender to be immediately admitted to hospital.

Essentially, this section allows for an offender to be transferred from hospital to prison at any time during sentence when the Secretary of State for Justice directs on the recommendation of the responsible clinician or tribunal, presumably when treatment is no longer needed or is no longer effective. The section can only be used at the sentencing stage where the court is satisfied on the evidence of two doctors, at least one approved under Section 12, that:

- the offender suffers from a mental disorder of a nature or degree which makes it appropriate for the offender to be detained in hospital for medical treatment; and
- appropriate medical treatment is available

and where

- the court has first considered making a Hospital Order, but has instead decided to impose a sentence of imprisonment (or equivalent for young offenders); and
- the court is advised by the responsible clinician or representative of him or her that arrangements have been made for admission to hospital within 28 days.

If the offender is still in hospital at the end of what would otherwise be the prison sentence, he or she is treated as though on a Hospital Order.

Statistics on the use of Part III powers

The numbers of restricted patients detained in hospital has increased from 2,749 in 1996 to 3,937 on 31 December 2008. Of these, 477 were female and 3,490 were male. Six per cent of female restricted patients were detained in high secure hospital compared to 17 per cent of the male patients. The overwhelming majority were subject to a Hospital Order with a Restriction Order and entered hospital straight from court, but 937 were transferred from prisons either before or after sentence (Ministry of Justice, 2010b).

Mental Health Act 2007: summary

The main changes brought about by the 2007 Act are:

- a simplified definition of mental disorder;
- changed criteria for detention, introducing a new 'appropriate medical treatment' test and abolishing the treatability criterion;
- a broadening of professional roles;
- provisions for patients to replace the individual identified as their nearest relative and for civil partners to be named as the 'nearest relative';
- the introduction of supervised community treatment;
- reductions in the timescales for referral to a review tribunal;

- requirement to provide age-appropriate services for under-18s (not yet implemented);
- introduction of independent advocacy schemes effective from April 2009;
- new safeguards for patients in relation to electro-convulsive therapy.

While there are aspects of the Act that may result in more restricted practices, the speedier access to tribunals and the establishment of advocacy schemes are important measures to help safeguard the rights of patients.

Sentencing mentally disordered offenders

The Magistrates' Court Act 1980 enables magistrates to adjourn cases for medical examination and reports and this has since been an important provision for ensuring that vulnerable offenders are dealt with appropriately.

Section 147 of the Criminal Justice Act 2003 requires the court to consider a medical report before passing a custodial sentence on any offender who is or appears to be mentally disordered, unless the court considers this unnecessary or the offence is one for which the penalty is fixed by law.

The courts may also look to PSRs for guidance on sentencing. Interestingly, a recent joint inspectorate report found that PSR authors were tending to discuss offending and mental health separately, whereas appropriate assessment and analysis should address the interplay between the two (CJJI, 2010a).

Assessments should look carefully at the issue of culpability where mental disorder is concerned, and the extent to which the offender should be held responsible for his or her behaviours. Any proposals for a community order should consider the feasibility and suitability of the suggested requirements and any strategies that might need to be put in place to engage the offender and help him or her to comply. The implications of a custodial sentence and how this might affect the offender should also be addressed, where custody is a possible outcome.

The Criminal Justice Act 2003 allows a mental health treatment requirement to be included on a community order, similar to the treatment condition that could previously be added to a Probation Order under the Criminal Justice Act 1991. These both differ from the supervised Community Treatment Order in needing the offender's consent which means that treatment cannot therefore be imposed against his or her will. It seems significant that neither of these provisions has been extensively used despite the evidence of high levels of mental disorder among probation caseloads, indicative perhaps of a lack of practitioner confidence in addressing mental health, but also reflecting the practical difficulties in obtaining psychiatric reports (Khanom et al, 2009).

Indeterminate and extended sentences under the Criminal Justice Act 2003 are particularly concerning in relation to MDOs and have potential to impact detrimentally on sentencing and decisions about release (Peay, 2007). The Prisoner Cohort Study, in fact, did find a significant overlap in the dangerous and serious personality disordered (DSPD) offenders and prisoners with indeterminate and extended sentences in their study sample (Cold et al, 2007).

Risk and dangerousness

There is a key conundrum at the heart of work with MDOs, which is that research suggests that on the whole they re-offend at lower rates than offenders without a mental disorder (Winstone and Pakes, 2005; Peay, 2007), yet at the same time there has been a ratcheting up of concerns about dangerousness following a small number of high profile killings by former psychiatric patients (Crow, 2001). Clearly some MDOs are very dangerous but exactly who or in what circumstances can be difficult to determine, as Peay (2007) notes when she says:

> Offenders with mental disorders are particularly "at risk" of being perceived as posing an unquantifiable danger, and thus, particularly apt for the ubiquitous focus on risk management. (2007, p 497)

This is especially ironic as MDOs in general may pose more danger to themselves than to others (Crow, 2001). Herschel Prins (2005, 2007) suggests that there are three types of myths around mental disorder that cause anxiety and that these irrational, if understandable fears, have contributed to the construction of the mentally disturbed (his preferred term) as 'folk devils'. He identifies these myths as:

- uncertainties as to the cause of such disorders;
- our personal fears of madness;
- our very real concerns about the intractability of some of the more serious forms of mental disorder.

Further problems lie in the lack of understanding about causal relationships between mental disorder and offending, and this is particularly so in cases where substance misuse is also involved (known as 'dual diagnosis'). Prins concludes from a 1995 review of the literature discussing the links between mental disorder and crime that:

1. Most mentally disordered people do not present an increased risk of violence to others
2. The strongest predictors of offending are the same for mentally disturbed offenders as for others
3. People with a functional psychosis may present an increased risk of harm to others when they have active symptoms, especially if they are also substance mis-users
4. By definition, people with severe personality disorder present an increased risk of violence. (Prins, 1999, p 66, cited in Canton, 2002, p 250)

More recently, Prins has specifically considered the association between mental disorder and crime, and notes that:

> All the conditions described in this contribution need to be viewed against the social and political climate prevailing currently. This climate is much preoccupied with public protection, the assessment of risk and the over-hasty implementation of more and more criminal justice measures to deal with our current "folk devils". Professionals have a responsibility to keep their heads above these turbulent waters and to remain calm. (2005, p 354)

This implicitly refers to the attempts of professionals to conduct assessments objectively and fairly. Clearly the use of assessment tools, such as OASys, could be seen to assist in this. However, there are concerns about current probation practice and whether the relationships between offender managers and offenders are likely to be sufficiently close and sufficiently strong to allow symptoms of mental disorder or incipient mental illness to be recognised. Canton (2002) notes a greater distance between supervisors and offenders, and a relationship transformed by the emphasis on punishment and enforcement as well as changes in practices involving fewer home visits and opportunities to gain a deeper understanding of the lived reality of individuals' lives.

Furthermore questions have been raised about assessment and case management practices. A review of the use of OASys in 10 selected cases from a large metropolitan service found that there was sensitivity shown towards the needs of offenders where the officer had time to build a rapport, but that staff turnover and movements had a negative impact and in some instances changed the focus from support to procedural concerns. There were also issues about confidence, experience and knowledge levels among officers, leading to inaccurate and defensive assessments which tended not to explore and use the evidence fully, even where it was available on case files (Fitzgibbon and Green, 2006).

This raises key dilemmas for the probation service in working with MDOs and ensuring that their rights which, as Canton (2002) notes, are always 'precarious', are upheld in the face of both the criminal justice and mental health systems. Many practitioners in the criminal justice system are not confident with this area of work, and research (see, for instance, Bhui, 1999) has pointed to the cultural biases in mental health services which ensure that black men in particular are over-controlled, if not by the mental health services themselves then through criminalisation of their behaviours.

In countering these difficulties, Canton (2002) and Farrow et al (2007) point to the value of effective multi-agency work in determining risk and appropriate intervention. The latter have produced a useful matrix around risk and intervention, adapted from work by Hazel Kemshall (see Figure 16.1).

However, multi-agency work is not without its problems, and the current orientation towards risk and enforcement may move the probation service further from other, more welfare and health-based services. One area where this is most

Figure 16.1: Matching practitioner contact with severity of mental illness symptoms and risk of harm and re-offending

Low   *Severity of mental health symptoms*   High

Persistence and/or danger may not be linked primarily to mental illness **– Work focusing on re-offending** **– Surveillance/monitoring** **– Frequent contact with supervisor**	Persistence/danger may be connected to mental illness **– Work focused on offending and treatment for condition** **– Surveillance/monitoring** **– Frequent contact with supervisor *and* mental health services**	High *Risk of harm and re-offending*
Beware deterioration of mental health condition **– Monitor for signs of escalation** **– Less frequent contact**	Appropriate intervention with focus on mental health need **– Diversion from criminal justice system** **– Monitoring** **– Referral to mental health support services**	 Low

Source: Farrow et al (2007, p 111)

evident is with offenders explicitly assessed as being dangerous who have been the object of Home Office policy since the late 1990s.

Dangerous and Severe Personality Disorder Programme

In the light of the current risk culture in criminal justice it is probably not surprising to find a policy focus on MDOs assessed as potentially dangerous. Add to this the longstanding controversies about diagnoses of personality disorder and questions about the extent to which such disorders are 'treatable', and the rise of the DSPD offender becomes understandable.

DSPD is an invention of politicians and policy makers, not a clinical category (Farrow et al, 2007). Personality disorder itself is not easily defined and is subject to debate within the fields of psychology and psychiatry. However, a useful description by John Milton helps centre this discussion:

> Personality disorder can be defined in several ways, but, essentially, represents enduring patterns of thinking, feeling, interpersonal style and impulse control which deviate markedly from cultural norms, leading to considerable personal distress and disruption in most aspects of the individual's life and/or of those around him or her. (2007, p 206)

Milton goes on to note that, although personality disorder should sit within mental health services, frequently it has not because the 'treatability' requirements of key sections in the original Mental Health Act 1983 excluded those more serious personality disorders that could not be treated, whether by medication, counselling, cognitive behavioural therapy or other means. Personality disordered offenders nevertheless frequently come before the court for sentencing under the mentally disorder offender provisions and 'in short, we do not know what to do with them, or what to do for them' (Winstone and Pakes, 2005, p 228).

The White Paper, *Reforming the Mental Health Act Part II: High risk patients* (DH, 2000b), noted the difficulties that DSPD offenders had posed historically for mental health and criminal justice services. It suggested that before making more definite proposals for changes in legislation for the DSPD group of offenders, more evidence from research and from pilots was needed. The DSPD Programme was launched in 2003 following such pilots, bringing together criminal justice agencies with the Department of Health and the NHS to deliver services for a relatively small but worrying number of high-risk individuals. New units have been established in two hospitals, Rampton and Broadmoor, and in two prisons, HM Prisons Whitemoor and Frankland, providing an initial 300 places for men. Services for 12 women are being developed at HM Prison Low Newton in the North East. A further five prisons are designated as democratic therapeutic communities with 538 beds, many of which are taken by DSPD offenders. It is estimated that the total number of DSPD offenders may be 2,400 (Peay, 2007), so these provisions are likely to grow and to demand a substantial amount of resources. Indeed, under the Coalition government plans, the number of places will increase to 570 by 2014 (Ministry of Justice, 2010a).

The objectives of the programme are:

- to protect the public;
- to provide high quality services to improve mental health outcomes; and
- to understand better what works in the treatment of this group.

The offenders being considered for the DSPD Programme must be rigorously assessed and a range of tools are in use, depending on the profile of the case, in addition to OASys and OGRS. The main tool is the PCL-R (or Psychopathy Checklist – Revised), but for sex offenders SARN, Risk Matrix 2000 or Static 99 may also be used. Similarly, for violent offenders, the Violence Risk Appraisal Guide (VRAG) or the Violence Risk Scale (VRS) might be employed.

Alongside the DSPD, the Prisoner Cohort Study was established to help build the evidence base around work with DSPD offenders. The first report from the Study concentrated on the effectiveness and predictive accuracy of the assessment tools in use, as this would give an indication of whether or not the study was targeting the 'right' offenders.

The findings suggested that, of the 1,396 offenders in the study sample, 212, or 15 per cent, had a DSPD. That subset of offenders was significantly more likely to be reconvicted on release and there was a strong association with violent and acquisitive crime, which seems to confirm the benefits of the programme. All the assessment instruments covered in the study predicted re-offending better than chance, but overall OGRS was the most accurate. The authors concluded by suggesting that a combination of clinical and actuarial assessment is recommended for determining risk in any one individual (Cold et al, 2007) – this is interesting given the discussion on risk assessment in Chapter Seven.

Nevertheless, there is profound scepticism about the DSPD Programme, and Peay (2007) voices her suspicions that the initiative stems not from concerns about treatment, justice or due process, but from anxiety about the possibility of individuals 'prematurely' released from the hospital or prison system re-offending. She goes on to say:

> Generally, the DSPD initiative does not bode well ... if there is no agreed definition, no diagnosis, no means of assessing when the predicted risk might have been reduced, and no obvious link between the alleged underlying condition and the behaviour, how could outcome measures be agreed upon and then evaluated? (p 518)

Further details and referral information can be found in PC 21/2008.

Care Programme Approach

The DSPD explicitly deals with offenders at the more severe end of the spectrum in detention. Criminal justice practitioners may more frequently find themselves working with other offenders who are vulnerable because of their mental disorder. Release into the community after a period of compulsory in-patient treatment can be an unsettling experience, and the Care Programme Approach (CPA) is intended to ensure that there is support and coordination of aftercare arrangements for discharged patients forming an integrated care pathway. The CPA is used to support individuals subject to supervised Community Treatment or Guardianship Orders (DH, 2008). It should also be in place in prison settings, although evaluation suggests that this has not developed as quickly as envisaged following the transfer of responsibility for providing health services in prisons to the NHS (DH, 2008).

When a patient is discharged from compulsory detention, there will usually be a period during which outpatient support is available. Section 117 of the Mental Health Act 1983 places a duty on health and social care to provide aftercare services beyond that period, in order to assist individuals in the community. These arrangements were strengthened first by the introduction of the CPA in 1991 and the Mental Health (Patients in the Community) Act 1995. This Act allows for the responsible clinician to apply for a supervised discharge in order to ensure that the patient in question receives and complies with services under Section 117.

The four elements of the CPA are:

- systematic assessment of the needs of the patient and their carers;
- a care plan to meet those needs;
- a key worker to monitor and coordinate the care plan; and
- regular reviews. (Farrow et al, 2007, p 112)

Although primarily for health and social care professionals, criminal justice practitioners may well be part of the multi-agency group that comes together in care planning. Indeed, it may be important that they are present to ensure equity of support and services for offenders with mental health needs. The care plan should, wherever possible, be developed with the patient and carers, but in MDO cases the views of victims and protection for victims may also need to be considered, and this is a role that is likely to fall to the probation service (see Chapter Thirteen).

Interestingly, Farrow et al (2007) discuss the inter-relationship between care planning and MAPPPs for more high-risk MDOs. They suggest that any restrictions on the offender proposed by the MAPPP for the offender's release should feature in the care plan, as this would ensure that all professionals were aware of arrangements for the safe return of the offender to the community and the agreed roles and responsibilities of each. They quite rightly emphasise that:

> A diagnosis of mental illness does not render the practitioner peripheral to the offender. Although mental health services will be providing treatment to remedy symptoms, practitioners should see themselves as integral to the process. They should feel confident in their own knowledge base and take an active part in inter-agency collaboration, which is essential to the effective management of mentally disordered offenders. (Farrow et al, 2007, p 113)

Inter-agency practice: future directions?

MDOs have been a neglected group both within health and criminal justice services, most particularly in prison settings. While official policy has continued to endorse the emphasis on diversion from the court system and from custody, there has been little strategic lead (CJJI, 2010a), and in many areas the risk agenda has taken precedence over treatment options. Accordingly, in 2007, Lord Bradley was engaged to conduct a review of the health problems or learning disabilities of people in the criminal justice system which was reported in 2009 (Bradley, 2009). Although initially focusing on courts and diversion, its remit was extended and ultimately what came out of the review is an 'ambitious, possibly even an inspired report' (Pakes and Winstone, 2010, p 180). The key themes are early assessment, continuity of care support, quality of partnership work and improved information flows. This latter is particularly important as offenders are physically moving and are passed between agencies at successive stages of the criminal justice process, but also because of the sensitivity expected of health services in dealing with confidential patient information.

While the report contained key recommendations in relation to national and regional structures driving strategy and working across departmental boundaries, the crux of the changes proposed is the creation of local criminal justice mental health teams. These will operate flexibly to deliver the following core elements:

- liaison with local community services;
- screening and assessment;
- coverage of police custody and courts, with links to prison mental health in-reach services and re-settlement to ensure continuity of care;
- management of information concerning an individual's needs throughout the criminal justice system and back into the community.

There will be a focus on service user involvement in development of services, which is not often a feature of services to offenders. Criminal justice, health and social care staff should be jointly trained. Over and above the direct services that such teams will deliver, the expectation is that they and the governance structures around them will support and inform the involvement of other mainstream agencies with offenders with mental disorders.

New Labour, while still in government, endorsed the recommendations of the Bradley Report and subsequently published *Improving health and supporting justice: The National Delivery Plan of the Health and Criminal Justice Programme Board* (2009). This established a clear objective:

> To develop care pathways that enhance health and social care provision and contribute to the delivery of justice. Pathways will focus on assessment and intervention at as early a stage as possible, and will support improved risk management and continuity of care. (DH, 2009, p 7)

It is still early days and, with a change of government, it is unclear whether the intended transformations will stay so firmly on the agenda. However, one hopeful assessment suggests that 'if it does bring about the envisaged change, the report will be the best thing that has happened in this field for 20 years' (Pakes and Winstone, 2010, p 180).

Summary

This chapter began negatively by identifying MDOs specifically, and offenders with lower level mental health problems more generally, as awkward and unwanted by both criminal justice and health systems. This could change dramatically in the wake of the Bradley Report, but it is by no means certain that the level of proactive multi-agency work proposed will materialise. However, change is imperative as current service delivery structures are variable and inconsistent, and practitioners in health and criminal justice agencies typically lack the understanding and confidence needed to access each other's professional expertise. This is very much to the detriment of offenders, leaving those with more severe mental health problems and offending patterns vulnerable to punitive rather than constructive or rehabilitative responses. It also means that many offenders with less obvious mental health needs do not receive appropriate assessment, support or services.

Of course, criminal justice practitioners will not become mental health experts overnight, and the developmental training and support advocated in the Bradley Report is vital. However, over and above any formal training programme, practitioners have much to learn from colleagues in health services and from offenders themselves about their experiences of the world and the agencies supporting them. It is also important to be sensitive to the individual's social context and how this might impact on his or her well-being and mental state, bearing in mind vulnerability and risk to self as well as to others. This is one area of work where skills in advocacy and willingness to provide practical help and support may be needed, particularly for individuals who are distressed or in crisis.

Further reading

Bradley, K. (2009) *The Bradley Report: Lord Bradley's review of people with mental health problems or learning disabiities in the criminal justice system*, London: Department of Health.

Farrow, K., Kelly, G. and Wilkinson, B. (2007) *Offenders in focus: Risk, responsivity and diversity*, Bristol: The Policy Press.

These edited collections contain useful chapters on mental health:

Green, S., Lancaster, E. and Feasey, S. (eds) (2008) *Addressing offending behaviour: Context, practice and value*, Cullompton: Willan.

Pyecroft, A. and Gough, D. (eds) (2010) *Multi-agency working in criminal justice*, Bristol: The Policy Press.

Winstone, J. and Pakes, F. (eds) (2005) *Community justice: Issues for probation and criminal justice*, Cullompton: Willan.

SEVENTEEN

Sex offenders

Offending of a sexual nature is deeply problematic for the criminal justice system, entangled as it is with values and notions of sexual norms. The sexual behaviours targeted by the criminal justice system have changed over the years, reflecting the way that society's preoccupations have shifted from questions of public morality to the abuse of children and vulnerable adults. Clearly there are deeply moral aspects to the commitment to protect the vulnerable, but frequently the discourse tips over into moralising and condemnation of offenders. Debates in the public domain about sex offenders are not typically balanced and pragmatic; their offending impinges on areas of private life and bodily integrity and so touches on the deeply personal. It is therefore more important than ever that professionals should bring balance, pragmatism and principles to bear.

This chapter outlines legislation relating to sex offences/sex offenders and analyses current policy and interventions, before exploring alternative approaches that might hold more promise for integration and social inclusion than the measures presently in place. As with other chapters, the end discussion returns to rights and possibilities for helping this particularly stigmatised group of offenders to build better and safer lives.

What exactly is sexual offending?

The whole question of sexual offending is vexed. Knowledge about the prevalence and types of 'sex offences' – and whether they have altered over time – is partial and confused. Official statistics and research studies give some indications but it is difficult to accurately assess the scale of the problem due to the levels of denial and the general secrecy that surrounds it, affecting rates of disclosure and reporting. The situation is not helped by lack of a common methodological approach or even a standard definition of what constitutes a 'sex offence' (Brown, Sarah, 2005b). The views of society also change, and legislation and law enforcement activities are adapted accordingly to reflect public opinion (Matravers, 2003).

Examples of these shifts can be found in the way that legal measures have been used and are currently used to regulate street sex work or homosexual activity. Although certain areas such as these are now less or differently controlled, many sexual acts are still regulated or banned by law (Sampson, 1994). However, for the purposes of this chapter, the definition of sexual offending offered by the *Dictionary of probation and offender management* (Canton and Hancock, 2007) is used and discussion focuses on adult male sex offenders.

> The engagement in sexual activity by penetration, touching, viewing or causing others to engage in sexual activity or exploitation, where there is an absence of consent between the offender and the victim. In this consent is taken to include whether the victim had the capacity to consent, whether by age, the use of coercion or mental disorder.
>
> *Source:* Middleton (2007, p 295)

Background to the legislation on sexual offending

The major recent legislation in this area is the Sexual Offences Act 2003, which updated the previous legislation that had remained largely unaltered since the Sexual Offences Act 1956 and the Street Offences Act 1959. The intervening period, however, had seen significant changes in attitudes to sexual behaviours, including liberalisation in areas such as homosexuality. The impact of feminism in the 1970s had raised public awareness of crimes such as rape that predominantly targeted women in the private rather than the public sphere, and highlighted iniquities such as the then legality of rape within marriage. In the 1980s, the focus of attention became child sexual abuse, mainly within the family. Concern was additionally heightened by high profile cases, such as the Cleveland child sex abuse inquiry and also the spectre of alleged satanic abuse on Orkney (Kemshall, 2003).

At the beginning of the 1990s, the moral panic about sex offenders and predatory paedophiles in particular, began to reach a crescendo. Ironically, sex offences accounted for less than 1 per cent of all notifiable offences in 1998/99, and yet sex offenders dominated the political and policy agenda of the late 20th century, experiencing a unique level of 'criminal apartheid' (Kemshall, 2003, p 87).

Commentators have linked this construction of the sex offender – isolated, dysfunctional, predatory and paedophiliac – with the anxieties and insecurities of late modernity. It is an irrational and emotional response, but one that has nevertheless had a profound impact upon policy:

> While crime policy in general has become politicised, sex offender policy seems to have an especially knee jerk quality, reflecting a primary concern with public opinion and displaying a fine disregard for adverse side effects such as over-inclusiveness and erosion of offenders' rights. (Matravers, 2003, p 11)

Sex offender policy has stepped well outside the usual framework of actuarial justice (evidence-based practice, the impartial calculations of risks and concern with proportionality) to make sex offenders subject to ever more intrusive measures. In doing so the principles that guide decisions and actions towards other types of offenders have been brushed aside, principles such as innocence until proven guilty and the recognition of offender rights in balance with those of the community (Matravers, 2003).

Criminal Justice Act 1991

The Criminal Justice Act 1991 was the first significant piece of legislation to impact on the probation service's work with sex offenders. Sentencing under this Act was predicated on the principle of proportionality. However, at the same time, it singled out violent and sexual offenders for special treatment, with measures waiving this principle and freeing the courts to impose longer prison sentences and extended licence periods for these two groups.

These provisions, coupled with the overall increase in post-custody supervision brought about by the Act, greatly expanded the probation service's responsibilities for sex offenders. This was by no means uncontroversial, and Sampson (1994) describes ambivalence among probation officers about taking on this work and, indeed, some heated discussions at the 1991 Napo conference about the growth in sex offender programmes, noting a condemnatory attitude towards these offenders not evident in relation to other groups.

Measures placing restrictions on sex offenders

The penal climate of the 1990s proved conducive to the development of legislation designed to control and restrict the movements of known sex offenders. First, the Sex Offenders Act 1997 established the Sex Offender Register, currently governed by Part 2 of the Sexual Offences Act 2003. Despite any firm evidence that registration has a positive impact on re-offending, this later Act tightened up and extended notification requirements (Thomas, 2010). Any offender cautioned or convicted of sexual offences listed in Schedule 3 of the Act (even if still awaiting sentence) must now notify the police in person of his or her name and place of residence within three days. The offender must also notify the police of any alternative name used, change of home address or temporary residence at any other address within three days of the change. The Act thus permits what would otherwise be breaches of Articles within the Human Rights Act 1998 in relation to the offender's right to privacy and family life, as well as freedom to stay where he or she wishes and to associate freely with others (Grange, 2003).

Notification requirements also apply to individuals found not guilty of Schedule 3 offences by reason of insanity and to offenders convicted abroad.

The notification periods are dependent on the disposal received. These are halved for young people under the age of 18 (see Table 17.1).

The Sex Offender Register only applied to offenders convicted after it came into force. A further measure, the Sex Offender Order, which could be applied retrospectively, was therefore introduced by Section 2 of the Crime and Disorder Act 1998. Like ASBOs, created by Section 1 of that Act, these were civil orders that were punishable by imprisonment in the event of breach – a kind of hybrid order favoured by New Labour (Kemshall and Maguire, 2003).

At the same time, the Crime and Disorder Act gave the courts more powers to extend post-custody licences for sexual and violent offences beyond what would

Table 17.1: Sex Offender Register notification periods

Sentence	Notification period
Life imprisonment and IPP sentences	Indefinite
Imprisonment 30 months or more	Indefinite
Admission to hospital under Restriction Order	Indefinite
Imprisonment 6-30 months	10 years
Imprisonment less than six months	7 years
Admission to hospital without Restriction Order	7 years
Caution	2 years
Conditional discharge	Period of discharge
Any other	5 years

otherwise be the sentence expiry date. Finally, the Criminal Justice and Court Services Act 2000 made the Restraining Order available in Crown Courts and the Court of Appeal on conviction for specified sexual offences.

Background to the Sexual Offences Act 2003

Despite introduction of these control measures, in essence, the legislation relating to sex offences had changed little since the 1950s. The sentencing framework created by the Criminal Justice Act 1991 involved more supervision of sex offenders. The Sex Offender Order and Restraining Order offered some protection from known sex offenders, if their behaviour was considered to pose a risk of serious harm. Similarly, the MAPPPs introduced by Sections 67 and 68 of the Criminal Justice and Court Services Act required more effective cooperation between agencies working with sex offenders, most specifically the police and probation services.

The Home Office, nevertheless, was still looking at how it could tackle sexual offending more effectively. In 1999, it therefore established a Sex Offences Review, which in July 2000 published its report, *Setting the boundaries* (Home Office, 2000). The title is significant, as one of its intentions was to examine the extent to which the law was justified in intruding into private life (Matravers, 2003).

At the same time, and with an eye on public sentiment, the then Home Secretary announced a review of the 1997 legislation and arrangements for the Sex Offender Register. When this was followed shortly after by the murder of Sarah Payne, there were strident calls and a press campaign for a 'Sarah's law' similar to the 'Megan's law' in the US, which had been passed as a response to the death of Megan Kanka (Kemshall and Maguire, 2003). Such a law would permit local communities to be informed of the identities of sex offenders living in their neighbourhoods. Public pressure of this kind clearly had an influence on the Halliday report, *Making punishments work* (Home Office, 2001), and its proposals for extended and indeterminate sentences later enacted in the Criminal Justice Act 2003. The

White Paper, *Protecting the public* (Home Office, 2002b), attempted a more difficult balance, and tried to respond to both the hawkish public protection agenda and the more considered approach of *Setting the boundaries* (Matravers, 2003).

While the conception of public protection in the White Paper (Home Office, 2002b) did hark back to the predatory paedophile, it nevertheless acknowledged and attempted to address some of the complex issues around sexual offending and sex offenders. The resulting legislative measures are detailed in the following section.

Sexual Offences Act 2003

The Sexual Offences Act 2003 sets out to deal exhaustively and systematically with all sexual offences, starting with rape – defined as involving vaginal, anal or oral penetration with a penis – and assault by penetration. The Act gender neutralises certain offences that previously referred only to women (for example, soliciting and loitering for the purposes of prostitution), and in general seeks to update the legislation. It attempts to provide more effective legal protections for those unable to give free and informed consent to sexual activity – children, trafficked women and adults with mental disorders.

Particular parts of the Act to note are:

- Section 15, which creates an offence of 'meeting a child following grooming', which relates to adults over 18 arranging to meet a child under 16 in the UK or elsewhere with the intention of committing a sexual offence;
- Sections 16-24, which deal with abuse of positions of trust – these are at least partly motivated by cases of abuse of children in public care which have come to light;
- Sections 47-51, which cover offences relating to abuse of children through prostitution and pornography;
- Sections 57-60, which deal with trafficking into, within and out of the UK for the purposes of sexual exploitation;
- Section 61, which contains an offence of 'administering a substance with intent', consequent on allegations of drinks and so on being 'spiked'; and
- Sections 74-76, which attempt to clarify what have been historically difficult issues of consent, particularly in relation to rape of adult women.

The Act also creates two new orders, which are again civil orders, breach of which are criminal offences. These are:

- Sexual Offence Prevention Orders (Section 104) – these replace Sex Offender Orders and Restraining Orders. They can be made at the time of sentence or by application by the police to the Magistrates' Court, for offenders convicted of an offence in Schedules 2 or 3 of the Act. They can also be used in cases where an individual has been found not guilty of a sexual offence by reason of insanity. They should contain whatever prohibitions are considered necessary to protect the public from serious sexual harm for a specified period of not less than five years.

- Risk of Sexual Harm Orders (Section 123) – these differ from the previous preventative orders in that they can be made against individuals without a prior conviction for a sexual offence. They last for a minimum of two years and can contain only those prohibitions deemed necessary to prevent serious sexual harm. The police can apply for a Risk of Sexual Harm Order if they have reason to believe that an individual has committed the following acts on at least two occasions:
  a) engaging in sexual activity involving a child or in the presence of a child;
  b) causing or inciting a child to watch a person engaging in sexual activity or to look at a moving or still image that is sexual;
  c) giving a child anything that relates to sexual activity or contains a reference to such activity;
  d) communicating with a child, where any part of the communication is sexual.

These two orders extend the powers of control and surveillance in relation to sex offenders. In terms of sentencing, the provisions for indeterminate and extended sentences in the Criminal Justice Act 2003 also permit the state to assume greater control over sex offenders and intrusion into their lives.

Community notification and other disclosure of information

Reference has already been made to the demands from some quarters to be notified when a sex offender moves in or is living in a neighbourhood. This has been subject to much debate, particularly in the aftermath of the murder of Sarah Payne by a man on the Sex Offender Register and known to the local MAPPA structure. The initial response to Sarah's death was highly emotional, but by the time of Roy Whiting's trial and conviction, a more considered largely professional debate was developing (Kemshall, 2003).

Although Home Office officials and ministers had visited various States within the US to see their individual notification systems in action, until recently the official view in the UK has been that any such system would be unworkable (Thomas, 2008). Concerns centred on the potential for harassment, vigilantism and further instability for offenders which might increase their risk or cause them to 'go underground'.

However, while still acknowledging the need to respect offenders' rights, some commentators have considered whether community notification could be beneficial, if managed appropriately. Terry Thomas (2003), for instance, has looked at good practice in running community notification meetings in Minnesota, while Hazel Kemshall and Mike Maguire (2003) examined a more open system operating in Scotland. They concluded that success seemed to depend upon controlled disclosure, adequate information and support to those who received information, and assistance to parents, children and communities to enable them to self-manage risk. They further emphasised the local nature of such schemes and network of relationships between various professional groups, parents and communities needed to sustain them.

In terms of exchange of information between professionals, this is facilitated by Section 115 of the Crime and Disorder Act 1998 which allows information to be disclosed for crime prevention purposes. The extent to which public authorities are able to disclose to private parties has been much more restricted. It is therefore interesting that Section 140 of the Criminal Justice and Immigration Act 2008 has now amended the powers in the Criminal Justice Act 2003 to allow for disclosure about previous convictions to specific members of the public where an offender is considered to pose a risk of serious harm to a particular child or children. This measure has been piloted and is now subject to national rollout as the child sex offender disclosure scheme.

Sex offender treatment programmes

Sarah Brown (2005) notes that, despite the more punitive approach to sex offenders outlined here, rehabilitation in the form of cognitive behavioural treatment has gradually developed and expanded. The history of sex offender treatment has three identifiable phases in which the following approaches have been dominant:

• psychoanalytical therapy;
• behavioural therapy; and
• cognitive behavioural treatment.

Psychoanalytical therapy was most developed in the US, but largely fell out of use during the 1970s and the era when it was believed that 'nothing works'. At the same time behavioural approaches were receiving attention and initially focused on such goals as desensitisation and reducing deviant patterns of arousal. However, as time went on, practitioners recognised the complexity of sexual deviance and began to add other elements to intervention programmes (Sarah Brown, 2005).

In a separate line of development, during the 1980s and early 1990s, academics began to examine the patterns emerging from large numbers of evaluations of interventions on general offender populations. These meta-analyses suggested that cognitive behavioural work produced more promising results than other approaches and greater impact on reconvictions. The findings also indicated that the most effective programmes:

• responded to level of assessed risk;
• targeted criminogenic needs;
• paid attention to responsivity – adapting to the offender's learning styles, for instance; and

- operated with a high level of programme integrity – not drifting away from or subverting the original aims of the programme.

These studies were mainly of young male offenders and it should not be assumed, because such programmes are effective with a general offender population, that their successes are necessarily replicated when applied to sex offenders. Indeed, Sarah Brown (2005) identifies that the adoption of cognitive behavioural approaches with sex offenders was due to changing beliefs in the discipline of psychology rather than the emergence of positive empirical evidence. This development happened in two ways: first, behavioural practitioners in the US adding more cognitive elements to their programmes and, second, the introduction of sex offender treatment programmes to the prison service in England and Wales.

Cognitive behavioural work looks at the complex relationships between thoughts, feelings and actions. The early conceptual models used included an influential framework established by Finklehor (1984) originally for the field of sexual abuse and Wolf's (1985) sexual offence cycle. From the early 1990s, approaches have also been borrowed from the field of addictions and relapse prevention has been added as a component of many programmes. A more recent theoretical development still is the pathways model relating to child sexual abuse and proposed by Ward and Siegert (2002). This is predicated on the dysfunction of four psychological mechanisms:

- intimacy deficits;
- sexual arousal;
- emotional regulation; and
- cognitive distortions (deviant sexual scripts).

Although these developments are interesting, they are based on large and questionable assumptions about the characteristics of sex offenders who are a varied and complex group (Scott and Codd, 2010). They also see sexual offending as caused by individual pathology, with no reference to the impact of social context and wider societal attitudes to sexual behaviours and norms.

The Sex Offender Treatment Programme

In the UK, sex offender treatment is available in the community via the probation service, NSPCC and certain health providers. Accredited programmes are also available in prison establishments where a range of interventions has been established to cater for offenders with differing levels of risk and need. These are briefly outlined in Table 17.2.

The Sex Offender Treatment Programme was set up in 17 establishments in 1992, with evaluation and monitoring as an integral part, which is highly unusual for treatment programmes (Brown, 2005b). Initially places were limited and not all sex offenders could be treated, but places have since been expanded and the

Table 17.2: Sex Offender Treatment Programme (SOTP)

Name	Length	Target group	Intervention
Core programme	85 sessions over 26 weeks	Offenders with IQ over 80, accepting some responsibility for behaviour	Lifestyles, relationships etc Victim empathy Relapse prevention
Adapted programme	70 sessions over 26 weeks	Offenders with IQ under 80 and also those whose first language is not English	As for core programme, but method of delivery is adapted
Rolling programme	45-60 sessions over 26 weeks	Low-risk offenders or those who have completed the core programme but still have treatment needs	Same as core programme but with a changing rather than static group
Extended programme	74 sessions over 26 weeks	Offenders who have completed the core programme but are assessed as having high deviance and further treatment needs	Similar to core programme, but may be supplemented by individual therapy
Booster programme	35 sessions, usually over 12 weeks	Offenders who have successfully completed the core programme and are preparing for release or move to open conditions	Motivational work and reinforcement of work on core programme

Source: Adapted from Snowden (2007)

development of additional programmes as outlined in Table 17.2 has ensured that intervention is available for a greater proportion of those assessed as suitable and willing (the programmes are voluntary). Prisoners who are vulnerable because of mental ill health, suicide risk, extremely low intelligence or certain personality disorders would not be considered suitable.

By 2002, programme completions of all types reached 1,046 (HM Prison Service, 2004, cited in Sarah Brown, 2005), so it is an extremely large programme. It has been identified by Mann and Thornton (1998, cited in Sarah Brown, 2005) as having five aspects that distinguish it from other programmes:

- operation over a large number of sites;
- commitment to systematic evaluation;
- use of lay therapists to develop treatment (that is, prisoner officers, probation staff);
- the emphasis on therapeutic style as well as programme content; and
- a system of annual accreditation.

The creation of NOMS and closer working relationships between prison and probation services should, in theory, result in better monitoring of sex offenders after completing the programme in the community and reinforcement of their learning and positive behaviours (Home Office, 2002a).

Sex offender programmes in the probation service

The probation service began to develop sex offender programmes in earnest during the early 1990s, as work with sex offenders became more of a service priority. The type and form of treatment differed considerably but was generally found in a HMI Probation review (1998) to be cognitive behavioural in orientation. Programme provision was standardised in 1999 with the introduction of accredited programmes across the probation service. At that point three sex offender programmes had been accredited and were allocated to regions of the country:

- Community Sex Offender Groupwork Programme (C-SOGP) – London, Wales, West and East Midlands
- Thames Valley Sex Offender Groupwork Programme (TV-SOGP) – the East, South East and South West of England
- Northumbria Sex Offender Groupwork Programme (N-SOGP) – North East, North West and Yorkshire & Humberside

These programmes are available for adult males with IQs of 80 or above and subject to assessment by a treatment manager. They are split into components, so that some high-risk offenders complete the full range of sessions, whereas lower risk offenders may complete certain modules only. All three focus on relapse prevention. A further programme has since been accredited focusing on work with sex offenders who abuse through use of the internet.

Effectiveness of treatment

Obviously determining effectiveness depends on the goals of the particular programme, and different programmes emphasise victim empathy, reducing denial, cognitive restructuring or reduction in sexual arousal/sexual fantasy.

In discussing these treatment goals, Sarah Brown (2005) notes that, while they may seem logical and intuitive, they are actually quite limited in usefulness and there is little empirical support for them. Research has failed to demonstrate a link between progress towards any of these treatment goals and recidivism, although this may be due more to the lack of robust evaluation evidence rather than an absence of a link. These difficulties are due to reasons such as lack of methodological rigour, small sample sizes, the ethical issues in establishing control groups and lack of information about re-offending (as opposed to reconviction) (Brown, 2010).

Although evaluations of general offender programmes have shown a correlation between performance in treatment and positive outcomes, this may not be so in sex offender treatment. Seto (2003), however, suggests that, while treatment performance may not be a static risk factor, it may be a valid indicator of dynamic risk and of imminence of re-offending, although further research is needed to 'unpick' how this might operate. What is known from the research is that offenders who drop out of programmes tend to re-offend more frequently than completers or often those offenders who are unprogrammed (Sarah Brown, 2005).

There are few large-scale evaluations of sex offender programmes with robust methodologies, although a growing body of research evidence is available from the US and from our own Sex Offender Treatment Programme, which has produced data over a number of years. This seems to indicate that the programmes available are more effective with men who offend against children rather than adults, and also that programmes which require offenders to take responsibility for their actions are less likely to succeed with offenders who believe they have little influence over what happens, that is, with an external locus of control (Beech and Fisher, 2002, cited in Sarah Brown, 2005). It has also been found that there is likely to be a lower rate of sexual recidivism for those offenders who receive aftercare and services in the community, thus bolstering the relapse prevention elements of programmes.

Brown ends her recent analysis of evaluation evidence by bemoaning the lack of conclusive evidence for the efficacy of sex offender treatment, and indications of which types of programmes are most effective for particular subsets of sex offenders (Brown, 2010).

Sex offenders and the probation service

HMI Probation has published two thematic reports on work with sex offenders (1991, 1998). The later report commended the work of the service while also noting that the development of policy and strategy had been outpaced by the increase in sex offender cases (Crow, 2001). Nevertheless, more systematic approaches to working with sex offenders were appearing and this was subsequently strengthened by the adoption of accredited programmes and the introduction of the MAPPA framework.

Despite these developments, a further joint inspection by HMI Probation and HM Inspectorate of Constabulary, *Protecting children from potentially dangerous people* (2002), raised a number of issues. Some of these, such as the lack of engagement of agencies with MAPPA, were addressed in the Criminal Justice Act 2003 and other legislation. However, other concerns about not reviewing and evaluating the effectiveness of MAPPA were still present in a subsequent joint inspection, *Managing sex offenders in the community* (2005). This also found weak links between the SMBs for MAPPA and Area Child Protection Committees (now SCBs). More operationally, it also identified that:

- demand for sex offender treatment programmes outstripped supply;
- only 37 per cent of cases inspected started programmes within the 20 days national standard;
- there were a spread of views among staff about the appropriate balance between offender rights and public protection;

- diversity issues were reasonably well addressed when highlighted at a practice level but were not prioritised at a managerial or strategic level;
- there was no specific support for case managers dealing with sex offenders outside of normal supervisory arrangements, although this was available for officers running sex offender programmes;
- risk of harm assessments were poor and were not reviewed at appropriate points; and
- OASys were similarly found to be poor in terms of quality, timeliness and management input.

The inspectors concluded that despite some improvements, the findings were disappointing, with a lack of integrated and accountable case management in the community. Delivery was inconsistent and poorly coordinated, with inadequate use of to OASys to inform interventions and ensure that supervision remained purposeful (HMI Probation and HMIC, 2005).

Predating this review, the National Probation Service had published a *Sex offender strategy for the probation service* (2004) that had set a series of objectives for the service:

- timely assessment using evidence-based tools;
- interventions to reduce risk;
- interventions to manage risk;
- develop a range of accommodation options commensurate with risk and need.

The findings of the joint inspection the following year demonstrate the difficulties of implementing these strategic aspirations, particularly in the midst of tensions about level of resources, training and experience of staff and organisational change.

In the light of the comments from the Inspectorates, the National Probation Service and individual services progressed their plans for work with sex offenders and prioritising resources based on accurate assessment. PC 17/2007 gives guidance on the use of the main specialist assessment tool, Risk Matrix 2000, in pre-sentence and parole reports and prior to sex offender programmes. It should also be used as the first part of the SARN reports required from April 2007 at the close of any sex offender programme (see PC 9/2007).

In 2010 the Inspectorates again returned to the subject of sex offenders, reporting under the theme of *Restriction and rehabilitation: Getting the right mix* (CJJI, 2010b). Although progress was evident and inter-agency working had improved, the overall judgement was that the right balance of restriction and support/ rehabilitation was not being achieved in too many instances. Risk management plans tended to focus on restrictions, understating the role of rehabilitative or constructive interventions, and where several plans existed on one offender, these were not always coordinated. Although good practice was apparent for higher risk cases, offender managers were not engaging well with offenders who were not allocated to treatment programmes and needed more support and guidance to deliver individual offence-focused work. The report also observed that sentence plans were often completed without active offender involvement and lacked outcome-focused objectives. The fact that the Inspectorates also highlighted that reporting frequencies tended to be determined by the minimums set by national standards rather than according to the assessed risk posed by the offender further suggests significant room for improvement and responsiveness in risk management practices.

Could it be done differently?

The current approach to work with sex offenders in the UK sits firmly within the community protection model. This has its strengths and research has indicated that within a MAPPA context, positive relationships can be established, acting as a sound basis for work that is responsive to individuals' social and personal problems (Wood and Kemshall, 2010). However, the indications from *Restriction and rehabilitation* (CJJI, 2010b) suggest that this level of good practice does not extend across the whole sex offender group and that work with lower risk offenders is often less confident and less geared to responding to individual risks and needs. Given also the context where sex offenders are the focus of acute popular and professional concerns, and the availability of an increasing range of restrictions that can be applied – licence conditions, curfews, exclusions, Sexual Offence Prevention Orders, registration requirements – potential exists for cautious practice and the over-use of control measures, not sufficiently balanced by constructive intervention. The effects may be disintegrative, rather than reintegrative (McAlinden, 2010), increasing social isolation and, ironically, creating the pre-conditions for further offending.

Interest in the academic world and currently at the margins of UK practice suggests that there are other approaches that may be more socially inclusive and more effective in managing risk through the use of more targeted control measures and greater social support. However, these approaches are not developed on the basis of their instrumental benefits in reducing re-offending, but advocate a different ethic in terms of recognising the humanity and the rights inherent in each individual offender. And this is particularly important with sex offenders as a highly stigmatised group, where substantial legal powers and public sentiment can combine to erode rights in the name of public protection.

Good Lives Model

Reference has been made in previous chapters to the Good Lives Model, which proposes work with sex offenders based on learning from the field of positive psychology in relation to *primary social goods*. These are outlined in full in Chapter Four, but briefly,

> Basic human needs cause us to want and require certain outcomes – for example relationships, autonomy, food and warmth – in order to function in an optimal manner. There is a range of distinct goods, and a (good) life represents the presence of each of these. (Ward and Stewart, 2003, p 353)

All individuals are programmed – hard-wired, if you like – to seek these primary goods. Where legitimate and pro-social means of doing so are frustrated – perhaps due to factors in the individual's psychological make-up or external environmental conditions that limit opportunities – the individual may try to achieve the goods in other ways. This may involve offending or other behaviours that directly or indirectly damage others. In relation to a sex offender, offending may be motivated by the need for intimacy and a feeling of relatedness that the individual is trying to fulfil inappropriately. The Good Lives Model entails complex work with individuals exploring needs and motivations, but, put at a very simplistic level, it is about enabling individuals to understand what it is they want to achieve and to find ways of reaching their goals and fulfilling needs in pro-social ways:

> It is always much easier to motivate individuals if they are reassured that the goods they are aiming for are acceptable; the problem resides in the way they are sought. (Ward and Maruna, 2007, p 129)

Managing risk is a fundamental principle within the Good Lives Model, because the rights of victims are taken into account alongside those of the offender. Offenders, as well as having rights of their own, have duties towards the rights of others and it is useful to consider this in relation to sex offenders (Connolly and Ward, 2008). Restraints limiting freedoms should be put in place but these should impinge upon the offender's rights only insofar as is necessary to contain harmful behaviours and in proportion to the level of risk. Accurate and sensitive assessment is therefore central to the approach and this should take place within the context of a respectful and collaborative relationship. Later in the process, intervention should focus on creating opportunities and capacities for the offender to build human and social capital, and to create an alternative identity dissociated from offending (again, this is discussed in more depth in Chapter Four).

There is much that can be taken from the Good Lives Model in terms of its approach to risk which is seen in its cultural and social context, rather than being a fixed property residing in the individual (Ward and Maruna, 2007). It takes a positive humanistic stance and focus on strengths rather than deficits, which is not always the case in the RNR model. It may be criticised for being overly optimistic and questions could be raised about its basic assumptions; for instance, whether *primary human goods* are as universally sought as it assumes and whether there is sufficient consensus about what constitutes a *good life* (McNeill and Weaver, 2010). Nevertheless, it suggests a powerful and different attitude to sex offenders and the focus of agency interventions supporting desistance.

Circles of Support and Accountability

Circles of Support and Accountability (COSA) developed initially in Canada in an attempt to enhance formal supervisory mechanisms and reintegration of sex offenders into the community through the involvement of volunteers. In Canada, circles can operate at three different points in the criminal justice process:

- sentencing, perhaps operating as an alternative to custody or as well as custody:
- on release from prison, supporting parole supervision; and
- at the end of custodial sentences in the absence of statutory supervision. (Kemshall, 2008, p 76)

Through the COSA, the offender is held to account and is subject to a degree of social control, but is also able to access support for rehabilitation and changes in lifestyle. They typically involve a partnership between professionals and volunteers, which in the UK pilot in Thames Valley was formalised and linked to the local MAPPA structure (Kemshall, 2008). The UK model is therefore more systemic than the original Canadian initiatives, which tended to develop organically (McAlinden, 2010) and to some extent, because of its role in relation to MAPPA, has been co-opted into the community protection model with resultant tensions and conflicts (Kemshall, 2008).

Evaluations of effectiveness in Canada have indicated successes in the use of COSA for high-risk offenders, with recidivism rates reduced by 50 per cent (McAlinden, 2006). The goals, however, are rather broader than just reducing offending, and aim to achieve greater degrees of social cohesion and to enhance the ability of communities to respond appropriately to individuals whose behaviours may pose a risk in their midst. Further evaluations should explore these wider goals and also investigate the potential for community engagement, particularly in larger communities.

Stop It Now!

Originating in Vermont, USA, Stop It Now! UK and Ireland is run under the umbrella of the Lucy Faithful Foundation. It adopts a public health approach and incorporates three strands of work:

- a helpline for sex offenders and their families or partners;
- treatment and counselling for sex offenders; and
- public awareness, public education and media campaigning.

As well as providing direct services, Stop It Now! aims to influence and inform policy makers as well as professionals working in child protection and members of key community groups (Kemshall, 2008).

The work of Stop It Now! is interesting, if small scale due to limited access to funds. There are also issues about circulating public health messages about sensitive subjects such as sex offending as these may be distorted or undermined by a hostile media (Kemshall, 2008). Nevertheless, it exemplifies a different approach, attempting to address offending from outside the criminal justice system and seeking to harness the capacities of communities and other agencies, such as local authority children's social care.

Summary

Work with sex offenders is a difficult area of practice and can challenge practitioners' values and beliefs as well as being exceptionally emotionally demanding. As individuals, sex offenders have rights to fair treatment and privacy, but these must be balanced by the need to protect both specific victims and, in some cases, the community at large. There can therefore be complex decisions and judgements about what degrees of intrusiveness or restriction would be both appropriate and effective in individual cases. This is one of the areas where the dilemmas about rights and responsibilities towards public protection is uppermost for practitioners, aware that being too risk-averse may ironically increase stigma and social isolation, thus in turn increasing risk.

Intervention with sex offenders is conventionally based on the community protection model, using the principles of risk, need and responsivity. Other frameworks may be able to offer more inclusive ways of working and certainly practitioners should seek to exploit opportunities to engage offenders in self-managing their risk and to build a life that is more fulfilling as well as offence-free.

Further reading

Brown, S. (2005) *Treating sex offenders: An introduction to sex offender treatment programmes*, Cullompton: Willan.

Harrison, K. (ed) (2010) *Managing high risk sex offenders in the community: Risk management, treatment and social responsibility*, Cullompton: Willan.

Ireland, J.L., Ireland, C.A. and Birch, P. (eds) (2008) *Violent and sexual offenders: Assessment, treatment and management*, Cullompton: Willan.

EIGHTEEN

Indeterminate sentence prisoners

Ending this book with an analysis of indeterminate sentencing is particularly apt, because the policy developments concerning individuals serving indeterminate sentences encapsulate some of the trends and characteristics of criminal justice policy making more generally. These include a focus on risk, moves towards multi-agency assessment and decision making, and a more stringent approach to enforcement/recall. The key concerns about balancing individual (offender) rights and risks to specific victims or to the public are of particular interest in relation to these offenders, and supervision demands much of experienced practitioners who invest knowledge, skills and emotional connection in what is sometimes long-term work with individuals in prison serving indeterminate sentences or post-release on licence. The population of such offenders includes those convicted of sexual crimes, MDOs and young people detained at Her Majesty's Pleasure. In this sense, this chapter provides a useful rounding up of previous discussions.

The law in relation to life sentences

In common with many other aspects of sentencing, legal provisions relating to life sentences for adults have changed as a result of the Criminal Justice Act 2003. However, as practitioners may find themselves working with individuals serving a sentence who were convicted a considerable time ago, a historical perspective is needed more than ever.

Murder

The provisions vary according to age and are mandatory:

- Over 21
  Imprisonment for life (Section 1 of the Murder [Abolition of Death Penalty] Act, 1965)

- 18-20 at the time of the offence
  Custody for life (Section 93 of the Powers of the Criminal Court [Sentencing] Act 2000). Prior to that Act sentences were imposed under Section 8(1) of the Criminal Justice Act 1982

- Under 18
  Detention during Her Majesty's Pleasure (Section 53(1) of the Children and Young Persons Act 1933 as updated by Section 90 of the Powers of the Criminal Court [Sentencing] Act 2000)

Discretionary life sentences

Certain offences such as manslaughter, rape, buggery or arson, may also attract life sentences and these again vary according to age:

- Over 21
  Imprisonment for life

- 18–20 at the time of the offence
  Custody for life (Section 94 of the Powers of the Criminal Court [Sentencing] Act 2000). Prior to that Act, sentences were imposed under Section 8(2) of the Criminal Justice Act 1982

- Under 18
  Detention for Life (Sections 53(2) and (3) of the Children and Young Persons Act 1933 as updated by Section 91 of the Powers of the Criminal Court [Sentencing] Act 2000)

Automatic life sentences

Section 2 of the Crime (Sentences) Act 1997 required the court to pass a life sentence on any individual convicted of a second 'serious' offence (that is, violent or sexual offence) unless there were exceptional circumstances. What constitutes 'exceptional circumstances' caused intense debate at the time and was ultimately refined by case law, including the ruling by the Lord Chief Justice, Lord Woolf, which reinterpreted exceptional circumstances to cover those cases where the offender was not felt to present a significant risk to the public. Automatic life sentences were a controversial provision, intended to limit the discretion of the judiciary in cases involving serious offences, and lowering the bar in terms of the public protection considerations previously required before a discretionary life sentence could be passed. However, as indicated, the judiciary found ways of subverting or circumventing the legislation (Jones and Newburn, 2006).

Section 2 has been effectively superseded by the IPP sentences in the Criminal Justice Act 2003. Nevertheless, many lifers within the system have been sentenced under this provision and transitional arrangements will remain in place to ensure their continued supervision.

Sentences of imprisonment for public protection (IPP)

Offenders serving IPP sentences under Section 225 of the Criminal Justice Act 2003 (and young people serving detention for public protection [DPP] sentences under Section 226) were initially subject to the same processes and procedures as prisoners serving life. However, the number of IPP sentences passed exceeded expectations and planning projections, and created resource pressures for the probation service. From January 2008, therefore, they have been dealt with through the OMM as part of the Phase III implementation, which means that offender managers will manage the sentence, in contrast to life sentence prisoners where responsibility for OASys completion as well as sentencing planning and review remains with the prison service.

Punitive periods of an indeterminate sentence: 'the tariff'

The 'tariff' denotes the minimum term that an IPP sentence prisoner must serve in prison before being considered for conditional release. The process of setting tariffs has been the subject of debate over the years. In cases of mandatory life sentences for murder, the tariff was customarily determined by the Home Secretary but, following an appeal from life sentence prisoner, Anthony Andrews, the House of Lords ruled in 2002 that this was incompatible with the ECHR (see PC 28/2003). Subsequently, Section 269 of the Criminal Justice Act 2003 stipulated that the sentencing court should decide the minimum term following the passing of the sentence. Schedule 21 of that Act sets out the statutory framework for determining the tariff and, significantly, contains provision for 'whole life' sentences. When determined by ministers, the tariff or punitive period of the sentence would run from the date of incarceration, so all remand periods would be taken into account, but this is no longer the case, as the tariff now runs from the date of court sentence.

The process for discretionary life and also IPP sentences differs in that the sentencing judge must declare what is known as the 'relevant part' of the sentence in open court, except in certain extremely serious cases where the judge is able to decline such open declaration. In these circumstances, the case is then treated as similar to a mandatory life sentence case. The time spent on remand is taken into account.

In line with the growing awareness of prisoners' rights and openness in the sentence planning process, the prisoner is now informed of the tariff set, which was not the case when the tariff system was introduced by the then Home Secretary, Leon Brittan, in 1983. The tariff expiry date is calculated by the Public Protection Casework Section in NOMS and this information and the date of the first Parole Board Review is communicated to the prison establishment, the prisoner and the probation service.

Reviews and recalls of indeterminate public protection sentence prisoners

Oversight of the lifer system has historically been undertaken by the Lifer Management Unit in the Home Office that has since been replaced by a specialist team working within the NOMS Public Protection Casework Section. It has a range of functions including monitoring the Parole Board's review processes for lifers and IPP sentence prisoners, monitoring progress of those on indeterminate sentences in the community and questions of recall or cancellation of supervision, and, more broadly, policy development in work with lifers.

Relevant statistics

Later sections develop arguments about the way that indeterminate sentences are viewed and changes in their use. It is useful first, however, to consider some basic information about changing patterns of sentencing and specifically the number of lifers currently in the prison system. Table 18.1 charts sentences of life imprisonment made during the period 1995-2008 by age and gender (Ministry of Justice, 2009d).

This shows that the number of life sentences rose by almost 100 per cent between 1995 and 2008, with a sharp rise in 1999 that coincided with implementation of the Crime (Sentences) Act 1997. England and Wales has the dubious distinction of having the highest number of life sentence prisoners in Europe, more in fact

Table 18.1: Sentences of life imprisonment 1995-2008

Sex and age	1995	1997	1999	2000	2001	2002	2003	2004	2005	2006	2007	2008
Males												
10-17	10	24	26	19	28	21	11	15	27	16	23	24
18-20	13	29	38	9	27	21	47	24	50	46	70	54
21+	226	293	401	418	429	494	431	509	517	469	378	417
All males	249	348	465	445	484	536	489	548	595	531	471	495
Females												
10-17	1	3	3	2	1	1	0	1	1	0	3	1
18-20	2	2	2	1	3	2	4	2	4	2	3	2
21+	21	16	14	18	15	16	20	19	26	14	15	25
All females	24	21	19	21	19	19	24	22	31	16	12	28
Males + Females												
10-17	11	27	29	21	29	22	11	16	28	16	26	25
18-20	15	31	40	10	30	23	51	26	54	48	73	56
21+	247	309	415	436	444	510	451	528	543	483	393	442
All ages	**273**	**367**	**484**	**467**	**503**	**555**	**513**	**570**	**625**	**547**	**492**	**523**

than Germany, France, Italy, the Russian Federation and Turkey combined (Prison Reform Trust, 2009).

In terms of IPP and DPP sentences, the figures have risen from 426 when they first became available in 2005, to 1,538 in the course of 2008. Greater discretion in the use of IPP sentences introduced by the Criminal Justice and Immigration Act has reduced the number of such sentences being imposed, but the rate of release from these sentences is slow. This means that by the end of 2009, 5,788 offenders had been made subject to DPP/IPP sentences but only 99 had been released from prison, 24 of whom had been subsequently recalled (CJJI, 2010c).

On 30 June 2010, there were 13,134 prisoners serving indeterminate sentences, comprising 12,753 men and 381 women, and including 54 young people under the age of 18. This represents an increase of 8 per cent compared to June 2009 (Ministry of Justice, 2010d).

Explaining the increase in life sentences

Although homicide rates have not significantly increased, the number of life sentences being imposed clearly has grown, and this coincides with the rise of the public protection agenda and the climate of popular punitiveness referred to in previous chapters. Michael Howard, as Home Secretary in the early 1990s, signalled disillusion with the 'just deserts' sentencing philosophies that had only too briefly held sway, and flirted with the idea of automatic life sentences, as had been adopted in the US.

Jones and Newburn's (2006) exploration of the adoption of US-style 'three strikes and you're out' sentencing indicates a more complex picture than has been popularly supposed. The idea was first promoted by campaigners in Washington State following the murder of Diane Ballasiostes by a previously convicted rapist. It was subsequently adopted by California, again in the wake of a high profile murder by a known offender. However, despite the publicity that these policies have received and the introduction of mandatory minimum sentences in 50 states, there is considerable variation in the laws currently in place and their impact, with California being the state that has most aggressively made use of such laws. In certain other states, the eligibility criteria are rather stricter.

In contrast, the introduction of mandatory minimum sentencing in the UK for violent and sexual offences, as well as other provisions relating to drugs and burglary offences, was part of a general move towards more punitive sentencing, rather than a response to particular crimes and to the victims' lobby. However, as in the US, the symbolic power of 'tough' mandatory minimum sentences was attractive to both the Conservative administration who made the original proposals and to New Labour who enacted and implemented them. Jones and Newburn (2006) identify that for politicians on both sides of the House, this legislation was intended to have considerable teeth, but that in practice they were significantly blunted by the opposition from professionals and the judiciary, among others.

A further development in the US has been the use of Life Without Parole (LWOP) sentences as an alternative to the death penalty. Appleton and Grover (2007) tellingly cite a 2004 survey which found that 33,633 prisoners, or approximately one in every four life sentence prisoners in the US, were serving LWOP sentences, a hugely disproportionate increase over the last 30 years. The same article points to a stark contrast with countries such as Croatia, Norway, Portugal and Slovenia which make no provision for life sentences at all.

Sadly, the UK is moving in the direction of the US rather than colleagues in Europe, with Schedule 21 of the Criminal Justice Act 2003 outlining three starting points for the consideration of judges in setting tariffs for life sentence prisoners. These are, briefly:

- A whole life minimum term for exceptionally serious offences committed by offenders over 21 – these might include cases involving sexual or sadistic conduct, particularly with a minor.
- Thirty years for particularly serious cases such as murders of police or prison officers in the course of duty, murders involving firearms or murder that was racially aggravated. This length tariff could be available for any offender over 18 years at the time of commission.
- Fifteen years for other murders by over-18s.
- Twelve years for murders by under-18s.

While there are few UK prisoners serving what are known here as 'whole life sentences'(currently fewer than 50 in England and Wales), a general lengthening of tariffs clearly is taking place. Furthermore, there are serious implications in imposing whole life sentences, not least the management of such prisoners who have even less incentive than other life prisoners to comply with sentence planning requirements and to behave appropriately in the prison. Whole life sentences are difficult for the individual to cope with and may be viewed as harsher than the death sentence, despite the arguments of those in the US, for instance, keen to promote LWOP in order to hasten abolition of the death penalty. Appleton and Grover (2007) also raise concerns about whether whole life sentences are proportionate to the crime committed, particularly in key States that have used 'three strikes and you're out' sentencing for offences less than murder. They go on to comment that:

> We would argue that LWOP faces many, if not all, of the objections of the death sentence and, therefore, is equally untenable in civilised society. To lock up a prisoner and take away all his or her hope of release compromises principles of human rights and human dignity, ignores the capacity for redemption and rehabilitation, and denies individuals any right to be considered for release. (2007, p 612)

A further implication of longer sentences, including whole life sentences, is the need for the prison estate to cope with growing numbers of older or indeed elderly prisoners, who differ physically and psychologically from the majority of inmates. At present the numbers are small: on 31 March 2009, there were 7,358 prisoners over 50 years old and 518 over 70, almost exclusively men, out of a population of more than 80,000 (Prison Reform Trust, 2009). However, their needs will become more significant and will require change within prison environments, new medical services and provision of appropriate purposeful activity (Wahidin et al, 2007).

Sentences and tariffs are important factors influencing the numbers of life sentence prisoners in custody, but at the other end of the process so too are the decisions made by the Parole Board about release. Hood and Shute (2000) have examined the decision making of the Board and found a decline in the use of parole alongside what they identified as a tendency to overestimate the risk posed by many prisoners. This, coupled with a growing use of recall to prison, has also contributed to the increase in numbers of lifers in prisons.

To summarise, the number of life sentence prisoners have been affected by:

- a generally more punitive sentencing climate, resulting in longer sentences and greater use of indeterminate sentences;
- specific legal provisions and specified 'starting points' for setting tariffs;
- concerns about public protection resulting in cautious decision making about release of prisoners on parole; and
- a greater tendency to use powers to recall offenders to prison.

The impact of being given a life sentence

For a life sentence prisoner, the start of the sentence can be traumatic, as the following quote illustrates:

> Being sentenced to life imprisonment brings with it unique feelings and experiences. Prisoners serving even long determinate sentences (despite many uncertainties) know, as do their families, that there is a date when they must be released. A life sentence brings no such certainty. Prisoners facing this prospect react in complex ways and commonly go through stages – from denial (of the offence and its consequences), withdrawal, frustration, rage and disappointment. Accepting responsibility for a grave crime inevitably occasions overwhelming guilt and distress. These emotions make unusual demands on those working with them throughout their sentence. (Baldwin and Canton, 2007, p 156)

IPP and DPP sentence prisoners may share some of these same reactions simply because of the uncertainties surrounding not having a fixed release date. But there may be an additional emotional impact for a life sentence prisoner in coming to terms with the traumatic nature of their offence, particularly where there is no previous history of offending.

Organisation of an indeterminate sentence

Lifers used to have specific planning processes of their own, but have now been brought closer to the NOMS standard offender management processes and the approach used for the IPP prisoners.

The initial sentence planning meeting should take place within 16 weeks of sentence. For mandatory life sentence prisoners, a Multi-Agency Lifer Risk Assessment Panel (MALRAP) must be held and this will have access to a summary of evidence about the index offence supplied by the police. Similar meetings may be held in respect of discretionary life and IPP/DPP prisoners, but are not compulsory.

The second sentence planning meeting should be held within 26 weeks of the initial planning meeting – by which time the offender should be involved in interventions – and subsequent meetings should take place annually. The home probation officer/offender manager will be required to prepare reports for these meetings. Sentence planning and reviews are the responsibility of offender managers for IPP prisoners.

Guidance states that the indeterminate sentence should be managed in accordance with the risk of harm that the offender poses to the public, rather than the index offence or length of tariff. Sentence planning should identify relevant interventions and support to help reduce risk, inviting offender participation as much as possible in setting goals and targets and working on the principle that the ultimate responsibility for demonstrating a reduction in risk lies with the offender. Some work will necessarily be offence-specific (such as the Sex Offender Treatment Programme), but it is important that other needs relating to mental disorders, emotional states or educational development are also addressed, especially where these involve needs or goals identified by the offender. PSI (Prison Service Instruction) 36/2010 states that:

> Sentence planning for indeterminate sentence prisoners must be realistic, spanning work whilst in custody and in the community. There is an expectation that sentence planning should be achievable, not aspirational, and that where interventions are recommended they can be delivered ... interventions are not limited to accredited programmes and can include a range of other work with an offender to address and help them reduce the risk of harm they pose to the public. Sentence plan targets must identify the prisoner's risk to be reduced, rather than identifying interventions to be completed. (HM Prison Service, 2010, p 1)

All moves within the prison system are subject to careful multi-disciplinary assessment that informs the successive sentence plans and the progressive steps leading to release on licence.

A virtual pre-requisite for progress through an indeterminate sentence is for the offender to demonstrate acceptance of guilt and appreciation of the harm that has been caused. There are, however, a number of offenders who continue to deny the offences for which they have been convicted, and these individuals present challenges for the indeterminate sentence system. Samuels (2003) felt that the small number of lifers who persist in denial are unfairly treated in terms of the opportunity for parole, particularly as many of the courses and groupwork programmes that lifers are expected to attend require that all participants admit their offences, and this is also clearly the case for the more recent IPP prisoners. Although accepting that deniers pose some difficulties for the prison service, Nigel Newcomen, former Head of the Sentence Management Group, argued that constructive work can still take place with offenders and that a realistic assessment of risk is still feasible, thus making parole still a possibility, if less straightforward than for other prisoners (2003).

Chapter 4 of the *Indeterminate sentence manual* (HM Prison Service, 2010) addresses denial of guilt and emphasises that the focus of work should be on assessing and reducing risk, recognising that professionals involved with indeterminate sentence prisoners who maintain their innocence have to work on the basis that the conviction is a correct one, but that there may be cases where there has been a wrongful conviction. Denial, in itself, should not prevent progress through the indeterminate sentence system as long as the level of risk can be assessed as acceptably low.

Progress towards release

Prison Service Order 6010 details the generic parole process that is followed in assessing readiness for release. The Parole Board may already have reviewed the case before any planned move between security categories. The relevant team in the NOMS Public Protection Casework Section should refer cases to the Parole Board again approximately eight months before the tariff expiry date in order to consider whether release on that date would be appropriate.

Every indeterminate sentence prisoner has the right under Article 5 of the ECHR to have his or her continued detention reviewed by the Parole Board once the tariff has expired and every two years thereafter if still remaining in custody.

A skeleton parole dossier will be prepared by the Public Protection Casework Section in NOMS. Further reports from the sentence review process as well as an updated OASys and a report from the home probation officer/offender manager in the PAROM1 template will be added according to a strict timetable 18 weeks before the parole review date. Home probation officers/offender managers should be aware of situations where a psychiatric or psychological report may be required and should initiate this if necessary. Documentation is routinely shared with the prisoner unless there are overriding considerations of public protection or national security.

Prison Service Order 6010 details the assessment process and the timetable over 26 weeks that must be adhered to. Unless the prisoner has already expressed a wish to have an oral hearing, a single member of the Parole Board will assess the documentation and may make a decision not to proceed on the basis of that information. Otherwise the case will either be subject to a further assessment on paper by three panel members or be referred straight to an oral hearing. The Secretary of State's case, in a standard form of words, may be put to the hearing by an advocate from the Public Protection Casework Section or a designated senior manager from the prison. The majority decision of the Parole Board panel, however, is binding on the Secretary of State, even where this does not accord with the Secretary of State's view. If release is not recommended, the panel may make alternative recommendations in relation to a move to open conditions and this will be then considered by the Public Protection Casework Section.

Release on licence

Life sentence prisoners are released on life licence issued under Section 28(5) of the Crime (Sentences) Act 1997, and those subject to IPP sentences are also covered by the same arrangements by virtue of Schedule 18 of the Criminal Justice Act 2003.

Details of the licence are contained in Chapter 13 of the *Indeterminate sentence manual* that states that:

> The licence:
>
> • remains in force for the rest of the individual's life, except for those serving an IPP sentence
> • may be revoked and the licensee returned to prison at any time if he/she no longer represents a safe enough risk to remain in the community.
>
> All life sentence and IPP prisoners are released on a licence which contains seven standard conditions. On the recommendation of the Parole Board, a life licence may include additional conditions related to that particular individual. The inclusion of additional conditions on a life licence is usually recommended by the supervising officer in his/her report to the Parole Board. In making such recommendations the supervising officer should explain in terms of risk the reasons why the additional conditions are required. All such conditions must be lawful by being reasonable, necessary and proportionate.
>
> Additional or non-standard conditions are included in a life licence in order to:
>
> • ensure the continued safety of the public by providing a means to help assess and manage the risk the licensee presents;
> • help the licensee reintegrate into the community as a law-abiding citizen. (HM Prison Service, 2010, p 2)

'Reasonable, necessary and proportionate' are important principles to bear in mind in relation to suggesting licence conditions, which is primarily the role of the home probation officer/offender manager. The offender should be allowed sufficient opportunity to engage in activities that promote reintegration and rehabilitation. Certain licence conditions involving treatment will require the expressed willingness of a named medical or other specialist practitioner to deliver the treatment, although the offender's consent is not required.

The home probation officer/offender manager should provide a report to the Public Protection Casework Section one month after release and then quarterly for the first two years. These will be endorsed by a senior officer of at least assistant chief officer level who will add his or her own comments. Templates for progress reports are provided within the *Indeterminate sentence manual* in Annex 6 of Chapter 13, while Annex 8 contains a template for requesting the revocation of a life or IPP licence where concerns about public protection arise and/or where the offender breaches licence conditions.

Probation service and life sentence prisoners

The probation service has had a distinct role in relation to life sentence prisoners since the inception of the lifer system. The *Lifer manual* (which pre-dated the *Indeterminate sentence manual*) noted that:

> The National Probation Service needs to be involved at all key stages of the sentence. They need to work with lifers before conviction, through seconded Probation Teams in prisons and then supervise the offender following release back into the community during the course of the sentence. Lifers remain on licence until they die, but they may have their licence conditions cancelled after a period of trouble-free living in the community. (HM Prison Service, 2002, Chapter 1, p 6)

The involvement of the service starts once the offender is charged and follows the case through the trial and/or sentencing process. The role now encompasses work with victims but the focus remains on risk assessment and management in relation to the life sentence prisoner. There are key points immediately post-sentence and in preparation for release where the probation service contribution is most needed, but the present-day expectation is that contact will be maintained throughout the prison part of the sentence. Closer working arrangements with the prison service under NOMS should facilitate communication and consistency between staff in the prison and in the community to the benefit of offenders. This was identified as necessary in the joint thematic inspection conducted by HMI Prisons and HMI Probation in 1999 (Home Office, 1999). The report was critical of some aspects of the prison service management of life sentence prisoners, including the lack of central direction in relation to this work and quality of regimes in main lifer centres. It was also critical of the Lifer Management Unit in the Home Office, which it found to be overly bureaucratic. However, the probation service's work was found to be positive on the whole:

> In recent years the number of life sentences has continued to rise and the pressures upon the prison system in managing them has become acute resulting in unacceptable levels of delays. However, the work undertaken in prison, coupled with close supervision by the probation service following release, is likely to have contributed to the fall in reconviction rates for male lifers for serious offences, in marked contrast to the higher reconviction rates for other types of offenders. Probation services have clearly demonstrated their ability to effectively supervise lifers over extended periods following their release from prison. (Home Office, 1999, p 7)

Nevertheless, challenges were identified for the probation service, including engaging managers more in proper oversight and support around cases, moving towards more multi-disciplinary ways of working and ensuring that staff are appropriately trained and confident to undertake this skilled and demanding work.

Involvement with lifers is distinct from other areas of probation involvement and requires practitioners to draw on considerable reserves of professional expertise and personal qualities, but it is rewarding work nonetheless:

> It was clear that work with lifers should be regarded as different from other types of supervision, because of its intensity, the nature of the offence, the indeterminate nature of supervision, the high level of sensitivity in these cases and the responsibility of reporting to prison headquarters. (Home Office, 1999, p 100).

Imprisonment for Public Protection prisoners

Whereas work with life sentence prisoners has historically attracted a certain cachet, this has not been the case with IPP and DPP prisoners who place different demands often because their tariff dates are relatively short (an average of 3 years and 140 days in 2008; Prison Reform Trust, 2009). The sheer number of such sentences has also created resource problems for prison and probation services. One response to this has been to bring IPP prisoners within scope of Phase III of the OMM and therefore to remove them from the onerous and bureaucratic paperwork that was in place for life sentence prisoners. However, two joint inspections by HMI Prisons and HMI Probation have been extremely critical of the sentences themselves and lack of strategic thinking about resources and staff training and also the agencies involved – prisons, probation and YOTs – in working with individuals with indeterminate sentences in custody.

The first thematic review (CJJI, 2008) pointed to

• the wide range of offences that could attract an IPP/DPP sentence;

- the typically low lengths of the tariffs set by court, meaning that these prisoners would be eligible for parole review within a relatively short period of time;
- inadequate planning for implementation, despite predictions that a large number of these sentences would be imposed;
- an already overcrowded prison system;
- cuts in the section of the Home Office that was overseeing life sentence prisoners at a point where they were also expected to take on these new sentences;
- a probation service that was poorly prepared and trained for the demands of this work; and
- an under-resourced Parole Board.

All this added up to what the Inspectors called 'a perfect storm' (CJJI, 2008). At the time of this inspection, two IPP prisoners had already taken the government to judicial review on the basis that they had not been provided with the interventions necessary for them to prove that they had addressed and reduced their risks before their tariffs expired. The Court of Appeal found that the Secretary of State had acted unlawfully in not making suitable provision, thus creating what the Inspectors referred to as a 'Kafkaesque predicament' (CJJI, 2008) for prisoners where they were being held because of presumed risk but were not being allowed the opportunity to address that risk.

The Inspectors had further criticisms of the quality of probation reports and specifically risk assessments, which did not recognise the relevance of diverse needs such as mental health, substance misuse and learning difficulties to offending or future risk. Risk of Harm assessments were particularly singled out and identified as inadequate to assist the courts in their determination of dangerousness and whether or not to impose an IPP sentence. Lack of ongoing involvement with the prisoner also affected the quality of probation reports prepared for parole reviews (although the greater frequency of contact required within the OMM may assist with this). These quality issues around assessment were also found in the follow-up inspection, where it was noted that inadequate recognition of, for instance, learning disabilities and mental ill health, may affect sentencing and success in meeting sentence plan objectives if significant were not addressed (CJJI, 2010c)

Interestingly, women generally had a more positive experience of indeterminate sentences largely because the lifer system for women was less stretched at the point where IPP sentences came on stream. However, there are different issues for women, particularly the prevalence of mental health needs among the much smaller IPP group and the disproportionate number of cases where arson was the index offence. Additionally, the Inspectors noted that:

> The sentence seemed to impact differently on women. For many there was a sense of disbelief that they were deemed a risk to the public. They felt the sentence was unfair and harsh in proportion to their offences and only one of the 12 said she had been forewarned of potentially receiving an IPP. (CJJI, 2008, p 32)

The situation of young people was equally worrying. Planning on their sentences was conducted through an uncomfortable amalgam of lifer processes and conventional training plans for young offenders. The young people receiving DPP sentences typically have persistent patterns of criminal activity and multiple personal needs, but these were inadequately assessed in many cases. Vulnerability was also poorly assessed and quality of risk management planning by YOTs was found to be variable. In part, this is due to lack of appropriate guidance and clear processes appropriate for young people, but it is also indicative of the fact that these more complex young offenders are a real challenge for YOTs who are not well prepared and trained to take on this work.

The follow-up inspection in 2010 was intended to focus on the probation service and the quality of the processes in preparation for release. However, at the time of the inspection only 99 prisoners had been released from IPP sentences and of these only 75 remained in the community. The report of the review was again very critical, and specifically highlighted the difficulties of expecting offender managers to take responsibility for sentence planning and implementation when they are in a weak position in terms of being able to command the necessary resources within the prison system (CJJI, 2010c). This harks back to some of the issues raised in Chapter Two and the challenges of creating closer working relationships between prisons and probation and confidence in working across agency boundaries.

Planning for IPP and DPP prisoners is particularly important in ensuring at least some measure of responsiveness to risks and needs. Sadly the 2010 Inspection found little evidence of the active involvement of prisoners in sentence planning (CJJI, 2010c), and this seems a missed opportunity to encourage participation and create the conditions for improved compliance and engagement post-release. In addition, parole reports were judged inadequate in too many cases, with only about half of them containing risk management plans of a sufficient standard (CJJI, 2010c).

Clearly the influx of so many IPP and DPP prisoners has stretched the capacities of prison, probation and youth justice services and some of the difficulties they are experiencing are not of their own making. Nevertheless, the lack of holistic assessment and consistently robust risk management is worrying and could have profound implications for a category of offenders whose rights are explicitly being limited because of public protection concerns.

Summary

Prisoners serving indeterminate sentences are a growing proportion of the prison population and the nature of work with them is changing, as an increasing number have a relatively short tariff period set. This creates pressures on sentence planning and parole processes, with difficult questions where prisoners are unable to access appropriate interventions and resources to enable them to progress towards release.

The nature of indeterminate sentence prisoners is also changing, as the IPP and DPP populations tend to have greater levels of need and more entrenched patterns of offending behaviour than the 'traditional' lifer population. The expansion in indeterminate prisoner numbers is relatively recent and as yet little research is available, although the two reports from HMI Prisons and HMI Probation contain much critical material and recommendations for action. Their findings suggest that practice in assessment, planning and risk management is inconsistent. This may disproportionately impact upon these prisoners who can only be released at the direction of the Parole Board and whose freedoms and rights are consequently so vulnerable.

Further reading

HM Prison Service (2010) *Indeterminate sentence manual*, Prison Service Order 4700.
Stone, N. (2008) *A companion guide to life sentences* (2nd edn), Crayford: Shaw and Sons.

References

Abbott, D., Townsley, R. and Watson, D. (2005) 'Multi-agency working in services for disabled children: what impact does it have on professionals?', *Health and Social Care in the Community*, vol 13, no 2, pp 155-63.

ACOP (Association of Chief Officers of Probation) (1994) *Guidance on the management of risk and public protection*, Wakefield: ACOP.

Allen, R. (2005) *From punishment to problem-solving: A new approach to children in trouble*, London: King's College.

Andrews, D.A. and Bonta, J. (1995) *The level of supervision inventory – Revised*, Toronto: Multi-Health Systems.

Anglin, M.D. and Hser, Y.I. (1987) 'Sex Differences in Addict careers' in *Americal Journal of Drug and alcohol Abuse* Vol 13: 253-80

Anning, A., Cottrell, J., Frost, N., Green J. and Robinson, M. (2002) *Developing multi-professional teamwork for integrated children's services*, Maidenhead: Open University Press.

Annison, J., Eadie, T. and Knight, C. (2008) 'People first: probation officer perspectives on probation work', *Probation Journal*, vol 55, no 3, pp 259-71.

Ansbro, M. (2006) 'What do we learn from serious incident reports?', *Probation Journal*, vol 53, no 1, p 57.

Appleton, C. and Grover, B. (2007) 'The pros and cons of life without parole', *British Journal of Criminology*, vol 47, p 597.

Ashworth, A. and Redmayne, M. (2005) *The criminal process* (3rd edn), Oxford: Oxford University Press.

Attrill, G. and Liell, G. (2007) 'Offenders' views on risk assessment', in N. Padfield (ed) *Who to release? Parole, fairness and criminal justice*, Cullompton: Willan, pp 191-201.

Audit Commission (1994) *Seen but not heard: Co-ordination community child health and social services for children in need*, London: HMSO.

Audit Commission (1996) *Misspent youth: Young people and crime*, London: Audit Commission.

Bailey, R., Knight, C. and Williams, B. (2007) 'The Probation Service as part of NOMS in England and Wales: fit for purpose?', in L. Gelsthorpe and R. Morgan (eds) *Handbook of probation*, Cullompton: Willan, pp 114-30.

Baker, K. (2010) 'More harm than good? The language of public protection', *The Howard Journal of Criminal Justice*, vol 49, no 1, pp 42-53.

Baldwin, L. and Canton, R. (2007) 'Lifers', in R. Canton and D. Hancock (eds) *Dictionary of probation and offender management*, Cullompton: Willan.

Bale, D. (1987) 'Uses of a risk of custody scale', *Probation Journal*, vol 34, no 4, pp 127-31.

Barry, M. (2006) *Youth offending in transition: The search for social recognition*, Abingdon: Routledge.

Barry, M. (2007) 'The transitional pathways of young female offenders: towards a non-offending style', in R. Sheehan, G. McIvor and C. Trotter (eds) *What works with women offenders*, Cullompton: Willan, Chapter 2.

Barry, M. and McIvor, G. (2010) 'Professional decision-making and women offenders: containing the chaos', *Probation Journal*, vol 57, no 1, pp 27-41.

Bean, P. (2008) *Drugs and crime* (3rd edn), Cullompton: Willan.

Beaumont, B. (1999a) 'Assessing risk in work with offenders', in P. Parsloe (ed) *Risk assessment in social work and social care*, London: Jessica Kingsley Publishers, Chapter 6.

Beaumont, B. (1999b) 'Risk assessment and prediction research', in P. Parsloe (ed) *Risk assessment in social work and social care*, London: Jessica Kingsley Publishers, Chapter 5.

Beckett, C. (2007) *Child protection: An introduction*, London: Sage Publications.

Beckett, C. (2010) *Assessment and intervention in social work*, London: Sage Publications.

Beech, A.R. and Fisher, D.D. (2002) 'The rehabilitation of child sex offenders', *Australian Psychologist*, 37(3): 206-14.

Bennett, T. and Holloway, K. (2005) *Understanding drugs, alcohol and crime*, Maidenhead: Open University Press.

Bennett, T., Holloway, K. and Farrington, D. (2008) 'The statistical association between drug misuse and crime: a meta-analysis', *Aggression and Violent Behaviour*, vol 13, pp 107-18.

Bhui, H.S. (1999) 'Race, Racism and Risk Assessment: Linking theory to practice with mentally disordered offenders' in *Probation Journal* Vol 46(3): 171-181

Bhui, H.S. (2006) 'Anti-racist practice in NOMS: reconciling managerialist and professional realities' in *Howard Journal* Vol 45(2): 171-190

Bhui, H.S. (2009a) 'Introduction: criminal justice and race equality', in H.S. Bhui (ed) *Race and criminal justice*, London: Sage Publications, pp 1-8.

Bhui, H.S. (2009b) 'Prisons and race equality', in H.S. Bhui (ed) *Race and criminal justice*, London: Sage Publications, pp 83-101.

Boeck, T. (2007) 'Social capital', in R. Canton and D. Hancock (eds) *Dictionary of probation and offender management*, Cullompton: Willan.

Bottoms, A. (2001) 'Compliance and community penalties', in A. Bottoms, L. Gelsthorpe and S. Rex (eds) *Community penalties: Change and challenges*, Cullompton: Willan, pp 87-116.

Bottoms, A., Gelsthorpe, L. and Rex, S. (2001) *Community penalties: Change and challenges*, Cullompton: Willan.

Bradley, K. (2009) *The Bradley Report: Lord Bradley's review of people with mental health problems or learning disabiities in the criminal justice system*, London: Department of Health.

Brayford, J., Cowe, F.B. and Deering, J. (eds) (2010) *What else works? Creative work with offenders*, Cullompton: Willan.

Braithwaite, J. (1989) *Crime, shame and reintegration* Cambridge: Cambridge University Press.

Broom, D. and Stevens, A. (1991) 'Doubly deviant: women using alcohol and other drugs' in *International Journal of Drug Policy* Vol 2: 25-7.

Brown, Sheila (2005a) *Understanding youth and crime: Listening to youth?*, Maidenhead: Open University Press.

Brown, Sarah (2005b) *Treating sex offenders: An introduction to sex offender treatment programmes*, Cullompton: Willan.

Brown, Sarah. (2010) 'An introduction to sex offender treatment programmes and their risk reduction efficacy', in K. Harrison (ed) *Managing high risk sex offenders in the community: Risk management, treatment and social responsibility*, Cullompton: Willan, pp 81-104.

Buchanan, J. (2008) 'Understanding and engaging with problematic substance use', in S. Green, E. Lancaster and S. Feasey (eds) *Addressing offending behaviour: Context, practice and value*, Cullompton: Willan, pp 246-64.

Burnett, R. (2004) 'To reoffend or not to reoffend? The ambivalence of convicted property offenders', in S. Maruna and R. Immarigeon (eds) *After crime and punishment: Pathways to offender reintegration*, Cullompton: Willan, pp 152-80.

Burnett, R. and Stevens, A. (2007) 'Not much of significance (yet): NOMS from the perspective of prison staff', *Prison Service Journal*, issue 172, pp 3-11.

Burnett, R., Baker, K. and Roberts, C. (2007) 'Assessment, supervision and intervention: fundamental practice in probation', in L. Gelsthorpe and R. Morgan (eds) *Handbook of probation*, Cullompton: Willan, pp 210-47.

Burney, E. (2005) *Making people behave: Anti-social behaviour, politics and policy*, Cullompton: Willan.

Calverley, A. (2009) *An exploratory investigation into the processes of desistance amongst minority offenders* Unpublished PhD thesis, University of Keele

Calverley, A. et al (2004) *Black and Asian offenders on probation*, Home Office Research Study 277, London: Home Office.

Calverley, A., Kaur, G. and Sadeghi, S. (2006) 'Introduction: race, crime and community penalties', in S. Lewis, P. Raynor, D. Smith and A. Wardek (eds) *Race and probation*, Cullompton: Willan.

Canton, R. (2002) 'Rights, probation and mentally disturbed offenders', in D. Ward, J. Scott and M. Lacey (eds) *Probation: Working for justice*, Oxford: Oxford University Press, pp 238-56.

Canton, R. (2007a) 'Probation and the tragedy of punishment', *The Howard Journal of Criminal Justice*, vol 46, no 3, pp 236-54.

Canton, R. (2007b) 'Compliance', in R. Canton and D. Hancock (eds) *Dictionary of probation and offender management*, Cullompton: Willan.

Canton, R. (2008) 'Working with mentally disordered offenders', in S. Green, E. Lancaster and S. Feasey (eds) *Addressing offending behaviour: Context, practice and value*, Cullompton: Willan, pp 318-43.

Canton, R. and Eadie, T. (2002) 'Practising in a context of ambivalence: the challenge for youth justice workers', *Youth Justice*, vol 2, no 1, pp 14-26.

Canton, R. and Eadie, T. (2007) 'National standards', in R. Canton and D. Hancock (eds) *Dictionary of probation and offender management*, Cullompton: Willan.

Canton, R. and Eadie, T. (2009) 'Accountability, legitimacy and discretion: applying criminology in professional practice', in B. Stout, J. Yates and B. Williams (eds) *Applied criminology*, London: Sage Publications, pp 86–102.

Canton, R. and Hancock, D. (2007) *Dictionary of probation and offender management*, Cullompton: Willan.

Carlen, P. (1985) *Criminal women*, Cambridge: Polity Press.

Carlen, P. (1988) *Women, crime and poverty*, Milton Keynes: Open University Press.

Carlen, P. (ed) (2002) *Women and punishment*, Cullompton: Willan.

Carlen, P. and Worrall, A. (2004) *Analysing women's imprisonment*, Cullompton: Willan.

Carter, P. (2003) *Managing offenders, reducing crime*, London: Home Office.

Cavadino, M. and Dignan, J. (2006) *The penal system* (4th edn), London: Sage Publications.

Cavadino, M., Crow, I. and Dignan, J. (1999) *Criminal justice 2000: Strategies for a new century*, Winchester: Waterside Press.

Cherry, S. (2005) *Transforming behaviour: Pro-social modelling in practice*, Cullompton: Willan.

Chigwada-Bailey, R. (2003) *Black women's experience of criminal justice, race, gender and class: A discourse on disadvantage*, Winchester: Waterside Press.

Christie, N. (1980) 'The Ideal Victim' in Fattah, E. (ed.) *From Crime Policy to Victim Policy*

CJJI (Criminal Justice Joint Inspection) (2008) *The indeterminate sentence for public protection: A thematic review*, London: HMI Prisons.

CJJI (2009) *Prolific and other priority offenders*, London: HMI Probation.

CJJI (2010a) *A joint inspection on work prior to sentence with offenders with mental disorders*, London: HMI Probation.

CJJI (2010b) *Restriction and rehabilitation: Getting the right mix*, London: HMI Probation.

CJJI (2010c) *Indeterminate sentences for public protection*, London: HMI Probation.

Cobley, C. (2003) 'The legislative framework', in A. Matravers (ed) *Sex offenders in the community: Managing and reducing the risks*, Cullompton: Willan, pp 51–71.

Cold, J., Yang, M., Ulrich, S., Zhang, T., Roberts, A., Roberts, C., Rogers, R. and Farrington, D. (2007) *Predicting and understanding risk of re-offending: The prisoner cohort study*, Research Summary 6, London: Ministry of Justice.

Commission for Racial Equality (2003a) *The Murder of Zahid mubarek: A formal investigation by the Commission for Racial Equality into HM Prison Service for England and Wales Part 1* London: CRE.

Commission for Racial Equality (2003b) *A formal investigation by the Commission for Racial Equality into HM Prison Service for England and Wales Part 2 Race Equality in Prisons* London: CRE.

Connolly, M. and Ward, T. (2008) *Morals, rights and practice in the human services*, London: Jessica Kingsley Publishers.

Cook, D. (2006) *Criminal and social justice*, London: Sage Publications.

Corston, Baroness J. (2007) *A report by Baroness Jean Corston of a review of women with particular vulnerabilities in the criminal justice system*, London: Home Office.

Coyle, A. (2008) 'The treatment of prisoners: international standards and case law', *Legal and Criminological Psychology*, vol 13, pp 219-30.

Crawford, A. (2007) 'What impacts on quality assessment using OASys', *Probation Journal*, vol 42, no 2, pp 157-70.

Crawford, A. and Enterkin, J. (2001) 'Victim contact work in the Probation Service: paradigm shift or Pandora's box?', *British Journal of Criminology*, vol 41, pp 707-25.

Crawford, A. and Newburn, T. (2003) *Youth offending and restorative justice: Implementing reform in youth justice*, Cullompton: Willan.

Crow, I. (2001) *The treatment and rehabilitation of offenders*, London: Sage Publications.

CSCI (Commission for Social Care Inspection) (2005) *Safeguarding children: The second joint Chief Inspector's report on arrangements to safeguard children*, London: CSCI.

Dalrymple, J. and Burke, B. (1995) *Anti-oppressive practice: Social care and the law*, Maidenhead: Open University Press.

Davis, L. (2009) *The social worker's guide to children and families law*, London: Jessica Kingsley Publishers.

Dawson, J. (2007) *The national PPO evaluation – Research to inform and guide practice*, Home Office OLR 09/97, London: Home Office.

Dawson, J. and Cuppleditch, L. (2007) *An impact assessment of the Prolific and other Priority Offender programme*, Home Office OLR 08/07, London: Home Office.

DCA (Department for Constitutional Affairs) (2006a) *A guide to the Human Rights Act 1998* (3rd edn), London: DCA.

DCA (2006b) *Review of the implementation of the Human Rights Act*, London: DCA.

DCSF (Department for Children, Schools and Families) (2010) *Working together to safeguard children*, London: DCSF.

Deering, J. (2010) 'Attitudes and beliefs of trainee probation officers: a "new breed"?', *Probation Journal*, vol 57, no 1, pp 9-26.

DH (Department of Health) (1999) *Reform of the Mental Health Act 1983*, London: DH.

DH (2000a) *Framework for the assessment of children in need and their families*, London: The Stationery Office.

DH (2000b) *Reforming the Mental Health Act Part II: High risk patients*, London: DH.

DH (2008) *Refocusing the Care Programme Approach*, London: DH.

DH (2009) *Improving health and supporting justice: The National Delivery Plan of the Health and Criminal Justice Programme Board*, London: DH.

Dhami, M.K. (2004) 'Conditional bail decision making in the Magistrates' Court', *The Howard Journal of Criminal Justice*, vol 43, no 1, pp 27-46.

Dignan, J. (2005) *Understanding victims and restorative justice*, Maidenhead: Open University Press.

DrugScope (2005) *Using women* (www.drugscope.org.uk).

Durrance, P., Dixon, L. and Bhui, H.S. (2009) 'Creative working with minority ethnic offenders' in Brayford, J., Cowe, F. and Deering, J. (eds.) *What else works? Creative work with offenders* Cullompton: Willan, pp 138-54.

Eadie, T. (2007) 'Discretion', in R. Canton and D. Hancock (eds) *Dictionary of probation and offender management*, Cullompton: Willan.

Eady, D. (2007) 'Prisoners' rights since the Woolf Report: progress or procrastination?', *The Howard Journal of Criminal Justice*, vol 46, no 30, pp 264-75.

Edwards, I. (2001) 'Victim participation in sentencing: the problems of incoherence', *The Howard Journal of Criminal Justice*, vol 4, no 1, pp 39-54.

Edwards, I. (2004) 'An ambiguous participant: the crime victim and criminal justice decision-making', *British Journal of Criminology*, vol 44, no 6, pp 967-82.

Farrall, S. (2002) *Rethinking what works with offenders: Probation, social context and desistence from crime*, Cullompton: Willan.

Farrall, S. (2007) 'Desistance studies vs cognitive behavioural therapies: which offers most hope for the long-term?', in R. Canton and D. Hancock (eds) *Dictionary of probation and offender management*, Cullompton: Willan.

Farrall, S. and Calverley, A. (2005) *Understanding desistance from crime*, Maidenhead: Open University Press.

Farrall, S., Mawby, R.C. and Worrall, A. (2007) 'Prolific/persistent offenders and desistence', in L. Gelsthorpe and R. Morgan (eds) *Handbook of probation*, Cullompton: Willan, pp 352-80.

Farrington, D. (1989) *The origins of crime: The Cambridge study of delinquent development*, Research Bulletin No 27, Home Office Research and Planning Unit, London: Home Office.

Farrington, D. (1994) 'Human development and criminal careers', in E. Maguire, R. Morgan and R. Reiner (eds) *The Oxford handbook of criminology*, Oxford: Clarendon Press.

Farrow, K., Kelly, G. and Wilkinson, B. (2007) *Offenders in focus: Risk, responsivity and diversity*, Bristol: The Policy Press.

Faulkner, D. (2002) 'Probation, citizenship and public service', in D. Ward, J. Scott and M. Lacey (eds) *Probation: Working for justice*, Oxford: Oxford University Press, pp 276-96.

Faulkner, D. (2008) 'The new shape of probation in England and Wales: values and opportunities in a changing context', *Probation Journal*, vol 55, no 1, pp 71-83.

Feeley, M. and Simon, J. (1992) 'The new penology: notes on the emerging strategy for corrections', *Criminology*, vol 30, no 4, pp 449-75.

Feilzer, M. and Hood, R. (2004) *Differences or discrimination? Minority ethnic young people in the youth justice system*, London: Youth Justice Board.

Fenwick, H. (1995) 'Rights of victims in the criminal justice system: rhetoric or reality?', *Criminal Law Review*, November, pp 843-53.

Fenwick, H. (2007) *Civil liberties and human rights*, Abingdon: Routledge-Cavendish.

Finklehor, D. (1984) *Child Sexual Abuse* New York: The Free Press

Fitzgibbon, W. and Green, Dr R. (2006) 'Mentally disordered offenders: challenges in using the OASys risk assessment tool, *British Journal of Community Justice*, vol 4, no 2, p 33.

Flatley, J., Kershaw, C., Smith, K., Chaplin, R. and Moon, D. (eds) (2010) *Crime in England and Wales: Findings from the British Crime Survey and police recorded crime*, Home Office Statistical Bulletin 12/10, London: Home Office.

Francis, P. (2007) 'Race, ethnicity, victims and crime', in P. Davies, P. Francis and C. Greer (eds) *Victims, crime and society*, London: Sage Publications, pp 109-41.

Frost, N. and Parton, N. (2009) *Understanding Children's Social Care: Politics, Policy and Practice*, London: Sage.

Frost, N. and Robinson, M. (2007) 'Joining up children's services: safeguarding children in multi-disciplinary teams', *Child Abuse Review*, vol 16, pp 184-99.

Frost, N., Robinson, M. and Anning, A. (2005) 'Social workers in multi-disciplinary teams: issues and dilemmas for professional practice', *Child and Family Social Work*, vol 10, pp 187-96.

Furlong, A. and Cartmel, F. (2007) *Young people and social change: New perspectives* (2nd edn), Maidstone: Open University Press.

Gelsthorpe, L. (2001) 'Accommodating difference and diversity in probation practice, in A. Bottoms, L. Gelsthorpe and S. Rex (eds) *Community penalties: Change and challenges*, Cullompton: Willan, pp 146-67.

Gelsthorpe, L. (2002) 'Critical decisions and processes in criminal courts', in E. McLaughlin and J. Muncie (eds) *Controlling crime*, London: Sage Publications, pp 101-56.

Gelsthorpe, L. (2006) 'The experiences of female ethnic minority offenders: the other "other"', in S. Lewis, P. Raynor, D. Smith and A. Wardak (eds) *Race and probation*, Cullompton: Willan, pp 100-20.

Gelsthorpe, L. (2007) 'Probation values and human rights', in L. Gelsthorpe and R. Morgan (eds) *Handbook of probation*, Cullompton: Willan, pp 485-517.

Gelsthorpe, L. and McIvor, G. (2007) 'Dealing with diversity in probation', in L. Gelsthorpe and R. Morgan (eds) *Handbook of probation*, Cullompton: Willan, pp 485-517.

Gelsthorpe, L. and Morgan, R. (eds) (2007) *Handbook of probation*, Cullompton: Willan.

Gelsthorpe, L. and Morris, A. (1994) 'Juvenile justice 1945-1992', in M. Maguire, R. Morgan and R. Reiner (eds) *The Oxford handbook of criminology*, Oxford: Clarendon Press, pp 949-93.

Gelsthorpe, L. and Morris, A. (2002) 'Restorative Youth justice: the last vestiges of welfare?', in J. Muncie, G. Hughes and E. McLaughlin (eds) *Youth justice: Critical readings*, London: Sage Publications, pp 238-54.

Gelsthorpe, L., Sharpe, G. and Roberts, J. (2007) *Provision for women offenders in the community*, London: Fawcett Society.

Gilling, D. (2005) 'Partnership and crime prevention', in N. Tilley (ed) *Handbook of crime prevention and community safety*, Cullompton: Willan, pp 734-56.

Goldson, B. (2006) 'Penal custody: intolerance, irrationality and indifference', in B. Goldson and J. Muncie (eds) *Youth crime and justice*, London: Sage Publications, pp 139-56.

Goodey, J. (2005) *Victims and victimology: Research, policy and practice*, Edinburgh: Pearson Education Ltd.

Gorman, K., O'Byrne, P. and Parton, N. (2006) 'Constructive work with offenders: setting the scene', in K. Gorman, M. Gregory, M. Hayles and N. Parton (eds) *Constructive work with offenders*, London: Jessica Kingsley Publishers, pp 13-32.

Gough, D. (2010) 'Multi-agency working in corrections: co-operation and competition in probation practice', in A. Pyecroft and D. Gough (eds) *Multi-agency working in criminal justice*, Bristol: The Policy Press, pp 21-34.

Graham, J. and Bowling, B. (1995) *Young people and crime*, Home Office Research Study No 145, London: Home Office.

Grange, T. (2003) 'Challenges for the Police Service', in A. Matravers (ed) *Sex offenders in the community: Managing and reducing the risks*, Cullompton: Willan, pp 219-32.

Green, S., Lancaster, E. and Feasey, S. (eds) (2008) *Addressing offending behaviour: Context, practice and value*, Cullompton: Willan.

Haines, K. and Morgan, R. (2007) 'Services before trial and sentence: achievement, decline and potential', in L. Gelsthorpe and R. Morgan (eds) *Handbook of probation*, Cullompton: Willan, pp 182-209.

Halliday, J. (2001) *Making punishments work: Report of a review of the sentencing framework for England and Wales*, London: Home Office.

Hancock, D. (2007a) 'The Halliday Report', in R. Canton and D. Hancock (eds) *Dictionary of probation and offender management*, Cullompton: Willan.

Hancock, D. (2007b) 'Prison probation teams', in R. Canton and D. Hancock (eds) *Dictionary of probation and offender management*, Cullompton: Willan.

Harding, T. (2006) 'Gender, drugs and policy'. in R. Hughes, R. Lart and P. Higate (eds) *Drugs: Policy and politics*, Maidenhead: Open University Press, pp 18-30.

Hearnden, I. and Millie, A. (2004) 'Does tougher enforcement lead to lower reconviction?', *Probation Journal*, vol 51, no 1, pp 48-58.

Heath, B. (2010) 'The partnership approach in drug misuse', in A. Pyecroft and D. Gough (eds) *Multi-agency working in criminal justice*, Bristol: The Policy Press, pp 185-200.

Hedderman, C. and Gelsthorpe, L. (1997) *Understanding the sentencing of women*, Home Office Research Study No 170, London: Home Office.

Hedderman, C. and Hearnden, I. (2000) 'The missing link: effective enforcement and effective supervision', *Probation Journal*, vol 47, no 2, pp 126-8.

Heidensohn, F. (1985) *Women and crime*, Basingstoke: Macmillan.

Hendrick, H. (2006) 'Histories of youth crime and justice', in B. Goldson and J. Muncie (eds) *Youth crime and justice*, London: Sage Publications, Chapter 1.

Hilder, S. (2007) 'Anti-discriminatory practice', in R. Canton and D. Hancock (eds) *Dictionary of probation and offender management*, Cullompton: Willan.

HM Government (2008) *Drugs: Protecting Families and Communities – the 2008 Drug Strategy* London: TSOHM Government (2008) *Safe, Sensible, Social: Next Steps in the National alcohol Strategy* London: TSO

HM Prison Service (2002) *Lifer manual*, London: HM Prison Service.

HM Prison Service (2004) *Annual Report 2004*, London: HMSO.

HM Prison Service (2010) *Indeterminate sentence manual*, Prison Service Order 4700, London: Prison Service.

HMI Prisons (2008) *Annual report 2007/8*, London: HMI Prisons.

HMI Prisons (2009) *Annual report 2008/9*, London: HMI Prisons.

HMI Probation (1991) *Exercising constant vigilance: The role of the Probation Service in protecting the public from sex offenders*, London: HMSO.

HMI Probation (1998) *The work of the Probation Service with sex offenders*, London: The Stationery Office.

HMI Probation (2000a) *Towards race equality*, London: HMI Probation.

HMI Probation (2000b) *Serious incidents: Probation Service's compliance with the notification requirements of PC 71/1998*, London: HMI Probation.

HMI Probation (2002) *Safeguarding children: The National Probation Service role in the assessment and management of child protection issues*, London: HMI Probation.

HMI Probation (2003) *Valuing the victim: An inspection into national victim contact arrangements*, London: HMI Probation.

HMI Probation (2004) *Towards race equality: Follow-up inspection report*, London: HMI Probation.

HMI Probation (2006a) *An independent review of a Serious Further Offence case: Anthony Rice*, London: HMI Probation.

HMI Probation (2006b) *Putting risk of harm in context*, London: HMI Probation.

HMI Probation (2006c) *An independent review of a serious further offence case: Damien Hanson and Elliot White*, London: HMI Probation.

HMI Probation and HMIC (HM Inspectorate of Constabulary) (2002) *Protecting children from potentially dangerous people*, London: HMI Probation.

HMI Probation and HMIC (2005) *Managing sex offenders in the community*, London: HMI Probation.

Home Office (1968) *Children in Trouble* London: Home Office

Home Office (1990) *Crime, justice and protecting the public*, London: Home Office.

Home Office (1991) *Safer communities: The local delivery of crime prevention through the partnership approach* (known as the 'Morgan Report'), London: Home Office Standing Conference on Crime Prevention.

Home Office (1995) *Tackling drugs together: A strategy for England and Wales 1995-98*, London: Home Office.

Home Office (1997a) *The prisons and probation review*, London: Home Office.

Home Office (1997b) *No more excuses*, London: Home Office.

Home Office (1998a) *Joining forces to protect the public*, Green Paper, London: Home Office.

Home Office (1998b) *Tackling drugs to build a better Britain: The government's 10-year strategy for tackling drug misuse*, London: Home Office.

Home Office (1998c) *Speaking up for justice: A report of the Interdepartmental Working Group on the treatment of vulnerable or intimidated witnesses in the criminal justice system*, London: Home Office.

Home Office (1999) *Lifers: A joint thematic review by Her Majesty's Inspectorates of Prisons and Probation*, London: Home Office.

Home Office (2000) *Setting the boundaries*, London: Home Office.

Home Office (2001) *Criminal justice: The way ahead*, London: Home Office.

Home Office (2002a) *Justice for all*, London: Home Office.

Home Office (2002b) *Protecting the public*, London: Home Office.

Home Office (2002c) *Updated drugs strategy*, London: Home Office.

Home Office (2003a) *A new deal for victims and witnesses*, London: Home Office.

Home Office (2003b) *Youth justice: Next steps*, London: Home Office.

Home Office (2004a) *Reducing re-offending national action plan*, London: Home Office.

Home Office (2004b) *Joint inspection report into persistent and prolific offenders*, London: Home Office.

Home Office (2004c) *Reducing Crime, Changing Lives* London: Home Office

Home Office (2006) *Rebalancing the criminal justice system in favour of the law-abiding majority*, London: Home Office.

Home Office Statistical Bulletin 05/07, London: Home Office.

Home Office (2009) *ASBO statistics* – Crime Reduction website. http://webarchive.nationalarchives.gov.uk/20100413151441/crimereduction.homeoffice.gov.uk/asbos/asbos2.htm

Home Office (2011) *More Effective Responses to Anti-Social Behaviour* London: Home Office

Home Office/DH (Department of Health) (1999) *Managing dangerous people with severe personality disorder: Proposals for policy development*, London: Home Office/DH.

Hood, R. and Shute, S. (2000) *The parole system at work: A study of risk based decision-making*, Home Office Research Study 202, London: Home Office.

Horsefield, A. (2003) 'Risk assessment: who needs it?', *Probation Journal*, vol 50, no 4, pp 374-9.

Howard, P. (2006) *The Offender Assessment System: An evaluation of the second pilot*, Home Office Research Findings 278, London: Home Office.

Howard League for Penal Reform (1995) *Banged up, beaten up, cutting up: Report of the Howard League Commission of Inquiry into violence in penal institutions for teenagers under 18*, London: The Howard League.

Howard League for Penal Reform (2005) *Children in custody: Promoting the legal and human rights of children*, London: The Howard League.

Hucklesby, A. et al (2007) *The evaluation of the restriction on bail pilot*, Home Office online report 06/07, London: Home Office.

Hudson, B. (1987) *Justice through punishment*, London: Macmillan.

Hudson, B. (2001) 'Human rights, public safety and the Probation Service: defending justice in the risk society', *The Howard Journal of Criminal Justice*, vol 40, no 2, pp 103-13.

Hudson, B. (2003) *Justice in the risk society*, London: Sage Publications.

Hughes, G. (2007) *The politics of crime and community*, Basingstoke: Palgrave Macmillan.

Hughes, G. and Follett, M. (2006) 'Community safety, youth and the "anti-social"', in B. Goldson and J. Muncie (eds) *Youth crime and justice*, London: Sage Publications, pp 157-71.

Hughes, R. and Anthony, N. (2006) 'Drugs, crime and criminal justice', in R. Hughes, R. Lart and P. Higate (eds) *Drugs: Policy and politics*, Maidenhead: Open University Press, pp 75-91.

Humphrey, C., Carter, P. and Pease, K. (1992) 'A reconviction predictor for probationers', *British Journal of Social Work*, vol 22, pp 33-46.

Huntington, J. (1981) *Social work and general medical practice: Collaboration or conflict?*, London: Allen & Unwin.

ICPR (Institute of Criminal Policy Research) (2007) *National evaluation of criminal justice intervention teams*, London: ICPR.

Ireland, C.A. and Worthington, R. (2008) 'Treatment approaches for sexual violence', in J.L. Ireland, C.A. Ireland and P. Birch (eds) *Violent and sexual offenders: Assessment, treatment and management*, Cullompton: Willan, pp 179-97.

Johnstone, G. and Ward, T. (2010) *Law and crime*, London: Sage Publications.

Jones, T. and Newburn, T. (2006) 'Three strikes and you're out', *British Journal of Criminology*, vol 46, p 781.

Keith, Justice Mr B. (2006) *Report of the Zahid Mubarek Inquiry*, London: The Stationery Office.

Kemshall, H. (1995) 'Offender risk and probation practice', in H. Kemshall and J. Pritchard (eds) *Good practice in risk assessment and risk management 1*, London: Jessica Kingsley Publishers, pp 133-45.

Kemshall. H. (2003) *Understanding risk in criminal justice*, Maidenhead: Open University Press.

Kemshall, H. (2008) *Understanding the community management of high risk offenders*, Maidenhead: Open University Press.

Kemshall, H. and Maguire, M. (2001) 'Public protection, partnership and risk penalty: the multi-agency risk management of sexual and violent offenders', *Punishment and Society*, vol 3, no 2, pp 237-64.

Kemshall, H. and Maguire, M. (2003) 'Sex offenders, risk penality and the problem of disclosure to the community', in A. Matravers (ed) *Sex offenders in the community: Managing and reducing the risks*, Cullompton: Willan, pp 102-24.

Kemshall, H. and Wood, J. (2007a) 'High risk offenders and public protection', in L. Gelsthorpe and R. Morgan (eds) *Handbook of probation*, Cullompton: Willan, pp 381-97.

Kemshall, H. and Wood, J. (2007b) 'Beyond public protection: an examination of community protection and public health approaches to high risk offenders', *Criminology and Community Justice*, vol 7, p 203.

Kemshall, H., Mackenzie, G., Wood, J., Bailey, R. and Yates, J. (2005) *Strengthening Multi-Agency Public Protection Arrangements (MAPPAs)*, Home Office Development and Practice Report 45, London: Home Office.

Kemshall, H., Canton, R., Bailey, R., Dominey, J., Simpkin, B. and Yates, S. (2002) *The effective management of programme attrition*, Leicester: De Montford University.

Khanom, H., Samele, C. and Rutherford, M. (2009) *A missed opportunity? Community sentences and the mental health treatment requirement*, London: Sainsbury Centre for Mental Health.

Kropp, P.R., Hart, S.D., Lyon, D.R. and Lepard, D.A. (2002) 'Managing stalkers: co-ordinating treatment and supervision' in J.C.W. Boon and L. Sheridan (eds) *Stalking and psycho-sexual obsession: Psychological perspectives for prevention, policing and treatment*, Chichester: Wiley, pp141-63.

Laming, Lord (2003) *The Victoria Climbié Inquiry: Report of an Inquiry by Lord Laming*, Cm 5730, London: The Stationery Office.

Lancaster, E. (2008) ''Values' talk in the criminal justice system' in Green, S., Lancaster, E. and Feasey, S. (eds.) *Addressing Offending Behaviour: Context, Practice and Values* Cullompton: Wilan, pp 367-84.

Lart, R. (2006) 'Drugs and health policy', in R. Hughes, R. Lart and P. Higate (eds) *Drugs: Policy and politics*, Maidenhead: Open University Press, pp 92-112.

Lavoie, J.A.A., Guy, L.S. and Douglas, K.S. (2008) 'Violence risk assessment', in J.L. Ireland, C.A. Ireland and P. Birch (eds) *Violent and sexual offenders: Assessment, treatment and management*, Cullompton: Willan, pp 3-26.

Lewis, S. and Olumide, J. (2006) 'Not black and white: mixed heritage experiences of criminal justice', in S. Lewis, P. Raynor, D. Smith and A. Wardak (eds) *Race and probation*, Cullompton: Willan, pp 121-42.

Lieb, R. (2003) 'Joined-up worrying: the multi-agency public protection panels', in A. Matravers (ed) *Sex offenders in the community: Managing and reducing the risks*, Cullompton: Willan, pp 207-18.

Loader, I. and Sparks, R. (2007) 'Contemporary landscapes of crime, order, and control – governance, risk and globalisation', in M. Maguire, R. Morgan and R. Reiner (eds) *The Oxford handbook of criminology* (Fourth edn), Oxford: Oxford University Press, pp 78-101.

Macpherson, W. (1999) *The Stephen Lawrence Enquiry: Report of an Inquiry by Sir William Macpherson of Cluny*, London: The Stationery Office.

McAlinden, A.-M. (2006) 'Managing risk: from regulation to reintegration of sex offenders', *Criminology and Criminal Justice*, vol 6, no 2, pp 197-218.

McAlinden, A.-M. (2010) 'Restorative justice and the reintegration of high-risk sex offenders', in K. Harrison (ed) *Managing high risk sex offenders in the community: Risk management, treatment and social responsibility*, Cullompton: Willan, pp 133-58.

McConville, M. and Wilson, G. (2002) *Handbook of the criminal justice process*, Oxford: Oxford University Press.

McCulloch, T. and McNeill, F. (2007) 'Consumer society, commodification and offender management', *Criminology and Criminal Justice*, vol 7, no 3, pp 223-42.

McCulloch, T. and McNeill, F. (2008) 'Desistance-focused approaches', in S. Green, E. Lancaster and S. Feasey (eds) *Addressing offending behaviour: Context, practice and value*, Cullompton: Willan, pp 154-71.

McIvor, G. (2007) 'Restorative justice', in R. Canton and D. Hancock (eds) *Dictionary of probation and offender management*, Cullompton: Willan.

McIvor, G. (2009) 'Therapeutic jurisprudence and procedural justice in Scottish drugs courts', *Criminology and Criminal Justice*, vol 9, pp 29-49.

McIvor, G. (2010) 'Drug courts: lessons from the UK and beyond', in A. Hucklesby and E. Wincup (eds) *Drugs interventions in criminal justice*, Maidenhead: Open University Press, pp 135-60.

McIvor, G., Murray, C. and Jamieson, J. (2004) 'Desistance from crime: is it different for women and girls?', in S. Maruna and R. Immarigeon (eds) *After crime and punishment: Pathways to offender reintegration*, Cullompton: Willan, pp 181-200.

McLaughlin, J. (2003) *Feminist social and political theory*, Basingstoke: Palgrave Macmillan.

McNeill, F. (2003) 'Desistence focused probation practice', in W.H. Chui and M. Nellis (eds) *Moving probation forward: Evidence, arguments and practice*, Harlow: Pearson Longman, pp 146-62.

McNeill, F. (2006a) 'A desistance paradigm for offender management', *Criminology and Criminal Justice*, vol 6, no 1, pp 39-62.

McNeill, F. (2006b) 'Community supervision: context and relationships matter', in B. Goldson and J. Muncie (eds) *Youth crime and justice*, London: Sage Publications, pp 125-38.

McNeill, F. (2009a) 'What works and what's just?', *European Journal of Probation*, vol 1, no 1, pp 21-40.

McNeill, F. (2009b) *Towards effective practice in offender supervision*, Glasgow: Scottish Centre for Crime and Justice Research.

McNeill, F. and Weaver, B. (2010) *Changing lives? Desistance research and offender management*, Glasgow: Scottish Centre for Crime and Justice Research.

Maguire, M. (2007) 'The resettlement of ex-prisoners', in L. Gelsthorpe and R. Morgan (eds) *Handbook of probation*, Cullompton: Willan, pp 398-424.

Maguire, M. and Raynor, P. (2010) 'Putting the OM into NOMS: problems and possibilities for offender management', in J. Brayford, F.B. Cowe and J. Deering (eds) *What else works? Creative work with offenders*, Cullompton: Willan, pp 236-53.

Mair, G. (2004) 'The origins of what works in England and Wales: a house built on sand?', in G. Mair (ed) *What matters in probation*, Cullompton: Willan, pp 12-33.

Mair, G. (2007) 'Community penalties', in R. Canton and D. Hancock (eds) *Dictionary of probation and offender management*, Cullompton: Willan.

Mair, G. and Canton, R. (2007) 'Sentencing, community penalties and the role of the Probation Service', in L. Gelsthorpe and R. Morgan (eds) *Handbook of probation*, Cullompton: Willan, pp 248-91.

Mair, G., Cross, N. and Taylor, S. (2008) *The Community Order and Suspended Sentence Order: The views and attitudes of sentencers*, London: Centre for Crime and Justice Studies, King's College.

Malloch, M. and Louckes, N. (2007) 'Responding to drug and alcohol problems: innovations and effectiveness in treatment programmes for women', in R. Sheehan, G. McIvor and C. Trotter (eds) *What works with women offenders*, Cullompton: Willan, pp 91-109.

Mann, R.E. and Thornton, D. (1998) 'The evolution of a multi-site sexual offender treatment programme' in W.L. Marshall, Y.M. Fernandez, S.M. Hudson and T. Ward (eds) *Sourcebook of treatment programmes for sexual offenders*, New York: Plenum Press.

Martinson, R. (1974) 'What Works? – questions and answers about prison reform' in *The Public Interest* Vol 35 p22-54

Maruna, S. (2001) *Making good: How ex-convicts reform and rebuild their lives*, Washington, DC: American Psychological Association.

Maruna, S. and Farrall, S. (2004) 'Desistance from Crime: A Theoretical Reformulation' in *The Cologne Journal of Sociology and Social Psychology* Vol 43

Maruna, S., Immarigeon, R. and LeBel, T.P. (2004) 'Ex-offender reintegration: theory and practice', in S. Maruna and R. Immarigeon (eds) *After crime and punishment: Pathways to offender reintegration*, Cullompton: Willan, pp 3-26.

Maruna, S., LeBel, T.P., Naples, M. and Mitchell, N. (2009) 'Looking-glass identity formation: Pygmalion and Golem in the rehabilitation process', in B.M. Veysey, J. Christian and D.J. Martinez (eds) *How offenders transform their lives*, Cullompton: Willan, pp 30-55.

Matravers, A. (ed) (2003) *Sex offenders in the community: Managing and reducing the risks*, Cullompton: Willan.

Matthews, R. and Briggs, D. (2008) 'Lost in translation: interpreting and implementing ASB policies', in P. Squires (ed) *ASBO nation*, Bristol: The Policy Press, pp 87-100.

Mawby, R.I. (2007) 'Public sector services and the victim of crime', in S. Walklate (ed) *Handbook of victims and victimology*, Cullompton: Willan, pp 209-39.

May, C. and Wadwell, J. (2001) *Enforcing community penalties: The relationship between enforcement and reconviction*, Home Office Research Findings 155, London: Home Office.

Mead, J. (2007) 'Resettlement', in R. Canton and D. Hancock (eds) *Dictionary of probation and offender management*, Cullompton: Willan.

Melrose, M. (2006) 'Young people and drugs', in R. Hughes, R. Lart and P. Higate (eds) *Drugs: Policy and politics*, Maidenhead: Open University Press, pp 31-44.

Melrose, M. (2009) 'Out on the streets and out of control? Drug using sex workers and the prostitution strategy', in J. Phoenix (ed) *Regulating sex for sale*, Bristol: The Policy Press, pp 83-98.

Mental Health Alliance (2007) *The Mental Health Act 2007: The final report*, London: Mental Health Alliance.

Merrington, S. and Stanley, S. (2007) 'Effectiveness: who counts what?', in L. Gelsthorpe and R. Morgan (eds) *Handbook of probation*, Cullompton: Willan, pp 428-58.

Metcalfe, C. and Kennison, P. (2008) 'Constructing childhood and child abuse', in P. Kennison and T. Goodman (eds) *Children as victims*, Exeter: Learning Matters, pp 1-14.

Middleton, D. (2007) 'Sex offenders', in R. Canton and D. Hancock (eds) *Dictionary of probation and offender management*, Cullompton: Willan.

Miller, C., Freeman, M. and Ross, N. (2001) *Inter-professional practice in health and social care*, London: Arnold.

Millie, A. (2009) *Anti-social behaviour*, Maidenhead: Open University Press.

Millie, A. and Erol, R. (2006) 'Rehabilitation and resettlement: a study of prolific offender case management in Birmingham, United Kingdom', *International Journal of Offender Therapy and Comparative Criminology*, vol 50, no 6, pp 691-710.

Milton, J. (2007) 'Personality disorder', in R. Canton and D. Hancock (eds) *Dictionary of probation and offender management*, Cullompton: Willan.

Ministry of Justice (2007a) *Offender management caseload statistics 2006*, London: Ministry of Justice.

Ministry of Justice (2007b) *Application of the offender management model to indeterminate sentence prisoners*, London: Ministry of Justice.

Ministry of Justice (2007c) *National standards for the management of offenders*, London: Ministry of Justice.

Ministry of Justice (2008a) *The National Offender Management Service: Agency framework document*, London: Ministry of Justice.

Ministry of Justice (2008b) *National Service Framework: Improving services to women offenders*, London: Ministry of Justice.

Ministry of Justice (2009a) *National Offender Management Service: Strategic and business plans 2009-2010 to 2010-2011*, London: Ministry of Justice.

Ministry of Justice (2009b) *NOMS risk of serious harm guidance*, London: Ministry of Justice.

Ministry of Justice (2009c) *MAPPA guidance*, London: Ministry of Justice.

Ministry of Justice (2009d) *Judicial and court statistics 2008*, London: Ministry of Justice.

Ministry of Justice (2009e) *Public Protection Manual: Chapter 2 Section 1 Safeguarding Children Statutory Guidance Section 11 of the Children Act 2004*, London: Ministry of Justice.

Ministry of Justice (2010a) *Breaking the cycle: Effective punishment, rehabilitation and sentencing of offenders*, London: Ministry of Justice.

Ministry of Justice (2010b) *Statistics of mentally disordered offenders 2008, England and Wales*, London: Ministry of Justice.

Ministry of Justice (2010c) *Population in custody June 2010*, London: Ministry of Justice.

Moon, D. and Walker, A. (eds) with Murphy, R., Flatley, J., Parfrement-Hoskins, J. and Hall, P. (2009) *Perceptions of crime and anti-social behaviour: Findings from the British Crime Survey 2008/9*, Home Office Statistical Bulletin, London: Home Office.

Moore, R., Gray, E., Roberts, C., Taylor, E. and Merrington, S. (2006) *Managing persistent and serious offenders in the community: Intensive community programmes in theory and practice*, Cullompton: Willan.

Morgan, P. and Joe, K.A. (1996) 'The private and public Lives of women in the illicit drugs economy' in *Journal of Drug Issues* Vol 26(1): 125–42

Morgan, R. (2007) 'Probation, governance and accountability', in L. Gelsthorpe and R. Morgan (eds) *Handbook of probation*, Cullompton: Willan, pp 90–113.

Morgan, R. and Newburn, T. (2007) 'Youth justice', in L. Gelsthorpe and R. Morgan (eds) *Handbook of probation*, Cullompton: Willan, pp 292–321.

Morris, A. (1987) *Women, crime and criminal justice*, Oxford: Blackwell.

Muncie, J. (2004) *Youth and crime*, (2nd edn) London: Sage Publications.

Muncie, J. (2009) *Youth and crime* (3rd edn), London: Sage Publications.

Munro, E. (2008) *Effective child protection*, London: Sage Publications.

Munro, E. (2010) *The Munro Review of child protection part one: a system's analysis*, London: Dept of Education.

Munro, E. (2011) *The Munro Review of child protection final report: a child-centred system*, London: Dept of Education.

Murphy, M.C. (2001) *Natural Law and Practical Rationality*, New York: Cambridge University Press.

Nacro (2000) *Let's get it right: Race and justice 2000*, London: Nacro.

NAO (National Audit Office) (2005) *Facing justice: Tackling defendants' non-attendance at court*, London: NAO.

Nash, M. (1999) 'Enter the polibation officer', *International Journal of Police Science and Management*, vol 1, pp 360–8.

National Probation Service (2004) *Sex offender strategy for the probation service*, London: National Probation Service.

Nellis, M. (2001a) 'Community values and community justice', *Probation Journal*, vol 48, no 1, pp 34–8.

Nellis, M. (2001b) 'Community penalties in historical perspective', in A. Bottoms, L. Gelsthorpe and S. Rex (eds) *Community penalties: Change and challenges*, Cullompton: Willan, pp 16–40.

Nellis, M. (2005) 'Dim prospects: humanistic values and the fate of community justice', in J. Winstone and F. Pakes (eds) *Community justice: Issues for probation and criminal justice*, Cullompton: Willan, pp 33–51.

Nellis, M. (2007) 'Probation values', in in R. Canton and D. Hancock (eds) *Dictionary of probation and offender management*, Cullompton: Willan

Nellis, M. and Gelsthorpe, L. (2003) 'Human rights and the probation values debate', in W.H. Chui and M. Nellis (eds) *Moving probation forward: Evidence, arguments and practice*, Harlow: Pearson, pp 227–44.

Nettleton, H., Walklate, S. and Williams, B. (1997) *Probation Training with The Victms in Mind: Partnership, Values and Organisation* Keele: Keel University Press

Newcomen, N. (2003) 'Lifers who maintain their innocence', *Probation Journal*, vol 50, no 1, p 90.

Nicholls, G. (2007) 'Enforcement', in R. Canton and D. Hancock (eds) *Dictionary of probation and offender management*, Cullompton: Willan.

NOMS (National Offender Management Service) (2006) *The NOMS Offender Management Model*, London: Home Office.

NOMS (2009) *MAPPA Guidance 2009*, London: NOMS.

NTA (National Treatment Agency) (2006) *Models of care for treatment of adult drug misusers, Update 2006*, London: NTA.

Nutt, D., King, L.A., Saulsbury, W. and Blakemore, C. (2007) 'Development of a rational scale to assess the harm of drugs of potential misuse', *The Lancet*, vol 369, pp 1047-53.

Osborne, S. (2010) 'Extents and trends', in J. Flatley, C. Kershaw, K. Smith, R. Chaplin and D. Moon (eds) *Crime in England and Wales: Findings from the British Crime Survey and police recorded crime*, Home Office Statistical Bulletin 12/10, London: Home Office, pp 9-44.

PA Consultancy Group and MORI (2005) *Action research study of the implementation of the National Offender Management Model in the North West Pathfinder*, Home Office OLR 32/05, London: Home Office.

Pakes, F. and Winstone, J. (2010) 'Offenders with mental health problems in the criminal justice system: the multi-agency challenge', in A. Pyecroft and D. Gough (eds) *Multi-agency working in criminal justice*, Bristol: The Policy Press, pp 169-84.

Parfrement-Hopkins, J. and Green, B. (2010) 'Public perceptions', in J. Flatley, C. Kershaw, K. Smith, R. Chaplin and D. Moon (eds) *Crime in England and Wales: Findings from the British Crime Survey and police recorded crime*, Home Office Statistical Bulletin 12/10, London: Home Office, pp 109-48.

Partridge, S. (2004) *Examining case management models for community sentences*, Home Office OLR 17/04, London: Home Office.

Patel, S. and Stanley, S. (2008) *The use of the Community Order and Suspended Sentence Order for women*, London: Centre for Crime and Justice Studies, King's College.

Paylor, I., Hucklesby, A. and Wilson, A. (2010) 'Drug interventions in prison', in A. Hucklesby and E. Wincup (eds) *Drug interventions in criminal justice*, Maidenhead: Open University Press, pp 190-216.

Payne, M. (2000) *Teamwork in multi-professional care*, Basingstoke: Palgrave Macmillan.

Peay, J. (2007) 'Mentally disordered offenders, mental health and crime', in M. Maguire, R. Morgan and R. Reiner (eds) *The Oxford handbook of criminology*, Oxford: Oxford University Press, pp 496-527.

Peckover, S., Broadhurst, K., White, S., Wastell, S., Hall, C. and Pithouse, A. (2011) 'The fallacy of formalisation: practice makes process in the assessment of risks to children' in Kemshall, H. and Wilkinson, B. (eds) *Good practice in assessing risk: current knowledge, issues and approaches*, London: Jessica Kingsley.

Philips, D. (2008) 'Beyond the risk agenda', in S. Green, E. Lancaster and S. Feasey (eds) *Addressing offending behaviour: Context, practice and value*, Cullompton: Willan, pp 172-89.

Piquero, A.R. (2004) 'Somewhere between persistence and desistance: the intermittency of criminal careers', in S. Maruna and R. Immarigeon (eds) *After crime and punishment: Pathways to offender reintegration*, Cullompton: Willan, pp 102-28.

Porporino, F.J. (2010) 'Bringing sense and sensitivity to corrections: from programmes to "fix" offenders to services to support desistance', in J. Brayford, F.B. Cowe and J. Deering (eds) *What else works? Creative work with offenders*, Cullompton: Willan, pp 61-86.

Power, H. (2003) 'Disclosing information on sex offenders: the human rights implications', in A. Matravers (ed) *Sex offenders in the community: Managing and reducing the risks*, Cullompton: Willan, pp 72-101.

Powis, B and Walmsley (2002) *Programmes for Black and Asian Offenders on probation: Lessons for developing practice,* Home Office Research Study 250.

Prins, H. (2005) 'Mental disorder and violent crime: a problematic relationship', *Probation Journal*, vol 52, no 4, p 333.

Prins, H. (2007) 'Mentally disordered offenders', in R. Canton and D. Hancock (eds) *Dictionary of probation and offender management*, Cullompton: Willan.

Prison Reform Trust (2007) *Indefinately maybe? How the indeterminate sentence for public protection is unjust and unsustainable*, London: Prison Reform Trust.

Prison Reform Trust (2009) *The Bromley Briefings*, London: Prison Reform Trust.

Putnam, R. (2000) *Bowling alone: Collapse and revival of the American community*, New York: Simon & Schuster.

Raine, J. (2001) 'Modernisation and criminal justice', in D.M. Ward, M. Lacey and J. Scott (eds) *Probation: Working for justice*, Oxford: Oxford University Press, pp 257-75.

Ray, L., Smith, D. and Wastell, L. (2002) 'Racist violence and probation practice', *Probation Journal*, vol 49, no 1, pp 3-9.

Raynor, P. and Lewis, S. (2006) 'Black and Asian men on probation: who are they, and what are their criminogenic needs?', in S. Lewis, P. Raynor, D. Smith and A. Wardek (eds) *Race and probation*, Cullompton: Willan, pp 61-80.

Raynor, P. and Vanstone, M. (2007) 'Towards a correctional service', in L. Gelsthorpe and R. Morgan (eds) *Handbook of probation*, Cullompton: Willan, pp 59-89.

Raynor, P., Kynch, J., Roberts, C. and Merrington, S. (2000) *Risk and need assessment in probation services: An evaluation*, Home Office Research Study No 211, London: Home Office.

Rex, S. (1999) 'Desistance from offending: experiences of probation', *The Howard Journal of Criminal Justice*, vol 38, no 4, pp 366-83.

Roberts, J. (2002) 'Women-centred: the West Mercia community-based programme for women offenders', in P. Carlen (ed) *Women and punishment*, Cullompton: Willan, pp 110-24.

Roberts, J. (2003) 'Evaluating the pluses and minuses of custody: sentencing reform in England and Wales', *The Howard Journal of Criminal Justice*, vol 42, pp 229-47.

Roberts, J. (2007) 'Custody plus, intermittent custody and custody minus', in R. Canton and D. Hancock (eds) *Dictionary of probation and offender management*, Cullompton: Willan.

Robinson, G. (1999) 'Risk management and rehabilitation in the Probation Service: collision and collusion', *The Howard Journal of Criminal Justice*, vol 38, no 4, pp 421-33.

Robinson, G. (2005) 'What works in offender management', *The Howard Journal of Criminal Justice*, vol 44, no 3, pp 307-18.

Robinson, G. and Burnett, R. (2007) 'Experiencing modernisation: frontline probation perspectives on the transition to a National Offender Management Service', *Probation Journal*, vol 54, no 4, pp 318-37.

Robinson, M. and Cottrell, D. (2005) 'Health professionals in multi-disciplinary and multi-agency teams: changing professional practice', *Journal of Inter-professional Care*, vol 19, no 6, pp 547-60.

Robinson, G. and McNeill, F. (2004) 'Purposes matter: examining the "ends" of probation', in G. Mair (ed) *What matters in probation*, Cullompton: Willan, pp 277-304.

Roll, J. (2007) *The Mental Health Bill*, Research Paper 07/33, House of Commons Library.

Rosenbaum, M. (1981) *Women on heroin* New Brunswick, NJ: Rutgers University Press

Rumgay, J. (2003) 'Partnerships in the Probation Service', in W.H. Chui and M. Nellis (eds) *Moving probation forward: Evidence, arguments and practice*, Harlow: Pearson Education, pp 195-213.

Rumgay, J. (2004a) 'The barking dog? Partnership and effective practice', in G. Mair (ed) *What matters in probation*, Cullompton: Willan, pp 122-45.

Rumgay, J. (2004b) 'Scripts for safer survival: pathways out of female crime', *The Howard Journal of Criminal Justice*, vol 43, no 4, p 358.

Rumgay, J. (2007) 'Partnerships in probation', in L. Gelsthorpe and R. Morgan (eds) *Handbook of probation*, Cullompton: Willan, pp 542-64.

Sampson, A. (1994) *Acts of abuse: Sex offenders and the criminal justice system*, London: Routledge.

Samuels, A. (2003) 'In denial of murder: no parole', *The Howard Journal of Criminal Justice*, vol 42, no 2, p 176.

Sanders, T., O'Neill, M. and Pitcher, J. (2009) *Prostitution: Sex work, policy and politics*, London: Sage Publications.

Scott, J. (2002) 'Human rights: a challenge to culture and practice', in D. Ward, J. Scott and M. Lacey (eds) *Probation: Working for justice*, Oxford: Oxford University Press, pp 3-24.

Scott, D. and Codd, H. (2010) *Controversial issues in prisons*, Maidenhead: Open University Press.

Senior, P., Crowther-Dowey, C. and Long, M. (2007) *Understanding modernisation in criminal justice*, Maidenhead: Open University Press.

Sentencing Guidelines Council (2004) *Over-arching principles: Seriousness*, London: Sentencing Guidelines Council.

Sentencing Guidelines Council (2005) *New sentences: Criminal Justice Act 2003*, London: Sentencing Guidelines Council.

Seto, M.C. (2003) 'Interpreting the treatment performance of sex offenders', in A. Matravers (ed) *Sex offenders in the community: Managing and reducing the risks*, Cullompton: Willan, pp 125-43.

Shaw, S. *(1987)* Conviction Politics: A Plan for Penal Policy *(Fabian Society Pamphlet No. 522), London: Fabian Society.*

Shiner, M. (2006) 'Drugs, law and the regulation of harm', in R. Hughes, R. Lart and P. Higate (eds) *Drugs: Policy and politics*, Maidenhead: Open University Press, pp 59-74.

Silvestri, M. and Crowther-Dowey, C. (2008) *Gender and crime*, London: Sage Publications.

Skodbo, S., Brown, G., Deacon, S., Cooper, A., Hall, A., Milar, T., Smith, J. and Whitham, K. (2007) *The Drugs Intervention Programme (DIP): Addressing drug use and offending through 'Tough Choices'*, Research Report 2, London: Home Office.

Smith, D. (2006a) 'Racially motivated offenders and the Probation Service', in S. Lewis, P. Raynor, D. Smith and A. Wardak (eds) *Race and probation*, Cullompton: Willan, pp 25-40.

Smith, D. (2006b) 'What might work with racially motivated offenders?", in S. Lewis, P. Raynor, D. Smith and A. Wardak (eds) *Race and probation*, Cullompton: Willan, pp 200-16.

Smith, D. (2009) Criminology, contemporary society and race issues' in Bhui, H.S. (ed.) *Race and Criminal Justice* London: Sage, pp 30-48.

Smith, R. (2003) *Youth justice: Ideas, policy, practice*, Cullompton: Willan.

Snowden, A. (2007) 'Sex offender treatment programmes', in R. Canton and D. Hancock (eds) *Dictionary of probation and offender management*, Cullompton: Willan.

Social Exclusion Unit (2002) *Reducing re-offending by ex-prisoners*, London: Social Exclusion Unit.

Solomon, E. and Garside, R. (2008) *Ten years of New Labour's youth justice reforms: An independent audit*, London: Centre for Crime and Justice Studies, King's College.

Souhami, A. (2007) *Transforming youth justice: Occupational identity and cultural change*, Cullompton: Willan.

Souhami, A. (2008) 'Multi-agency practice: experiences in the youth justice system', in S, Green, E. Lancaster and S. Feasey (eds) *Addressing offending behaviour: Context, practice and values*, Cullompton: Willan, pp 208-28.

Spencer, S. and Stern, B. (2001) *Reluctant witness*, London: Institute for Public Policy Research.

Squires, P. and Stephen, D. (2005) *Rougher justice: Anti-social behaviour and young people*, Cullompton: Willan.

Stevens, A. (2010) 'Treatment sentences for drug users: contexts, mechanisms and outcomes', in A. Hucklesby and E. Wincup (eds) *Drugs interventions in criminal justice*, Maidenhead: Open University Press, pp 161-89.

Stevenson, O. (1989) *Child abuse: Public policy and professional practice*, London: Harvester Wheatsheaf.

Stone, N. (2007a) 'The Criminal Justice Act 1991', in R. Canton and D. Hancock (eds) *Dictionary of probation and offender management*, Cullompton: Willan.

Stone, N. (2007b) 'The Criminal Justice Act 2003', in R. Canton and D. Hancock (eds) *Dictionary of probation and offender management*, Cullompton: Willan.

Tarling, R. et al (2000) *Victim and witness intimidation: Key findings from the British Crime Survey*, London: Home Office.

Taylor, A. (1993) *Women Drug Users: An ethnography of a female injecting community* Oxford: Oxford University Press

Thomas, T. (2003) 'Sex offender community notification: experiences from America', *The Howard Journal of Criminal Justice*, vol 42, no 3, pp 217-28.

Thomas, T. (2008) 'The sex offender "register": a case study in function creep', *The Howard Journal,* Vol 47(3): 227-37.

Thomas, T. (2010) 'The sex offender register, community notification and some reflections on privacy', in K. Harrison (ed) *Managing high risk sex offenders in the community: Risk management, treatment and social responsibility*, Cullompton: Willan, pp 61-80.

Thompson, N. (2006) *Anti-discriminatory practice 4th Edn* Basingstoke: Palgrave Macmillan

Thompson, S. and Thompson, N. (2008) *The critically reflective practitioner*, Basingstoke: Palgrave Macmillan.

Timms, N. (1983) *Social work values: An enquiry*, London: Routledge & Kegan Paul.

Trotter, C. (2006) *Working with involuntary clients: A guide to practice*, London: Sage Publications.

Turnbull, P. and Skinns, L. (2010) 'Drug Intervention Programme: neither success nor failure?', in A. Hucklesby and E. Wincup (eds) *Drug interventions in criminal justice*, Maidenhead: Open University Press, pp 64-83.

UK Drug Policy Commission (2008) *Tackling Drug Use, Reducing Re-offending,* London: UKDPC

Vanstone, M. (2006) '"Room for improvement": the history of the Probation Service's response to race', in S. Lewis, D. Raynor, D. Smith and A. Wardak (eds) *Race and probation*, Cullompton: Willan, pp 13-22.

Wahidin, A. et al (2007) 'Older offenders', R. Canton and D. Hancock (eds) *Dictionary of probation and offender management*, Cullompton: Willan.

Wallace, S. (2000) 'Responding to the Human Rights Act', *Probation Journal*, vol 47, pp 53-5.

Walmsley, R.K. and Stephens, K. (2006) 'What works with Black and minority ethnic offenders: solutions in search of a problem?', in S. Lewis, P. Raynor, D. Smith and A. Wardek (eds) *Race and probation*, Cullompton: Willan, pp 164-80.

Ward, T. and Marshall, W.L. (2004) 'Good lives, aetiology and the rehabilitation of sex offenders: a bridging theory', *Journal of Sexual Aggression*, vol 10, no 2, pp 153-69.

Ward, T. and Maruna, S. (2007) *Rehabilitation*, Abingdon: Routledge

Ward, T. and Siegert, R.J. (2002) 'Towards a comprehensive theory of child sexual abuse: a theory knitting perspective', *Psychology, Crime and Law*, vol 8, no 4, p 319.

Ward, D. and Spencer, J. (1994) 'The future of probation qualifying training', *Probation Journal*, vol 41, no 2, pp 95-8.

Ward, T. and Stewart, C. (2003) 'The treatment of sex offenders: risk management and good lives', *Professional Psychology: Research and Practice*, vol 34, no 4, pp 353-60.

Weaver, B. and McNeill, F. (2010) 'Travelling hopefully: desistance theory and probation practice', in J. Brayford, F.B. Cowe and J. Deering (eds) *What else works? Creative work with offenders*, Cullompton: Willan, pp 36-60.

Webster, C. (2007) *Understanding race and crime*, Maidstone: Open University Press.

Wenger, E. (1998) *Communities of practice*, Cambridge: Cambridge University Press.

White, R.C.A. (1999) *The English legal system in action*, Oxford: Oxford University Press.

Whitehead, P. (2010) *Exploring modern probation: Social theory and organisational complexity*, Bristol: The Policy Press.

Williams, B. (1995) 'Introduction', in B. Williams (ed) *Probation values*, Birmingham: Venture Press, pp 1-28.

Williams, B. (1997) 'Rights versus risks: issues in work with prisoners', in H. Kemshall and J. Pritchard (eds) *Good practice in risk assessment and risk management 2: Key themes for protection, rights and responsibilities*, London: Jessica Kingsley Publishers, pp 255-66.

Williams, B. (1999a) 'The Victim's Charter: citizens as consumers of criminal justice services', *The Howard Journal of Criminal Justice*, vol 38, no 4, pp 384-96.

Williams, B. (1999b) *Working with victims of crime: Policy, politics and practice*, London: Jessica Kingsley Publishers.

Williams, B. (2002) 'Justice for victims of crime', in D. Ward, J. Scott and M. Lacey (eds) *Probation: Working for justice*, Oxford: Oxford University Press, pp 67-82.

Williams, B. and Goodman, H. (2007a) 'Working for and with victims of crime', in L. Gelsthorpe and R. Morgan (eds) *Handbook of probation*, Cullompton: Willan, pp 518-41.

Williams, B. and Goodman, H. (2007b) 'The role of the voluntary sector', in S. Walklate (ed) *Handbook of victims and victimology*, Cullompton: Willan, pp 240-54.

Williams, J. (2008) *Child law for social work*, London: Sage Publications.

Williams, P. (2002) 'The competent boundary spanner', *Public Administration*, vol 80, no 1, pp 103-24.

Winstone, J. and Pakes, F. (2005) 'Marginalised and disenfranchised: community justice and mentally disordered offenders', in J. Winstone and F. Pakes (eds) *Community justice: Issues for probation and criminal justice*, Cullompton: Willan, pp 219-38.

Wolf, S. (1985) 'A multi factor model of deviant sexuality', *Victimology: An International Journal*, vol 10, p 359.

Wood, J. and Kemshall, H. (2007) *The operation and experience of Multi-Agency Public Protection Arrangements (MAPPA)*, London: Home Office.

Wood, J. and Kemshall, H. (2008) 'Risk management, accountability and partnerships', in B. Stout, J. Yates and B. Williams (eds) *Applied criminology*, London: Sage Publications, pp 135-53.

Wood, J. and Kemshall, H. (2010) 'Effective multi-agency public protection: learning from the research', in K. Harrison (ed) *Managing high risk and sex offenders in the community: Risk management, treatment and social responsibility*, Cullompton: Willan, pp 39-60.

Woodin, J. (2007) 'Drug action teams', in R. Canton and D. Hancock (eds) *Dictionary of probation and offender management*, Cullompton: Willan.

Woolf, H. and Tumin, S. (1991) *Prison disturbances April 1990: Report of an enquiry*, Cm 1456, London: HMSO.

Worrall, A. (1990) *Offending women*, London: Routledge.

Worrall, A. (2002a) 'Targeting and treatment? Do prolific offender projects have a future?', *The Probation Journal*, vol 49, pp 287-95.

Worrall, A. (2002b) 'Missed opportunities? The Probation Service and women offenders', in D. Ward, J. Scott and M. Lacey (eds) *Probation: Working for justice*, Oxford: Oxford University Press, pp 134-48.

Worrall, A. and Gelsthorpe, L. (2009) '"What works" with women offenders: the past 30 years', *Probation Journal*, vol 56, no 4, pp 329-45.

Wright, L. and Kemshall, H. (1994) 'Feminist probation practice: making supervision meaningful', *Probation Journal*, vol 41, no 2, pp 73-80.

YJB (Youth Justice Board) (2009) *National standards for youth justice services*, London: YJB.

Zehr, H. (1990) *Changing lenses: A new focus for crime and justice*, Scottsdale PA, Herald Press.

Appendix: List of probation circulars

PC 41/1995	*Incident reporting*
PC 79/1996	*Serious incident reporting*
PC 71/1998	*Serious incident reports: Analysis*
PC 3/1999	*Enforcement*
PC 62/2001	*Victim contact work guidance*
PC 28/2003	*Victim Contact work: Guidance on recent court judgements*
PC 19/2005	*Bail information schemes*
PC 22/2005	*Implementing Section 10 of the Children Act 2004: Inter-agency co-operation to improve the well-being of children – Children's Trusts*
PC 25/2005	*Criminal Justice Act 2003: Implementation on 4 April*
PC 56/2005	*Delivering intensive community orders under the Criminal Justice Act 2005*
PC 57/2005	*Effective management of the Drug Rehabilitation requirement (DRR) and the Alcohol Treatment Requirement (ATR)*
PC 63/2005	*Statutory guidance on implementing Section 11 of the Children Act 2004 and the* Working together to safeguard children *consultation*
PC 9/2007	*Definition of programme completions for accredited offending behaviour programmes*
PC 17/2007	*Assessment and management of sex offenders*
PC 29/2007	*Post-release enforcement – Licence conditions*
PC 14/2008	*Post-release enforcement – Recall and further release*
PC 21/2008	*Managing high risk of serious harm offenders with severe personality disorder*
PC 23/2008	*Mental Health Act 2007: Rights to information under the Domestic Violence, Crime and Victims Act 2004*

Index

A

Abbott, D. 44
abusive behaviour
  defining 120, 139
  see also child sex abuse
accountability 13, 20, 107–8, 114, 128
ACE (Assessment, Case Management and
  Evaluation) system 106
ACOP (Association of Chief Officers of
  Probation) 190
actions, and values 4
actuarial justice 105
acute risk factors 109
aftercare 173, 174, 183–5, 279
agencies *see* criminal justice agencies
aims, and values 4
Alcohol Treatment Requirement (ATR) 167,
  169, 195
alcohol use 254, 261
Allen, R. 243
Ansbro, M. 115–16
anti-discriminatory practice 6, 86–7
anti-racism 6, 89–91, 93–4
anti-social behaviour 240–2
Anti-Social Behaviour Act (2003) 241
Anti-social Behaviour Orders (ASBOs) 75,
  240–1
Appleton, C. 304
Area Child Protection Committees 129, 293
Ashworth, A. 145–6
assessment
  in children's services 127, 132
  mental health assessment 267–8
  see also risk assessment
Assessment, Case Management and Evaluation
  (ACE) system 106
assessment tools
  Asset 107–108
  and mental disorder 276, 278
  see also risk assessment tools
Association of Chief Officers of Probation
  (ACOP) 190
ATR (Alcohol Treatment Requirement) 167,
  169, 195
Attrill, G. 116
Audit Commission 227
automatic life sentences 300

B

bail 145–50
Bail Act (1976) 146, 147–8
bail information schemes 149–50
Barry, M. 56–7
BCS (British Crime Survey) 208
Bean, P. 245, 257
Beaumont, B. 105–6

Beckett, C. 121, 140
behavioural change
  and compliance 202
  see also desistance
behavioural therapy 289
Bennett, T. 246
Bhui, H.S. 89
BME (black and other minority ethnic) groups
  88
  and court system 151
  and desistance 99
  experience of probation 91–2
  and mental health 276
  in prison 89
Boeck, T. 56
bonding capital 56–7
Bottoms, A. 201
Bradley Report 280–1
breach proceedings 145, 153–4, 190, 191–2,
  193–6, 238
breach rates 190, 236
breach reports 155
*Breaking the cycle: Effective punishment, rehabilitation
  and sentencing of offenders* 31–2
bridging capital 56, 57
British Crime Survey (BCS) 208
brokerage 29, 43
Brown, Sarah 289, 290, 292, 293
Bulger, James 224
Burke, B. 86
Burnett, R. 30

C

CAF (Common Assessment Framework) 127
Cafcass (Children and Family Court Advisory
  and Support Service) 21, 161
Calverley, A. 88, 91–2, 93, 99
Canton, R. 4, 107–8, 188, 189–90, 191, 200–1,
  202, 263–4, 276
care orders 138
Care Programme Approach (CPA) 279–80
Carter, P. 21–2, 162, 185
case administrators 29
case management approach
  of DIP 255
  Offender Management Model 25–31, 185–6
  and reducing offending 61–4
cautions 224, 231
Cavadino, M. 74
CDRPs (Crime and Disorder Reduction
  Partnerships) 37, 40, 254
change **see** behavioural change; desistance
child abuse 120, 139, 284, 287, 288
Child Assessment Orders 134
child protection 119, 120, 139–40
  background to system 120–3

Children Act (1989) 123–4, 125–6
Local Safeguarding Children's Boards 130
multi-agency process of 131–8
child protection case conferences 134–6, 138
child protection plans 135–8
Child Protection Register 135
child sex abuse 284, 287, 288
child sex offender disclosure scheme 289
children
in care 138, 139
criminal intent and the principle of *doli incapax* 230–1
multi-agency work with 43–5, 126, 127–38
societal attitudes to 120–1
as vulnerable witnesses 213
and women's drug use 253
Children Act (1908) 222, 225
Children Act (1989) 123–6, 138–9, 226
section 47 enquiries 125, 132–4
Children Act (2004) 126–9
Children and Family Court Advisory and Support Service (Cafcass) 21, 161
Children (Leaving Care) Act (2000) 139
Children and Young Persons Act (1933) 225, 238
Children and Young Persons Act (1969) 223, 225–6
Children's Hearing system 222
children's homes 236, 237
children's services 122–6, 138–9
assessment 127, 132
Children Act (2004) 126–9
multi-agency and inter-agency working 43–5, 126, 127–38
Children's Trusts 127
Christie, N. 209
Circles of Support and Accountability (COSA) 297
citizenship 11
civil rights 9
CJITs (Criminal Justice Intervention Teams) 168, 255, 256
co-ordination 35
see also multi-agency working
Codd, H. 247
coercion, and drug treatment 255, 256–7
cognitive behavioural work 289–90
collaboration 13, 35, 62
see also multi-agency working
Combination Orders 159, 192
Common Assessment Framework (CAF) 127
community, rights and offenders in 78–9
community engagement 297
community notification 286, 288–9
community orders 164–6
Alcohol Treatment Requirement 167, 169, 195
amendment of 193–5
Drug Rehabilitation Requirement 167–9, 195, 256, 257
intensive community orders 167
and mentally disordered offenders 195, 274
relationship with custodial sentences 177, 178–9

Supervision Requirement 167
use of 169–70
community protection model 51–2
see also public protection
community protection orders 242
Community Safety Partnerships (CSPs) 37, 40, 254, 255, 261
community sentencing
Crime and Disorder Act (1998) 161
Crime (Sentences) Act (1997) 161
Criminal Justice Act (1991) 159–61
Criminal Justice Act (2003) 164–6
Alcohol Treatment Requirement 167, 169
background 162–4
Drug Rehabilitation Requirement 167–9, 256
Mental Health Treatment Requirement 274
supervision requirement 167
Criminal Justice and Court Services Act (2000) 161–2
enforcement of *see* enforcement
historical perspectives 157–8
use of community orders 169–70
in youth justice 233–6
community service 159
community treatment, mental health 267, 269–70
Community Treatment Orders 269–70
compliance
and offender engagement 190, 200–2
see also enforcement
compulsory hospital detention
for mental assessment 267–8
patient discharge from 279
for treatment of mental disorder 268–9
conditional bail 147–9
conditions, of licences 178, 196–8, 237–8, 308–9
Connolly, M. 10, 61
contractual partnerships 36
Core Assessment 132
COSA (Circles of Support and Accountability) 297
Cottrell, D. 45
Court of Appeal 154
court proceedings
breach proceedings 145, 153–4, 191–2, 193–6, 238
first appearance and bail 145–50
and mental health legislation 271–2
trials 150–4
and youth justice 232, 237, 238
court system 143–5
and probation service 154–5
role in drug treatment 258–9
Coyle, A. 76
CPA (Care Programme Approach) 279–80
CPPCs (Critical Public Protection Cases) 113
CRASBOs 241
Crawford, A. 217, 233
crime
perceptions about 208
relationship with mental disorder 275–6

relationship with substance misuse 245–7
reporting of 208, 210, 211
see also re-offending
Crime and Disorder Act (1998) 161, 176, 228–32, 237, 239, 240, 256, 285, 289
Crime and Disorder Reduction Partnerships (CDRPs) 37, 40, 254
Crime, justice and protecting the public 157
crime prevention injunctions 242
Crime (Sentences) Act (1997) 161, 175
crime statistics 208
criminal behaviour orders 242
Criminal Care Orders 226
Criminal Injuries Compensation Scheme 211–12
criminal intent 165, 230–1
Criminal justice: The way ahead 212–13
Criminal Justice Act (1991)
  enforcement under 191–2
  impact on probation service 6, 187–8
  and sentencing 157–8, 256
    community 159–61
    custodial 174
  and sexual offending 285
  and youth justice 224, 226
Criminal Justice Act (2003) 154, 171, 274, 304
  background 162–4
  community sentencing 164–6
    Alcohol Treatment Requirement 167, 169
    Drug Rehabilitation Requirement 167–9, 256
    enforcement 193–5
    Mental Health Treatment Requirement 274
    Supervision Requirement 167
  court procedures 146, 151, 154
  custodial sentencing 176–7
    custody plus 178, 179
    extended sentences for public protection 181
    indeterminate sentences for public protection 181–3
    intermittent custody 180
    life sentence tariffs 304
    standard determinate sentence 180–1
    Suspended Sentence Orders 178–80
  deferred sentences 171
criminal justice agencies
  future changes 31–2
  human rights and duties of 75–6
  modernising agenda 19–20
    managerialism 20–1
    service reorganisation 21–2
  National Offender Management Service 22–5
  Offender Management Model 25–31
  risk culture of 17–19, 51–2
  see also inter-agency working; multi-agency working; partnership structures
Criminal Justice and Court Services Act (2000) 21, 161–2, 176, 216–17, 286
Criminal Justice and Immigration Act (2008) 164, 182, 183, 199, 289
Criminal Justice Intervention Teams (CJITs) 168, 255, 256

Criminal Justice Joint Inspection (CJJI) report 294–5, 310–12
Criminal Justice and Public Order Act (1994) 175
criminal justice system
  and diversity 83
  impact of human rights on 74–5
  and mental disorder 263–4
  and 'race' 88–9, 151
  risk management approach 17–19, 51–2
  see also criminal justice agencies
Criminal Procedure and Investigation Act (1996) 150–1, 154
criminalisation
  of drugs 247, 248
  of individuals 88
Critical Public Protection Cases (CPPCs) 113
Crown Courts 143, 144, 147, 150–4
  breach proceedings 193, 194
  and mental health legislation 271–2
  and youth justice 237
Crown Prosecutor 145
CSPs *see* Community Safety Partnerships
cultural resources, and desistance 99
Curfew Orders 159–60
custodial licences
  breach of 192
  conditions of 178, 196–8, 237–8, 308–9
  period of 174, 176, 178, 181
  for sex offenders 176, 285–6
custodial period, of Suspended Sentence Orders 179
custodial remands 146–7
custodial sentence
  re-settlement following 183–5
  release on licence following see custodial licences
  work with offenders in custody 173, 185–6
custodial sentencing
  breach of Suspended Sentence Orders 195–6
  Crime and Disorder Act (1998) 176
  Crime (Sentences) Act (1997) 175
  Criminal Justice Act (1991) 174
  Criminal Justice Act (2003) 176–7
    custody plus 178, 179
    extended sentences for public protection 181
    indeterminate sentences for public protection 181–3
    intermittent custody 180
    standard determinate sentence 180–1
    Suspended Sentence Orders 178–80
  Criminal Justice and Court Services Act (2000) 176
  Criminal Justice and Public Order Act (1994) 175
  custody threshold, the *so serious* criterion 158, 178, 193, 235, 237
  and mentally disordered offenders 274
  recall and re-release 198–9, 305
  for young offenders 175, 176, 224, 236–9, 312
custody minus **see** Suspended Sentence Orders
custody plus 178, 179

D

DAATs (Drug and Alcohol Action Teams) 168, 254
Dalrymple, J. 86
dangerous and serious personality disordered (DSPD) offenders 274–5, 277–9
dangerous and serious personality disordered (DSPD) Programme 278
dangerousness
  of mentally disordered offenders 275–7
  see also harm
data protection 38–9
DATs (Drug Action Teams) 248, 254–5
death penalty 304
defendants' rights 152–3
  to bail 146, 149
  to jury trial 151
deferred sentences 170–1
depressants 251
deprofessionalisation 188
desistance
  and diversity 87, 98–100
  factors in increasing 58–9
  and offender management 55–6, 201
  and Offender Management Model 58–9, 61–4
  and resettlement 184
  role of Good Lives Model 13–15, 59–60
  role of human and social capital 56–7
desistance debate 54
Detention for Public Protection (DPP) 238, 301, 303, 305, 310–12
Detention and Training Orders 176, 237–8
Dhami, M.K. 148
difference
  respecting 12–13
  see also diversity
Dignan, J. 208, 209, 210, 214
DIP *see* Drugs Intervention Programme
direct discrimination 84
disability 84
discretion 13, 107–8, 122, 139–40, 192, 199–200, 231
discretionary life sentences 300, 301
discrimination
  layers of 86
  see also racism
Dispersal Orders 241
diversity 12–13, 83, 98–100
doli incapax 230–1
domestic violence 114–15
Domestic Violence, Crime and Victims Act (2004) 218
'double jeopardy' 95, 154
DRR *see* Drug Rehabilitation Requirement
Drug Abstinence Orders 162
Drug Action Teams (DATs) 248, 254–5
Drug and Alcohol Action Teams (DAATs) 168, 254
drug classification 249–50
drug courts 258
drug dependence 247–8, 252

drug interventions
  Drugs Intervention Programme 39, 41, 168, 255–6, 257, 260
  multi-agency partnerships 159, 248, 253–5, 260
  in prisons 259–61
  see also drug treatment
drug policy, transformations in 247–9
Drug Rehabilitation Requirement (DRR) 167–9, 195, 256, 257
drug testing 248–9, 257
drug treatment
  policy on 248–9
  in prisons 260
  role of courts 258–9
  for women 253
  see also drug interventions
Drug Treatment and Testing Orders (DTTOs) 167, 256, 257, 258
drug use/misuse
  bail restrictions 148–9
  patterns of use 251–2
  regulatory framework 249–51
  women and 252–3, 255
  working with drug using offenders 261–2
drugs
  effects of 251
  relationship with crime 245–7
Drugs Act (2005) 255
Drugs Intervention Programme (DIP) 39, 41, 168, 255–6, 257, 260
DTTOs *see* Drug Treatment and Testing Orders
dual discrimination 84
duties *see* obligations
dynamic risk factors 109

E

Eadie, T. 107–8, 188, 199–200
ECHR *see* European Convention on Human Rights
ECtHR (European Court of Human Rights) 71
Edwards, I. 208, 215–16
effectiveness
  of MAPPAs 114
  of sex offender treatment 292–3
elderly prisoners 304–5
electronic monitoring 148, 159–60
emergency admission for assessment 268
Emergency Protection Order (EPO) 125
empowerment 86–7, 259
end-to-end offender management 22–3, 25, 31
enforcement
  changes in 2000 192–3
  custodial licences 196–8
  defining 187
  development in probation work 189–91
  discretion 199–200
  recall procedures 198–9
  of Suspended Sentence Orders 195–6
  of treatment requirements 195
  under Criminal Justice Act (1991) 191–2
  under Criminal Justice Act (2003) 193–5

see also breach proceedings
engagement model 63
engagement of offenders 190, 200–2
Enterkin, J. 217
equality *see* diversity; gender; 'race'; women
    offenders
Equality Act (2010) 83–5
equality duty (public sector) 85
Equality and Human Rights Commission 85
ethnicity 88
    and desistance 99
    mixed ethnicity offenders 92–3
    see also BME groups; 'race'
European Convention on Human Rights
    (ECHR) 71–2, 301, 307
    and Human Rights Act (1998) 72–3, 75–6
European Court of Human Rights (ECtHR) 71
    Every Child Matters 126, 227
evidence-based programmes 53
Exclusion Orders 162
extended sentences for public protection 181,
    196–7, 199, 238, 274–5
extremism 89

F

Farrow, K. 97, 276, 280
Feeley, M. 105
Feilzer, M. 93
Fenwick, H. 212
final warning scheme 231
First Tier Tribunal–Mental Health 268, 271, 272
fixed term recall (FTR) 199

G

Garside, R. 242
Gelsthorpe, L. 13, 83, 87, 92, 157, 219
gender 94
    information on 160
    see also women; women offenders
Goldson, B. 236
Good Lives Model 14–15, 59–62, 295–6
Goodey, J. 207
Goodman, H. 214
governance structures 20, 229–30
Grapes, T. 26
Grover, B. 304
Guardianship Orders 269

H

Halliday Report 162, 163, 176, 193, 286
hallucinogens 251
Hancock, D. 176–7
harm
    and drug classification 249–50
    risk of serious harm 108–10, 111–12
    see also child protection; dangerousness; risk
harm reduction approaches to drug misuse 248
hearings 152
High Court 147
Hilder, S. 86
HM Inspectorate of Constabulary 293
HMI Prisons 309–11

HMI Probation 90, 113, 129, 190, 218, 293,
    309–11
Holloway, K. 246
Home Detention Curfews 160, 196
Hood, R. 93, 305
hospital and limitation direction 272–3
Hospital Orders 271
Howard, Michael 303
Hudson, B. 9, 10, 70
human capital 56, 58, 60, 61
human rights 9, 10–11
    balance with risk management 80
    duties for public authorities 75–6
    Equality and Human Rights Commission 85
    human rights and offenders in community
        78–9
    impact on criminal justice system 74–5
    international human rights 70–2, 77
    and prison system 76–8
    see also rights-based approach
Human Rights Act (1998) 72–4, 75–6, 285

I

ideal victim 209, 211, 212
imminent risk of serious harm 110
imprisonment *see* custodial sentence
Improving health and supporting justice 281
indeterminate sentences *see* Detention for Public
    Protection; indeterminate sentences for
    public protection; life sentences
indeterminate sentences for public protection
    (IPP) 181–3, 301, 310–12
    impact on offenders 305
    and mentally disordered offenders 274–5
    release on licence 197, 308–9
    reviews and recalls 302
    sentencing planning and reviews 306
    statistics 303
    tariffs 301
indictable offences 143, 150
indirect discrimination 84
individuality, respecting 12–13
inequality
    layers of 86
    see also diversity; gender; 'race'
information disclosure
    and court proceedings 152
    and multi-agency work 38–9, 42–3
    and sex offenders 285, 286, 288–9
Institute for Public Policy Research (IPPR) 210
Integrated Offender Management Units 41
intensive community orders 167
intensive supervision and surveillance (ISS)
    schemes 234–6
inter-agency working
    in children's services 43–5
    in criminal justice system 46–7
    with mentally disordered offenders 280–1
    rights-based approach in 48
    see also multi-agency working; partnership
        structures
Intermediate Treatment Initiative 223–4

intermittent custody 180
International Covenant on Civil and Political
Rights 77
international human rights 70–2, 77
interventions 28–9, 31
  and anti-social behaviour 241
  in context of change process 55–6
  What Works movement 53
  for women 96–7
  see also treatment
intimidation of victims 211
IPP *see* indeterminate sentences for public
  protection
IPPR (Institute for Public Policy Research) 210
ISS (intensive supervision and surveillance)
  schemes 234–6

J

Johnstone, G. 145
joined-up programmes 38–41
Jones, T. 303
'judge in chambers' application 147
jury trials 151
  see also Crown Courts
'just deserts' policy 160, 163, 223, 226
juvenile courts 222, 225

K

Kemshall, H. 42, 96–7, 103–5, 107, 113, 114,
  202, 288–9
key workers 29, 47, 59, 65, 185

L

labelling 88
Laming Report 122
'law-abiding majority' 209–10
legitimate differentiation 13
Level of Service Inventory – Revised (LSI-R)
  107
licence period 174, 176, 178, 181
licences
  post-custody
    breach of 192
    conditions of 178, 196–8, 237–8, 308–9
  for sex offenders 176, 285–6
Licensing Act (2003) 261
Liell, G. 116
life sentence prisoners, work with 309–10
life sentences
  assessment for parole 307–8
  impact on offenders 305
  law relating to 299–300
  organisation of 306–7
  reasons for increasing 303–5
  release on licence 308–9
  statistics 302–3
  tariffs 301, 304–5
  and youth justice 238
  see also indeterminate sentences for public
    protection
Life Without Parole (LWOP) 304
linking capital 56, 57

local authorities, youth justice services 228–9
local authority children's social care 122, 123–6,
  138–9
  case conference and protection plan 134–8
  referrals to 131–4
  section 47 enquiries 125, 132–4
local authority secure children's homes 236, 237
Local Criminal Justice Boards (LCJBs) 37
local governance 20
Local Safeguarding Children's Boards (LSCBs)
  129–30
Lucy Faithful Foundation 297
LWOP (Life Without Parole) 304

M

McNeill, F. 51, 54, 58–60, 87, 202
Magistrates' Court Act (1980) 151, 274
Magistrates' Courts 143–7
  breach proceedings 191–2, 193
  committal to Crown Court by 150–1
  and mental health legislation 271
  youth justice 232, 237
Maguire 184, 185
Maguire, M. 184, 185, 288–9
Mair, G. 170, 189–90, 191
  Making punishments work see Halliday Report
managerialism 20–1, 36
Managing offenders, reducing crime 21–2
Mann, R.E. 291
Maruna, S. 54
masculinity 94
Matravers, A. 284
media, victims in 209
medical model 247–8, 252, 264
medical reports 274
Megan's Law 286
mental disorder
  defining 264–5
  relationship with crime 275–6
Mental Health Act (1983) 265, 279
  Part II 267–70
  Part III 270–3
Mental Health Act (2007) 218, 265
  amendments to Mental Health Act (1983)
    267–73
  summary 273–4
Mental Health Alliance 266
mental health legislation
  admission for assessment 267–8
  admission for treatment 268–9
  Guardianship Orders 269
  guiding principles 266–7
  hospital and limitation direction 272–3
  Hospital Orders 271
  reforming 265–6
  remand to hospital for medical report 270–1
  Restriction Orders 271–2
  supervised community treatment 267, 269–70
  transfer to hospital from prison 272
Mental Health (Patients in the Community)
  Act (1995) 279
Mental Health Review Tribunal 268, 271, 272

mental health system, and MDOs 263–4
mental health treatment
  amendments to mental health legislation 267
  compulsory detention 268–9
  hospital and limitation direction 272–3
  Hospital Orders 271
  supervised community treatment 267, 269–70
  transfer between prison and hospital 272–3
  enforcement of 195
  as requirement of community order 274
mentally disordered offenders (MDOs)
  Care Programme Approach 279–80
  in context 263–4
  dangerous and serious personality disordered
    (DSPD) offenders 274–5, 277–9
  Guardianship Orders 269
  and inter-agency practice 280–1
  remand to hospital for medical report 270–1
  Restriction Orders 271–2
  rights of 266–7
  risk and dangerousness 275–7
  sentencing 274–5
  treatment of see mental health treatment
Milton, J. 277
Misspent Youth 227–8
Misuse of Drugs Act (1971) 249
mixed ethnicity offenders 92–3
Models of Care framework 254
modernisation 19–20
  and managerialism 20–1
  Offender Management Model 25–31
  service reorganisation 21–5
Moore, R. 235
Morgan Report 37
Morris, A. 219
motivational work 202
Multi-Agency Lifer Risk Assessment Panel
  (MALRAP) 306
Multi-Agency Public Protection Arrangements
  (MAPPAs) 18, 110–14, 293, 297
Multi-Agency Public Protection Panels
  (MAPPPs) 111, 113, 280, 286
Multi-Agency Risk Assessment Conferences
  (MARACs) 114–15
multi-agency working
  and drug interventions 159, 248, 253–5, 260
  and mental health 280
  relationships in 41–3
  risk assessment and intervention 276
  and safeguarding children 43–5, 126, 127–38
  in youth justice 228, 229, 242
  see also inter-agency working; partnership
    structures
Muncie, J. 222
Munro, E. 120, 122–3
murder 299–300
Muslim prisoners 89

N

Nacro (National Association for the Care and
  Resettlement of Offenders) 90, 264

Narrowing the Justice Gap (NJG) initiative
  39–40
Nash, M. 17
National Audit Office 149–50
national drugs coordinator 248
National Offender Management Model (OMM)
  25–31, 61–4, 185–6
National Offender Management Service
  (NOMS) 18, 22–5, 109, 185, 188, 260, 301,
  302
National Probation Service strategy 217, 294
national standards 160, 187–9, 190–1, 192, 217,
  234, 239
National standards for youth justice services 234
National Treatment Agency 254
negative rights 70
Nellis, M. 3, 4–6
Newburn, T. 233, 303
Newcomen, N. 307
Nicholls, G. 187
No more excuses 226
NOMS **see** National Offender Management
  Service
North West Pathfinder scheme 22–3, 30
Nutt, D. 249–50

O

OASys *see* Offender Assessment System
obligations 10–12, 296
occupational identity 44, 46–7
offences
  categories of 143
  related to drug use 246
Offender Assessment System (OASys) 107, 108,
  109, 276
Offender Group Reconviction Scale (OGRS)
  106
offender management
  and desistance 55–6, 58–9
  and human rights 79
  and lifestyle change 13–15
  with prisoners 185–6
  values in 3–5
Offender Management Act (2007) 23
Offender Management Model (OMM) 25–31,
  61–4, 185–6
offender management process 28–9
offender managers
  and community sentences 167, 169
  and licence conditions 198, 309
  role of 29, 31, 43, 59
  and safeguarding children 132
  and substance using offenders 169, 261–2
  use of discretion 13, 199–200
  work with indeterminate sentence prisoners
    306, 309
  work with offenders in custody 185–6
offender rights 11
  at trial 152–3
  balance with public protection 80
  in community 78–9
  in prison system 76–8

offender supervisors 29, 47, 59, 65, 185
offenders
  aftercare 279–80
  assessment and categorisation of 18–19,
    111–12, 115–16
  engagement and compliance of 190, 200–2
  impact of life sentence on 305
  lifestyle change 13–15, 53–5
    see also desistance
  non-compliance see enforcement
  previous convictions 160, 163
  racist/racially motivated 93–4
  relationships with professionals 54, 62, 188–9,
    201–2, 276
  social construction of victims and 209–10
  taking responsibility 306–7
  views of risk assessment 116–17
  see also mentally disordered offenders; prisoners;
    'race'; sex offenders; women offenders; young
    offenders
offending *see* crime; re-offending
OGRS (Offender Group Reconviction Scale)
  106
OMM *see* Offender Management Model
open teamwork 45
operational partnerships 38–41
operational period, of Suspended Sentence
  Orders 179, 195, 196
organisations *see* criminal justice agencies

P

Pakes, F. 266
parental responsibility 138–9
Parenting Orders 239–40
parents, partnership with 123–4, 139
Parole Board 173–4, 181, 182, 198, 199, 305,
  307–8
Parole Unit 192
participatory rights 9
partnership structures 20, 22, 29, 30–1
  defining partnerships 35–6
  multi-agency teams 41–7
  operational partnerships 38–41
  rights-based approach in 48, 64
  and safeguarding children 127–31
  strategic partnerships 36–8
  and substance misuse 253–5, 256
  work with offenders in custody 185–6
  working with parents 123–4, 139
  see also inter-agency working; multi-agency
    working
Partridge, S. 26
Patel, S. 95
pathways model 290
'payments by results' (PBR) 32
Payne, M. 45
Payne, Sarah 286, 288
PCS model of inequalities 86
Peay, J. 265, 275, 279
penalties
  first tier penalties in youth justice 231–3
  see also sentencing

performance targets 20
persistent young offenders (PYOs) 39, 227, 242
personality disordered offenders 274–5, 277–9
plea and direction hearings (P&DH) 152
police powers under Mental Health Act 270
Police Reform Act (2002) 241
police service, and partnership work 39, 41
positive rights 70
power, and women's drug use 252
Powers of the Criminal Court (Sentencing) Act
  (2000) 238
Powis, B. 90
PPO (prolific and other priority offender)
  programme 39–41
pre-sentence report (PSR) 148, 155, 160, 168,
  169, 274
predictive tools **see** risk assessment tools
preliminary hearings 152
prevention activities, and anti-social behaviour
  241
primary goods 14–15, 59–60, 295–6
Prins, H. 275–6
Prison Reform Trust 182–3
prison service
  and child protection 119
  management of life sentence prisoners 309
  and risk management 18
  working with probation service 30–1, 309
prison system
  and human rights 76–8
  'race' and racism in 88–9
Prisoner Cohort Study 274–5, 278–9
prisoners
  aftercare and re-settlement of 173, 174, 183–5
  human rights of 76–8
  older prisoners 304–5
  release of 174, 176, 180–1
    on licence see custodial licences
    re-release 199
  work with 173–4, 185–6
prisons
  Care Programme Approach in 279
  drug interventions in 259–61
  probation work inside 173, 185–6
  transfer between hospital and 272–3
  see also custodial remands; custodial sentencing
pro-social modelling 202
probation
  BME offender experiences of 91–2
  functions of 161
probation boards 21
Probation Orders 159, 167, 192, 256, 274
probation service
  and community resources 57
  and court proceedings 145, 149–50, 153–5
  enforcement by see enforcement
  and managerialism 20–1
  'race' and anti-racism in 6, 89–91, 93–4
  reorganisation of 21–2, 23, 24
  rights and practice of 79
  risk assessment in 103–8
  and risk management 18

and safeguarding children 119, 127–9
Serious Further Offence (SFO) reviews 115–16
values 5–7, 10
work with IPP prisoners 301, 311, 312
work with life sentence prisoners 309–10
work with other agencies *see* inter-agency working; multi-agency working; partnership structures
work with prisoners 173, 185–6
work with sex offenders 285, 292, 293–5
work with victims 216–18
work with women offenders 95–8
working with prison service 30–1, 309
and youth justice 221
see also community sentencing
probation service standards 160, 187–9, 190–1, 192, 217
probation trusts 23
problem-solving partnerships 36
professional identity 44, 46–7
professional judgement
in child protection work 139–40
see also discretion
professionalism
deprofessionalisation 188
and risk assessment 107–8
prolific and other priority offender (PPO) programme 39–41
property crime, reporting 211
proportionality 158, 162, 163, 194, 198, 224, 226, 285
protected characteristics 84
Protecting the Public 287
psychoanalytical therapy 289
public health approach 113, 297–8
public protection
and background to Sexual Offences Act (2003) 286–7
balance with rights 10, 18, 80
community protection model 51–2
and life sentences 305
MAPPAs 110–14
as value base 7–8
see also extended sentences for public protection; indeterminate sentences for public protection; risk assessment; risk management
public sector equality duty 85
punishment-based enforcement 201
Putnam, R. 56
PYOs (persistent young offenders) 39, 227, 242

R
'race'
BME offender experiences of probation 91–2
and criminal justice 88–9, 151
and desistance 99
and gender 92
information on 160
and mental health 276
mixed ethnicity offenders 92–3

in probation service 6, 89–91, 93–4
racialisation 88
racism, in prison system 88–9
racist/racially motivated offenders 93–4
rape trials 212
re-offending
assessing risk of see risk assessment
desistance debate 54
desistance and offender management link 55–6
and effectiveness of sex offender treatment 292–3
factors in reducing 58–9
and Good Lives Model 13–15, 59–60
and inequalities 87, 98–100
involving others in change process 64–5
and Offender Management Model 58–9, 61–4
and re-settlement 183–5
rights-based approach to reducing 61–5
role of human and social capital in reducing 56–7
What Works movement 53
and youth justice 236
re-release of prisoners 199
re-settlement of prisoners 183–5
recall 198–9, 305
Redmayne, M. 145–6
Referral Orders 232–3
Reforming the Mental Health Act Part II: High risk patients 278
reintegrative shaming 219
relational values in OMM 27
release of prisoners *see* prisoners
remand
custodial 146–7
to hospital for medical report 270–1
Reparation Orders 231–2
repeat victimisation 210
resentencing 191, 194
resource targeting and risk assessment 28, 96, 184
'respecting diversity' 12
restorative justice 218–20, 232, 233
Restorative Justice Consortium 218–19
Restraining Orders 286, 287
Restriction Orders 271–2
Restrictions on Bail (RoB) schemes 148–9
retrials 154
review case conferences 138
reviews, of DRRs 169
revocation of community sentence 191
Rice, Anthony 80
rights 10–12
balance with risk management 80
of defendant 152–3
right to bail 146, 149
right to jury trial 151
defining 69
and drug treatment 255, 256–7
duties for public authorities 75–6
Human Rights Act (1998) 72–4, 75–6, 285
impact on criminal justice system 74–5
international human rights 70–2, 77
of mentally disordered offenders 266–7

and offenders in community 78–9
prison system 76–8
of sex offenders 285, 295
of victims 208–9
of young people 223, 226, 238–9
rights-based approach 8–13, 48, 61–5, 79, 87, 97
risk
concept of 103–4
dangerous and serious personality disordered
offenders 274–5, 277–9
of mentally disordered offenders 275–7
as value base 7–8
risk assessment
and child protection 121, 122
defining 103
of IPP prisoners 311, 312
and mental disorder 276–7, 278–9
Multi-agency Public Protection Arrangements
18, 110–14, 293, 297
Multi-Agency Risk Assessment Conferences
114–15
offenders' views of 116–17
in probation service 103–8
Serious Further Offence Reviews 115–16
serious harm 108–10, 111–12, 165–6
and targeting resources 28, 96, 184
risk assessment tools 18, 104–8, 276, 278, 294
risk culture of 17–19, 51–2
Risk of Custody Scale 104
risk management 51–2
balance with rights 10, 18, 80
and Good Lives Model 59–60, 296
in Offender Management Model 62–4
and sentencing planning for indeterminate
sentence prisoners 306
see also public protection
Risk Matrix 2000 294
Risk of Sexual Harm Orders 288
risk-need-responsivity (RNR) approach 52–3,
60–1
RoB (Restrictions on Bail) schemes 148–9
Roberts, J. 177
Robinson, G. 27, 104
Robinson, M. 45
role boundaries in teams 44
Rosenbaum, M. 252

S

safeguarding children 119–20
Children Act (1989) 123–6, 138–9
Children Act (2004) 126–9
children in care 138, 139
Local Safeguarding Children's Boards 129–30
multi-agency work 126, 127–38
parental responsibility 138–9
referrals to local authority children's social
care 131–4
see also child protection
Sampson, A. 285
Samuels, A. 307
SCBs (Safeguarding Children's Boards) 129–30,
293

Scott, D. 247
Scott, J. 69, 79
secondary victimisation 210
secure training centres 236, 237
sentence management see enforcement;
engagement
sentence planning, for indeterminate sentences
306, 312
sentence plans 186
sentencing
court system 150, 151
Crime and Disorder Act (1998) 161
Crime (Sentences) Act (1997) 161
Criminal Justice Act (1991) 157–8, 159–61,
256
Criminal Justice Act (2003) 164–6
Alcohol Treatment Requirement 167, 169
background 162–4
Drug Rehabilitation Requirement 167–9,
256
Mental Health Treatment Requirement 274
Supervision Requirement 167
Criminal Justice and Court Services Act
(2000) 161–2
deferred sentences 170–1
and human rights 74
of mentally disordered offenders 274–5
purposes of 164
and 'race' 91
and substance misuse 256–7
use of community orders 169–70
of women offenders 94–5
and youth justice 231–6, 240–1
see also custodial sentencing
Sentencing Council 163
Sentencing Guidelines Council 163, 165–6,
170–1, 194, 196
sequencing 29, 31
Serious Further Offence (SFO) reviews 115–16
serious harm 182
risk of 108–10, 111–12, 165–6, 286, 288
Serious Incident Reviews (SIRs) 115
seriousness of offence
and community sentencing 165, 166, 167–8
and court system 143, 150
and custodial sentencing 158, 163, 174, 175,
178, 181, 182, 193
life sentences 300, 304
and victim impact 215
and youth justice 231–2, 235, 237
Seto, M.C. 292
Setting the Boundaries 286
Sex Offender Orders 285, 287
Sex Offender Register 285, 286
Sex Offender Treatment Programme (SOTP)
290–2
sex offender treatment programmes 289–93
sex offenders
alternative approaches to work with 295–8
probation work with 285, 292, 293–5
rights and restrictions 285–6, 288, 295–6
and risk management 112, 113

sentencing 181
social construction of 284
Sex Offenders Act (1997) 285
sex workers, and drug misuse 253, 255
Sexual Offence Prevention Orders 287–8
Sexual Offences Act (2003) 285, 286–8
sexual offending
and criminal justice system 152, 211, 212
defining 283–4
legislation
background 284, 286
Criminal Justice Act (1991) 285
restrictive measures 285–6
Sexual Offences Act (2003) 286–8
notification and disclosure 285, 286, 288–9
SFO (Serious Further Offence) reviews 115–16
Shaw, S. 76
Shute, S. 305
Siegert, R.J. 290
significant harm, and child protection 120, 125–6, 132–4
silence, right to 153
Simon, J. 105
SIRs (Serious Incident Reviews) 115
SMBs (Strategic Management Boards) 111
Smith, D. 93–4
'so serious' criterion 158, 178, 193, 235, 237
social capital 56–7, 58, 60, 61, 62, 78, 262
social construction
of sex offenders 284
of victims and offenders 209–10
social resources, and desistance 99, 100
social work
and identity in inter-agency teams 46–7
see also children's services
Social Work (Scotland) Act (1968) 222
social work values 5–6, 12
Solomon, E. 242
SOTP (Sex Offender Treatment Programme) 290–2
Souhami, A. 46
Speaking up for justice 212
Squires, P. 240
standard determinate sentence 180–1, 196–7, 198, 199
standards
for probation service 160, 187–9, 190–1, 192, 217
for youth justice 192, 234, 239
Stanley, S. 95
static risk factors 109
statistical prediction tools 104–6
see also risk assessment tools
statutory partnerships 36
Stephen, D. 240
Stevens, A. 257
Stevenson, O. 139–40
Stewart, C. 15
stimulants 251
Stone, N. 158, 163–4
Stop It Now! 297–8
Strategic Management Boards (SMBs) 111

strategic partnerships 36–8, 253–5
strategic priorities 36–8
substance misuse
Alcohol Treatment Requirement 167, 169, 195
approaches to alcohol 261
and bail restrictions 148–9
changing policy on 247–9
drug effects 251
drug interventions in prisons 259–61
Drug Rehabilitation Requirement 167–9, 195, 256, 257
Drugs Intervention Programme 39, 41, 168, 255–6, 257, 260
multi-agency partnerships 159, 248, 253–5, 260
patterns of use 251–2
regulatory framework 249–51
relationship with crime 245–7
role of courts in drug treatment 258–9
sentencing and treatment 256–7
women and drug use 252–3, 255
working with substance using offenders 261–2
summary offences 143, 150
supervised community treatment 267, 269–70
supervision
intensive supervision and surveillance schemes 234–6
post-release for young offenders 237–8
as requirement of community order 167
Supervision Orders 226
supervision period
of Suspended Sentence Orders 179, 196
see also licence period
Suspended Sentence Orders 178–80, 195–6
symbolic capital 57

T

Tackling drugs to build a better Britain 248
Tackling drugs together 248
tariffs 182, 301, 304–5
Tarling, R. 211
Taylor, A. 252–3
Thomas, T. 288
Thornton, D. 291
Together Women Programme 96, 98
transfer, between hospital and prison 272–3
treatment
as condition of life licence 309
for drug misuse see drug interventions; drug treatment
enforcement of 195
for sex offenders 289–93
see also mental health treatment
'triable either way' offences 143, 150
trials 144–5, 153–4
Tumin, S. 77, 183

U

UN Convention on the Rights of the Child (UNCRC) 71, 226
Universal Declaration of Human Rights (UDHR) 71

urgent admission for assessment 268

V

values 3–5
  core values in inter-agency teams 45, 48
  and defining abuse 120
  and good lives 13–15
  and managerialism 21
  probation service 5–7
  relational values in OMM 27
  respecting individuality and difference 12–13
  rights-based approach 8–10
   rights and obligations 10–12
  and risk prediction tools 107
  risk and public protection as basis 7–8
Victim Impact Statements 215
Victim Personal Statements 213, 214–16
Victim Support schemes 212, 214
victim surveys 208
victimisation, types of 210
victims 280
  changing approach toward 207–9
  offender release and wishes of 212, 213, 216
  policy development 211–12
  probation service work with 216–18
  Reparation Orders 231–2
  and restorative justice 218–20
  rights of 208–9
  social construction of 209–10
  support for 214
  as witnesses 210–11
  and youth offender panels 233
Victims' Charters 212
Victims' Code of Practice 212
violent crime
  domestic violence 114–15
  reporting 211
Violent Crime Reduction Act (2006) 261
violent offenders, sentencing 181
voluntary agencies 10, 39, 119, 214
voting rights 76
vulnerable witnesses 212–14

W

Wallace, S. 79
Walmsley, R.K. 90
Ward, T. 10, 15, 61, 145, 290
warnings 224, 231
Weaver, B. 202
welfare, in youth justice 123, 222–3, 225–7
What Works movement 53
Wilberforce judgement 76
Williams, B. 214
Williams, P. 43
Winstone, J. 266
witnesses
  victims as 210–11
  vulnerable witnesses 212–14
women, and drug use 252–3, 255
women offenders 94–6
  BME offenders 92
  desistance 99

indeterminate sentences 311
  probation responses to 95–8
  youth justice 239
Wood, J. 42, 113, 114
Woolf, H. 77, 183
Working together to safeguard children 120, 129,
  130–8, 139
Worrall, A. 94, 95
Wright, L. 96–7

Y

YJB *see* Youth Justice Board
YOTs *see* youth offending teams
young offender institutions 236, 237
young offenders
  persistent (PYOs) 39, 227, 242
  rights of 238–9
young people
  and court proceedings 152–3
  and drug use 246
youth courts 226
Youth justice: Next steps 227
youth justice
  anti-social behaviour 240–2
  community sentencing 233–4
  criminal intent 230–1
  custodial sentencing 175, 176, 224, 236–9, 312
  first tier penalties 231–3
  intensive supervision and surveillance 234–6
  Parenting Orders 239–40
  policy development 19, 222–5
  post-custody licence 196–7
  pre-court interventions 231
  and probation service 221
  reform
   background to 227–8
   Crime and Disorder Act (1998) 228–32
   evaluating 242–3
  standards 192, 234, 239
  welfare in 123, 222–3, 225–7
Youth Justice Board (YJB) 192, 229–30, 239
Youth Justice and Criminal Evidence Act (1999)
  213, 232–3
youth justice services 228–9
youth offender panels 232–3
youth offending teams (YOTs) 46–7, 192, 229,
  231, 242–3, 312
  Youth Rehabilitation Orders (YROs) 233–4,
  235